Travels on the _
Cambodia, Laos, and Yunnan

The Political and Trade Report of the Mekong

Exploration Commission (June 1866 - June1868)

by
Louis de Carné
Member of the Mekong Exploration Commission

White Lotus Press

Originally published as *Voyage en Indo-Chine et dans l'Empire Chinois*, 1872, Dentu Ed., Paris.

G.P.O. Box 1141
Bangkok 10501
Thailand

Telephone:	(662) 332-4915 and (662) 741-6288-9
Fax:	(662) 741 6607 and (662) 741-6287
E-mail:	ande@lox2.loxinfo.co.th
Webpage:	http:/ thailine.com/lotus

Printed in Thailand

ISBN 974-8496-31-7 pbk White Lotus Co. Ltd., Bangkok

Front cover:	Annamite, Cambodian and Siamese Costumes. Garnier Mission, 1873 (Janet Lange & L. Delaporte)
Back cover:	Festivities in Bassac— Illumination of the River, Garnier Mission, 1873 (L. Delaporte)

Travels on the Mekong

Preface

It is customary to provide a rather in-depth introduction to historical reprints. Especially so when dealing with the description of an important event, in this case, the French Commission for the Exploration of the Mekong which traveled from Saigon to Yunnan over a period of two years. However, in this English translation the father of the author, Count de Carné, has written an excellent introduction to the Commission as well as to the short life of his son, Louis de Carné, secretary and representative of the Ministry of Foreign Affairs in the expedition who died, probably due to tuberculosis, shortly after returning to France. His views, as a representative of Foreign Affairs and a diplomat amongst Navy men, were not always welcomed by those advocating France's involvement in Indochina. More so because he was a relative of the superior of the Commission's officers.

This rare book which was published before the main report of the Commission, written mostly by Francis Garnier, appeared in book form is focused on the aspects with which the author was entrusted in particular, politics and commerce. This being said, the main focus of the expedition is also clearly stated: gaining political influence to benefit from trade in and out of the area. Greedy eyes were cast at the time by traders mostly on Yunnan but also on China as a whole—hence the somewhat misleading original title of the British edition. These motives were not new but, at that time, the magnitude of the undertaking must have been staggering. The courage and perseverance of the members of the expedition deserves respect and admiration, whatever the ultimate political motives of the government or the colonial circles backing the expedition were. Furthermore, as there is no translation in English as yet of the main report of the Commission— these days an undertaking perhaps *a par* in terms of cost with the expedition itself—this book is a welcome addition to our limited knowledge of these areas in the mid-nineteenth century.

Rather than editing and re-setting the text of the book, the publisher has wisely refrained from replacing a number of place names that are written in unusual spellings. There is rarely any confusion regarding these places and the names can be seen in other books or on maps. The inclusion of a map from the original main report of the mission—the vulgarizing 1885 edition has been used here—and of a number of engravings from the first reports of the expedition, published in the magazine *Le Tour du Monde*, help to create an adventure that can be savoured in an armchair, far away from the jungles and rapids in which it was first experienced.

Dr. Walter E.J. Tips
November 1994

Plate 1 *A niece of the King of Luang Prabang (Drawing by L. Delaporte from life)*

TRAVELS IN INDO-CHINA

AND

THE CHINESE EMPIRE

BY

LOUIS DE CARNÉ,

MEMBER OF THE COMMISSION OF EXPLORATION OF THE MEKONG.

WITH A

NOTICE OF THE AUTHOR BY THE COUNT DE CARNÉ.

Translated from the French.

LONDON:

CHAPMAN AND HALL, 193 PICCADILLY.

1872.

Plate 2 *The French Commission upon arrival in Han Kéou. From left to right: L. de Carné, L. Joubert, F. Garnier, Cl. Thorel, L. Delaporte (Drawing by Émile Bayard, based on a photograph).*

CONTENTS.

CONTENTS.

X

NOTICE OF THE LIFE OF THE AUTHOR.

ALREADY struck by the disease to which he finally succumbed, my son had prepared everything for the publication of the narrative of the journey in which he had exhausted his strength; and I now only carry through what he had himself arranged. This book, the composition of which was his last delight, will preserve at least a trace of him in that country where a great future awaited him, even in the opinion of those more able to judge, and more disinterested, than a father. I cannot but think that, in these ingenuous pages, some traits will be seen of that noble nature, in which the glowing ardour of youth showed itself associated with a precocious maturity; a nature which cast across the sallies of a fine mind a shadow of sadness too much in harmony with his fate. Closed at the age of twenty-seven, his brief career was summed up in the long journey which was the object of his keenest desires, the perils and fatigues of which he never regretted, even when he could no longer deceive himself as to the price he would soon have to pay for them.

Admitted in 1862, after having finished his studies, to the Ministry of Foreign Affairs, Louis de Carné was attached to the commercial department. The consular service, isolating him, for the time, from politics, had the advantage of opening before him those vast distant perspectives, to which he felt himself specially drawn.

Having a taste for political economy and ethnography, the numerous documents, which he had to consult daily, were exactly what his inclination would have chosen. He studied the different schemes of colonisation tried in our day with special delight, and the travels published in England and Germany were familiar to him. He read them pen in hand, and thus they form precious relics, in which I love to retrace, as if it were a breath of his spirit, the outline of his first thoughts.

In hardly legible notes, referring to his daily occupations, I notice these words, under date of Jan. 27, 1864: 'We try to defend ourselves against the Socialists by argument, by laws, and, if need be, by bayonets; and all this is well enough; but a hungry stomach has neither reason nor ears, and ideas will not triumph over want, especially when it has the ballot-box in its control.

'If, then, France be not able to find, at a distance, the "Far West," which the happy fortune of the United States has set close at their hand, she will assuredly see the sunset of civilisation in that of liberty.'

Five years later, in the project of a colonial establishment at the mouths of the Songkoï, which the young writer recommended to public notice, I find the same fear and the same prepossession, expressed in almost identical terms. In the interval between the two dates, the expedition took place in which he engaged with so brave a heart, because it seemed the consecration of his reigning thought.

In the spring of 1865, Admiral La Grandière, my brother-in-law, obtained leave to come to France for his family, and take them to Cochin-China, the territory of which he was soon to double without shedding a drop of blood. My son took part in the frequent conversations as to the future of this rich country, peopled by an intelligent race, in no way hostile to our own; he asked his uncle the condition of Cambodgia, of which France had just assumed the protectorate, and listened to the Admiral as he expressed the hope of some day seeing our colony connected with China, by a magnificent river communication, the mouth of which would be under the control of France.

The Governor of Cochin-China believed that he could attract to Saïgon, a city laid out for half a million inhabitants, the important commerce which is carried on by caravans between Laos, Burmah, Thibet, and the western provinces of the Chinese Empire, thinking it by no means impossible to secure for its chief artery the Mekong, which diverts into the Indian Ocean the waters of the Himalayan plateaux. To secure for Europe, in its trade with the Celestial Empire, a vast entrepôt, of easy access, and at the same time free the route from China, shortened by twelve hundred miles, from that part of the voyage in which the periodical monsoons are to be especially dreaded, would have been no inconsiderable service to the general commerce of the world, as well as to our own colony, which must, as the result, have become one of its principal centres.

Since the establishment of France in Cochin-China, England had redoubled its efforts to find, at last, that route from India to China, by Burmah and Yunan, hitherto sought for in vain: efforts quite natural, since this route would enable her to draw this great commercial current to her Asiatic possessions, by the upper valleys, along which flow the rivers of Indo-China. To get the start of our rivals was, then, a matter of the utmost importance.

These considerations struck the Marquis de Chasseloup, then Minister of Marine and Colonies, strongly;

and it is to his persistency France owes the preservation of Cochin-China, long threatened in the councils of the Second Empire. This minister approved the scheme of a grand scientific mission, which, ascending the Mekong from its mouth to its still undiscovered sources, should report fully on the navigability of that great river, then almost unknown beyond the lake of Angcor. He thought it especially necessary to display the flag of France to the swarming populations on the river-sides, an establishment among whom would be an introduction to us to those countries. This mission of exploration, designed to serve at once the interests of science, and colonial interests of the first importance, was to have been composed, as first planned, independent of servants, and of a military escort of about twenty-five soldiers, as follows :

A superior officer of the navy—chief of the expedition.

Two officers charged with hydrographic matters, astronomical observations, surveying, and sketching.

A naval surgeon, as botanist, as well as to act professionally.

Some one appointed by government to act as mineralogist and geologist, especially in the relations of these sciences to the industrial arts.

Some one appointed by the Minister for Foreign Affairs as secretary to the commission, charged also with the study of whatever concerned politics and commerce.

M. Drouyn de Lhuys, Minister of Foreign Affairs, threw himself heartily into the project of his colleague. He was pleased to appoint my son to represent his department, authorising him to correspond with him during the expedition; and, crushed as my heart is to-day, I cherish a lively remembrance of this honour; for one can die for his country on the battle-field of science as truly as on that of war.

Louis de Carné left France in the autumn of 1865. He spent some happy weeks in Egypt, of which he retained that fond recollection, which their first steps in a foreign land leave in the heart of the young. He had the pleasure of there meeting his brother, then connected with M. Lesseps' great undertaking, and with him was able to examine the works of the canal, in which France, then in the height of its confidence and strength, flattered itself to see a marvellous way opened to the extreme East, where it had just raised its flag.

On his arrival at Saïgon, at the close of December 1865, the young attaché devoted the first weeks of his residence to visiting the three provinces of Lower Cochin-China, the only ones then belonging to France; and in his correspondence with the department of Foreign Affairs reported on their condition with that entire freedom which was at once his characteristic and his duty. This visit ended, the governor of Cochin-China sent him to Cambodgia, where he was able, during the months that necessarily elapsed before the receipt of passports demanded at Bangkok and Pekin, to continue his personal observations, before returning to Saïgon, to join the members of the scientific expedition, at last assembled.

It was during this first stay at Cambodgia he met M. de Lagrée, who had been intrusted, through the admiral, to conduct this difficult enterprise. The rare ability of this officer will be seen in the introduction to my son's book, in the way he induced the king, Norodom, at whose court he was the military agent of the governor, to ask the protectorate of France, after long hesitation, caused by the threats of the Siamese government. By nature brave and sympathetic, M. de Lagrée

hid a generous heart under the inflexible rigour befitting
a military command, of which he seemed the living em-
bodiment. Always master of himself in the most terrible
extremities, he took minute precautions for the safety
of others, which he would have disdained for his own.

Already threatened by disease, this eminent officer,
whose name heads the list of deaths closed by that of
Louis de Carné, accepted the command of the expedition,
to which the public voice called him, only from his devotion to science, and in spite of a presentiment, felt from
the outset, of the fate awaiting him. He required, as
indispensable to the unity of direction, and the success of
the enterprise, material alterations of the plan arranged
at Paris, and thus, under the naval discipline which he
enforced, the special agent of the Ministry of Foreign
Affairs found himself seriously hampered, being unable,
till the end of the journey, to correspond with the department to which he belonged. The prohibition from
doing so, which was only communicated on the eve of
starting, put him in a painful dilemma. He must either
submit to it, contrary to the text of his private instructions, or decline to set out, at the risk of seeming to
have deserted his post, at the approach of danger. He
felt that this was impossible, lodged a protest, and started
with the rest.

The expedition, which so many vows attended, left
Saïgon in June 1866. A gunboat bore it over the deep
waters of the Mekong, which spread into a wide and
tranquil lake before disclosing its roaring current, its
impassable rapids, and the terrors of its fathomless
whirlpools. The final arrangements were made in the
territory of the tributary prince, and some days of study
and of initiation into their work were devoted to the
ruins of Angcor, as imposing as the ruins of Thebes or

Memphis, and more mysterious. Soon after, they reached Laos, whose putrid exhalations had proved fatal to all the missionaries who had encountered them, and, still more recently, to M. Mouhot, the only traveller who, for two centuries, had set foot on this ill-omened soil.

This was the moment of the last adieus and the most poignant emotions. In these waters, now bottomless, now barred by sandbanks, it was necessary to use boats managed by natives, and to separate themselves, with farewell letters to France, from the steam gunboat, whose flag and black streaks symbolised still, in these deserts, civilisation and home.

I shall not describe this voyage, in which tried sailors and accomplished men had to put their lives at the mercy of barbarians, depending on their skill for help, which science could no longer supply : a navigation unparalleled, which led the voyagers from a sheet of water, of which the eye could hardly take in the expanse, to unsoundable gorges overhung by Alpine precipices, and bore them, from the burning heat of a fiery sky, to the shade of impenetrable woods, where the Mekong lost itself in a labyrinth of islets, of weeds, and of trees rising from the bosom of the waters. It is not for me to repeat either the hazards of that life of adventure, supported chiefly by fishing and hunting, or the violence of a torrent-like stream, which soon forced the admission of its being unnavigable, as an indisputable conclusion, on three naval officers, whom it grieved to the heart to have to own it. I shall say nothing of the long wintering in the marshes of Burmah, where, already, the unhappy travellers, forced to dismiss the greater part of their escort, exhausted by fever and by privations, their feet naked and their limbs torn, disputed what remained of their impoverished blood with myriads of leeches, vampires more terrible than the tigers and serpents of Laos.

This book will show what these trials were, of which each day, during eighteen months, varied the nature and agony. It will disclose the wiles of a half-barbarous diplomacy, and will set in the clearest light the almost insurmountable difficulties of the leader of the expedition among the petty independent chiefs of Central Asia, with whom the recommendations of the court of Bangkok had no influence, and who paid no regard even to those of the court of Pekin. All this is told, as it seems to me, with a circumstantiality and naturalness, which bring the reality before the reader. If the narrative is coloured, it is because the picturesque rises from the subject itself; if, in spite of the gaiety with which such miseries are borne, tears sometimes come to the eyes, they are the true *lacrymæ rerum*, called forth neither by the art nor the design of the author.

The days during which it was necessary to struggle against the cataracts of the stream, or to seek food from the creatures of the virgin forests, were not, however, the worst to pass, for the sufferings of the mind and the tortures of the heart were thus escaped. I have often heard my son say, that the members of the expedition preferred these times of struggle to the intervals of comparative ease, when safety, assured for the moment, carried back the travellers, deprived, for eighteen months, of all news from Europe, to sad recollections, which woke the thought of their absent families, and of that France, whose very name was unknown in those regions. At such seasons they kept long silence, each unwilling to be the first to broach the one subject which interested all alike. But when at drum-beat, each morning, they rose with the dawn,—the camp surmounted by the

national colours,—each could see, on the clouded brow
of his neighbour, what tender visions had passed in the
troubled dreams of the night.

Meanwhile, they advanced a little each day, and the
prospect of return, now realised as possible, rekindled
their spirits. If it had been necessary to give up the
hope of making the Mekong the grand maritime route
of Indo-China, and Saïgon one of the first ports of the
world,—if, with this, the great end of the expedition had
failed,—still, geography and the natural sciences continued to yield the courageous travellers the most important observations, and the most precious collections.[2]

Moreover, it was found that the perfect navigability
of the Songkoï—a fine river, which flows into the gulf
of Tonkin, and is every way fitted to promote the commercial intercourse of the Celestial Empire with our
new colony—was proved beyond question. The earnest
desire to find, at last, that route to China—the discovery
of which, reserved to France, would mark the hour
when they could prepare for the inexpressible happiness
of returning—was redoubled by this stimulus.

It will be told in this narrative how the travellers,
having reached, in January 1868, the borders of Yunan,
on the other side of a range of mountains, thought impassable, came all at once, when they were not expect-
ing it, on the soil of the great empire. It will be seen
with what joyful shouts they saluted this land, sought
for so long; a land in which, thanks to a powerful civilisation, they were as safely protected, at eight hundred

2 Europe will be able to judge of the value of the labours of the Commission of the Mekong when the great publication, prepared for the Minister
of Marine and the Colonies, at last sees the day. Delayed by the sad events
of the war, it has been recommenced, and is continued steadily by naval
Lieutenant Garnier, with the assistance of naval Lieutenant Delaporte, and
Doctors Joubert and Thorel.

leagues from Pekin, by the official letters of Prince Kong, as they could have been in a faubourg of that capital.

Notwithstanding the obsequious respect shown by the Chinese functionaries to the strangers in rags, whom the prestige of an official despatch served in lieu of decent clothing, it was in China they met their most cruel trial. In order to penetrate, in compliance with his instructions, to the sources of the Mekong, hidden in the highest mountains of Thibet, Commandant de Lagrée, then lying on a bed of sickness, determined that some of the commission should proceed by the northwest into the part of the Celestial Empire disturbed by a Mussulman insurrection, and that they should try, by letters obtained in Yunan from the secret chiefs of that strange movement, to reach to the very capital of the new kingdom founded by the rebels. Appointed to this task, with two officers, the author of this book has been able to give Europe the first correct details of the vast social convulsion, which, springing originally from Arabia, wrestles with Bouddhism, even at Pekin and Lhassa.

The earlier stages of this daring enterprise, which had the assistance of one of our devoted missionaries, gave, for a moment, a flattering hope of success. The adventurous travellers were able to reach Tali-Fou, the citadel of a faith wandered a thousand leagues from its cradle; but they did so only after passing through a country covered with ruins and with whitened bones of men and beasts, to find themselves face to face with a capricious tyrant, and an excited population which demanded their heads. Escaping, as by a miracle, from this bloody den, but disappointed in their most cherished geographical hope, they reëntered the territory of the Son of Heaven, only to learn the death of the leader, who, after having so skilfully directed the expedition, had just succumbed, rather to the weight of his responsibilities than to the blow of disease. But M. de Lagrée's work was done, and his name will for ever be connected with the history of discovery in these regions.

Having, through his care, reached within a few days' march of the Blue River, which, from west to east, washes the empire through its whole course, the members of the commission were able to embark with his precious remains, which they carried with them. A Chinese junk, which was soon exchanged for a smart American steamer, bore to Shanghai, in some weeks of easy navigation, through the most populous provinces on the globe, the *grand ambassadors* of the West, who had hardly been able to get shoes for their feet; and the French of that city welcomed the travellers, long given up as dead, with an enthusiasm in which all the European population joined.

Although, outside the provinces of Yunan and of Setchuen, he only came in contact with the towns on the river, Louis de Carné bore away ineffaceable impressions of the country. In his daily conversations he reverted continually to these strange regions, which he called the intellectual antipodes of the Christian world. The petrifaction of a whole race, which has not changed since the dawn of history, seemed to him an inexplicable moral phenomenon.

'The Chinese are not only old, they are decrepit,' he writes, in his manuscript notes of 1869; 'and the amazing thing is that this world of old people has never been young, as far back as we can trace them. It speaks, thinks, and feels to-day as it did three thousand years ago. The language, the system of writing, the laws, and the rites, uniting to destroy all human spontaneity, have paralysed in its cradle this fossil race, which is senile without having ever been anything else.

'The small success made by the missionaries in China may at times surprise us; for it is hard to understand how doctrines so noble as those they preach should have so little influence on the crowds of mandarins, whose life is spent in study. But may not any one see, that the more educated the Chinese are, the more memory gains, in these perfected machines, at the expense of intelligence? Christianity, which aspires to develop human individuality, strives vainly in this sad country against a creed which has succeeded in crushing it; it is life trying to galvanise death. China is Lazarus in the grave: it "*already stinks;*" to raise it, by making it Christian, needs, as of old, the hand of God. Our missionaries seem to me like Daniel in the lions' den; only the lions are, nowadays, toothless; but, besides having filed their teeth, the naval powers will need also to clip their claws, or they will, before long, use them fiercely enough.

'The Chinese question, which is at once religious, naval, and territorial, will thrust itself on cabinets in spite of doctrinaire economists; for the tutelage of barbarism is an obligation of civilisation. The admiration which the philosophy of last century affected for China, is, in my opinion, one of its greatest crimes. An abyss separates the most corrupted Christian nation from Chinese depravity.'[3]

This moral and political problem of China filled the soul of the young traveller. It was the subject to which he most readily reverted to the close of his life; and the fever must have been fierce indeed, or the prostration intense, when a conversation on it did not rouse and re-

[3] *Notes inedites de* 1869.

animate my dear sick one, bringing me for the moment a fond illusion of hope. When, for a time, he revived, and began to think he might still recover, he delighted to sketch out a plan of study, which would naturally have led him to treat this great question. He proposed to describe, some day, the state of Christianity in the extreme East, and hoped to be sent to Japan, to be able to study it there. In a narrative in which the Catholic missions would have had the first place, he rejoiced in advance at the pleasure he would have in making known a crowd of details respecting the poor converts, always trembling under a yoke hardly yet lightened; and, above all, in repeating what he had felt, when, on a Christmas night, he heard for the first time, resounding under a roof of bamboos, in the midst of the mountains which divide China from Thibet, the chants which had cradled his infancy, and how he, a worn traveller, received the strengthening sacrament from the mutilated hands of an old confessor.

After a sojourn of some weeks in Cochin-China—which he found completed by the annexation of three fine provinces, but in which he met the bitter disappointment of not seeing his family, who had already left—he was able, at last, to set sail for France. He reached it at the close of 1868, bearing in his breast, though without any outward apparent symptom as yet, the seeds of the mortal malady by which ancient Asia seems to wish to defend itself against the invasion of Europe. I have not the courage to recall the joys of his return, which Providence made so brief, while the succeeding anguish has been so long.

Deputed by the Minister of Foreign Affairs to the exploration of the Mekong, the young traveller bent all his energy to present to his department, in the course of 1869, an extended report of the results: what little leisure he had from this task, he devoted to these papers in the *Revue des Deux Mondes*, often a literal reproduction of the journal written during the journey, at times on the bench of a canoe borne on the course of the stream, at times in the depth of the forest, in a tent set up for the night.

A good constitution bore for long the steady progress of a disease, which the invalid hid from others without concealing from himself; a steady progress, which neither the lights of science, nor the assiduous care of the dearest companion [4] of his journeys, could conjure away.

At last, in compliance with the desire of his chiefs, who very much wished to procure him a post in Egypt, of whatever kind would most perfectly suit him, he made a trial of his strength in the first months of 1870, in a short excursion to England. The experiment was not encouraging; and my son, with too sure a presentiment of the fate that awaited him, returned to seclude himself in the home of his childhood, which he quitted no more, and where we comforted him with our loving attentions, though its well-loved landscapes, alas, only pleased his eyes without reviving his heart.

The feverish agitation increased when he heard our earlier disasters, and when unfavourable bulletins reached me, I had to bear not only what I suffered as a Frenchman, but what the effect made me endure as a father.

The agony became more intolerable when all our Breton youth set off to defend their country. When he stood in front of his brothers, to give them the farewell salute, he was overwhelmed by the disclosure of

---

[4] Dr. Joubert, member of the scientific commission of the Mekong, now medical inspector of the thermal baths of Bagnoles.

his own weakness. From that day, the world, where there remained no longer a place for him, in the extremity of our public perils, seemed to fade and disappear from his eyes; and, separating himself, without effort, from a future which was awanting alike to him and his country, his thoughts rose, as of themselves, to those regions where, only, the future is never clouded. In going over some scattered pages, written with a trembling hand, after all was ended, I found this:

'The life of man has no value except in proportion as he has learned to contemn it by rising above it. To be devoted, is truly to live; to be devoted to the end, is to live beyond it.'

These words are, perhaps, the last he wrote before leaving earth: they contain the expression of his assurance and mine.

COUNT DE CARNÉ.

Plate 3 *Louis de Carné in a big Cambodian barge (Drawing by Émile Bayard, based on a sketch done by L. Delaporte).*

TRAVELS IN INDO-CHINA,

ETC.

INTRODUCTION.

ESTABLISHMENT OF THE FRENCH PROTECTORATE OVER THE

KINGDOM OF CAMBODGIA.

THOUGH it is easy for theorists to attack the colonial system, by contrasting its returns with its cost, men called to
direct affairs, to whatever school of economy they belong,
are forced, by an irresistible impulse, to those generous pro-
digalities which honour the youth of nations and profit their
riper age. Greece colonised Asia Minor, Sicily, and Italy;
Rome moulded the world to its image by manners as well
as by arms; and England would have been to-day no more
than a third-rate power, if the brave Anglo-Saxon race, which
covers two continents, had acted on the recent and hardly
serious theory of isolation. The doctrine of 'every one by
himself and for himself,' is fundamentally opposed to the
genius of France, of which expansion is the law. However many her mistakes in colonial matters, her faith has
fortunately survived her disappointments. The French government has opened for us, by a victory, the gates of the
Celestial Empire, amidst universal applause, and has justly
counted on the approval of all schools of politics in planting the national flag between India and Japan, at the mouth

B

of one of the greatest water-courses of Upper Asia. The Frenchman who arrives from Europe, after having seen Persia and Malacca, and having touched at Aden, at Point de Galle, and at Singapore, views with an unspeakable joy the flag which floats on the summit of Cape St. Jacques, sheltering more than three millions of men, subjects of France, whose laws, manners, and interests, we have known how to respect, while we have widened all their prospects.

I do not propose at present, either to enter into the condition of Cochin-China, or to sketch the future which all who know the fertility of its soil, and the intelligent aptitude of its people, anticipate for it. Other competent writers have already done so. But our possessions include one territory— Cambodgia—the value of which is less understood. The brilliant success of Admiral Rigault de Genouilly à Touranne, the happy inspiration which took him to Saïgon, the decisive victory of Admiral Charner at Kihoa, are henceforth part of our military annals, and by no means their least glorious pages; but it is hardly well enough known how we acquired Cambodgia, the necessary complement of a territory which, without it, must be permanently insecure. I shall try to tell the story. It was, besides, from this country that the expedition started charged to trace to its sources the immense river which fertilises it; and it will therefore surprise no one if, having lived in it for some time before the Commission set out, I give it such special notice as will form a natural introduction to the long story of our journey.

I.

The six provinces which now form our colony of Cochin-China were formerly part of the kingdom of Cambodgia. It is not yet 200 years since the emperor of Annam, anxious respecting the turbulent disposition of a great number of Chinese who had fled from their country rather than submit to Tsing, the victorious head of the dynasty of Ming, assigned them, very cleverly, lands in the south of his territories which did not belong to him. They established themselves in them and drove out the inhabitants. More recently, the Annamite government resolved to 'levy and gather together numbers

from among the common people, especially from among the
vagrants and worthless, from the province of Quang Binh,
above Hué, to Binthuan, and to transport them as colonists
into these new provinces.[1] These vagabonds have made the
stock of an honest race, and have multiplied in less than two
centuries, under the influence of Chinese legislation, which
honours and guards that central principle of civilisation, the
rights of property, to a population of three million souls,
who pay us to-day nearly eight millions of taxes. The Cambodgians, forced towards the west, henceforth formed only
a small part of the inhabitants of Lower Cochin-China. To
study their civilisation, so different from that which flourishes
in Annam, it was necessary to visit them; and I therefore
determined to take advantage of the interval at my disposal
before the starting of the Commission appointed by the governor of Cochin-China to explore the basin of the Mekong,
and do so.

I left Saïgon at the beginning of the year 1866, on one
of the little gunboats so well called by the police, *arroyos*.
On board, close to a missionary with a long beard, and some
French officers, a number of Cambodgians formed a separate
group, and chatted as they smoked. They were kinsmen
of the King Norodom, returning home, after having attended
the industrial and agricultural Exposition, which had inaugurated in Cochin-China the era of the fêtes of peace. Their
heads were full of what they had just seen. What puzzled
them most was, how we could not only give rewards, but
leave the exhibitors free to sell what they had brought. Such
magnanimity confounded them, and set them on healthy self-
reflection. These mandarins, powerful and rich in spite of
their poor pay, which hardly rises, even for the highest officers, to more than a thousand francs a year, make it up from
the people, who are left all but defenceless under their pitiless and arbitrary exactions. Their extortions have no limit,
indeed, but their interest, which too grievous a rapacity
would injure, by inducing emigration to another province.
The nephew of the king, a child of eight, had bracelets of
gold on his legs and arms. His neck was ornamented by a

[1] *Histoire et Description de la Basse Cochin-Chine*, traduction de M. Aubaret.

motley collar of gold plates, joined by a thread to bits of
glass, and some stones more or less precious. He wore no
hair except on the front half of the head, and only on the
right side of that. The back was clean shaved, except two
locks. His dress, like that of all the Cambodgians, was a short
jacket and a *langouti*, which is a kind of cotton or silk petticoat encircling the lower part of the body to the knees, one
end, lifted between the legs, being fixed behind to the waist-
band, the calves remaining bare. It thus recalls the Celtic
breeches, and the baggy knickerbockers of the Greeks and
Albanians. This dress, more manly than the long robe of
the Annamites, is generally adopted by the Siamese and the
Laotians.

Princes as these travelling companions were, it was not
without some repugnance that I found myself forced to lie
down at their side, when night came, to try to sleep. The
prejudices of caste, after centuries of often bloody struggle,
have almost disappeared from France, thank God; but for a
European,—however free he may think himself from such
feelings,—contact with other races—yellow, black, or copper-
coloured—is always a trial. It is only after long effort that
one is able, if not entirely to conquer these inner aversions,
at least to keep them under due control. At this moment
we left the Donnaï to enter the Soirap. We were close to
the sea, which sent us its fresh smell and its rough waters.
The wind came, with the south-east monsoon, from the side
next France, and I breathed it long, before burying myself
anew in these lands. We soon cleared the two Vaicos, to
fall into the *arroyo* of the Poste—a channel scooped out partly
by nature, partly by human labour—which unites the great
stream of the Mekong to the river of Saïgon. It runs like a
river in an English park, between banks covered with cabbage-palms, palm-trees, and a thousand other trees and
plants of every colour and of varied foliage. There are no
longer those eternal monotonous mangroves of the other
arroyos of Cochin-China—amphibious shrubs, busily conquer-
ing the waters of vast provinces by the entanglements of
their encroaching roots. The boats which pass us are covered,
according to custom, with flags; so that one would think the
crew busy drying its linen, if they had any, and if the three

colours of France were not seen floating in the place of honour.

The arroyo of the Poste is famous in Cochin-China, in which rice shoots up wondrously, but where there is a sad want of the picturesque. We near Mytho, the chief place of one of the three ancient provinces. This little town, situated at the confluence of the arroyo of the Poste and of the Mekong, is of some importance; but since the recent annexation of Vinh-long, the Chinese have partly deserted it, and its growth is somewhat arrested. Amidst the houses that press close to the quays, one notes the establishment of the Sisters of the Holy Infancy, who could not fail in attracting children if they could only inspire in them the desire to be well harboured from the snares of this world. The citadel is a vast *enceinte* constructed by the Annamites, enclosing nearly all the dwellings of Europeans at Mytho. That of the naval commandant is an old cottage, carried there and set up again at great expense at the time when the enthusiasm of the first organisers of the conquest led them to admire everything connected with our new subjects, without exception, and to copy everything without judgment from them —their institutions no less than their architecture.

Leaving Mytho, a superb landscape presents itself. The Mekong, which will bear comparison with the noblest rivers of Asia, stretches beyond the horizon, its waters fading in the distance into the clouds, with which the burning sun, raising a veil of transparent vapour, unites them. It was not without emotion I felt myself floating on its stream. I was about to ascend it, and to do my part in tracing it to its sources; and I involuntarily did so in advance in my thoughts, picturing myself now burning under a tropical sun, and next frozen by the cold in the mountains of Thibet. I never realised so vividly the idea of ancient mythology, which gave great rivers a god or a genius for father. At the sight of the Mekong, the image of Camoens, who composed his paraphrase of the Psalm, 'On the rivers of Babel,' on its banks, rose in my mind; and I shared the sadness of the great exile, tempered by his manly hope, and felt myself strengthened by the recollection thus suddenly evoked.

The Mekong runs at this part between the province of

Dinh-Tuong and the three provinces which the treaty of
1862 have left to the Annamites. It is covered with a crowd
of boats, of which a great number carry the French flag. All,
indeed, have not the right to show it who do so, but they
hoist it fraudulently, because it covers their cargo. The
French Annamites are, in fact, free of the Cambodgian cus-
tom-duties in virtue of the treaty of the protectorate. The
waters were very low, and the navigation difficult, even for
our small gunboat. I at last reached the place where the
Mekong divides into four arms, each like a great river. The
position which we hold on it is unique; a concession of
ground having been cleverly chosen on the tongue of land
which separates the great stream descending from Laos from
the arm which leads to the lake. The town of Pnom-Penh,
to which the king had just removed his capital, proclaims itself from a distance by a grand pyramid built on a height,
leading the traveller to hope that he is about to come upon
another Bangkok, reflecting in a river much nobler than the
Meïnam monuments whose singularity is not wanting in
grandeur. But the illusion is short-lived, for Pnom-Penh is
only a crowd of petty wooden and bamboo houses, most of
them raised above the ground on posts, round which pigs
and chickens live in a familiarity which brings the inhabitants inconvenience of more kinds than one. A winding
street runs from one side to the other of the town, which is
pretty populous, and indeed the largest in Cambodgia. It
was once a place of 50,000 inhabitants; but invasions, to
which it was peculiarly exposed from its nearness to Hatien,
had reduced them to about 5000 or 6000. Since our protectorate, however, they have tripled. The natives huddle
together in it in the strangest way. There were about 100
of them lodged in the three houses assigned by the king as
the residence of the French officer who represents at his
court the governor of Cochin-China. The king, since he has
become our protégé, thinks he must copy France in everything, and has ordered a great many of his subjects to leave
their houses, that they may be rebuilt in a uniform style. He
wants his capital to be worthy of him, and expropriates as
he likes, by his royal caprice, without thinking of indemnity.
To set the example, he has bargained with a French work-

man, who never in his life was an architect, to build him a brick villa. As to the cost, it does not trouble him: the Cambodgians have to bear that.

I put off my presentation to the king to another day, and went up the arm of the lake to Compon-Luon, a large village on the banks, about six kilometres from Houdon, the capital which had just been abandoned. The French resident lived there, with his gunboat moored close to his house, near enough to the king to direct and watch him. At the time of my visit the post was held by M. de Lagrée, a captain of a frigate. Seconding the views of Admiral de La Grandière with equal energy and ability, he planted and established the French flag in Cambodgia. It was under his command I ascended the great river whose mysteries he had for years endeavoured in vain to solve, the information given by the natives being as cloudy as the troubled waters of the Mekong. When it was offered him to lift the veil, he accepted without hesitation. I lived with him while waiting till the expedition was completely organised, and I owe to his thorough knowledge of Cambodgia most of the details respecting it which I shall copy from my notes. His house was of wood, thatched; but he had been his own architect, and not a mandarin could boast of having a more elegant, a smarter, or a better-arranged mansion. At the side, and within the same enclosure, an infirmary, a guard-house, a magazine, and various offices completed the residence, which was made known from a distance by a flag-staff from which floated our colours. The erection of this small French establishment on soil consecrated by the presence of a magnificent banyan, the sacred tree which commonly covers only bonzeries, pagodas, and tombs, had marked the close of the struggle between the two rival influences which sought to prevail in Cambodgia. It will perhaps not be without interest to recall the principal incidents of that long strife, which we often all but lost, but from which we at last came out victorious,—and this the rather, since being now definitely established in these regions, it is well to know both our friends and those who for long will be our enemies.

When the emperor of Annam, by the treaty signed at Hué in 1862, had recognised the rights of France over the

three provinces of Lower Cochin-China, the first care of the
governor of our new colony was to secure the peace of our
frontiers. We had just cut in two the dominions of Tu Duc,
who retained, on the south-east of our possessions, the provinces of Vinh-long, Angiang, and Hatien. One of the conditions of the treaty being, in effect, the re-cession of Vinh-
long, we could not dream of extending our rule to the Gulf
of Siam, its natural limit, at once. The necessity of holding
these provinces, which we have since been led to occupy,
was forced on the author of the treaty of 1862 by the evidence of events which were not long in showing themselves.
On the west and south-east we were bounded by the Annamite territory, and by the sea; on the north-east we touched
Cambodgia, a little kingdom then unknown. The few travellers who had visited it had told us nothing of its history.
Owing to the apparently impenetrable mystery which veiled
the meaning of inscriptions carved on the walls of ruined
buildings, it was the general belief that the history of Cambodgia would be found written, in the fashion of the Egyptian
annals, on the walls of temples—a belief now hardly probable. I have seen the chief bonze of Cambodgia read, in the
grand pagoda of Angkor, some inscriptions chosen from
among those which, from the place where they occurred,
seemed the most important. He easily understood the fragments written in the ancient Cambodgian language while it
was still free from any foreign alloy, and they were found to
refer only to pilgrimages, religious ceremonies, and confused
incidents of Buddhist legend, without offering anything of
historical interest. It is quite possible that some inscription
may one day be found which will throw light on the past of
this kingdom, but there is too good ground to fear that the
events of which it has been the theatre have never been
written. Unless some bonze convent preserve the record
of these problematic annals, we must give up the hope of
having anything like full light thrown on the times of the
glory and prosperity of Cambodgia. About the middle of the
sixteenth century Portuguese came to settle in the country,
some traits of the race still remaining recognisable in their
descendants. They left writings, which would have been
a precious source of information on the history at least of

that era, but the Siamese have destroyed them. These Portuguese, on their arrival, asked the king for a small piece of land, and he allowed them to take as much as they needed. They humbly answered that they only wanted as much as a buffalo-hide would cover, and then, repeating the trick of Dido, they appropriated a considerable tract; so that the Cambodgians till this day say of a Christian that he belongs to the ' village of the stretched-out skin.'

Some passages of Chinese books speak of Cambodgia as one of the numerous kingdoms tributary to the Celestial Empire. They even say that, till the seventh century of our era, it was dependent on the province of Founan or Tonkin, which was then Chinese. If they can be believed, the country of Cambodgia, which they call Tchinla, began to pay tribute, and to send ambassadors to the Son of Heaven, in the year A.D. 616, under the reign of Yong-ti, of the dynasty of Soui. One of the kings of Cambodgia, in the year A.D. 625, shook off the Tonkin yoke, and even took possession of that province itself, and of the kingdom of Thsan-pan. This latter country is, perhaps, the ancient Ciampa, visited by Marco Polo, and now included in the Annamite province of Binthuan, on which we touch by ours of Bienhoa. Under the Ming, the armies of Tchinla overran all Cochin-China. The emperor of China, in his struggles with Tonkin, did not disdain to ask the help of the king of Tchinla, in 1016. Alliances seem then to have been common between the grand empire and this powerful kingdom. The Chinese traveller, whose narrative is translated by Abel Rémusat, relates that in his time the people of Tchinla gave their country the name of Kamphoutchi, which soon became Kamphoutche. The Cambodgians now call themselves Khmer, and say, in speaking of their country, Sroc Khmer—the country of the Khmer. Nevertheless, one cannot but recognise in the Kambodia of the Portuguese, of which we have made Cambodgia, an evident corruption of the word Kamphoutche.

On the other hand, one reads in the Siamese annals that the country of Sajam was long under the rule of the king of Kamphoxa, and paid him tribute. Phra-Ruang, prince of Sajam, freed his country, which took then the name of

Thaï, which means 'free,' and modified the Cambodgian alphabet, which in the end was employed exclusively in religious writings. It would thus appear that at one time Cambodgia included in its extended frontiers most of Indo-China. But I shall not spend time in retracing the dark story of these ages. One thing is certain: the past of Cambodgia must have been very brilliant. Enormous ruins bear glorious witness of this even to our day, and we found ample and ready confirmation of it during our residence at Laos. In a country tributary to Burmah, and close to the frontier of China, an old bonze eagerly asked us about the state of Cambodgia, which bore in his books the name of Tepada-Lakhon, or 'Kingdom of Angels.' The Cambodgians themselves know nothing either of their origin or of their history. Degenerate as they are in such matters, they have no idea that their forefathers could have constructed the monuments whose ruins cover their country. M. de Lagrée, who continually interrogated them for years on this point, ended by getting from a bonze who was reputed to be very wise the name of the founder of Angcor; but when he came to compare it with others which he had already collected, he found that it was simply a fancy word, meaning in French 'Architect of Heaven.' We, ourselves, at the time of our arrival in Cochin-China, were absolutely ignorant alike of the past and the present condition of the Cambodgians, and a first glance at the position of the kingdom showed, in the character of its relations with its neighbours, a serious obstacle to the legitimate extension of our influence in Indo-China.

II.

Cambodgia has at present a population of hardly a million souls, including in this number forty thousand slaves, and twenty thousand savages inhabiting the mountains, where they enjoy a kind of independence. This petty kingdom, with fewer inhabitants than some French departments, could not, in itself, be either a source of danger to us, or even become a cause of anxiety; but the law of nations, as it is known in Europe, is very little known in the East, and Cambodgia touches Siam, a neighbour comparatively power-

ful, which has filched provinces from it by force or cunning
in turn. The court of Bangkok and that of Hué alike
hankered after what remained of this dismembered kingdom. In 1795 the king of Siam carried off from Cambodgia
the young Ang Eng, to protect him from the violence of his
revolted subjects, and caused him to be crowned, some time
after, at Houdon. To reimburse himself for these services,
he took possession of the provinces of Battam-bang and
Angcor; and the emperor of Annam, on his side, had not
been less active. The Siamese government ought, from
the first, to have rejoiced at our intervention, which put a
check to the political ambition of the Annamites, who, invited in 1810 by Ang-chan to help him against the Siamese,
conquered the six provinces which we hold to-day under the
name of Lower Cochin-China, and established themselves
even at Pnom-Penh, from which they governed the country
down to 1834. Not content with holding the unfortunate
Cambodgians under their yoke, they tried to impose on
them their customs. The historian of Gyadinh, in his triple
pride of conqueror, literary man, and Chinese, does not hesitate to write that the emperor of Annam appointed to the
different Cambodgian mandarins, civil and military, a costume of ceremony. Thus, he continues, disappeared, day
by day, those barbarous manners which showed themselves
in their cutting their hair, in wearing clothes not slit at the
sides, in covering their body round with a langouti, in eating with their fingers, and sitting squat on their heels.

The dislike, which has always divided the two races,
changed, on the one side, into an inextinguishable hatred,
on the other into a profound contempt. A Cochin-Chinese
law went so far as to punish with strangling any Annamite
who married a Cambodgian woman. The Annamite emperor's intention to conquer the whole kingdom was clear,
and the declaration to the contrary of the minister of state,
Phan-tan-gian, published by M. Aubaret, is of no weight in
the face of undoubted facts. 'To begin,' says he; 'we have
no intention to take possession of this country; we wish,
like heaven, to leave men to live in peace. No, we do not
wish the destruction of this little kingdom, as others do,
who have hearts full of bitterness;'—that is, the Siamese,

who, not content with the two provinces taken from Ang
Eng,—under the pretext of upholding the interests of Ong-
duong, the legitimate king, advanced to drive out the Annamites. The struggle between the two rivals lasted more
than ten years. Whichever side won the victory, Cambodgia was fated to disappear; but the peace was signed,
each retaining what he held before the war, and the partition was indefinitely postponed. Ong-duong agreed to pay
a yearly tribute to his two neighbours; and at this price the
Siamese set him on the throne of Cambodgia, though not
without requiring him to leave his children at Bangkok, to
receive an education worthy of their birth. In reality, the
Siamese king wanted to have hostages for the present, and
to prepare instruments for his purposes in the future.

On the death of his father, Norodom mounted the throne,
thanks to his interested protector. Si-vata, one of his brothers, rebelled on the instant, claiming the crown, because
he was the son of a king who had been crowned, while
Norodom, the elder, had been born before his father Ong-
duong had assumed the diadem in the solemn ceremony, regarded, according to Cambodgian rites, as specially important. An uncle of the princes, Senong Soo, supported the
cause of Si-vata, stirred up the province of Baphnum, which
was next Pnom-Penh, and made Norodom flee to Bangkok
without attempting resistance. In the month of February
1862 he was led back to his states by the soldiers of the
king of Siam, and reëstablished at Houdon, on the condition
that he would inaugurate his reign by ceding the provinces
of Compong-soaï and Pursat, as his father had begun his by
letting himself be plundered, for the benefit of Laos, of two
provinces bordering that country, over a part of which Siam
exercised absolute sovereignty. In haste to possess the
power, Norodom subscribed everything, so that the king of
Siam might well be proud of his pupil. At Bangkok his
promise was duly recorded, with the assurance, however,
that its performance would not be insisted upon if the king
of Cambodgia showed himself docile to the counsels of his
friends. Norodom was only too well inclined for the part
of vassal-king which they wished to make him play. The
arrival of the French in Cochin-China finally took from the

Annamites, wholly engrossed with defending themselves, all idea of conquest; and the king of Siam set himself to the task of gaining over the rest of a nation, of which he had, as it were, kneaded the king to his liking with his own hands.

Things stood thus when Saïgon was taken; and this short statement of them will explain the reason which forced us to intervene, and how for a time there were difficulties which stood in our way. It was a critical moment. The English, though they cannot complain of being straitened for want of room in India, saw their designs thwarted by our presence in the empire of Annam. The fear they inspired at the court of Siam had for long kept it from granting European nations the right to have a consul at Bangkok. They hold at this time a piece of ground there, and enjoy considerable influence in the counsels of the Siamese government. They would have reckoned it a great stroke if they could have got the king Phra-maha-mongkut, who was very much inclined to follow their wishes, to annex Cambodgia without any more ado. It is too well known what any tenderness shown by England to her clients commonly hides, not to doubt the disinterestedness affected in her expression of so much solicitude for Siam. Her amazing success in the past justifies all her dreams for the future; and she was annoyed to find in her way rivals she had thought she had for ever driven away from Asia. From Moulmein she already watches Bangkok; and not being able herself to take Cambodgia, she was willing to enrich a friend of whom she expects to be heir. Meanwhile she plotted to secure our being surrounded by enemies in our new establishment. Still more: the kingdom of Cambodgia commands the lower valley of the Mekong; a battery placed on the custom-house point would close the four branches of that river to trade; and we could not permit the prosperity of our colony of Saïgon, in whose port the products of the whole interior were one day to be gathered, to depend absolutely on a foreign nation, which was under influences certain to make it, as a rule, hostile to us. These considerations were decisive, and the independence of Cambodgia was soon seen to be an essential condition to the development, or almost

the existence, of French Cochin-China. But in the weak
state of the kingdom this was impossible, except by a protectorate. The rights of French suzerainty substituted for
those of Tu Duc, being from the first at least equal to those
of Siam, we could proclaim these at once annulled by a fair
compensation. A treaty would create new and exclusive
rights for us, and Siam would be finally put aside. It was
to this end all the efforts of the French officers, who had
become diplomatists, were henceforth turned.

A Cambodgian noble, Senong-soo, the uncle of King Norodom, having sought a refuge on our territory, to escape
the Siamese, the prime-minister of Siam at once demanded
his extradition from Admiral Bonard, who, however, refused
to permit it. This was of itself enough to show the court
of Bangkok our intentions with regard to Cambodgia, and,
in some degree, was a beginning of hostilities. To induce
Norodom to treat with us, it was important to mark the
difference of our idea of a protectorate from the oppressive
way in which the king of Siam had employed his humiliating suzerainty. It was no question with us of homage or
service; we had only one end to secure—the autonomy of
Cambodgia; and all our negotiations were directed to this
object. The king, moreover, had for long wished some over-
ture from us; for he knew that Siam would abate its exactions as soon as it saw it had to reckon with us. For the
same reasons, this latter power dreaded a French intervention, and the Siamese general, Phnéa-rat, who lodged at the
gates of the royal palace, redoubled his vigilance. He devoted himself to his task of watching and guiding a weak
conscience; and no scrupulous duenna ever took greater
pains to guard her precious trust. The king never spoke
a word that was not repeated; never made a movement that
was not watched; and even the letters he had to write to
the French commandant of one of the frontier circles commenced with the words, 'The king and the Siamese general.'
It was necessary to avoid, in the opening of our relations
with the court of Houdon, anything startling; to act with
prudence; to free the king, without causing a shock, from a
subjection as incompatible with his own dignity as with our
interests. Under various pretexts our vessels entered the

Mekong. The officers took care not to stay long at any one place, that they might not excite premature resistance; but they got, little by little, into direct relations with the king. Their instructions forbad their recognising in any way the Siamese tutelage, or suffering any third party to come between them and his Cambodgian majesty. The advice-boat Gyadinh was the first French vessel appointed by Admiral de La Grandière to cruise in the waters of Cambodgia. The king received its captain, M. de Lagrée, with cordiality, and allowed him permission, there and then, to establish a coaling-station, on the spot which we yet hold, opposite Pnom-Penh. He even extended his courtesy so far as to come without delay on board the Gyadinh; though it is true he was accompanied by the Siamese,—and he expressed a wish to visit the new governor of Cochin-China; but this was only the caprice of a curious child, and was at once given up on his tutor showing him the political significance of such an act.

In proportion as the representative of the court of Bangkok became alarmed, and caught a glimpse of the approaching emancipation of his pupil, he became more exacting. Though he was not permitted to be present at any audience granted to the French, he so arranged as not to lose a word of what was said. He never showed himself in public except in sumptuous robes, which quite eclipsed those of the king. He assumed the airs of a master in everything; and his soldiers, copying the ways of their chief, plundered the market daily. This conduct, though very obnoxious to the people, degraded as they were, failed to excite a revolution in favour of Phra-kéo-féa,[2] younger brother of the king, whose hatred of the Siamese gave him a kind of popularity. Our presence alone hindered it; and the Siamese general, seeing this, and being no longer able to bear the sight of the evident progress of our influence, seized the occasion to announce that he must return for new orders, and would leave his brother to hold his post beside the king. He judged it advisable, moreover, to take the author of an insurrection which threatened to disturb the peace of a state

[2] Since imprisoned at Saïgon. The revolt of 1866, excited by Pouquambo, was sanctioned by his name.

tributary to Siam to Bangkok, in the hope that a year passed in a bonze monastery, and in bonze dress, might inspire the young prince with better sentiments. It was thus he masked his retreat. As to us, we had done a service which helped on our protectorate. The moment was favourable to secure its formal recognition, without at once drawing attention to all that it implied.

Admiral de La Grandière, taking advantage of these circumstances, now appeared on the field at Houdon. The king, perhaps a little surprised, and hardly perhaps comprehending the meaning of the word protectorate, which is as hard to define in Cambodgian as in French, readily consented to set his seal to a treaty of nineteen articles, in which the protectorate of France over Cambodgia, solemnly proclaimed, was surrounded by all the guarantees we wished to obtain. It was understood that, until it was ratified by the Emperor of the French, the convention had only a conditional force. We had succeeded in getting the king to do an act of free sovereignty; and we took away with us an agreement which we could not help thinking a first success. But hardly had the news reached Siam before it raised a storm, the echo of which almost frightened our new protégé into forgetting his word, and caused us serious embarrassments.

The Kalahom—the prime-minister of the king of Siam—told Commandant Forbin, our envoy to Bangkok on the death of the French consul, distinctly, that the king of Cambodgia was a mere viceroy vassal of Siam, who had no right to treat with us, and that his affairs could be decided only at Bangkok; then, becoming calmer, he gave it very clearly to be understood that his master would be disposed to divide with us what remained of the old Cambodgian kingdom. His assertions were definite, and the answers needed to be categorical also. It was therefore officially communicated to the Kalahom that this pretended vassalage of the king of Cambodgia had never been recognised by France, which was resolved to have nothing to do with any third party, in treaty with him. They raised an argument against us from M. de Montigny's mission in 1855, trying to prove that he had always acknowledged the vassalage of Cambodgia in his conferences with the Siamese

government. This was entirely untrue; and the mere statement of the facts suffices to refute it. It will require only a
short digression, but its exposure will show the tricks to
which Siamese policy resorted to gain its ends.

M. de Montigny having announced his intention of making a commercial treaty with Cambodgia, so far from any
opposition being offered, he was even advised to take possession in the name of France of the island of Phu-Quoc,
lying over against the Cambodgian port of Compot, in the
gulf of Siam, and peopled by Annamites. The Siamese states-
men evidently sought in this way to bring on a dispute, by
which they might profit, between France and Annam. On
the one hand, the king of Siam wrote to M. Miche, now bishop
of Saïgon, begging him to put the knowledge of the country and of the language he had acquired at the service of
M. de Montigny; on the other, he caused the king of Cambodgia to be secretly told, that if he were unfortunate
enough to treat with the French, he would be sorry for it.
The king, Ong-duong, on the news of the arrival of the
French ambassador, had ordered the road between Houdon
and Compot to be repaired, and set himself to give M. de
Montigny a magnificent reception; but the despatch from
Bangkok fairly terrified him. When he farther learned that
the same vessel which brought the ambassador bore also an
agent of the king of Siam, his alarm knew no limits; he
no longer thought of going to Compot to the meeting he
had himself appointed, and instantly began his annual visit
to the pagodas, in order that M. de Montigny might not
find him in his capital, if he came there after him.

Since it was thus necessary in 1855 to use threats to
keep Ong-duong from treating with us, it is clear that his
right to do so was acknowledged. Why should his successor be affirmed to have lost a right which belonged to
his father? After having for long been forced to submit to
Siamese interference in his affairs, the king of Cambodgia,
by a convention freely granted us, had created rights and
duties, against which the protests of the Siamese government were henceforth of no weight.

The general, Phnea-rat, who took Phrakeo-fea to Bangkok, had gained such an ascendancy over the king, that we

C

should probably have hardly succeeded so easily had he remained at Houdon.   Fortunately he left only his brother
behind him, a mandarin of little influence; who, keeping by
his instructions, and maintaining a careless surveillance from
a distance, neither foresaw nor prevented anything.   When
he learned that the convention was signed, he felt hurt in
his pride as a Siamese, and in his *amour propre* as a diplo-
matist; became violent, like all timid persons suddenly
waked from their torpor, and threatened Norodom with the
anger of his master, the terrible consequences of which the
French would be unable to avert.   He invited him, besides,
to add a letter of regrets and excuses to his own despatch
to Bangkok, in which he broke to the Kalahom the news of
the grave events which had just happened.   Norodom, quite
distracted, had the weakness to consent.   He said that he
confessed his fault; that he had no right to sign without
consulting the king of Siam; but that he had been taken by
surprise, and had not turned over the matter long enough
to reflect on the consequences of an act of which he now,
too late, repented.   Those who knew the king saw that
there was quite as much calculation as fear in his language.
His letter might be taken as an index of the policy he intended to follow.   He wished to appear to yield to a pressure
on our part, not doubting that Siam would give way to our
wish.   Knowing that we had no design on his territory, and
thoroughly aware of the value we set on the independence
of his kingdom, he was determined to leave us to manage
matters; to raise obstacles, as necessity might require, which
he knew we were strong enough to surmount, that he might
get himself out of his difficulty; to hold himself ready, in a
word, to enjoy the liberty which we should give him, without
Siam being able, whatever happened, to throw on him the
whole responsibility.

The future had, it must be granted, some dark points
which justified the uneasiness of Norodom.   The Annamite
ambassador was at that time in Paris; his mission was no
secret to any one in Cochin-China, and it was presently
made known in Cambodgia.   The Siamese spoke of the approaching evacuation by the French as certain; and an agent
of Tu Duc, still more confident, came to demand at Houdon

the triennial tribute. It was certainly not probable that Phan-tan-gian should succeed in the negotiations; nevertheless, when one knows the facts, and the hesitation, which was natural enough, before France came to a final decision, one is led to find in the clear-sightedness of the king a kind of excuse for the feebleness of his conduct. Norodom was, besides, the more troubled, from not taking into account the interval necessary for communication with France, and because Bangkok, confident in the resources of its diplomacy, alleged that the treaty would not be confirmed by Napoleon III.

Meanwhile the anger of the king of Siam, who had just heard of the events in Cambodgia, suddenly passed off; for he thought he had discovered in the letter of Norodom a way to draw down a terrible revenge on us, which he left to his faithful Phnea-rat to carry out. That clever agent, whose sudden departure had so greatly aided our success, was ordered to get ready to return to Houdon. He took with him a draft of a treaty, which he was told to get the king of Cambodgia to sign at any cost; the means to be used being left to him, as a man, skilful, and full of resources and energy. This treaty had for its end to define and emphasise more than hitherto the vassalage of Norodom, who was called in it the 'viceroy,' and mere 'governor of Cambodgia.' The king of Siam had taken the trouble to write the preamble of this diplomatic missive with his own hand. He wished, he said, to let all men know that Cambodgia is a state tributary to the kingdom of Siam, owing it homage, and for long under its protection. The right was granted him by article 6, in spite of an illusory restriction, to name the governors of Cambodgia henceforward at his pleasure; and the 7th article, in the same way, reserved to the court of Bangkok the right to nominate governors for the Cambodgian provinces. As to the French treaty, no notice was taken of it; it was not thought worth discussing, and indeed was not recognised as in existence. Phnea-rat, arriving at Houdon unexpectedly, acted with promptitude, ability, and vigour. Without giving Norodom time to collect himself, he told him that the king of Siam, though profoundly irritated at his conduct, assented to his becoming a subject of France; for his treaty with us

meant nothing less—the consuls of other nations at Bangkok
had made no secret of saying so; and they saw an incontestable proof of this subjection in the clause which shut out
from Cambodgia the representatives of all other European
powers. It was easy to divine the quarter from which insinuations of this kind came. The king of Siam, continued
Phnea-rat, had no intention of offering any opposition.
Only Norodom, in thus yielding up his sovereignty and
betraying his people, was, by the very fact, unworthy of the
throne, and Si-vata, till then detained at Bangkok, would be
set at liberty. The crown of the kings of Cambodgia was
kept at the capital of Siam; it would remain there, and even
if he retained his throne, he would never be a crowned king.
In addition, his Siamese majesty judged that the time had
come to accept the two provinces of Compong-soaï and
Pursat, so graciously offered him at the beginning of Norodom's reign. Phnea-rat added that the wishes of his master
were strictly within the limits of justice and moderation,
and did not shrink from saying that they would be imposed
on France itself by force in a war, in which the Siamese government had been assured of powerful allies. To turn aside so
many perils there was a last resource: Norodom had but to
sign a secret treaty, which was, in reality, only a precaution
taken against the French. The king of Siam would then
condescend to come personally to Compot, where Norodom
was to meet him, and all his faults would be forgiven.
These manœuvres were completely successful, for Phnea-rat
bore away from the palace the treaty signed by the king,
before M. de Lagrée knew of his being in Houdon. This was
in November 1863; the ratifications were sent to Siam on
the 22d of the January following; and it was not till the
month of August 1864 that we even heard of its existence,
from an English journal of Singapore, which published the
treaty at full length.

The artful Siamese diplomat knew well the interest he
had in misleading France as to the aim and the true result
of his mission. The arrival of a great mandarin at Houdon from the court of Bangkok awakened M. de Lagrée's
suspicions, for his watchful mind was beginning to get
acquainted with the tricks of Eastern diplomacy. This

difficulty had no way embarrassed Phnea-rat; he had a pretext ready. Determined to avoid any meeting with the representative of France, who would not readily have yielded to this change in his designs, he caused a letter to be sent by the king of Siam to M. Miche, telling him that Norodom was to be crowned in a fortnight. Feigning to be taken all at once with a holy zeal for the Catholic religion, and with a profound respect for the venerable head of the Cambodgian Christians, he came to see him at Pinhalu. He had an escort of two hundred guards, and a suite of a dozen elephants in scarlet housings worked with gold, one of them, the most richly caparisoned, bearing himself. What must have been the astonishment of the humble missionary bishop at seeing the ambassador of the king of Siam coming to his house in such pomp, and at his delivering him a letter from his sovereign! France having for long been known in these countries only by the missionary priests, Phnea-rat affected to believe that the bishop was its official representative, and passed contemptuously before M. de Lagrée's door without ever stopping. As to M. Miche, a stranger to politics by taste as well as by his functions, he took for granted that what he was told was really intended as it was spoken, and hastened to inform M. de Lagrée of the approaching coronation. Thus the treaty was made, and no one even suspected its existence : Phnea-rat had succeeded.

Meanwhile the report quickly spread to Cambodgia, that the king of Siam had determined to send to its legitimate possessor the ancient crown of the old Cambodgian princes, but that he would himself put it on the head of Norodom, when he conferred on him, on the day it might please him to fix, a solemn investiture, which should definitely make him his vassal. Public opinion gave the ceremony this meaning in advance, and every one asked himself curiously what we should do. It became urgent to enlighten the king, and to restore his confidence in us, which seemed very much shaken. M. de Lagrée did not hesitate to open his eyes on a state of things most annoying to France, and full of peril to himself, and Norodom thanked him with great heartiness for his advice. If one could have believed him, it was the first time he saw clearly whither the king of Siam wished to lead him. The court of Bangkok would consider itself sovereign of Cambodgia after the coronation, but he was resolved to disappoint their calculations. He wished to crown himself at Houdon, before his people, and he expressed a desire to see the governor of Cochin-China there, to assist at the ceremony. He loudly asserted that the day had not been fixed, and that he could easily find pretexts to delay it till the arrival of the answer expected from Paris about the protectorate treaty. 'Siam,' he said continually, 'has become kind to me.' Such a change, of which it was impossible for us to divine the causes, might well surprise us. The king of Siam had announced by a solemn and special message that the coronation would take place in a fortnight; and now, on the other side, we learned that the day was not fixed for it! They were clearly trifling with us at Bangkok. M. de Lagrée concealed his uneasiness. By his frankness and courtesy he exercised a strong personal influence on Norodom, who always yielded to him, though he all the time thought himself his own master. He had the imprudence to show his friendliness to the French officers publicly, with unusual demonstrativeness. His visits to M. de Lagrée became more frequent; he rejoiced at a truce, which he was as anxious to prolong as a scholar his holidays. Phnea-rat, who could not but notice this change in the king's mood, knew by experience how easily he was led, and believed the moment come to get him to enter into a fresh engagement with Siam.

It will be remembered that, at the time of the secret treaty, the king of Siam had promised to visit the Cambodgian port of Compot, to meet Norodom there. Phnea-rat announced that his master was about to leave his capital, and would come with his hands full of pardons. In order, however, not to embitter the joy of the king at the flattering news of this august visit, by fresh embarrassments, Phnea-rat subscribed at once to all the demands of the French, stipulating only that Norodom should agree to drink the water of the oath in presence of the king of Siam, which is the mode in which they pledge obedience and fidelity. He then tried once more to get Norodom to declare himself a subject of Siam, and merely the governor of Cambodgia.

While this was going on, some drunken French sailors caused some disturbance in the town, and even in the house of the king's mother. The Siamese mandarin made a great deal of this, exaggerating it extremely, and ended by getting a promise from the terrified Norodom to come to Compot. He hastened to spread the news, to speak of the water of the oath, and omitted nothing that could compromise the king. Satisfied with his success in this, he forthwith went off from Houdon, leaving M. de Lagrée thoroughly puzzled and Norodom more embarrassed than ever, neither daring to speak nor to be silent, bound on both hands by treaties, and reduced to play a passive part between two adversaries, who were each too strong for him, and with each of whom, in turn, he had signed contradictory engagements.

A few days after the Siamese had left, Norodom took advantage of his liberty to come on board the Gyadinh. He tried to be frank, but his courage could not get beyond half-confidences. 'I know Siam better than any one,' said he to the officers of the vessel; 'they fear you there, but are far enough from liking you. Don't believe what they say at the court of Bangkok about dislike of the English. They favour them as much as they are favoured by them. More than a year ago, the Siamese invited me to make a treaty with England; and they have lately made fresh overtures about it to me. The king of Siam wants me at Compot only to try to bring me under religious influence. It was he who made a bonze of me at Bangkok; I am his godson in religion, and it is a strong tie in our two countries. If he delay coming to Compot, the season will hinder me from making the voyage, and I should be glad of it; for, in reality, I have no love for him. When he wants to get a promise from me, an act, or, above all, a signature, I refuse, on the ground that I am under you.' He had not always had strength of mind to resist; and this last phrase hid a biting remorse. His words in other respects gave a clear enough view of how matters stood; and his calculations, which were more prudent than dignified, became daily more evident.

At last, on the 11th of January 1864, it was announced that a Siamese steamer had just anchored at Compot, and

the king immediately gave orders for his departure. This
was a check to our diplomat; and M. de Lagrée tried to
find a way of stopping him, on learning, not without surprise, that instead of the king of Siam, only a simple mandarin, with a letter from him for Norodom, had come. Under
some pretext the king excused himself from assisting in
the coronation, or even coming to Compot. He sent word,
however, that Phnea-rat would bring the famous crown
shortly.

The king of Siam is the object of a similar religious
veneration in the Buddhist part of Indo-China as the Sultan
at Constantinople is to the Mussulman. The prospect of a
visit from so great a personage flattered Norodom beyond
measure; and this consideration, which was made use of to
hasten the concluding of the secret treaty, was most likely
not without its influence in getting it signed. This end
once gained, the king of Siam soon lost all desire to come
to Compot, and Phnea-rat knew this well when he got Norodom to promise to go to drink the oath-water; but he cared
little at bottom whether the ceremony came off or not: every
one knew that the king of Cambodgia had agreed to it, and
that was enough.

Whilst M. de Lagrée saw in the sweetness and moderation of the court of Siam only a motive for keeping more
carefully on his guard than ever, Norodom, forgetting his
dignity, could hardly contain his joy. They might be treating him slightingly, but they were going to give him up his
crown. He thought only on that; he spoke only of that.
He ordered that nothing should be wanting to give splendour to the feasts, and the preparations began. The bonzes
having been consulted, gave themselves up to pious meditation, and at last announced that the 3d of February was
a day propitious and fixed by heaven. The governor of
Cochin-China was invited to Houdon, or at least to send a
representative, who would be received with all usual honours, and would occupy a position not less honourable than
that of the Siamese envoy, whoever he might be. Everything was arranged in advance. The king showed his joy
at being about to play the first part in an imposing ceremony. He waited impatiently for the French, before whom

Plate 4 *Commander Doudart de Lagrée (Drawing by Émile Bayard, based on a photograph)*

Plate 5 *The market in Parom Penh (Drawing by E. Boucourt, based on a watercolour by L. Delaporte)*

especially he wished to show himself in the ancient state-dress of the old kings of Cambodgia, long since disused.

The season favourable for religious ceremonies had now begun. The head of the staff of the governor of Cochin-China had arrived at Houdon: nothing more was wanting for the coronation but the crown. Couriers ran full speed to and from Compot; the bonzes redoubled their prayers; the king, greatly excited, lavished orders and counter-orders. Patience held out as long as it could; but at last there was nothing for it but to yield to evidence. Siam had merely wished to put Norodom in a false position with us, and to draw on ourselves an unbearable ridicule. Our protégé got out of his difficulty cleverly. He decided that, from regard for France, the fêtes should still take place, with no other omission than the want of the insignia necessitated. We could not have asked more. There could be no doubt of the good faith of the king, who had gathered round him the governors of the provinces. It was a good opportunity to bring under the eyes of these dignitaries the strange conduct of the Siamese government; and it was easy, by awakening their *amour propre*, to turn aside on the court of Bangkok, already disliked, the blow it intended for us.

The fêtes did take place, and also the ceremony of svett-rachat, or raising the parasol, which consists in setting over the throne a parasol of five stages, and is almost as neces-sary to complete a coronation as the crowning itself. Much elated at seeing this quintuple diadem for the first time over his head, Norodom cried out in a transport of gratitude and happiness, 'I look on the emperor of France as my father, and on the admiral as my brother!' He might have added that Siam insisted on being his mother—a mother exacting and crafty, who had not given up the hopes of supplanting the males of the family. The next day Norodom came on board the Mitraille in the uniform of an officer of marines,—of very fine cloth covered with embroidery. He wore, besides, white pantaloons, a heavy cap ornamented by a great deal of braiding, a gilded sword-belt, a sabre with an ivory handle, of European shape; but, as a protest against the exactions of etiquette which imprisoned him in such a make-up, he wore slippers, an extraordinary shirt strewn with rose-flowers,

and a necktie carelessly tied. The king was in a very merry
mood, and was pleasant even with the Siamese. 'Get ready
the rice,' said he to his mandarins squatted round him,
according to custom; 'the Siamese have arrived, and you
know they have come without any provisions.' The court
applauded the mirth of its master: Norodom did not mean
to speak so plainly.

Our great enemy, Phnea-rat, who had in reality been
charged to bring the crown, landed at Compot at the same
time as the French mission itself reached Houdon. The
Siamese dignitary learned that several officers who had come
from Saïgon, only for the purpose of adding to the *éclat* of
the ceremony by their presence, gave it quite a French character. This was so intolerable to him, that he took upon
himself to send back the crown to Bangkok, and stopped on
the way to Houdon, in order not to reach that town till after
the departure of M. Desmoulin, chief of the staff to Admiral
de La Grandière. He, now, conceived, on the instant, a new
and bold plan, by which he hoped to add a defeat to the
mystification he had already succeeded in giving us. The
moment the French naval officers left Houdon by one gate,
a little put-out by their mishap, the Siamese agent entered
by the other. He intended to take away the king to Bangkok, and crown him there, without consulting with us. It
was a daring scheme, and he set himself to it with his
usual ardour.

Attacking first the mandarins who were the ordinary
advisers of Norodom, he showed them the advantages they
and their master would reap from a voyage to Bangkok,
and the serious risks they ran if they displeased the king
of Siam. He knew how to use correspondents he had in
some of the provinces—notably in those of Compong-soaï
and Pursat, whose governors were creatures of the court of
Bangkok, and had protested against the French alliance—
so as to stir up the population. It will be remembered that,
but for our intervention, these two provinces were about to
share the fate of Angcor and Battam-bang, and be annexed
to the kingdom of Siam. Seeking the presence of the king
himself, presently, he reminded him of his treaty and his promises, which he could show, and thus make trouble between

him and us. He terrified him about the insurrection in the southern provinces, which demanded separation from Cambodgia; asserted roundly that the French were deceiving him shamefully; that their emperor had refused to ratify the treaty, and, moreover, that the English were determined at any cost to sustain the Siamese policy. In short, he ended by getting Norodom to consent, and even worked him up to the necessary pitch of courage for breaking the matter to us himself. The preparations for departure were kept secret till the arrival of some Siamese vessels at Compot, when the news broke like a thunder-clap on M. de Lagrée. He found the king, for the first time, in a fixed and invincible resolution. Norodom was unwilling to lose his crown; and since they would give it him only at Bangkok, he would go there to get it. Besides, the ratification of the treaty had not arrived; and this delay, which he was determined not to understand, justified all his suspicions and uneasiness. He announced that he would leave on the 3d of March; and on that day left his capital, intrusting the government of Cambodgia to his ministers. The agitation in Pursat and Compong-soaï ceased as by magic.

We were thus about to be beaten in our secret struggle with the court of Bangkok, which had lasted since the treaty of August 1863. It was hard to submit. When M. de Lagrée learned by public report the arguments that had led the king to consent to set out, he lost no time in exposing them. His majesty had started: it was a critical moment. M. de Lagrée acted on one of those sudden inspirations which redeem causes seemingly lost. The presence of a small Siamese garrison in the capital of Cambodgia authorised us to land some soldiers. The authorities readily consented to our doing so, and our men were lodged near enough the Siamese troops to watch all their movements. The French flag was raised over the barracks of the detachment of infantry, and saluted with twenty-one guns. It was this which retrieved our fortunes.

The king was not far on the way to Compot. Terrified at the sound of artillery, and thinking we were about to profit by his absence to make ourselves masters of Cambodgia, he at once called a halt; then came back part of the way. Phnea-rat himself hesitated. It was a doubtful success to have the king, and to lose the kingdom. He caused a letter to be written by Norodom to excite the French resident, who till then had lived on a footing of respectful courtesy with him, to use threats which he intended to urge against us before the assembled consuls: adopting in this phrase, one often employed by the Siamese plenipotentiary. The trap was badly set, and it was Phnea-rat who was caught in it. Without disputing the king's right to go to Bangkok, M. de Lagrée, in his answer, explained how the voyage, while distasteful to France, would compromise his own interests; and he reminded him especially of the bitter complaints the ambition of Siam had so often drawn from him, and of the behaviour commonly shown by the representative of that court at Bangkok. The Siamese general read before Norodom the letter of M. de Lagrée. Great was the rage of the one and the confusion of the other at the recital of the long string of troubles told us by Norodom's own lips as suffered from Siam. It was sought to drive us to violent language, and we had proof that our adversary owed his success only to his threats. Phnea-rat almost went into a fit with rage; then was abashed, and finally lost his self-control altogether. Usually as prompt to execute as to form a design, all at once he lost even the power to give a command. Our revenge began. Halted some leagues from his capital, Norodom announced one day that he had decided to go to Bangkok, and, the next, let it be known that he thought of returning to Houdon. After a time the mandarins got afraid of compromising themselves; regretted aloud the advice they had given their master. The Siamese saw all his prestige disappear; a moment's indecision had ruined all his clever manœuvres.

For several centuries Siam had favoured or frowned on Cambodgia as its own interests led it, always making its power sensibly felt. As to us, we were friends of yesterday, and had never given more than advice. However honourable this might be, it had the inconvenience of exciting the mistrust of our new protégé, the king Norodom, who could not see through it. By the simple political and social theories of these half-barbarous nations—theories consecrated by universal application—force is the best of all arguments. If

it was true that we were not afraid of the redoubtable power
of the king of Siam, why so much talking? why not tell him
our pleasure without so much circumlocution? why not require the immediate restoration of the crown? Norodom
always came back to this. We had shown moderation, and
he accused us of fear. Time passed, moreover, without bringing us the ratification of the treaty with France. Siam fought
against it at Paris, and continued to spread lying reports of
her success. What would become of the unhappy monarch,
if, by some impossibility, the Siamese negotiators carried
their point? His levity could not keep him from feeling
this.

Meanwhile, rebels, availing themselves of all this, had
risen in earnest in the south-west, and had massacred the
minister of war who had been sent to them. This insurrection gave the king an honourable pretext for returning to
his capital, which he did on the evening of the 17th March,
followed closely by Phnea-rat, beaten, furious, confused, but
yet not hopeless, for he began at once to do his utmost to
get our soldiers sent away. But he was unsuccessful. As to
Norodom, not daring to refuse anything to the irritated
general, whose humour became more unbearable than ever
after this last check, he tried to drag from M. de Lagrée
a declaration in writing that Phnea-rat had systematically
used coercion in his intercourse with him. It is not worth
while to say what came of a proposal like this, the knavery
of which almost loses its name, and turns half lovable for its
naïveté.

Our position was now very different from the half despair
in which we had been a fortnight before. The game, however, was not yet gained, as long as Phnea-rat remained at
Houdon, free to see the king all the time, and able to neu-
tralise our influence by his own. Happily, the ratification
of the treaty arrived at last, in the nick of time. The news
delighted the king. He burned with desire, he said, to see
the signature and the seal of the emperor of the French.
Phnea-rat tried hard to make him believe that the whole
thing had been concocted at Saïgon; but the king, full of the
prospect of a new ceremony, paid no attention to the un-
principled insinuations of the poor old despairing general,

who had the mortification of seeing our treaty carried with great pomp to the palace. The exchange of ratifications was conducted with great solemnity. The chief of the staff of Admiral de La Grandière, who had come once more to Houdon, asked the pleasure of an interview; but he unwisely declined it. Every one concluded from this that he was afraid of a public explanation of the facts, and that he thus felt himself not without ground of reproach. He decided at last to let us be masters of the field, and left Houdon on the 25th April, receiving the post of minister of justice in Siam, as the reward of his services and the consolation of his defeat. The Siamese flag was finally lowered in Cambodgia, and there was no longer any reason to delay the departure of the small French garrison, which might by its presence have irritated the people.

When the king of Siam saw his favourite mandarin return, the man on whom he had placed all his hopes, he felt that, the main point being lost, it was not worth while fighting over details. He was wise enough to yield with a good grace, and removed all hindrances to the coronation by restoring the crown. On the 26th May the Ondine left Saïgon, and carried to Cambodgia, along with a new French mission, the Siamese mandarin Phya-Montrey-Suriwan, who, by his breadth of mind and his courteous manners, made us pleasantly forget his insolent predecessor, in regard to whose management of Siamese policy he made no hesitation in repudiating what had been offensive. Thus the despairing efforts of an adversary, who had almost beaten us, were publicly disavowed. Phnea-rat, who had returned to Houdon with Phya-Montrey, and was lost in the crowd, devoured his mortification while he silently chewed his betel. Nothing was awanting in our triumph. The Siamese envoy wished himself to set the crown on Norodom's head, but the chief of the admiral's staff would not allow it. He then proposed that each party should take a side of it; but M. Desmoulin declined that proposition also, and made this arrangement: he received the crown from the hands of the Siamese, and then presented it to the king, who crowned himself, like Napoleon at Notre Dame. When he felt it at last really on his head, after having seen it vanish so often at the moment he seemed about to get hold of it, Norodom, overcome by his happiness, expressed the desire to salute his powerful protector, Napoleon III. He took some steps to the west, and, raising his hand to his crown, in imitation of M. Desmoulin, who took off his hat, repeated the same profound bows as had been made to himself. Phnea-rat, furious at this, now broke through the crowd, demanded that salutations be paid to the king of Siam, and, throwing himself on the ground, beat his forehead on it three times. Norodom, for courtesy, did the same, and all were pleased with the feeling which inspired this act of the unfortunate general in this his last public claim. The king of Siam did not, however, decide till long after this to recognise our protectorate officially, and to tear-up the secret convention negotiated by Phnea-rat, and demanded some concessions, which were granted by France, when he did so, particularly the definitive surrender to him of the two fine provinces of Battam-bang and Angcor. If the arrangement made in 1868 is not destined, as we may hope, however, it will be, to regulate for long our relations with the court of Siam, it will at least have the advantage of showing that our power did not abate our moderation. On learning our success, the part of the European colony at Bangkok which had been so hostile to us feigned themselves pleased.

I knew by what efforts the French flag had been finally hoisted at Houdon, and I could not help being astonished at the scornful indifference with which the king of Cambodgia spoke of his old friends the Siamese. At a collation which he gave us he was full of warmth, animation, and spirits. He seemed prouder of his dishes of figured English crockery than of his vases and waiters of massive gold. His palace is nothing more than a great thatched shed, in which a great number of women and servants lodge. Norodom is a little man, with a great inclination to corpulence. Certainly he is not good-looking even for a Cambodgian, but his face is expressive, intelligent, and mobile. He very soon acquired many of our ways, and one might say that he has hit on our characteristics. His conversation, which is very graphic, is mixed with sallies almost Voltairean. He despises his subjects, now he no longer fears them, and mocks at Buddha when he is in the mood. He treads under foot the ancient etiquette, which is the one surviving relic of the old civilisation of the Kmer, and seems disposed always to decide in favour of us, except on one point. He admits the different uses of steam, the many uses of electricity, the application of light to photography, and makes visible efforts to understand them; but he absolutely refuses to believe that there ever has been, or ever can be, a great nation without an absolute monarch. Despotism shows itself in him with a naïve candour, and he does not hesitate to reply, when recommended to open or repair a road necessary for commerce,—'There's no use for it—I never went by it.'

The Cambodgians are generally very dissolute. The Chinese traveller of the thirteenth century, whom I have already had occasion to quote, tells us, that if a husband be away on business, and stays over a week, his wife says, 'I'm not a demon: how can I sleep alone?' The naïve narrator adds, 'I have, however, heard say that there are chaste women.' I also have heard the same; but I doubt if there be virtue enough in any one to resist the seductions of the king, who knows the fact, and abuses it, which is one of the main causes of his great unpopularity. If we had not supported him in 1866, he would certainly have lost his throne. The Cambodgians have reason enough to ask a change of government; but they would gain nothing by a change of the individual. One cannot hope that the voice of political reason will make itself heard in the councils of these Asiatic princes, so long as that of the passions speaks so loud in their hearts. Subjects may hope in vain for security, while their master is not yet satiated in his pleasures. The brothers of a king, while still pretenders, publish declarations which they forget as soon as they are sovereigns. We have, therefore, done wisely in closing the throne against them, and in proclaiming our intention to uphold established authority. This revolt of 1866 has, moreover, created new rights for us over Cambodgia, while it has made it Norodom's duty to listen to our counsels. These will not be awanting, and this magnificent country, whose riches will rapidly develop under a more humane administration, is an admirable complement of our Annamite possessions. I had come to this conviction before returning to Saïgon to make my last preparations for the adventurous expedition, which would bring me in contact, at Laos,—side by side with the ancient vestiges of Cambodgian rule,—with the vigorous imprint of Siamese power, which bids fair to impose itself, unknown to Europe, on nearly all Indo-China.

CHAPTER I.

RUINS OF ANGCOR. STUNG-TRENG. RAPIDS OF KHON-KHONG.
ARRIVAL AT BASSAC.

The greatest European colonies have had modest beginnings; a fortified factory was the cradle of the immense empire which to-day embraces the whole Indian peninsula, and threatens to overrun China. Some points gained on the shore as the result of war, or of successful negotiations; some leaders, inspired by various motives, but all, alike, by the irresistible attractions of the unknown—have, most frequently, been the causes and instruments of progressive invasions, which have almost always ended in a definitive conquest. Like armies in the field, colonies have their advanced guards. They cannot suffer either barbarous or idle races on their frontiers: the tribes which leave a naturally fertile soil untilled are not less their enemies than those which are warlike. By a kind of natural law, which one can hardly admit without sadness, there is scarcely an alternative, for races outside European civilisation, between a melancholy transformation, or a remorseless extermination. The Eastern monarchs, who have not yet learned this from experience, divine it instinctively; and the wiser among them, opening among themselves a career to rival ambitions, seek safety in the competition thus established. It was on this account that the clause in our treaty, which shut out the representatives of other European powers from Cambodgia, irritated the king of Siam so gravely. It is thus easy to understand the repugnance with which Asiatic princes receive projects of expeditions into the interior of their countries.

The exploration of the valley of the Mekong, set afoot

in 1866, by order of the minister of marine, and by the labours
of the governor of French Cochin-China, could not fail to
excite such suspicions, however little ground there might
be for them. Passports were asked from four cabinets.
That of Pekin temporised, and sought to dissuade us from
an enterprise which would lead us to a part of the Celestial
Empire where we should meet no end of danger; that of
Hué declared that it sought to keep us from its tributary
subjects of the upper valley of the Mekong only from national self-love; these half-barbarous tribes in reality paying
them no homage at all. It has been said that this government, so full of coquetry, had sent presents to the chiefs,
urging them to murder us; but this disgraceful report is
perhaps only one of those mystifications of which the civilised press has not the monopoly. The Burmese empire had
just accomplished the revolution, during which the seat of
government had been transferred from Ava to Mandalay;
and the overtures of Admiral de La Grandière remained
without result. As to the cabinet of Bangkok, its position
towards us was more delicate. We had always refused to
recognise the rights of the king of Siam over Laos, and, he,
himself, had, besides, found it convenient, about that time, to
say that he exercised a purely nominal sovereignty over that
country, so that he could not, with a good grace, formally
shut us out of it. On the other hand, any bad treatment on
the part of functionaries set up by him might be a cause of
offence to France; and he questioned if the peaceful conquest of Cambodgia might not be a step on our march to
Indo-China, and could not refrain from looking on the projected journey as the preliminary to our taking possession.
The countries through which we must first pass had been
detached from the Cambodgian monarchy, or subjugated by
Siamese armies, who had committed horrible excesses, and
thus, as Siam had no other right over them but that of conquest, we should be in a position, on learning all this, to question the validity of its title to them. The king yielded,
however, and sent us passports. It was agreed at Saïgon
that the expedition would make a long halt in Lower Laos,
and would receive, some months after its setting out, the
letters expected from Pekin.

The principal results which were expected from the exploration of the Mekong may be summed up in a few words. It was desired, first, that the old maps should be rectified, and the navigability of the river tried, it being our hope that we might bind together French Cochin-China and the western provinces of China by means of it. Were the rapids, of whose existence we knew, an absolute barrier? Were the islands of Khon an impassable difficulty? Was there any truth in the opinion of geographers who, with Vincendon Dumoulin, believed that there was a communication between the Meïnam and the Mekong? To gather information respecting the sources of the latter, if it proved impossible to reach them; to solve the different geographical problems which would naturally offer, was the first part of the programme the commission had to carry out. We were required, besides, to report any miscellaneous facts which might throw light on the history, the philology, the ethnography, or the religion of the peoples along the great river, which was to be as much as possible the guiding thread of our expedition. We had instructions to seek for a passage from Indo-China to China; an enterprise in which the English have always failed as yet. It was, moreover, essential, since the establishment of France in Cochin-China, to know our neighbours of Laos better; the resources of their country, and their relations with the Indo-Chinese powers, of which they were vaguely known to be tributaries. No limit of time was fixed for us, nor any route for our return.

Laos, a vast region, which on the north touches China, and on the south Cambodgia, was reckoned at Saïgon one of the most unhealthy countries in the world. The missionaries who, in our time, had tried to carry the Gospel thither, had either very soon died or had returned grievously ill; and as the result of such disastrous experiments, the attemps to combat Bouddhism in one of its strongholds had been abandoned. The single lay traveller who had recently tried to explore these countries, our countryman Mouhot, had set out from Bangkok, after numerous excursions to Cambodgia, and had struck the Mekong only beyond the 18th degree of latitude, a little below Luan Praban, where he soon after died. But Crachè, the farthest point on the Mekong fixed by our naval hydrographers, is between the 12th and 13th degrees. Uncertainty begins within two degrees of Saïgon, the very inexact charts of the great river, beyond that, only misleading geography instead of serving it. The public will be able to judge the facts when Lieut. Garnier of the navy, who had special charge of the meteorological, hydrographical, and geographical section of the expedition, has finished his labours.

We left Saïgon on the 5th June 1866, at noon. Those who knew the indomitable energy of our leader shook hands with us as if we were doomed; but the majority predicted a speedy return, after an abortive attempt. For myself, when I try to recall to-day what I felt on seeing, from the bridge of the gunboat, the chief buildings of Saïgon, the infant capital of Asiatic France, receding from view, I find that my impressions are less vivid than they are of what I had felt at my first setting out, some time before, for Cambodgia. I had spent nearly six months in the enervating climate of Cochin-China, and it had brought me to a kind of universal indifference.

I could not leave Cambodgia without visiting the ruins which are at once its glory and its shame. They mark the spot where the heart of this great Khmer empire, now cold, once beat,—that empire whose scattered members we shall soon find on our course. The contemplation of these magnificent remains was well fitted to increase our zeal in the discovery of other traces of a civilisation that has disappeared. Leaving Compon-Luon, our little gunboat took the direction of the great lake—the Ton-le-sap, a true inland sea, not less than twenty leagues in length when the waters are lowest, but, when the inundation begins, spread over the country till it triples its surface. During the months of August and September there are no roads in the lower districts; boats sail over the fields, trees show their heads above the water, and the wild beasts flee, en masse, to the heights; so that nothing could give a more vivid idea of the deluge. The inhabitants of the plains betake themselves, with their domestic animals, to the mountains. The rise of the waters is not always the same; at times the rice suffers from want of moisture enough, at others it is drowned out in the lower tracts. There is, however, one kind, the stalk of which grows at the same rate as the waters rise, so that the ear is always at the surface.

We were in the month of June; the rains had hardly as yet begun to fall regularly every day, and the yellow waters of the lake were still comparatively shallow. The channels of this immense reservoir, which obscure traditions affirm to be comparatively recent, are narrow, and grow sensibly more obstructed year by year. At the entry, on the left, a chain of mountains runs in the direction of Pursat. Snows crown the peaks, and the sun, which does its best to melt them, without effect, gives them a pale, ethereal look. We meet, here and there, some fishing-boats which have stayed after the rest. Villages are scattered thinly along the banks, others come out over the water, the frail posts which support the huts bending under the force of the waves without its seeming to trouble the inmates. They are Annamites, and, like the buffalo, their faithful servant, if the land fail them, they take to the water. Presently the wind rises, it blows violently, ploughing deep furrows in the lake. The land is only a blue thread on our right, hardly seen above the waves; on our left the horizon is all sea.

An imaginary line, from two opposite posts placed on the banks, divides the great lake at two-thirds of its length, and marks the beginning of the Siamese dominions. When he took possession of the two provinces of Battam-bang and Angcor, the king of Siam appropriated part of the lake, of which, however, he can make little use, as the mouths still remain in the hands of the Cambodgians. The Annamites give themselves almost wholly to their fisheries. Some thousands of their boats are employed on the lake itself, and in the arm which connects it with the Mekong, and load very deep with the fish taken. Part of this astonishing harvest of the waters forms the food of the population at large: the rest is used to make oil.

This annual fishery is counted so good an affair that the Annamites sometimes give 100 per cent for money borrowed to buy the salt needed. The legal interest in Cambodgia is from forty to a hundred per cent a year! The Annamites ply, also, another industry in Cambodgia, which I must men-

tion. When the waters are high, they go up the arroyos
which enter the Mekong, and cut down the bamboos on the
banks, making them into huge rafts, which they commit to
the current. When these reach Pnom-Penh, prices fall so
low that you buy thirty or forty great bamboos for one
ligature, that is, a franc; but to raise their value, a very
simple means is taken—they burn up a fourth part of the
stock.

In the evening, as our gunboat anchors, some fisheries
show themselves by the flickering light of torches, which
illuminates them with the fiery-serpent-like beams it casts
on the waters: there is no human sound; nothing but the
rippling of the water, and the dying voice of the wind. The
fishing season is over, and the fish enjoy more peace throughout all their domain. The next day we see before us Mount
Khròme, which was formerly crowned by a pagoda, the ruins
of which we wish to visit before going on to Angcor. They
are hidden by a thick curtain of high trees, and consist of
seven towers, still standing. At the entrance of the last
enceinte, there are two of brick, and two of sandstone.
From their isolation, one cannot but notice them, but the
three which rise before them absorb all the attention. The
largest, which is the centre one, is the most broken down,
and perhaps owes part of its effect to the ravages of time.
On the side beaten by the winds and torrent-like rains, which
last five months of the year, it looks like a rock roughly
quarried over, but with some fragments of fine sculpture
here and there. A crowd of bats, disturbed by our presence,
flew whirling out of a large gap in the ruin. The two other
towers, which are better preserved, are covered with arabesques and ornaments, which increase our desire to see
Angcor. We are already in the province of that name, a
province lost by the grandfather of Norodom by a kind of
political swindle. The moral authority of the grandson has
not entirely disappeared from this land, where his grandfather reigned, and the governor of Angcor gave us a hearty
welcome, putting horses, elephants, and buffalo-wagons at our
disposal; and our caravan, thus made up, advanced towards
his residence. An enormous enceinte, built of iron-stone regularly cut, and probably taken from some ruins, recalls the

castles of the middle ages. A huge iron cannon, in which birds nestle, is mounted in front of the principal gate, and human heads fresh cut off, and set on long pikes fixed in the ground, show that the lord of the place has the right to inflict death-penalties. Some Cambodgian thatches are all you see inside the enceinte of this vast citadel. An air of cleanliness, which one does not commonly see even in the houses of great people, distinguishes the dwelling of the governor, who took no end of trouble with us, and wrote our names and rank on a slate; a form of politeness, but, perhaps, an act of policy as well, for this brave Cambodgian was the agent of the court of Bangkok. Some bad European engravings adorned the pillars and the walls, and a portrait of the Pope was hung at the entrance to the women's apartments.

Leaving this hospitable dwelling, we entered the forest, where the roughness of the road, which made my wagon perform a thousand fantastic somersaults, did not hinder my admiring the luxuriance of the tropical vegetation. Gigantic trees fought for room, and the branches, interlacing, a hundred feet above us, intercepted the light of the sun. The air circulated with difficulty through the verdure; gusts of heat came from the sun, as from a furnace. The feet of the animals raised the gray sand of the road; and it was necessary to strive against the physical discomfort, and make a constant effort to admire the wonderful arboreal columns, placed there by nature as a magnificent portal to the ruins of Angcor, described already by the Portuguese at the close of the sixteenth century, but buried till late years in unmerited obscurity. Some hours of this fatiguing march through the woods brought us to them.

Lions, stiff and fierce as those of heraldry, first met the eye. They stand erect at the entrance to a vast causeway, paved with large slabs, leading across immense ditches, now transformed to swamps, to a gallery, the three half-fallen towers of which interrupt the long line of building. I shall ever recall the profound impression this spectacle excited. Pompous descriptions had been given me; I had just re-read the pages of M. Mouhot on Angcor; but in spite of all, I felt overcome. I had, as it were, a shock of astonishment. I had hardly cleared the gate of the central pavilion when a second paved avenue, about 200 metres in length, opened before me to a huge building, the style of which is as different from any of our western forms of architecture as the Chinese fancies, of which I had already been able to study some examples. Wearied with the journey, and overcome by the heat, I thought I saw an incredible number of towers of strange outline dance before me, nothing supporting them in the air, and another higher tower rising above them. This kind of hallucination soon passed, and gave place to a just admiration. The general plan is simple. The edifice is made up of two rectangular, concentric galleries, rising in stories: the first,—of which the shortest side is not less than 180 metres, while the two lateral faces are about 250,—adorned at the corners by pavilions. The second is adorned with four towers, built like an immense tiara. In the middle of the second gallery a high mass of masonry rises, ended likewise by four towers. The centre of this wall, which is also the centre of the building, bears a tower of the same style as the others, but higher,[1] which seems to reign over the whole structure. In most Christian temples, the sanctuary, placed at the most secluded and gloomy end of the building, is, as it were, surrounded by shadows; no light reaches it but that of the coloured windows through which it streams. At Angcor, the holy of holies is in the highest tower, the part nearest light and day. This holy of holies is, nowadays, reduced to four very mediocre statues of Bouddha, to the foot of which the bonzes arrive by the avenues, which, cutting the two enceintes at right angles, abut on the four grand staircases of the central mass. With the exception of horizontal surfaces, there is not a stone of this colossal monument without carving. These sculptures are marvels from the chisel of incomparable artists, whose inspirations are graven on the stones for ever, but whose names have perished from the memory of man.

'The man most given to art, reading, in Paris, the truest description of the Coliseum, could not avoid thinking the author's exaggeration ridiculous, though he had had only the one thought, to keep the fear of his reader before his eyes.

[1] It is 56 metres above the level of the causeway.

and express himself with a studied moderation.' This reflection of Stendthal comes to my mind, and checks me from
continuing this rapid sketch of the noble temple of Angcor.
According to an almost legendary tradition, it was founded,
in fulfilment of a vow, by a king who was a leper, and lived
in the neighbouring town, where his monument may yet be
seen. It runs back to a date less distant than that of the
principal monuments of the capital, and is in a state of
comparative preservation, which makes the opinion very
probable, but nothing has as yet been discovered to enable
the date to be fixed exactly. Among the kings who have
reigned over Cambodgia, a number of those who have
thought themselves illustrious—and that happens often, one
would think, with sovereigns—changed the Cambodgian era,
and even introduced compulsory changes into the alphabet,
and hence there is a confusion almost hopeless. One can
hardly, however, doubt, that the development of architectural art, of which this temple seems the highest expression,
coincided with the triumphant blossoming of Bouddhism
among the Khmer people, perhaps when it had been chased
from India at the time of the great religious persecution. In
celebrating their new faith by imperishable works, these emigrants have imprinted on them the seal of the monuments
of their country—monuments whose image they had carried
with them in the depth of their hearts.

As to the town itself, Angcorthôm, Angcor the Great, the
walls alone are perfect. They are three metres broad; and
their great courses of cut stone, laid one on the other, without lime or cement, defy the ages, and resist the efforts of
a vigorous vegetation, still more destructive. Causeways
thrown over great ditches lead to the gates of the town,
guarded by fifty great stone giants, huge, grimacing sentinels, bound one to the other by the folds of a monstrous
serpent, which exhausts itself in impotent struggles to escape
their grasp. The gate by which we penetrated the interior
of the ancient city forms a vault six metres in depth, and it
is not without reason that M. Mouhot calls it a triumphal
arch. Elephant-heads adorn its summit, and the trunks led
down vertically, as great pillars, rest on a bundle of huge
leaves.

Sadness follows astonishment, when, having passed this magnificent entrance, one comes on a dense forest, filling the vast enceinte shut in by its great walls. It is necessary to pass through closely-tangled thickets to reach the ruins of the few buildings of which vestiges still survive, and to have recourse to the compass to keep from losing oneself in these solitudes, peopled only by wild creatures, which call and answer each other with hoarse cries, the echoes prolonging, and turning them, as it were, to groans. We had an excellent guide in M. de Lagrée. He had long before this studied, with the passion of a *savant*, all that remained standing within the walls of the town, and had discovered a temple and great buildings, seemingly, the residences of princes and the palace of the kings. The latter had fallen down under the efforts of roots and creepers, which force themselves between the stones like iron wedges. It appeared to have been the conception of an imagination of unheard-of richness, and was formerly surmounted by a prodigious number of towers, perhaps forty or fifty, some of which, representing heads of Bouddha, recalled the sphinxes of Egypt. Though it was impossible to judge of this monument fairly, mutilated as it was, invaded by vegetation, cumbered by ruins; and though an architecture, which makes great towers of monstrous human figures, is too remote from our notions not to bewilder our judgments, I cannot consent to put this fantastic structure in the same rank with the temple of which I have just spoken, which is a model of grandeur, harmony, and simplicity. According to Christoval de Jaque, one of the Portuguese who took refuge in Cambodgia during the sixteenth century, after having been driven from Japan, Angcor was no longer a royal residence in 1570. He seems to say that even at that period it had already been deserted by its inhabitants.

Was civilisation, in the complex meaning we give that word, in keeping, among the ancient Cambodgians, with what such prodigies of architecture seem to indicate? The age of Phidias was that of Sophocles, Socrates, and Plato; Michael Angelo and Raphael succeeded Dante. There are luminous epochs, during which the human mind, developing itself in every direction, triumphs in all, and creates masterpieces, which spring from the same inspiration. Have the nations of India ever known such periods of special glory? It appears little probable, and it is only necessary to read the Chinese traveller of the thirteenth century, whose narrative M. Abel Rémusat has translated, to be convinced that it was never reached by the Khmers. He describes the monuments of the capital, most of which were covered with gilding, and he adds that, with the exception of the temples and the palace, all the houses were only thatched. Their size was regulated by the rank of the possessor, but the richest did not venture to build one like that of any of the great officers of state. Despotism induced corruption of manners, and some customs mentioned by our author show actual barbarism. Let me add, when one goes over the ruins, it is impossible to refrain from a generalisation, which some exceptions do not invalidate. The human form was not understood; and if Cambodgia has had incomparable architects and marvellous carvers, it has had no sculptors.

In the presence of these grand wrecks of the past, one is struck with admiration; but there is little emotion, and the enjoyment is far from complete. The ruins of a monastery mouldering in the bosom of an English wood; the cracked walls of a deserted château which sheltered the feudal baron, move us more deeply. Men of our own race have thought behind these walls, have fought behind these battlements; we can reconstruct their lives, can follow the traces of their footsteps. Here, in this spot of the extreme East, all is dead, even to the memory of that brilliant theocracy, the mother of a material civilisation, greatly developed, we own, but which never reached a manly maturity. The research of science, which leads us, little by little, towards our origin, and shows us our brothers in the first castes of India, interests the mind rather than touches the heart; the separation is too remote, and these sepulchres seem too good for the race they entomb.

After eight days of painful journeying and incessant study, M. de Lagrée gave the signal of departure. Our camp, established in a thatched house, at the foot of the great temple, was struck before daybreak, and our caravan formed, as when we came;—of horses, buffalo-wagons, and

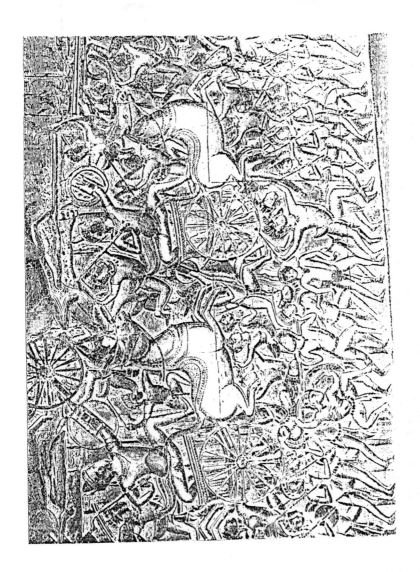

Plate 7 *Angkor Wat: North-Western construction (Drawing by E. Thérond, based on a photograph by Mr. Gsell)*

elephants. One of these, of huge size, with huge tusks, stood immovable between two pillars of the peristyle, and in the uncertain light of the early morning, seemed part of the basement of the edifice. We rejoined the gunboat, which quickly took us to Pnom-Penh, the capital of Cambodgia. Our first business was to run through the shops of the Chinese merchants, finally to complete our store of objects of exchange. We had brought from Saïgon pieces of velvet and silk, some arms of little value—a veritable venture—to which we now added cotton checks of all colours, glass trinkets, and brass wire. Besides the bags of Siamese *Ticaux*, which come from Bangkok, our treasure consisted of gold in leaf and bars, and some Mexican dollars—the whole representing hardly thirty thousand francs. The commission was formed of six members —MM. de Lagrée, head of the expedition; Garnier and De la Porte, naval officers; Joubert and Morel, navy surgeons; and L. de Carné, attached to the department for foreign affairs;—the escort consisted of two French sailors and two French soldiers; of two Tagals from the Philippines, chosen from the best of those who remained at Saïgon, after the departure of the Spanish soldiers; and of six Annamites. We took with us, also, a European interpreter, who spoke Siamese fluently, a Cambodgian interpreter, and an interpreter for Laos. The last, having lived long in Cambodgia, could speak Cambodgian. M. de Lagrée alone could hold communication with him and the Cambodgian.

The Cambodgians came to bid us farewell, and strove to dissuade us from setting out. These brave folks could not succeed in comprehending what motive could urge strangers living beyond the sea to undertake a journey which none of themselves would dare to try. They are kept back by fabulous stories and imaginary fears. The king himself, whose predecessors extended their rule over part of Laos, knew nothing of the country, except that the air and the water in it are mortal. Our Cambodgian interpreter, a young man full of intelligence and in high health, who had lived long among Europeans, drew back frightened at the last moment. He feigned sickness, and we were compelled to take him with us by force. As to the Laotian who accompanied us, he seemed glad to see his country again. The son of a travelling merchant, he had long followed his father across mountains and forests, sleeping under trees or in the pagodas, and living on rice, which the laws of hospitality secure to all travellers. One day, in the middle of one of these journeys, his father died. He closed his eyes, and confided his dust to the bonzes of a village; then continuing his travels as chance guided him, going on or stopping as he thought fit, ended by reaching Bangkok, whence he passed to Cambodgia. He had learned the virtue of plants during his sojourn in the forests; and having come from a distant and therefore a marvellous country—one of those which border the great river on the confines of the great empire—he did not fail to make use of these facts to gain himself respect. He put the topstone on his fortune by turning bonze, gained the confidence of the king's mother in this character, and spent his life loaded with dainties and honours. Sacrificing all this to his wish to get married, he had thrown his yellow frock to the nettles, and the plump and venerated bonze, the sage and rare oracle, who decided cases of conscience, became a badly-fed man and a deceived husband. He continued, by force of habit, to chant the praises of Bouddha all day; and fearing lest any one should steal his private idol —a little statuette in silver-gilt—he confided it to me, and I threw it into the bag that held my dollars.

Meanwhile king Norodom was not willing to let us go without giving a feast in our honour. In the shed which serves for the throne-room of his majesty, seats set in a line were prepared for us. That of the king was, naturally, the highest. As soon as the orchestra struck up, actresses presented themselves in their ordinary dress, and began an interminable ballet-pantomime, accompanied by recitatives, of which we did not understand a word, and singing, by a choir, in a snuffling tone. The king seemed to follow with interest the evolutions of his women, who stopped often before him, and gave him a special salute, with much sensual grace. The dancing-girls, squatted on the ground, raised their hands, little by little, above their heads—their bodies at first bent back, a brilliant dress showing their forms— straightened themselves at the sound of three beats given by the orchestra; then remained an instant on their knees, with their breasts bent forwards. The costumes were like those of the kings and lords which remain preserved on the bas-reliefs: there was a deal of gold and tinsel, of glass and precious stones, on them—a singular mixture of luxury and misery, which reminded one of the theatres at fairs. The king seemed in ecstasy, and could not refrain from asking his neighbour which of the actresses he thought prettiest. The interpreter, having been asked secretly, indicated by his eye which of them enjoyed the royal favours for the time; and Norodom appeared highly pleased with the answer. After the toasts and the shaking hands, new and familiar customs which a little shocked the upholders of the old etiquette, we left the palace, and our gunboat saluted the Cambodgian flag with twenty-one guns. The wretched pieces, which were all the artillery the king had, made an attempt at returning this farewell salvo, and we entered the great arm of the Mekong. It was a solemn moment; every one gave himself up to his own thoughts. The brows were grave, the lips were silent; but a secret joy lightened the face: our voyage had begun.

The provinces on the river seem to me the best-cultivated parts of Cambodgia. They raise a large quantity of maize, and especially of cotton. The island of Ko-Sutin yields, by itself, an annual revenue of 15,000 francs to the king's mother; and this represents hardly a tenth of the value of the total production. The villages, overshadowed by cocoa-trees, which hang out their heavy plumes over bamboo huts, have an air of elegance which increases as we recede from Pnom-Penh. Contrary to the European rule, nearness to the capital is no security in this country for the people liable to forced labour. In less than two days' journey above Pnom-Penh, the navigation of the Mekong becomes difficult, and the gunboat, which carried us as far as Crachè, made ready to return to Saïgon. Henceforth France was before, not behind us; for we were determined to get to it only by crossing China. All our aspirations went out towards that empire. M. de Lagrée was afraid of such enthusiasm; for he knew that it was near neighbour to despondency, and foresaw that our work would be pre-eminently one of patience. The governor of Crachè, who

was prepared for our arrival beforehand by a letter from
Norodom, took several days to collect the boats needed for
the expedition, and, after all, got together only half the
number we required. We were in a friendly country, and
the authorities showed us sincere good-will; and yet it was
already necessary, to avoid delay, that we should leave part
of our provisions behind. It was a foreshadow of the utter
destitution which awaited us hereafter.

The boats are narrow canoes, made commonly of a
single tree, hollowed out by fire, and provided with a con-
trivance which enables them to ascend the torrent-like current of the river. They are covered along all their length,
except at the ends, with a round roof of leaves, kept in their
place by a double trellis of bamboo slips. This cover is a
good-enough protection against the rays of the sun, but it
is often of little use against rain. Large bamboos fixed in
the sides of the canoes, and immersed in the water, give
them the stability they would otherwise want. A narrow
board forms an outside bench on which the boatmen get
about easily. Each of these, furnished with a long boat-
hook, catches it in the branches of trees or the roughnesses
of the rocks, while the steersman at the end skilfully guides
the paddle which serves as a helm. For eight hours a day
our unhappy Cambodgians go round us with the docility of
the blind horses used to turn wheels, their chief, if they seem
to fail, rousing them by crying that he will get them beaten
when they arrive. They are sweet-tempered and resigned,
often almost mirthful; yet they are men mostly dragged
away from their rice-fields, sent far from their families and
their interests, and they have no right to any wages; for in
Cambodgia every free man is liable to forced labour from
eighteen to sixty, and we were provided by the king's orders.
I was leaving civilisation behind, and entering on a savage
country; I had passed at one step from a steam-ship to a
canoe. The roof was too low to let me sit up; I had to
keep half lying down; and the rain-water collected in the
bottom, splashed my feet every moment. The captain was,
however, very attentive, for I was a great lord in his eyes,
and busied himself during the squalls by baling the boat
with a leaf of banana.

The stream is sown with islands, which divide it into a great many arms. The opposite bank could only be seen in the foggy distance. The waters, dashing against rocks which formed an almost uninterrupted series of rapids, made a great thundering in the air. Between the islands, these rapids offer a singular appearance; for an incredible quantity of shrubs have taken root on the rocks and shoals, and rise above the surface, their stems bent by the current, as if a forest had been flooded. Some high trees seem to hold on to the earth only by creepers, which bind them to the bank, like airy roots. Our boatmen showed extreme boldness and wonderful agility. They guided their skiff with precision along winding channels, among trees round which the water boiled as it rushed past. They were admirable equilibrists, and never failed to seize any rugged trunk or bending branch, which could serve them for a hold, and hinder the canoe from putting its side to the stream, which would have thrown it on the rocks. After some hours of this excitement, I always hailed the time of halting with pleasure. We had the forest for dining-room, and herds of wild boars had often to make way for us. Our bedroom was the narrow and damp jail of our canoes. Evening come, we cut down trees, cleared away the long plants streaming with rain; the fires kindled at last; every one exerted himself; and dinner began,—most commonly frugal enough, sometimes even sumptuous, as our fortune with the gun had been better or worse,—but almost delightfully happy. The remembrances of Paris, the prospects of our voyage, or perhaps political or religious discussions, sent round among the astonished echoes of these grand woods words new to them. A pertinacious grasshopper pursued us from station to station, and sounded at the same hour its single and long-drawn note, as if to give the pitch to the other musicians of these sombre green palaces. In these regions, life seems to awake at nightfall. The creatures, overcome, like man, by the heat of the day, take a long siesta till the sun is near sinking.

One evening we had stopped at the bottom of a little creek, thinking ourselves sheltered from the wind and rain. Our boats were drawn close to each other, and moored in a brook nearly dry, while we ourselves were sleeping quietly,

E

in spite of the loud cries of tigers, too near at hand. All at once a storm broke over our heads, and a deluge of rain fell on our camp,—one of those tropical rains which nothing can stand, and that form great floods in a few seconds, swelling the least thread of water into an impetuous torrent. The quiet brook, in which our boats hardly floated, rose high, at once, and it was all we could do to get them anchored once more to the bank. When the danger was over, we could enjoy, at our ease, the fair disorder of virgin nature around, to which the pale light of electricity lent mysterious charms.

At last, after nine days of this perilous and slow navigation, we reach Stung-Treng, the first village of Laos. It lies partly on the banks of the great river Attopée, the first large affluent of the Mekong. The province, of which it is the chief place, formerly belonged to Cambodgia, and was only separated from it during last century. It has some political importance, for it borders on our Annamite possessions, and the malcontents who were chased from Tay-ninh, one of our advanced posts, were able to take refuge there, to repair their losses, or form new plans of campaign.

We had, then, set foot in this terrible Laos: and were about to get a sample of it in our first relations with the authorities. The governor, a Laotian, six feet high, with a face stupid by the constant use of opium, and an interminable neck, received us dryly, and refused us the slightest services, under pretext that our demands were contrary to usage. The sight of our Siamese passport seemed to have some little effect on him; and we had brought a great many packages, which he took for granted were filled with everything precious; for M. de Lagrée had been styled a great mandarin in the letter from Siam, and our names had all been handed in to the chancellor's office at Bangkok as those of very great men. But well-taught people receive no gifts without giving some in return. He weighed all this in his wisdom, and ended by giving us a pig. He was presently told, that it was not our custom to accept hogs from governors of provinces. More and more humbled, he came himself with his excuses to the chief of the expedition. He declared, that having lately had a visit from a Frenchman,

whose violence had frightened the whole people, he thought
himself lost when he saw six come; but the quietness of our
manners and the strict discipline of our escort had quickly
reassured him. As a proof of his good feeling, he ordered
a small establishment to be set up for us at once; for we had
no lodgings but the canoes, and it may be readily believed
that we were anxious to quit them for *terra firma*. It took
only two hours to make. Woven bamboos formed a clean
floor for us; a roof of thatch kept us pretty well from the
rain; and a charming tap stry of large banana-leaves protected us from the sun, whose rays, thus sifted, coloured themselves green in passing through.

We had lived fifteen days in this fragile house, which
was shaken by the squalls; while the river kept steadily
rising, and after a time covered the floor. Our barrels of brandy
and wine, pierced by legions of invisible insects, ran empty
in a single night; and our flour stuffs, spoiled by a penetrating damp, were past using even before the water had covered the oven we had hastily built. We were hardly able to
save from this last disaster a few bottles of wine for the sick,
and a little flour, so indispensable for our quinine pills, of
which there was already a large daily consumption. Besides
cases of fever, the sad, but inevitable tribute to the climate
and the season, two members of the commission fell seriously
ill—the one of dysentery, which speedily took away all his
strength; the other of a typhoid fever, so severe our
doctors gave him up as hopeless. The forced stoppage of
rations of wine and brandy, and the wretched native chicken
substituted for beef, raised discontent among the Frenchmen
of the escort, which often broke out in murmurs; till it
became clear that they had not sufficiently realised the
expedition they had joined, to let us hope that it would be
possible to keep them long.

At Stung-Treng, Cambodgian is only used by the educated
and by travelling merchants. Laotian is in common use;
and yet our interpreter, who had never lived but at Bangkok, made himself easily understood from the first day. It
is a proof of the close relations between the Siamese and
Laotian languages. This resemblance of the two idioms was
confirmed at each station of our voyage, nor did it fail sen-

sibly till we were on the borders of Burmah. As far as that,
it is too general and too striking to be attributed to the
effect of conquest. Opposite Stung-Treng, however, on the
other bank of the river, there still exists a large village of
Cambodgians, who received us almost as if we were fellow-
countrymen, when we went to hunt among them.

The vast forest, which crowds their huts between its ancient trees and the tumultuous river, is full of savage creatures, in the pursuit of which we affected, at first, an ardour
which soon cooled. In one of these hunts, in which several
flocks of pea-fowl had been decimated, I was overtaken by
a storm, with one of my companions, and soon found that we
were lost. We had no compass; no mark by which we could
tell our way presented itself; all the trees looked alike; and
we could fancy, for the three hours during which we walked
on at random, what the feelings must be of a traveller hope-
lessly lost in these solitudes, full of shadows and sounds, a
hundred times more terrifying than deserts of sand. The
Cambodgians, who were uneasy at our non-appearance, happily came upon us towards evening, and, guided by them,
we discovered some brick walls, the last traces of an important town, and visited some monuments still standing.
The one in best preservation is an edifice, rectangular at
the bottom, terminating in a kind of tower. The base is decorated with a garland of birds interlaced, which surrounds
the monument about two feet from the ground. Over the
principal gate there is a sculptured sandstone pediment, let
into the wall, and supported by two brick pillars of elegant
form. These ruins, though inferior to those at Cambodgia,
may be regarded as the half-effaced signature of the old
Khmer masters of the soil, whose inhabitants have forgotten
them.

Siam has completely assimilated to itself these people,
who speak its language. It names their governors, and sends
them their collectors of customs; its silver money is the only
coin in circulation. For transactions of little value, a peculiar money is used at Stung-Treng, consisting of ingots of
iron narrowing towards the end, and about a décimètre in
length. These ingots are made by the savage Cuys, who
live in the north of the province of Compong-soaï, and are

tributary to Norodom. Barter was the easiest exchange for us among this half-barbarous population. Empty bottles and eighteen inches of red cotton secured us the good services of the housewives, who covered our table with the productions of the country—pumpkins and cucumbers, with rice boiled in water—a wretched feast, but cheered at times by a bottle of preserves. It was important, at our entrance to Laos, to establish our reputation. We, therefore, gave away glass collars, earthenware pipes, and other objects of similar value, to the principal personages. The governor got one of the four revolvers we could spare; and this generous act so moved him, that he at once got ready the boats we needed. He went so far as to beg us to put off our departure, because, on the day we had chosen, we might meet an evil spirit which runs on the waters, enticing after him voyagers foolish enough to brave them, and swallowing them up in a whirlpool. In spite of this alarming prediction, our Laotians went to work at the hour we had fixed; and we left Stung-Treng, carrying our sick. Of these one was nearly well again; the other, delirious, and seemingly near death, had, like us all, no other bed than the bamboo hurdle, which reached from end to end of the canoe, and caught the rain through numerous holes, which soon showed themselves in our roofs of leaves. He got better, however, and our confidence began to return.

The river continues of a great breadth; so much so, that the two banks are, in some places, more than two leagues apart, and nothing can give an idea of the violence of the current. Notwithstanding the vast width of its bed, it twists itself into the sharpest eddies, and drives against the land with fury. An enormous alligator, which had been hurled by it against the trees, had been killed by the shock; and we saw its carcass, carried among the branches and thrown up again, almost straight, like that of some hideous executed criminal. We followed, closely, the narrower and more tortuous channels, creeping along the edges of the islands, hooking ourselves on to creepers, roots, and the trunks of great trees. When one of these was too near the water to let us glide beneath it, the whole flotilla was stopped, and every one worked without intermission till the obstruction gave

way before their axes. It would have been perilous to leave
the bank; for the boats would have been carried away like
straws, by the violence of the current, had we done so.

After leaving Stung-Treng, the banks of the river were
a desert. Not a hut showed a sign of human presence. The
river and the forest join one to the other, and nothing is
heard but the noise of the wind in the high branches of the
trees, or the roaring of the waters round their roots. Some
few mountains show themselves at a distance from each
other, as far as we can see, and we also soon distinguish the
hills of Khong. The islands multiply beyond number; we
advance slowly through them; and our boatmen, who never
lose their way in this labyrinth, halt at last at the mouth of
the bed of a torrent. This torrent, though dry in spring-time,
is the one passage frequented, after some months of rain, by
the boats of the merchants; a channel always difficult, encumbered by shallows, and only passed through after several
times partially unloading the cargo on some rock, trusting
to get it on board again, after the obstacle has been surmounted, by hauling it along a rope of rattan. We had to
employ other means. Our letter from Siam gave us the right
to require the coöperation of the authorities in the organisation of our transport. It was, therefore, much easier to
cross the island on foot, and take new boats on the other
side of the cataracts. Mandarins always do this in travelling,
and the government maintain a buffalo-wagon on purpose,
for the transfer of baggage.

The hostelry to which we were taken, while everything
was being made ready for a new start, consisted of two small
dilapidated huts. We found only the wreck of the lodgings
prepared for the last mandarin who had crossed the island,
and had to content ourselves with it; for we had committed
the mistake of not announcing ourselves. It was easier to
do this on leaving a canoe, and the country made us forget
the poor shelter. Masses of trees, impenetrably thick, hid
the river, a considerable stretch of which ran along our left. It
made itself heard by a noise not unlike that which meets one
as he comes near the shore at Penmarch in Brittany; and
the sight which I soon had under my eyes can only be compared for effect to that of the sea dashing against the strand

after a storm. An arm of the river, about 800 metres in breadth, is obstructed from side to side by enormous blocks of rock. The current, ten times fiercer for these checks, hurls its furious waters against them. The projecting rock, on which I stood, was often covered by the spray; and as far as I could see, the white crests of the waves were mingled with the black tops of the rocks. The sheet of water seemed to enlarge, and lose itself insensibly in the distance, with no other limit than the blue mountains on the horizon. It is through this, mainly, that the waters of the Mekong precipitate themselves into the lower part of the valley, but they also escape by other outlets. Here, the water is broken up as it dashes into a gulf, raising a sparkling pillar of moist dust, on which there rests a rainbow. Farther off, a cascade, mostly open, recalls by its regular outline the bars of our rivers or lakes. Elsewhere, the water spreads out, half veiled by charming trees, which bend over it, and dip their ever-fresh leaves, and white and rose flowers, in its coolness.

These cataracts offer an insurmountable obstacle to steam navigation. The difficulty commences a little above Crachè, where the blocking of the stream is complete, and could only be removed by a large amount of labour. In the seventeenth century, it would appear, a Jesuit offered to the king a model for the construction of some dams, which would facilitate the passage. 'The king,' says an Italian missionary of the time, who tells the fact, 'has always been more concerned for the safety of his kingdom—the advantageous position of which serves him as a rampart against the insults of his neighbours—than for gain; about which, from a generous contempt he has for it, he gives himself no trouble. He very much approved the proposal, but he said it would give his enemies the key to his states.' The king of Siam will not likely have any need to weigh such considerations nowadays, for no one, for long to come, will dream of taking up again this project of dams. We have still too much to do in the delta of the Mekong to think of giving considerable sums for such an enterprise, which only the wants of an important commerce could justify. This vast gathering of islands, islets, and rocks, which form formidable rapids

during the rains, is turned into cataracts during the dry
season. Then the level of the water falls, the river shrinks,
and shows on the banks marbles equally remarkable for the
fineness of their grain and the brilliancy of their colours.

The island of Khong is inhabited by agriculturists. The
rice-fields seemed well cultivated, and we assisted at the
transplanting of the rice. The women of the country, bent
all day over the muddy furrows, have this as their task.
The authorities begged us not to shoot in the island, and
not to beat the gong, because the unwonted noise would
for certain lead tigers to devour a number of the people in
the course of the year. At a spot where several branches
of the river flow into it, the view opens as at the meeting of
different roads in a forest. The sheet of water is immense,
and all in one, like a lake, as if the Mekong were collecting
itself before the terrible confusions that await it lower down.
Serrated hills form the background of the picture, while,
nearer us, the eye is caught by a fantastic tree which seems
to rise out of the water, and by the thick mantle of green
which covers it, looks like an old line of wall kept up in its
ruin by the living embraces of creepers. We pass soon after
into a course winding among the islands, where we see the
river only at rare intervals, and have to cut ourselves a path,
by blows of the axe, through the forest. A tree which ran
out almost horizontally over the water, and which it was
necessary to cut down, was of huge diameter. My natives
every now and then fell into the water. A loud shout of
laughter announced the accident, which might have been
serious, if the Laotians were not marvellous swimmers; and
I saw the clumsy wight get on board again, leaving it to
the sun to dry his clothes on him. There were one or two
savages in my crew. They were easily known by their
manners, but still more so by their dress; for their langouti
was reduced to a kind of narrow drawers, twisted into a
rope behind. These brave creatures, levied for forced labour,
seemed, nevertheless, very happy; and I had nothing to say
against their mirth, except that it was, perhaps, a little too
expansive. Their bursts of laughter were like the neighing
of draught horses. They renewed them at each sally of one
or other, and sometimes howled like beasts at fault, to ex-

cite themselves when at some specially hard spot. I should
have got tired of so much noise, if it had not struck me
very opportunely, when I was getting cross, that so much
good-will deserved some allowance.

As you approach the province of Khong the valley contracts, but the river gains in depth by it. The bed, at last
free from rocks, becomes navigable. Large villages stretch
on all sides along the banks, surrounded by bananas and
cocoa-trees, giving the country a pleasant and prosperous
look. The governor, who had been informed of our coming
beforehand, had prepared a huge lodging for us; and likewise let us know that he would be delighted himself to
receive us. We found him an old man, squat, weak, and
fat, but with pleasing features. His white hair and saffron
robes made him look not unlike the gods of the country.
Though this excellent Laotian was governor of Stung-Treng
by direct appointment of the court of Bangkok, he seemed
to have no prejudice against us, and if he showed a little
kindly patronising, it was allowable in an old man. He had
not come back from his numerous journeys to Siam empty-
handed. With a simple cynicism he asked us to notice an
obscene photograph, inserted in the handle of a knife. To
show us, moreover, that Laotian art was capable of the same
conceptions as European, he made one of the numerous young
females, who assisted at the interview, bring two statuettes
in wood, coarsely carved, which were unfit for the lowest
place in the lowest of secret museums.

The houses of the natives, which are grouped, as usual,
round the enclosure of the governor's palace, are very like
the huts of the Cambodgians. They, perhaps, differ from
them in their height and in the steepness of their roofs,
which makes one think that the rains here are either more continuous, or heavier. The windows are narrow and few, which
seems to show, farther, that the Laotian values *home* more
than the Cambodgian, who lives almost in public. The men
have their heads shaved, as in Cambodgia, except on the top of
the head, which is ornamented by a short tuft. The women,
who wear a jupon, and a scarf of a bright colour, less to hide
their bosoms than to make their skin look a little lighter,
wear chignons. They have very little timidity; and became

soon familiar, and even bold, with our escort, carrying their
unceremoniousness so far as to bathe naked in the river
within a few paces of us. The province of Khong has given
the river the name it bears for a good part of its course.
As far as its entrance into China the natives call it Nam
Khong, or water of Khong, river of Khong; a name far more
rational than that of Mekong, which has been adopted by
European geographers, and means literally sea of Khong.
It was formerly part of Cambodgia, like the province of
Tonli-Repou, which borders it, and there is still a small Cam-
bodgian population on one of the islands.

The current borrowed, at this time, a fresh force from the
torrent-rains, which fell daily. The waters rose perceptibly
in twenty-four hours, and the total rise within a month and
a half could not be put lower than four metres. As the surface rose, the stream found an ample harvest of vegetable
wreck on its submerged banks, gathering it through its
whole course. The quantity is so great, that the natives, as
far as Pnom-Penh, and even to the borders of the great lake,
find their provision of wood in its bed. We saw huge trunks
of trees pass, like floating islands, or the vast remains of
some great shipwreck, as the great tangled roots bound
them together, or kept them apart. Enormous bamboos,
loaded with earth at their lower ends, floated perpendicularly; the eddies and thousand whirlpools, which they had
to pass, making them reel like drunken giants.

When we went to take leave of the old governor, he tired
himself with expressions of good-will, adding them, doubtless, to the good works which he was accumulating against
the close of his life, and thinking, perhaps, that provided he
employed part of the money, stolen through a long career,
rightly, Bouddha would forgive his having kept the rest.
He received with due acknowledgments a silver watch. It
would serve him, he said, as an ornament; for to put such a
thing in the hands of such a savage, was like giving an
ape a cocoa-nut, which he turns and turns, without knowing
how to open or make use of it. He told us he had sent on
a gang of Laotians, the day before, to cut the branches in
the course of our canoes, and to open the way for us to the
borders of the states of his confrère of Bassac.

The six long canoes which carried us were manned by fifty-three of a crew, who were guided and kept in order by five chiefs of an inferior grade. These petty mandarins were responsible for us to the governor, who had appointed them, and he, in his turn, was responsible, for any trouble we might meet, to the king of Siam. We had not to think of anything while we passed from one point to another, and M. de Lagrée confined himself to naming the spot which he thought suited for our stopping at night. The chiefs of the village came, according to custom, to offer us presents, which were not always enough for our wants, but they helped out our provisions, and were better than nothing. The bank served for kitchen; the ground for seat and table. Compared to the Laotians, who were with us, we lived luxuriously. They fed, commonly, on rice, with which they crammed themselves several times a day, adding pimento to it, some lumps of dry or stinking fish, and raw vegetables. When they had the chance of adding anything more substantial, they took care not to let it escape them. I have often seen them, the moment they landed, spread themselves through the villages, force the doors of the huts, and carry off fowls and ducks, which they cooked forthwith, without even plucking. They have a practice of acting in this way whenever they have a Siamese mandarin over them. We had made a rule to pay our boatmen, and always to leave behind us better souvenirs than the functionaries of the court of Bangkok, and, therefore, put a stop to these depredations—a step which astonished the spoilers and spoiled alike profoundly. Mandarins with tufted beards, who did not chew betel, who had no women, who paid for forced labour, and prohibited stealing—such a thing was never known. We united all these wonders, physical and moral. At first, every one laughed to hear such tales; but, on reflection, we seemed less ridiculous, especially to the chicken-breeders. This good name helped us; the doors, instead of being shut at our approach, were thrown wide for our entrance, every one brought what he had to sell, and the scruples of our conscience served the interests of our stomach.

At last we saw, before us, like Colossi ready to bar our way, the mountains of Bassac. They stood out black against

the purple sky, while the tops still reflected the last beams of
day. We reached our first station in Laos, where we were
to wait for the letters, which were to be sent from Pekin to
Saïgon since we started, and for the last French posts. We
had had a great deal of sickness among the members of the
commission and the ranks of the escort, but our numbers
were still complete. Sinister predictions had not been realised, and we all, in our confidence, felt a new zeal. It would
have been a mistake to have set out, on chance, without
having in our hands passports which might, indeed, prove of
no use, but the want of which, on the other hand, we might
one day repent bitterly. It was necessary, therefore, to wait,
and make ourselves as comfortable as possible, in anticipation
of a stay of three months.

Bassac was formerly the capital of the Laotian monarchy,
the nearest to that of Cambodgia, and freed itself from dependence on the latter only during last century. According
to vague information gathered on our way, important ruins
still remained to attest the rule of the Khmers. Our first
care was to be taken to see them. After two hours' march
through rice-fields, we came upon a rectangular piece of
water, the longest face of which measured about six hundred
metres. This regularity indicates, beyond doubt, the hand
of man; but we already knew our Laotians too well to attri-
bute to them the formation of this petty lake, admirably
placed at the foot of the mountains, which were reflected in
its tranquil waters. It could be nothing but a relic of the
past. Indeed, at some metres from the west corner we found,
hidden by tufts of bamboos and thick shrubs, the steps of
a monumental staircase, on the platform of which a long
avenue opened, on which a thick coating of soil covered a
paving of flags. Monolith columns, ending in the form of a
mitre, stood at the two sides, and it led to the foot of a very
high stair, in good preservation, but very steep, like those
at Angcor. A terrace surrounded by balustrades crowned
this first flight, from which a series of staircases, with land-
ings, and broken by large terraces, following the inclination
of the ground, led to a sanctuary which was a real bijou
enshrined in the mountain. The stone is dug out to a depth
which gives the subjects chosen an admirable relief, while

the sharpness of the edges shows a wonderful precision of chiselling. The art of ornamentation has rarely been pushed farther.

The whole is more injured by time and vegetation than what we had seen at Angcor; but there are parts as complete and perfect as on the first day. The site which has been chosen for it must have added to its splendour, and, indeed, does so even yet. From the foot of the mountain the structures rise, little by little, in a straight line, to where the rolling outline of the ground stops abruptly at a huge wall of rocks, against which the sanctuary is, as it were, set back to back, at about 150 metres above the level of the lake. These rocks, the tops of which are covered with trees, are of a striking form. Covered in some places with red paint, over which the piety of the faithful has fastened leaves of gold in honour of Bouddha, opening in gaps, rough, with murmuring springs trickling from them, they are imperishable and sad witnesses of the lost splendour of the temples, which seem to have come out of their sides. We found some statues, but they were very poor. The Khmer artists, while incomparable in creating the plan of a huge building, or spreading over each stone of a wall a marvellous lacework, did not know how to copy the human body. Without requiring them to attain our ideal, realised in Greek art, we might ask that they should have tried to imitate the forms under their eyes; but they have done just the reverse. The stiffness of the limbs and of the body, the awkwardness of the postures, the coarseness of the features—in a word, the exaggeration of every physical imperfection—make gross caricatures of nearly all these statues. Nothing more painfully surprises the visitor of these ruins than to see a bas-relief of some human figure, grotesquely carved, in the midst of arabesques of the most exquisite finish and perfection. Singular fact!—all the living creatures seem drawn in rough outline, and share this defect in common. The elephant alone is finished in better style. Whether it be in little or of natural size, the centre of a medallion, or carved on the basement of a building, where it has the appearance of bearing the weight, it is always found as in nature—terrible in its strength, charming in its gentleness; man, who has made a god of it, seeming to have forgotten himself in handing its image to posterity.

Behind a screen of tufted trees we found two monuments, pendents of the two sides of the avenue, at the foot of the peristyle which leads to the sanctuary. They were perhaps palaces inhabited by pious kings, who wished to have a temple near their dwelling.

On the left of this collection of buildings are others, half ruined, which were, according to the tradition of the country, the abode of Sita, perhaps the wife of Rama, the hero of the Ramayaná. It is useless, on this point, to ask the least explanation from any of the people of the country, cleric or laic. All that they know about it is, that Sita had two sons, two brother-enemies, who, not contented with having spent their lives in bloody combats in the mountains, come still to disturb the quiet of these ruins. Woe to him whom unwise curiosity makes the witness of this duel of ghosts! The Laotians, who guided us, advanced with awe, prostrated themselves at each step, and laid dry leaves on some holy stones, lest the terrible brothers should roll some head of a pillar or some mass of rock on us. These monuments, which bear the name of Vat-Phou—the Pagoda of the Mountain— are the last we met in the valley of the Mekong which could be assigned to Cambodgian architecture.

It was September, the season of the heaviest rains. The mountains were always enveloped in clouds, and sometimes, though they were very near us, the mist so completely hid them, that no one would have suspected their existence. For the most part they were seen darkened by the woods that covered them, with white vapours gliding along their sides like smoke, and losing themselves in the spray of the cascades which fell down their heights. The rice-fields were filled with water, and we had to let this deluge pass away before we could attempt some excursions we had planned. We were blockaded in a dark hut, into which the light of day hardly penetrated at noon. To make up for these troubles, however, we were on an excellent footing with the governor of Bassac, who had retained the title of king,—with the authorities, and the inhabitants of the country. We dined in the town, and at the court itself, and our stomachs, become accom-

modating, allowed us to do honour to these feasts, of which
boiled pork formed the base. We ate, for politeness, the most
Laotian dishes, such as bamboo-stalks seasoned with pimento,
duck-eggs salted; all this minced small, and served in a great
number of bowls, placed on the ground on a mat. Water
and rice-brandy (a sickening liquor, so strong as to destroy
the taste), are put into the strangest collection of dissimilar
phials, pickle-bottles, and toilet-vinegar flasks, brought with
all care from Bangkok. A cousin of the king did us the
honour to admit us to his intimacy, opened his heart to us
little by little, and ended by complaining bitterly that his
right to the throne had been contemptuously cast under-
foot.

We enjoyed here, in truth, a double prestige. To our
title of Europeans, which of itself would have been enough
to secure us respect, we added the dignity of protectors of
Cambodgia, and that served us to admiration. It was known
that we had dared to dispute with Siam, and that we had
driven her off. Every one wished to see M. de Lagrée, the
conqueror of Phnea-rat, of whom the great mandarins had
heard speak during their annual journey to Bangkok. If
we had had a liking for getting up intrigues, or if we had
been ordered to prepare for annexations, it would have been
easy to work on the feelings which cropped out in certain
personages. But we had no such design. We wanted to
profit by our forced stay at Bassac, only by making friends;
our hut, open to all comers, was the rendezvous of the curious, and the Laotians never abused our confidence. Honest
by nature, they have laws which severely punish thieves. I
had the opportunity of seeing them enforced. The criminal,
seated on the ground, his neck held tightly squeezed in a
vice, and his limbs stretched out to the utmost by rough
cords, received ten blows of a rattan on the back, each cut-
ing the flesh. They told me, that to be condemned to fifty
was equal to death; and I can readily believe it, after seeing
the effect of ten. Before striking, the executioner gathers
himself up, as if penetrated by the importance of his social
mission, and bows profoundly in the direction of the king's
palace. The task finished, he invites the sufferer to lie on
his belly, and helps him with good-will, by pressing his foot

on the bleeding flesh, to give a little elasticity to the muscles, contracted by pain. Punishments of this kind are not
reserved for criminals only. They are used also to force
confessions; and I could not recall without a shudder, on
seeing such sights, the fact that the *question* was in use
among ourselves less than a hundred years ago. When one
finds among peoples rightly called barbarous, customs allowed
by our fathers, such as the *question* or the ordeal, which also
I saw in use at Bassac, pride of race presently vanishes, and
one of the best fruits of travel is proved, beyond doubt, to be
a respect for humanity.

CHAPTER II.

IT is with civilisation as with health; one must feel the want of it before he knows its value. To sleep on a bed and to eat bread are very vulgar delights, seldom awanting, thank God, in Europe, even to those least favoured by fortune; and hence we do not realise the part they play in the happiness of life. Yet, after some weeks of wonder, and almost of pain, you feel the body bend, little by little, to new habits; but the privations, which each day made more grievous to us, in our sad camp at Bassac, were of another kind: we lived, forced back on ourselves, awaiting the end of the rainy season, without books or newspapers, at the time when, behind the illusions which flew away, and in place of the dream which faded off, nothing was seen but the austere forms of a painful duty. The first fine days would, however, allow us to seek, outside, that food of curiosity which is the one thing which can bear up the traveller; and when they came at last, I hailed them as the prisoners of the Ark might have done the end of the deluge, only they had been better housed than we.

Since the 26th of October 1866, the river had fallen six metres from the highest level it had reached. The immense lake that separated us from the mountains was nothing more than an ocean of mud; but this slime, at first fetid, was soon dried and hardened by the sun, and we were then able to take extended rambles round our hut. The town stretches along the banks of the river, on both sides of the royal dwelling. The narrow road that ran through it was, as yet, no better than a slough. The inhabitants had taken the trouble to lay trees of different sizes, from the thick palm to the slender bamboo, side by side in the mud, so as to form

F

a causeway, along which one could walk, though not without difficulty. The houses, which are not inelegant, and are solidly built, are almost all double. They consist of two huts of the same size, put side by side, or united by a terrace. The cabbage-palms, which shade them, give the whole town the look of a grove planted with slender and beautiful trees. At every step you meet little obscure sanctuaries, where huge statues of Bouddha receive the daily homage of bonzes. When I think that I am in a capital where the descendant of the ancient kings still resides, I feel myself overcome by sadness in visiting these ruined temples. The palace itself is nothing but a set of thatched huts, surrounded by a wooden fence. A steep stair leads to the royal terrace, and one gets to it over a shaking causeway of trunks of trees of unequal sizes, thrown down on the mud. The king has preserved nothing of the power of his ancestors but an empty title; and were it not for the gold basket, ewer, and spittoon, which some chamberlains carry behind him, he would not be taken for more than a simple governor. These utensils hold the place of badges and ribbons at Laos, and are provided by the king of Siam himself, in gold, silver, or copper, according to the rank of the functionaries. They make both langoutis, and silk and gold robes of ceremony, at Bangkok, as well, and send them to the principal personages. The king of Bassac is a young man of distinguished manners, and a pleasing but rather sad countenance, as suits the scion of a decayed race. Norodom, with his accustomed stupidity, had called him a man of the woods, but there were no grounds for saying so. His enemies accuse him of despising the customs and oppressing the people, but it is not his Cambodgian majesty who has the right to call such things crimes.

The kingdom of Bassac has always played a very subordinate part. It was too near a powerful neighbour ever to have been able to secure a great importance to Laos. The Dutchman, Gerard van Vhusthorf, who partly ascended the river in 1641, does not even mention this principality, the capital of which, at that time, was at a place called, now, Muong-Cao, not far from the present town. The kingdom of Bassac was then, in truth, only a Cambodgian province. Freed, a century later, this unfortunate kingdom was not long in again losing its independence. It has been absorbed, as the last wrecks of Cambodgia were threatened to be, by the younger and more vigorous power of Indo-China. When one sees the striking resemblance between Laotian and Siamese civilisation, and the almost complete identity of the two languages, it is evident that a recent conquest could not have brought about such a result, and that a common origin must be ascribed to the populations grouped on the borders of the Meïnam and the Mekong. Perhaps we might go farther, and look on the Burmans, settled in the valleys of the Irawady and of the Salwen, and the Cambodgians, established at the mouths of the Mekong, as two branches separated from the same trunk. In their migrations, the members of this great family must have left India by the mountains of the north-west, and would be guided to the south along the courses of the great rivers which furrow Indo-China. Wandering for a long time, they would still preserve in their characteristics the marks of their parentage, modified by the influences immediately affecting them. The Cambodgians and Laotians speak languages, the mechanism and genius of which, if not the very words, are identical. M. Aubaret remarks that the Cambodgian language is written in the characters of the Pali language, while the Siamese and Burman characters differ from it a little, although belonging to the same type. He adds, that the Bouddhism practised in these three countries is exactly the same as that of Ceylon, and this may also be said of that which flourishes in Laos. It may be understood from this, how the most ambitious of the Indo-Chinese powers had the opportunity of definitively assimilating to itself all these populations, from the one fact that it was the strongest. It found the most of its laws and customs, already, in vigour, among the conquered.

The religion which has impressed on the architecture of these countries a uniform character, has laid hold on all the manifestations of life. The feasts take place at the same time in all the countries bordering on the Mekong, and have the same half religious, half profane features. During our stay at Bassac, we saw the bonzes, one morning, collecting in the open green of the village, and directing their course to the king's palace. Each year, on the same day, a new

robe is given them.   M. de Lagrée, wishing to connect the
Commission with this pious gift, caused two copper candlesticks to be carried to the throne-hall, where the clergy
were assembled.   They were accepted with great demonstrations of pleasure.   The officiating ministers of the two
principal pagodas, forgetting the gravity of their character,
tried each to get them for himself; but the king, who had
to intervene, decided that each of the pagodas should get
one.

During the day, magnificent regattas excited a real interest.   The canoes, belonging to pagodas, and built expressly for these nautical jousts, were adorned with flags, supplied with a primitive orchestra, of drum, tom-tom, and bamboo organ, and manned by vigorous fellows, who came to
sustain the honour of their parish.   The longest, which was
twenty-six metres, was hollowed out of the trunk of a single
tree, and was made for sixty rowers.   The crew was composed
entirely of savages, all tributaries of the king of Siam, and
living within the limits of Bassac.   Dressed in a morsel of
cotton check tied round the loins, they, yet, seemed to give a
good deal of work to the women, each wearing, for ornament, a white crown, worked by them in leaves of maize,
which showed off their black and silky hair.   Three young
savages, dressed in red, with red cowls, like the old court
fools, set up an unknown fantastic dance in the midst of
their brothers bending to the paddles.   As their feet could
not leave the bottom of the canoe, the steps had to be exchanged for contortions of the arms and haunches, mingled
with obscene gestures, performed in cadence, and much
relished by the rest.   After the races, the wrestlers entered the lists before the tribune of the king.   With small
heads and huge chests, such as we see in the representa-
tions of combatants armed with the cestus, they made provoking feints long before they darted at each other.   At last,
springing together, they rolled in the dust, before the eye
could follow them.   The king gave each of them a tical—
a little less than three francs—and was pleased to receive,
afterwards, the presents in kind which all the great personages offered him, according to custom.   These wrestlers,
or rather boxers, for they do not spare blows, are forced to

this rough service. I am not sure about Bassac; but I know, in Cambodgia, one village which has to furnish, for its forced labour, royal elephant-drivers, and another which has to supply so many boxers. At night, rockets were let off on all sides, and bamboos charged with powder made loud reports. Floating lamps, left to the stream, sparkled over the water like fallen stars, and great fire-rafts, real fire-ships, descended without a pilot, wheeling round at each eddy. Inside the huts, numerous parties, stimulated by copious draughts of rice-brandy, listened to singers brought in by the master of the house, who accompanied themselves on a bamboo organ, and a monochord lyre. The Laotians have a number of ancient songs, but the troubadours most frequently delight their audiences by improvisations. The circumstances and the persons present furnished subjects, and, now gay and satirical, now romantic and tender, they had something for every one in the circle round them. Fertile in imagination, and almost beyond tiring, their voice fails sooner than their inspiration. They take part in all public feasts, as well as in all private rejoicings. I have seen one of these poets of love, in an address to a young girl, begin in accents the sweetest, most discreet, and most chaste, gradually kindling, till, as he ended, he reached expressions so pointed that she ran off blushing. Vocal and instrumental music seem in their infancy. In our European ears all the airs seemed to be the same monotonous recitative, ending uniformly in prolonged notes. But the people of the country do not think so; they can readily tell the difference between any two singers or performers.

Next day the savages had got back to their forests, where we proposed to visit them; the town resumed its wonted quiet; and the court went into mourning, the king having lost a great mandarin, his relation, in the night. This respectable personage had called in the medical man of the expedition; but the bonzes having persuaded him that the remedies prescribed were contrary to the sacred rites, he left himself piously to die. A funeral pile having been built for him, with great pomp, behind the royal pagoda, the bonzes arrived, riding astraddle the coffin, which was covered with flowers, and with ornaments in wax. When they had

got off, the bier was placed on the top of the wood, and
each approached to apply the fire. The flames, laying hold
of the dry wood, rose crackling. The crowd, however, found
the sight too tedious; and the bonzes, well-nigh drunk, setting the example, the assistants provided themselves with
bamboos, and set themselves to stir up the furnace, attacking the coffin itself, which, being almost burned, burst open.
The muscles of the body contracting with the fire, I saw
the two hands rise towards heaven in the midst of the
flames. This dismal spectacle appeared to give great amusement to the Laotians. I found nothing the day after, where
the pyre had been, but some ashes, and a few whitened
bones. The ravens flew in circles above, cursing, in their
hoarse language, the dogs, which they hindered from approaching. This kind of 'interment' is reckoned as of the
first class, and it is not every one who can hope for it: the
poor and the unknown are simply put some inches deep in
the ground.

We had entered the month of November; the river was
sinking daily, and the banks were fringed, as far as we
could see, with a long border of white sand. The perpetual
mists of the rainy season gave place to a transparent curtain
of vapour. While we were inhaling with delight the cooler
breezes of night and morning, the natives were shivering
under their cloaks. Covered by these large cloth mantles,
with floating folds, and of brilliant colours, the Laotians justified the opinion of their elegance, which they enjoy even
in Cochin-China. We rejoiced in the changes brought on
by the approaching winter—a season so mild as to remind
us of our summers in Europe. Our strength returned as the
leaves fell, and we resolved on two excursions.

The courier from France and the passports from Pekin
had not yet arrived. M. de Lagrée ordered M. Garnier to
descend the river as far as Stung-Treng, where we hoped
he would meet a messenger. The chief of the expedition,
Dr. Joubert, and myself, made ready to start for Attopée.
This point, which is situated on the stream which flows
into the great river at Stung-Treng, is a kind of advanced
post, in the country of the savages of the west. The Laotians have a repugnance to going there, pretending that

mortal fevers decimate the caravans, and the Chinese merchants, established at Bassac, loudly confirmed this, by adding that none of them would dare to go to seek in that province for the gold it produces in abundance. But God only knows what a Chinaman would not risk to get any profit! We listened to all which their sincere interest in us led these brave people to say; but at Cambodgia they had said of Laos, in general, all that they repeated here about Attopée, and we fancied we had acquired the right to be sceptical; and set out in two canoes furnished us by the king's order.

After having ascended the Mekong for some hours, we halted for the night in the pagoda of Vat-sei, where a hearty reception awaited us, for, without knowing it, we were benefactors of the establishment. Vat-sei had obtained one of the candlesticks lately given by M. de Lagrée. Our mats were spread upon the flags of the sanctuary, and we were lulled to sleep by the sound of evening song, the psalmody of which was in general monotonous, but sometimes interrupted by a shrill note, a kind of yell, which gave a strange character to these prayers, so unintelligible to us, and no less so to most of those who recited them. Side by side with some passages in modern language, their breviary contains a great number of pages written in Pali; and the bonzes read these without knowing the meaning, as some ladies in France read an office in Latin, mechanically. The religious Bouddhists do not, however, on that account fail any the more to meet each evening, with edifying regularity, to prayers. We have often slept in a caravanserai, which was at once the house of God and of travellers, and they never failed to give us the favour of an anthem. The bonzes might set an example to many a chapter of canons.

Beyond the village of Vat-sei, the Mekong speedily contracts. The mountains, whose base it washes, leave it no more than three hundred metres in breadth. This sudden strangling makes no apparent increase in the swiftness of the current, but its depth becomes terrifying. Great apes escorted us along the banks, and growled familiarly when we threw them bananas. The Se-don, a pretty river, which we entered after a day and a half's sailing, runs softly through a very garden. Plantations of cotton and tobacco, of gourds and of batatas, into which flocks of wild pea-fowl come to plunder morning and evening, surround huts hidden in high tufts of bamboos. The king of Bassac had told us that a letter from him to the village chiefs, preceded us, ordering them to supply us with food and means of transport. This letter of the king had not arrived. When the first rapids in the river forced us to land, the subordinate authorities refused to procure us elephants; prayers, threats, the exhibition of the Siamese passport, were equally unavailing: a regular order of the governor of the province was necessary. Not to lose time, we set out on foot, after having dispatched a courier to Bassac. We learned, after, that the functionaries thus ill-disposed to us had suffered some days' severe punishment in consequence. The look of the country was far from corresponding to that which the narrow belt bordering the river had led us to expect. It was covered with high undergrowth and woods, uncultivated, and generally uninhabited. It is almost always thus in Lower Laos.

Beyond the first fall of the Se-don, a cataract of about fifteen metres and very beautiful, the river becomes navigable again, and we hastened to take advantage of it The echo of our anger of the day before had preceded us to the villages, and they put canoes at our disposal, without even asking us to show our papers. We thus passed the bounds of the territory of Bassac, and reached the borders of the province of Kantong-niaï, where we found comfortable lodgings prepared for us. The governor of Kantong-niaï was a little old man of about sixty-five, with a bad, not to say a wicked, face. He read the Siamese letter, copied it, and put a thousand ridiculous questions about France to us, before he would allow us to continue our journey. We were expected with impatience in the next province, that of Simia. They led us, on our arrival, to a charming hut, made expressly for us, of bamboos and leaves still quite fresh. The children and women, who made a holiday to see us, had advised this attention, in the hope of keeping us at least a whole day; but we had become used to having a heart wholly immovable, and took only two hours' rest with them. The authorities, cheated in their curiosity and wounded in their self-love, carried our little baggage, but left us to get on on foot, in spite of our protestations. The soil is sterile, the rock showing itself everywhere under it, and yields only a scanty growth, soon burnt up by the sun. At noon the heat was overpowering; I felt as if needles of fire were running into my brain, and bringing on a continual giddiness. We could breathe only in the evenings and mornings. One night the thermometer had fallen to twelve degrees above zero, and we awoke shivering with cold.

Some isolated rice-fields, in burned parts of the woods, cultivated by the savages, were to be seen here and there. To protect themselves from the wild beasts, the proprietors of these miserable fields have chosen to live fifty feet up in the air. They have built gray huts, which look like huge nests of birds of prey, on the tops of the great trees, in part stripped of their branches. They get at them by long ladders, narrow and bending. In walking across this wretched country, we came on a troop of buffaloes. At sight of the French flag, carried by a native, they moved, and presently made ready to charge us, as we were hurrying to hide the colours from their sight; yet they are far less wild in Laos than in Cochin-China. In our colony, even close to Saïgon, the sight of a Frenchman exasperates them, as if they resented the conquest more than the Annamites themselves. The Laotians every moment refused to go farther. We had to drive them on. They are, however, able to make long journeys a-foot, only time is of no value to them. They like to lie down, as often as may be, at the side of a brook, to smoke a cigarette, or chew a quid of betel. To go on without stopping, as we made them, was contrary to all their habits; and they showed it by grumbling, by tricks always baffled, and by lies always discovered, which they renewed none the less with an obstinate candour, in hope of getting a halt in the long-run.

Saravane, the chief place of a third province, is seen from a distance by the projecting angles of the triple roofs of its pagodas. Savages were busy making ready lodgings for us; two houses were already finished, and we relieved them from making any more. As great mandarins never travel without a numerous suite of men, women, and elephants, the governor expected to see 150 Frenchmen behind us, and caused barracks to be prepared for them. The modesty of our escort,—a modesty in keeping with the tenderness of our resources, as well as of our habits and tastes,—always astonished our hosts, and often made them, at first, doubt our rank. The village was agreeably situated on the borders of the Se-don, and shaded by a crowd of great trees regularly planted. The houses were numerous, and in good condition; but what surprised us most, was to find, in this hidden corner of the Siamese possessions, such a pagoda as we had not met since leaving Cambodgia. It was built of bricks, whitewashed, and covered by several roofs, one over the other. The façade, a little contracted, was approached by a porch sustained on four slender pillars of unequal height, and united a-top by a festoon carved in wood. Farther on, in the middle of a little pond, rose, on piles, a small building of the same style, covered outside with gilding. It was reached by a long wooden causeway, a little out of repair, the last plank being removed by design. This mysterious sanctuary, which the bonzes made great difficulty of letting us enter, was the library of the sacred books. Their books were there, ranged on rich shelves, in elegant cases, which, again, were covered with silk, and slept in undisturbed repose—for not one of these religious could decipher the Pali text, though they paid it such profound respect—the water, which bathes the feet of their palace, preserving them from the two great scourges of the country, water and the white ants. In the villages of these countries, the pagodas, built of brick, show off with an air of relative richness and solidity over the wooden huts which surround them. Built in the middle of a great yard, they seem to keep profane habitations at a distance. It is always near them one finds the best cocoa-trees, the highest palms, the most flourishing cabbage-palms. In the shade of these the bonzery shelters itself, and the children come to learn to read and write. As in ancient Europe, culture and teaching are in Laos the monopoly of the clergy. Literature, properly so called, hardly exists, and one has finished his studies when he has read a certain number of Bouddhist books, and heard them explained.

Plate 8 *Cambodian people (Drawing by Janet Lange, based on a drawing by L. Delaporte)*

Plate 9 *Royal pagoda in Bassac. (Drawing by E. Tournois, based on a watercolour by L. Delaporte)*

The bonzes, who pass their whole life in the yellow dress, subject to the austerities imposed by the rule, are not numerous. Most of the young men who fill the pagodas stay longer or shorter, as suits their convenience, but none less than three months. This custom is followed by all who respect themselves. The king of Cambodgia wears the frock, and has his head shaved; and the king of Siam, himself, enters religion before mounting the throne. I once saw the son of a mandarin renounce the world for a time, and greatly admired the facility with which he was admitted into the convent. The postulant, clothed in white, followed by his parents and his friends, presented himself before the bonzes, sitting in council, and laid down those offerings which are obligatory in a thousand circumstances of life, for procuring a prayer or a placet, or instead of *cartes de visite*,—and form in this country a heavy tax on the poor. The first thing to be done when an act of favour, or even of justice, is desired from any one, be he chief of a village, a great mandarin, the governor of a province, or the king, is to send him a basket of poultry, or a quarter of buffalo or of pork.

The bonzes, who live luxuriously on alms, have no inclination to lose the benefit of such a custom, and my novice having complied with it, was received. In the examination he had to undergo, far greater concern appeared to be shown for the health of his body than for the state of his soul. He declared he had never been either insane or leprous; that he had the authority of his parents for what he was doing; and that he was provided with all that constitutes the wardrobe or the furniture of a Bouddhist monk— a yellow frock, a mat, and a copper saucepan. This done, the old man vanished, and the clergy who had assisted at the transformation, bowed before the new *phra*—the saint almost canonised. They henceforth spoke to him only in words pitched on the key of the most extravagant hyperbole.

The yellow frock, so universally respected, inspires in those who wear it—if only put on to-day, to be put off to-morrow—a kind of fantastic insolence. The Bouddhist religious give their services to those who ask, and to those who pay them, but they have no cure of souls. Without

responsibility to heaven, they are without love to their
neighbour. They also use their numerous privileges, treat the
great of the earth almost as equals with equals, and despise
the poor. Most of the young bonzes have a faculty of forgetting the monastic rules, some of which, however, it must
be owned, are troublesome to excess. Bouddha prohibited
his disciples from touching a woman, from speaking to her
in a secret place, from sitting on the same mat with her,
or from going on a boat which carried one. Indeed, he so
dreaded the influence of the female sex on his religious, as
to interdict their use of a mare or of a she elephant when
they made a journey.

The Bouddhist calendar has a great many festivals.
Every one was keeping holiday at Saravane; and the
bonzes, whom the faithful are bound to feast on pain of loss
of salvation, made a long breakfast the day after we arrived.

In the afternoon a procession went several times round
the pagoda. It recalled the Catholic ceremonies of the same
kind so thoroughly, as to make one forget himself. The
bonzes marched before, carrying emblems and banners; the
laics came after; and, lastly, closing the whole, appeared
the women, in full dress and full chignon, their hands filled
with flowers.

We exchanged visits of ceremony with the authorities.
After the inevitable presentation of the letter from Siam,
that magic talisman which opened every door to us, the
governor promised to procure us six elephants, apologising
that he could not get more; he was obliged to take away
five for his annual visit to all the pagodas of his province,
which would begin the next day. Six elephants were
enough for us. A kind of narrow and long seat, like a
child's cradle, set on several ox or deer skins, was kept in
its place on the back of our beasts by a strong surcingle of
rattan. When we left a village or came to one, we were
helped to mount or descend these living walls, by ladders;
but it was different when we had to halt in the forest. Some
of the elephants, very well trained, knelt at the word of command from the driver. It looked as if a hill had fallen in on
itself. Others were content to lift their fore foot, so as to
form a kind of stool, by means of which one could scramble

into his place. The driver, astraddle on the neck of his beast, let his legs hang behind the huge ears of the elephant, which kept going all the time like huge fans.

A word was commonly enough to guide these intelligent animals; but it was sometimes necessary to use an iron hook, which was stuck into the skin of the head till it drew blood. In leaving Saravane we twice crossed the Se-don, which has very steep banks. Our elephants, to get down the high sides of the river, had to trust themselves to an almost perpendicular path, hardly wider than their own feet. When the soil was loose, they stiffened their legs before them, let their hind legs drag, so that their thighs were on the ground, and their belly not much above it, and slid to the very edge of the precipice, without for a moment losing either their coolness or their balance. When they emerged in this way from a hollow, they looked like a huge block of rock which had become detached and was in motion. We had seen their strength before, but now admired their prudence. We had to climb a dry watercourse full of rolling stones. They scanned the huge tree above them, with its bare roots, or the rocks overhanging them, and kept their eye on every tuft of grass or grain of sand, never advancing a step till they felt sure that the ground would bear them. In some difficult places they took an hour to a kilometre; but they never stumbled once.

When the woods had replaced the rice-fields, we ceased to meet villages at which to make our evening halts, and it was necessary to carry provisions for several days. We went along roads which no horse, however strong or active, could have travelled, and our beasts performed wonders of strength and cleverness. Reaching at last, after much toil, the top of a steep ascent, we discovered at our feet, beyond the foliage, a stretch of water, in which the mountains reflected their rounded summits. We took it for one of those magnificent lakes, which are the ornament of virgin forests, so often described; but our Laotians undeceived us—it was the river Attopée.

We had passed long days, formerly, at its mouth at Stung-Treng, so that it was an old acquaintance, and we wished to rest on its banks. The idea of this halt was

pleasant, for several reasons. The motion of elephants is
very fatiguing. It is not strictly either rolling or pitching,
but a mixture of both these horrible things, complicated, on
the least sound, by a sudden and violent step backwards.
These animals, once tamed, if not specially trained for war,
are as timid as hares. I have been on one which, in spite
of its formidable tusks and huge size, shied at the sight of a
small dog. In the forest, which we had to cross to get to
the river's edge, they met more worthy objects of terror;
for we passed the lair of a rhinoceros, and a tiger crossed
our path. We found ourselves, in fact, in a part abounding
with these ferocious beasts, and our guides seemed no less
terrified than the creatures they rode. M. de Lagrée did
not the less give them the order to halt. We chose the dry
bed of a torrent, which pours itself in the rainy season into
the river Attopée, as our place of encampment. Our Laotians, always willing to halt, resisted this time energetically, and only yielded when they had exacted the promise,
as impertinent as useless, that we would neither fight nor
swear, nor get into any noisy discussions. For greater security they also forthwith built a little altar to Bouddha,
with branches torn from the trees. All right with heaven,
they thought it well to take the steps which worldly prudence dictated, and kindled huge fires round our camp.
We got under our shelter of leaves, necessary at this season
by the heaviness of the dews, and stretched ourselves on
our mats, having primed our arms afresh. As to our guides,
our drivers, and our baggage-carriers, they smoked their
cigarettes, and chatted in a low voice, but were too cautious
to close an eye. When, after a weary march, I recovered,
under the reviving influence of a cool night, entire possession of myself, my thoughts turned sadly to France, from
which no whisper had reached us for six months. My wandering life amidst silent forests, with every emotion quickened by close contact with the greatness of nature, filled
me with unknown joys, and kept off those tortures of uncertainty about friends and country, which were daily becoming more keen. But while I tried to watch the stars
twinkling through the interlaced branches of the gourbi, I
saw all the evil phantoms which, under the horrid forms of

war and death, had, perchance, in a half year, humbled
France, and ravaged my paternal hearth, pass before my
eyes like nightmares. The courier, who was close at hand,
brought us the news of Sadowa.

Notwithstanding the fears expressed the day before, the
night passed without any alarm. Next day, the forest became
extremely difficult of passage. The tracks made by the wild
elephants crossed each other, under the bamboos, which
made an impenetrable tangle, bristling with prickles, between
the trees. Our elephants showed wonderful cleverness in the
fatiguing work of breaking through this jungle, tearing down
branches of trees in the way, twisting them off with their
trunks, or crushing them under their feet. Each, in its turn,
took the head of the column, and obeyed the word of command of the driver as exactly as if it understood his language. If a great tree stopped our course, the elephant
leaned its huge forehead against the trunk, and presently,
without any apparent effort on its part, the tree bent, the
roots started from the ground, and it lay stretched on the
earth, trampled down at last by the huge feet of the animal. If one of the huge creepers, which hung from the
trees, threatened to hurt one of us whom it happened to
carry, the elephant would draw this immense cable to it, tear
it off, breaking it as a child would a thread, and would not
go on till it had opened a wide passage for itself and its
charge on its back, whose height above it, it seemed to have
measured. Our beasts had to toil thus for several days together. Laborious and gentle, they never showed ill-humour,
except when the drivers, not thinking it enough to shackle
them, thought it necessary to tie them up as well. This
happened at every halt in these districts, frequented by numerous troops of wild elephants, which, as the drivers will have
it, blushing for their race at the sight of their fellows enslaved,
never fail, when they come on them, to break their bonds,
and force them to join them and renew their wandering lives
in the depths of the boundless woods. Our animals, angry,
and in a pet, beat their trunks against the ground with
a loud noise, or uttered cries not unlike the sounds a bad
player makes on a hunting horn. Their ill-will always ended

with this, however, as if it were a faint protest against their ill-usage.

We at last reached the edge of the forest, and saw in the distance a chain of bare mountains. It is the high natural barrier which has prevented the Annamites spreading themselves over Laos, and has kept them penned up on the sea-coast. We had reached the point where the river Attopée, which probably has its source in these mountains, begins to be navigable. A large village stands at this spot, and we took twenty-four hours' rest in it. A Siamese mandarin, a tax-collector, who happened to be there at the time, hastened to pay us a visit, and was very grateful for an earthenware pipe, with the head of a Zouave for bowl, given him by the head of the expedition. The river Attopée is very pretty, and recalls some rivers of France. It flows rapidly through vast and magnificent forests. Our light canoes, borne noise-lessly on the stream, did not alarm the wild animals, which came to the banks of the water for coolness and shade. The wild boars, the deer, but, above all, the pea-fowl, revived our taste for the chase; and our table, so often bare, would some-times have roused the envy of knights of the middle ages.

The river Attopée had been described to us as another Pactolus. Gold is, certainly, found in its sand and on its banks, but the search for it has been left to the savages. I went to see a little improvised village of the unfortunates who follow this branch of industry on a sandbank, just left dry. They lodge in bamboo huts about twice the size of large dog-kennels, which they pretty closely resemble. Each of these cabins is the home of a family. Several gene-rations of women were crouched in them, from the old crea-ture, whose long white hair fell over her hollow cheeks and meagre shoulders, to the little daughter, who peacefully sucked the plump breast of its mother amidst her half-alarm at our visit. There were no men to be met with, such as we saw at a distance instantly hurrying away when they noticed us. Wishing to see other camps of these wild people, we took a stroll into the country, under the guidance of a Laotian.

M. de Lagrée was now struck by one of those attacks of fever, which begin by freezing the blood in the veins, and

end by making it burn like fire. We at once procured from
a neighbouring village some felt coverlets, cloaks, and langoutis, and whatever might help to restore heat in his
chilled body; and after two hours of mortal anxiety, we
were able to assure ourselves that his strong constitution
would get him over the danger. We left him to rest, and
were free to continue our journey. We had to march a long
time through jungle, crossing broad and deep streams on
slender trunks of trees, which had no parapet but a yielding creeper. A wretched caravanserai, buried in the bushes,
showed us our journey was ended. There is not in these
countries a group of ten settlers which does not provide a
shelter for travellers; hospitality being the first law in such
regions, as being the first necessity. Among the Laotians,
if there be no cottage for the purpose, the pagoda serves
for inn; but there are no pagodas among the savages.
They believe in fairies and ghosts, which do not live in
temples. Round the village to which we had come rose a
palisade, to keep off evil spirits; but it would not have stood
a good kick from a man of flesh and blood. A bit of bamboo,
covered with writing and conjurations, hung over our door.
The huts were ranged in a semicircle. We counted seventy
or eighty, all built upon the same plan, which was as simple
as could be imagined. They are two metres broad, and about
three deep, and two narrow and low doors correspond one
to the other in the gables. These wretched dwellings are
perched on posts, which leave a commodious abode underneath the family to whom they belong, for fowls and pigs.
The women ran off, at a signal from their husbands, so that
we found none but the old people. At the gold-seekers'
village we had seen them sitting sadly on their doorsteps,
their age making them look as if they no longer belonged
to either sex. The men are, in general, well-grown and well-
made; their projecting forehead set in a frame of long hair,
which they leave to fall in confusion, or twist up behind
their head. The end of the nose comes very low, and the
nostrils are much raised. The Laotians, on the other hand,
have short snub noses, and would be less good-looking than
their tributaries, but for the true savage expression of these
poor people, seen especially in their wild frightened looks,

G

as if they were stupid with wonder. They have elegant
ways, however, which may be remembrances of some distant past. They wear bracelets of brass wire, and necklaces
of glass beads, and make holes in their ears large enough to
insert great cylinders of wood. This last custom prevails
also among the Laotians, but to a smaller extent. Formerly,
the most powerful king of Laos — the only one, indeed,
who really deserved the name—gloried in the extraordinary
diameter of these holes, made, little by little, in the lower
lobe of his ears. They begin by using a little gold bodkin,
which they let stay in the flesh for a month, introducing
others, larger and larger, successively, till they get the ends
of the ears to fall over the shoulders. The savages of to-
day no longer fear to indulge in a luxury formerly reserved
exclusively to the king.

What is the origin of these tribes, which we found everywhere alongside the Laotians, throughout the course of
the Mekong? In a journey so rapid as ours, it was impossible to study ethnography very deeply. To get at a
scientific conclusion, it would have been necessary to live
a long time among them; to gain the confidence of some
of the most intelligent, and to converse with them; but we
had no such opportunity. We only passed through; and,
besides, had no interpreter · ho knew their different idioms,
so that we can hardly venture even on a few conjectures.

The Laotians occupy only a narrow strip on the banks
of the river, especially on the left bank. Between their
villages and the great mountain-chain which bounds the
Annamite empire, numerous tribes are scattered, from the
Tonkin to our province of Lower Cochin-China, some of
them including several encampments in their tribal jurisdiction. Those nearest the Laotians, who have likely enough
given sovereigns to Laos in some former day, have submitted to the king of Siam, and pay him a light tribute. This
subjection, nominal, or nearly so, as it is, brings them some
very substantial advantages. They need no longer fear the
incursions of slave-traders, who drive a flourishing trade
with the independent tribes. In Cambodgia, and probably
also in Siam, as in Laos, there are several classes of slaves:
those who are slaves for debt, the slaves of the king, and

the slaves of pagodas. Slavery for debt is not, strictly speaking, slavery; it is a temporary loss of liberty. When any one is unable to pay his creditor a sum due, he gives himself, or one of his children, up to him. The slave's labour is reckoned equivalent to the interest on the debt; but he is not freed till the principal is paid up. If he is discontented with his master, he borrows money and repays him, passing by this simple fact into a new ownership.

The king's slaves are really slaves, whether they have been taken in war, or reduced to slavery by legal sentence. Any one, pursued for a delinquency or a crime, who takes refuge in a pagoda, is protected by the right of asylum, on condition of becoming a slave, or rather a bonze, for life. True slavery, in all the horror of the word — slavery simply from being basely carried of, with no deliverance but by death or escape — is inflicted only upon savages. These, trapped by ambushments, or driven off like fallow-deer by the man-hunters, are torn from their forests, chained, and taken to the chief places of Laos, Siam, or Cambodgia. At Pnom-Penh they are in especial demand, and are paid for more liberally than Annamite or Cambodgian slaves. They are worth 800 francs there, while the Cambodgian is hardly worth more than 500, and no more than 200 will be given for an Annamite. The difference in the conditions of the slavery has something to do with this difference in value; but the main thing which determines it is the degree of confidence the master can put in the uprightness of the slave, according to the race to which he belongs. The Annamites on the one hand, and the Laotians and Cambodgians on the other, give themselves up to this shameful trade. When I asked a mandarin the worth of the chief articles of merchandise in his village, he never failed, after mentioning rice, cotton, or silk, to add the slaves, whose value fluctuates, like that of other things, according to the law of supply and demand. Young good-looking virgin girls are sold to the rich men, who buy a mistress for about the same sum as a pleasure-elephant costs.

Among the tribes which have preferred the chances of their almost nomadic life to the security of an easy vassalage, some, become fierce, pursue strangers in their hatred, and shoot them with poisoned arrows. On the left bank of

the Mekong, as far up as Tonkin, the Laotians, though quite
convinced of their own superiority, confessed that a hundred
of them would not dare to face ten of these wild children of
the woods. In their turn, these use reprisals, and traffic, as
they have the chance, in the liberty of their enemies. I have
seen an Annamite of the neighbourhood of Tourane, who had
been taken prisoner by the savages of the hills, sold and
resold, till he became, at the end of the transactions, the
property of a Laotian mandarin. These tribes have many
names. In the lower and middle part of the basin of the
Mekong we meet the Moïs, the Chiâmes—the old inhabitants
of the kingdom of Tsiampa—and professing the Mussulman
faith—the Stiengs, the Penongs, the Cuys, the Charaïs or
Giraïës, &c. They are, perhaps, the old owners of the soil,
beaten, and driven into the woods, by the invaders established
on the banks of the great rivers and principal streams.

There are radical differences between the Cambodgian
or Laotian and the idioms of the savage tribes—idioms
which seem connected with each other by striking features,
and by a general resemblance. According to the information
given M. Mouhot by the Stiengs, among whom he lived for
a time, the Chiâmes speak the Charaï, and the Cuys speak
the same language as the Stiengs themselves. The tribes
which have submitted to Siam or Cambodgia have a rude
organisation, somewhat like what obtains in Laotian or Cambodgian villages. Those, on the contrary, who have retained
their independence, practise absolute independence, and recognise no chief. All live in a kind of communism, sharing,
impartially, want or abundance, and show in this mistake,
characteristic of children and savages, that want of foresight
which is only one of the forms of absolute confidence in
nature.

The Charaïs surround two personages in their tribe with
veneration—the one enjoying the name of the King of Fire;
the other, that of the King of Water. The fire-king is the
more important. A great rusty sabre, without a sheath, is
his symbol of power; and it is hard to tell whether the
homage is paid the man or his weapon. I am assured that
the kings of Cambodgia and of Cochin-China send him ambassadors periodically; and he is known and honoured by

all the savage tribes to the very frontiers of China. A missionary, who wrote in the seventeenth century the history of Tonkin, hesitates to include in the limits of that kingdom, at the time when it embraced Cochin-China itself, the mountain peoples who acknowledged the fire and the water kings. Can we recognise, in this singular fact, the sign of an ancient sovereignty, marking out still, after so many centuries, the despoiled family of the old kings of Laos? Does the tribe of Charaïs, like that of Judah of old, hide in its bosom some Joash? Without writings and fallen out of memory, without history as without tradition, the savages, whom we addressed in Laotian, understood little of our meaning, and most commonly gave us no answer.

Attopée, which we had reached, is no more than a very poor village. It is one of the principal centres of the slave-trade. I have seen boats, loaded with this miserable human freight, descending the river, to get into the Mekong at Stung-Treng, and thence make for Cambodgia. The unhappy captives seemed more crushed by their griefs than by the irons that bound them. In the paths of their forests, fleeing at the lightest sound, like wild deer, or crouching like fallow-deer at the bottom of their bamboo hut, and trembling at the sight of us, they seemed nearer the brute, in the scale of being, than man. Here, on the contrary, immovable in their narrow floating prison, letting their sad looks wander as they might, they showed in their bearing that nobility which hopeless misfortune, profoundly felt, everywhere imprints on the human figure. We may, doubtless, regret that a public market for slaves should be held at Pnom-Penh, under the shadow of our flag; but it must not be forgotten that, as yet, we are only the protectors of Cambodgia. Our interference in the affairs of this country can only be exercised with extreme caution, under pain of creating perils for ourselves. King Norodom himself must be got to suppress this odious custom, consecrated by the practice of centuries.

The people of Attopée melt the gold found in the sands, in little earthen crucibles, and send a certain number of these ingots annually to Bangkok. They thus pay, in kind, their dues to Siam. Here, again, one sees how the king of Siam enriched himself while he affected to render a service. His

armies drove off the bands of soldiers, who, rushing from the
Annamite mountains, threw themselves on Attopée at the
time of the revolt of the Taysons,[1] and this province has
since been detached from Cambodgia.

We were in haste to get back to Bassac, and avail ourselves of the precious months of the dry season, to continue
our voyage towards China. Seven elephants awaited us
some hours below Attopée; two of them were mothers, and
their young ones went with them. Sixty men were given
us, or rather were forced on us, as escort, for we were unwilling to take so many from their homes and their occupations. But they told us thieves infested the woods through
which we must pass, and the governor was responsible for
our safety. The journey, it was said, would take five days.
We dived into the forests, making our way through a kind
of marshy flat, where the waters collected from the neighbouring mountains. We had to cross a great many streams;
some of them actual rivers, bearing no inconsiderable tribute
of waters to the Attopée. My beast divided its cares between
the serious difficulties of the route and its little one, which
it did not let out of sight for a moment, and it, frolicsome,
and cross as a child led for a walk against its will, roared
and stamped. At its cries the mother became indifferent to
the iron which the driver stuck into its head; she stopped,
and turned back to quiet her son; when he wanted a drink,
nothing would induce her to take a step ahead; and the
crafty thing chose always to ask the breast at the moment
when its mother, busy with the slope of a hill, was letting
herself slide down painfully on her stomach. If the water
was too deep, she helped her little one with her foot and
trunk, keeping him on the surface. To the very last this
admirable animal never for a moment lost its coolness, but
discharged its duties as a mother with tenderness, and as
a beast of burden with conscientiousness. As to the males,
they are lavishly gallant. They hide their mysterious am-
ours in the depths of the woods; but they do not the less,
on the march, use their trunk for the most immodest sport.

[1] Mountaineers famous in the history of Cochin-China. It was against
them that Gia-long asked and obtained help from Louis XVI. by the me-
diation of the Bishop of Adran.

After having met torrents of clear and running water in the heart of the forest, we halted each night in the midst of vast grassy glades, with a tainted pool in some central depression, to which all the beasts of the woods came to quench their thirst, and wash. Our elephants found in such places abundant pasturage, and it was necessary to think of them.

At last we came to immense marshes, the country lay open before us, and we, once more, distinguished clearly, after a trip of thirty-two days, the tops of the Bassac mountains. An odd-looking peak, like a woman's breast, stood out against the deep blue of the sky, and we strained our eyes for long before we could discover the flagstaff, which bore the French flag, over our encampment. At the foot of these mountains we should find ourselves reunited, should read the French papers together, discuss the news, open our letters, and draw fresh courage from these last communications with our country. The fatigues, the fevers, which we had had to suffer in crossing the woods and marshes, were all forgotten in the first transports which this sight caused us. The disappointment we were to meet was all the more bitter. M. Garnier had found neither message nor messenger at Stung-Treng. The revolt of the Cambodgians cut off our communications with the lower part of the river, and troops had been sent after us to bring us back. This report soon spread among the Laotians of Bassac, who several times informed MM. Delaporte and Thorel, who alone, with a part of the escort, remained in the camp, that the enemy was close at hand. A sailor and a French soldier, tired of the serious privations which circumstances imposed on us, had stolen some arms, sown terror in the village, and refused to return to duty. M. Delaporte had to go to the king, who armed twenty Laotians with cudgels. Guided during the night by a complaisant husband, these surprised the fugitives, whom we brought back in irons. In spite of threats of invasion, of which we were the cause; in spite of internal disorder, provoked around him by the French, the king of Bassac did not cease to show his hearty good-will to us. He knew our plans, realised our embarrassment, and tried to lessen it. As to the Cambodgian rebels,—giving up their useless pursuit, they came no farther than Stung-Treng, on the left bank of the Mekong, and Tonli-Repon, on the right.

If we had expected only letters and papers, the not getting them would, no doubt, have been a serious disappointment, but the success of the expedition would not have been compromised. The impossibility of communicating, by the river, with the French officer at Cambodgia threw us into serious anxiety. It threatened to involve us in the most disastrous consequences. We had no passports from Pekin; and to go without them, after our recent experience, and when it was clear that we could not have advanced a step in the Siamese provinces, if we had not been able to show the governors imperative commands from Bangkok, was to condemn ourselves to be stopped at the frontier of Laos. M. de Lagrée, however, gave the order to prepare to leave Bassac, resolved to make a new attempt to get the papers, which he like ourselves, thought indispensable.

The king redoubled his delicate attention on learning that we were about to leave Bassac. We presented him with portraits of the Emperor and Empress, and he instantly ordered them to be hung up on the walls of the grand pagoda. In the farewell visit we went to pay him he said a thousand kindly things to us, which would in France have been only polite commonplaces, but in his mouth were of value. However little enthusiasm one may feel for savage and half savages, they never say what they do not think. I was a real pleasure to speak about France with this young Laotian. He seemed struck with wonder at the narration of the miracles effected by European genius, and listened with a simple confidence, throwing out embarrassing questions in the middle of our descriptions; for it would have been difficult to have given him explanations he would have understood. He made himself the mouthpiece of the regrets of his capital. Our medical men were followed by the bows and the gratitude of the sick whom they had attended. Whole families carried offerings to the pagodas, that heaven might be entreated to favour their voyage, and to give them a thousand years of life. They had, in reality, distributed some pills, and struck the imagination by some happy operations. The bonzes, alone, concealed their dislike; for they had given up the sick persons, and a double hurt came from these cures to them—the injury to their prestige, and a heavy loss to the pagoda. Funerals cannot be performed without largesses from the family, and the dead are never better honoured than when the living feast round the funeral pile.

The king came, himself, to accompany us to the beach, where the boats he had caused to be made ready for us were waiting, and we left in the last days of December. The navigation had become easy; the steep banks of the river no longer presenting the same obstacles as at the commencement of our voyage. The trees and the shrubs, through the middle of which we must have passed six months before, were now ten metres above our heads. One of my rowers, to escape his forced task, threw himself into the water, gained the bank, and disappeared in the high undergrowth. The unfortunate creature would only suffer worse troubles if he were taken; and if he escaped, his family would have to pay for him.

Our flotilla stopped, and we went on foot to visit the ruins of Muongcao, the ancient capital of the kingdom of Bassac. The immense plain which we had to cross had a desolate look, for the natives had set it on fire. The sun scorched our heads, and the still-glowing ashes burned our feet. Some half-burned trees, here and there, without leaves, showed in this desert, like giants in mourning; others, completely burned through, lay on the ground; and we could not but regret the delightful shade they would have given us, and denounce a barbarous custom, which destroys for the sake of destruction. The Laotians sometimes burn parts of the forest to make dry rice-fields, but they often do it to satisfy the instinct of devastation—an instinct which stupidly spreads the ravages of fire over thousands of hectares. In Cochin-China the French administration has been forced to take measures to protect the forests, which are one of the chief sources of the wealth of the state. By these random conflagrations the natives, without intending it, create impenetrable thickets of bamboos. This plant, thanks to the vigorous roots it pushes into the ground, is the only one that survives, and meeting no more obstacles or rivals, ends by covering immense tracts, through which neither men, wagons, nor elephants can pass, except with extreme difficulty.

There is not much of Muongcao : some parts of walls of enclosures, some pagodas, a small slender pyramid, sculptured like one of those gothic spires that decorate our cathedrals, a fine wide street, and trees planted in order. The Mekong at the place where we went on board again is cut up by sandbanks. It makes a sharp elbow, which gives it the appearance of a huge lake, shut in behind by a chain of mountains of various heights, and curious shapes, bathed in vapour. Some green islands rose from the waters, which surrounded them with a white girdle of foam. We had some rapids to pass, through confused masses of piled-up sandstone, which looked like strange crouching monsters. The river has marked on the polished sides of these rocks the height of its periodical risings. The hills which run along the river's edge are wooded; but the leaves had lost their freshness, yellow spots showing here and there on the green. Presently, the Mekong contracted ; on the right bank, which we followed, the blocks of sandstone rose into a cyclopean wall ; rocks encumbered the bed of the river, which at some spots was of immense depth, the sounding-line finding no bottom.

Six days after our leaving Bassac we reached the entry of the river Ubone, called Sé-mun by the natives, which seems only a bifurcation of the Mekong. This latter was almost unnavigable as far as Khemarat, and M. Delaporte was sent off, alone, on the difficult task of exploring it. The bulk of the expedition turned to the west, and ascended the river Ubone. We were told that we should have ten rapids to ascend, and, therefore, took a reinforcement of men at the village of Pacmoun; a precaution, as it proved, by no means useless. The river was very soon obstructed by a huge bar of sandstone, twisted, worn, and overthrown by the waters. The sandstone is perforated by holes as round as if made by human hands, but caused during the flood by whirlpools charged with flints. We had to carry all our canoes over these obstacles, and to do this we had to unload them completely. The sun heated the stones, and there was no shelter whatever from its rays, which were tenfold hotter by the reflection. The men yoked themselves to the canoes; a singer roared verses at the top of his voice, a long scream from the rest serving for refrain; then came a grand pull, and the burden moved forward a few paces. The night had already long fallen, and the last canoe was yet behind. Our natives had been a whole day in the water, and after all this toil they had nothing to eat but a little rice, and no bed but the hard stone. The fire, however, warmed them as it kindled, and kept up their spirits.

The river at this place is a torrent of about four hundred metres in breadth. It is, however, very picturesque. The banks are covered with trees. Near the water the undergrowth is of a fine green; but on the higher level the yellow and red leaves, hardly holding on to the withered trees, are carried away by the lightest breath of wind. One sees just such landscapes in autumn in some districts of France. Here, perhaps, it is a trifle wilder; but there is nothing to recall the tropics, except the sun. Our canoes made no more than three kilometres in twelve hours; and while our Laotians were dragging them, with great labour, in the middle of the rapids, we set out to hunt in the forest, which was inhabited by wild animals of all sizes and kinds, from the tiger, the elephant, and the wild boar, to the hare and the goat. The banks of the river and the edges of the smaller pools in the woods were marked by their footprints, but we saw no more of them than this. All, alike, flee from man, finding hiding-places in the impenetrable thickets and the vast wildernesses. It would be necessary to study their habits, and to surprise them by watching, and we had not the time. Fishing was at once easier and more successful. Fish is very abundant in the Ubone, and some kinds would, beyond question, be thought delicacies in Europe.

On the 3d of January 1867 we reached the foot of the last rapid. Other boats were needed to come to our aid, to get us over this barrier, and we halted till they arrived. We paid our men at the rate of four sous a day; but, in spite of the fatigue they had had, these bounties astonished them, and the report spread everywhere, as it had done in the past, that we scattered gold with open hand. Great trees protected us from the rays of the sun; the sound of the falling water—a little sad and monotonous —harmonised with our mood at the beginning of a new year, and we rested ourselves quietly in our boats. These Laotian canoes, narrow and long, covered with a low rounded roof, look curious by night. When I could not sleep, and saw before me only men, with shaved heads and of strange figures, crouching and watching round a torch which cast a flickering red light on them, I almost thought myself carried away to the low-arched fosses of some town on the Rhine. The windows had two square supports, and I saw through them a corner of the sky, which, with the water below, made the illusion still more complete.

We were near the village of Pimoun, which can hardly be called one. Great plants, and trunks of trees cut off at a man's height, still stood round the huts, and disputed the space intended for kitchen-gardens. The head of this straggling infant place sent to the rice-fields for labourers liable to forced work, and we quietly ascended the Ubone in new canoes, finding it easily navigable to that town, where we arrived on the 6th of January. Fifteen horses of the country, hardly larger than the dogs of the Pyrenees, wa ted us, saddled, beribboned, and with a silver ornament on their forehead, outside the row of mandarins of every grade, in full official costume, who had come to greet us. In spite of all that might be imposing in Europeans with great beards and soiled clothes, we felt a little put out by the solemnity of such a reception; for our blue flannel frock-coats, already threadbare and torn, contrasted too strongly with the glory of robes of gold, and langoutis of silk, not to give our self-love a real humiliation. It was not without some surprise we found, in the house which had been made ready for us, a table covered with a white cloth, set out with wine and finger-glasses, and with comfortable seats round it. Calico hangings made a good imitation of plaster ceiling. It looked as if we had been spirited away to a farm in Normandy. Messengers from the governor arrived, in numbers, with presents.

All this showed that he was a man who had some ideas of civilisation, and we hastened to pay him a visit with all

the ceremony we could. The palace was like a bazaar, it
was so heaped up with looking-glasses, cloth, and European
carpets, recently brought from Bangkok. It turned out that
they were intended to heighten the splendour of the coronation fêtes, at which we were present soon after. The
governor had, in fact, obtained the title of king. He belongs to the family of the princes of Vien-Chan, and having
been brought up at Bangkok since the conquest of this
kingdom by the Siamese armies, had done his best to gain
the favour of the king of Siam, who had placed him at the
head of the province of Ubone. He told us naïvely, that it
was the grand presents he had made his sovereign that had
won him his good fortune. His countenance is not pleasing; he is of middle height, lean and angular, and his shining eyes throw every instant a yellow light over his cat-like
parchment-coloured face. He was, however, well enough
disposed towards us. In one of the excursions which we
made outside the town he ordered some men to follow our
horses; and to be the more sure that nothing would hinder
their keeping up with them, they were forbidden to take
their little bag of rice with them, the chief who went with
them being, moreover, required to give any of them a beating, if they felt hungry and let it be known.

The coronation ceremony was partly civil, and partly
religious. To reach the new palace which he had had built
for himself, the king crossed the whole plain where we were
encamped. Music opened the procession. Next came some
cavaliers; and behind them marched an imposing troop of
twenty-two elephants, between two files of Laotians armed
with lances, and carrying banners. On the back of the first
sat the king in a tunic of green velvet, with a crown like a
Prussian helmet, and protected by a great parasol of silver
thread. The people followed in a crowd, and were ordered
to make holiday. I saw some collected by force, and driven
towards the royal cortége by blows of a rattan. The great
hall of the palace was full of bonzes, and their chief began
the long prayers usual on such occasions. Lustres in brass
gilt, which were a very fair imitation of a model seen at
Bangkok, hung from the ceiling, and wax-lights were burning, sending their smoke up along with that of cigarettes

and the perfume of fragrant woods. The prayers, alone, were not glowing; for every one chatted, smoked, or chewed his betel, except the old bonze, who, spectacles on nose, laboured to make out his Pali. At rare intervals the audience associated itself with him by a general inclination or a murmur, which was not unlike the response to our own prayers. The crown prince had his own part in the ceremony. Richly dressed in a langouti of cloth of gold, and a tunic of net starred with silver spangles, he had, in spite of his childish age, the haughty, solemn, and tired air of a youngster who feels his importance. He prepared to submit to the operation of cutting his hair; an observance in use in Siam and Cambodgia, as well as in Laos, to mark that the child has passed from boyhood to youth. When the heavens had been sufficiently invoked, the sovereign took his place under a kind of daïs, raised in the court, on an artificial rock, and communicating with the terrace of the palace, on the same level. Then, stripping off his fine robes, he put on white, and the bonzes proceeded to pour a deluge of lustral water, perfumed, over him. Four doves were set free, one after the other, by the new king, and they flew away over the heads of the kneeling people. This gracious symbol seemed a cruel irony. The whole, in short, was more curious than imposing, and I could not help thinking of those pompous Oriental ceremonies of which I used to dream, after reading self-deluded or lying writers. Women were altogether excluded from the solemnity. They take advantage of chinks in the walls, in such cases, to indulge their most imperious weakness—curiosity. It is not the jealousy of the men which makes them hide themselves, as in Turkey, but simply that they are not thought good enough to appear in such fêtes. Amusements were furnished for the public in the evening, in the court of the palace; but when we came there, after our dinner, they had just finished, and the crowd was dispersing. The king, however, no sooner saw us than he ordered the gates of the court to be closed, forced all to take their places again, and the artists to recommence their feats. Nobody had dined except the king and ourselves; but that did not matter. Some acrobats exhibited simple performances before us; two

of them, however, deserve more special mention. The first
put one of the heavy troughs in which the rice is pounded,
successively on his head, on his back, and on his stomach,
three vigorous fellows doing their best to show us, by the
use they made of three pestles, that they were not con-
federates. They brought us some of the rice, which was
ground to meal, as if it had come out of a mill. The other
passed and repassed over a wide carpet of glowing embers,
as quietly as if he had been walking on grass.

The province of Ubone, created by the fugitives from
Vien-Chan, the ruined capital whose remains we were soon
to inspect farther on, appears to have a population of about
100,000 souls. Its principal wealth is in beds of salt, which
are worked over a district of about fifteen leagues, round the
chief town. The rain-water, which gets saturated with the
mineral when it has soaked down to the lower part of the
soil, rises to the surface again in the dry season, through the
heat, and deposits it on the ground, which appears as if
covered with hoar-frost. The natives sweep the fields, wash
the earth, and evaporate the water. This crop of salt does
not prevent rice from growing on the same ground, as soon
as the first rains have cleansed it. As to the town, it was
the largest we had yet met. The streets are broad, and
pretty well laid out, parallel or perpendicular to the river.
In the more important, there are even wooden pavements,
which are of the greatest use to the people when the rains
have soaked the thick coat of sand with which the ways are
covered. We had frequent interviews with the king, and he
often came to see us *incognito*. He begged us one day to go
out and quiet a band of Burmese pedlars, who were making
disorder, and whom he could not correct, because they had a
letter from the English authorities at Rangoon. The chief
of the expedition answered that, not being an Englishman,
he had no power to mix in such a dispute. It was several
days before we could root out of the king's mind the false
idea he had taken up of our nationality, and I hardly feel
sure that we succeeded in the end. This incident, which
repeated itself several times during our journey, would, of
itself, show the necessity of being careful in this particular.
Now that we are finally settled in Indo-China, it behoves our

honour that the population of the interior should lear to know our name, as that of the coast has already, and that England should no longer be imagined by these ignorant people to be the only Western power. At Ubone, this title of English, which they persisted in giving us, procure us more consideration than we should otherwise have met; but farther on, the unfortunate confusion, in two cases especially, was on the point of leading to the most disastrous results.

It had become indispensable to rid ourselves of the Europeans who composed our escort. The Frenchmen, who had already created trouble for us at Bassac, might bring on more serious complications, by their bad conduct in circumstances easy to foresee. M. de Lagrée determined to end these men to Pnom-Penh, and he also wished to make a last effort to get the letters from Pekin, for which we had waited so long and so vainly. In our absolute ignorance of what had passed in Cambodgia since our departure, it was not prudent to go thither by the river, which is the usual route; and the chief of the expedition directed M. Garnier to reach Pnom-Penh by the interior of the countries bordering the provinces of the protectorate. This journey, equally difficult and perilous, was destined to have the additional advantage of bringing to light what had been hardly suspected- the existence of a great country, which remained absolutely Cambodgian, under foreign domination. In the province of Suren, Coucan, Sanka, and Tchonkan, which border on Angcor, the population preserves, still, the language of the ancient kingdom, of which we protect what remains. This country separates the provinces situated on the Mekong to about the fifteenth degree of north latitude, from the other Siamese possessions, and has preserved a kind of autonomy, the king of Siam, in deference to the feelings of the people, giving them no governors who are not of their own race.

Nature, herself, thus seems to have marked out the field which we have to clear in the lower part of the Mekong valley. On both sides of the great river, the Se-mun or river Ubone, and the Se-don, bound the zone within which our influence behoves us to prevail. On the right bank, the ancient Cambodgian provinces I have just named seem to be inexhaustibly fertile. Their productiveness, stimulated by new markets, by the opening of roads, which the geological structure of the country makes easy, will increase the exports of Saïgon. On the left bank, on this side of the Sé-don, the country is less favoured, as we proved during our excursion to Attopée; but behind the strip occupied by the Laotians, and the narrow territory where some savage tribes live scattered in their forests, are the Annamites, of whom one cannot help thinking at the sight of a soil, naturally fertile, but only half inhabited and only half cultivated by a lazy population, whom the mandarins devour. The intelligent race, of whom we have already attracted a marvellous proportion into the six provinces of Lower Cochin-China, will, perhaps, some day cross the mountains which separate it from Laos, and will transform that country, at once by its industry and by its healthful example.

CHAPTER III.

IT had been predicted that we should have to pass some
months in Laos—a region of evil name, protected by the
rocks with which its river bristles, and still more by the
miasma exhaled by the sun's heat, from the curiosity or ambition of its neighbours. It was not, therefore, without some
feeling of joy, almost of pride, that in thinking of the road
we had already come, we recalled our hardships, running
over them as a soldier does his wounds, and finding that we
still survived. Our ranks were about to be thinned, but it
was an act of our own will. M. de Lagrée had sent away all
the Europeans of our escort but one, the rest having shown
that their courage was greater than their resignation, and
that they were fitter to fight visible enemies than to bear
the enforced delays of our progress, and the annoyances of
the climate. Attracted at first by the hope of adventure,
they soon got an inkling of the monotonous life before them,
and their enthusiasm sank, as their eyes opened to the reali-
ties of the case. We fancied, moreover, that we had nothing
to fear from the Laotians; for their extreme gentleness left
us without anxiety, so far as they were concerned. We were
called, it is true, to pass through the midst of other populations of very different tempers, but they were still far distant; and it was wise, since we could not in any case force
the mandarins to do what we wanted, to make sure, at least,
of the sympathy of the natives, by irreproachable conduct
and strict discipline.

About three degrees of latitude and one of longitude

already separated us from Crachè, the Cambodgian village where we had exchanged our steamer for canoes, and which we, therefore, regarded as our true point of departure. The windings of the river made the distance still greater. We had reached the limits of Lower Laos, and it may not be without use, if, in a few words, before leaving Ubone, to advance into Middle Laos, I note the results obtained in the first part of our journey. As I have said already, these results, so far as regards the hope of making the river a great commercial highway, were unfortunately negative. The difficulties it offers begin at first starting from the Cambodgian frontier; and they are very serious, if not insurmountable. If it were attempted to use steam on this part of the Mekong, the return would be very dangerous. At Khong an absolutely impassable barrier, as things are, stands in the way. Between Khong and Bassac the waters are unbroken and deep, but the channel is again obstructed a short distance from the latter. From the mouth of the river Ubone, which we had ascended, to Khemarat,—that is, over a distance of two-thirds of a degree of latitude,—the Mekong is nothing more than an impetuous torrent, whose waters rush along a channel more than a hundred metres deep by hardly sixty across. The truth began, at last, to force itself on the most sanguine among us. Steamers can never plough the Mekong, as they do the Amazon or the Mississippi; and Saïgon can never be united to the western provinces of China by this immense river-way, whose waters make it so mighty, but which seems, after all, to be a work unfinished. From other points of view, our labours had not been so barren. If the great hope faded away—if it seemed no longer likely that the produce of Setchuen and of Yunan should ever come to be stored on the wharves of Lower Cochin-China—it became, at least, certain, on the other hand, that the commerce of Lower Laos naturally flowed to Pnom-Penh, and that there was nothing like a forced direction of it to Bangkok, as had been feared at Saïgon. The great rafts of collected bamboos, and even canoes, guided by the sure skill of hardy crews, are already the agency used for the transport of bales of cotton and silk, of loads of rice, and troops of slaves. A course of exchange, of a kind, already exists, and it is only required that this be

developed. Annamites, Chinese, and Europeans, were use-
fully helping this commercial propagandism, which would
benefit our colony. An excellent plan, and one of which our
colonial government could try the effect, would be, to rouse
the Laotians from their torpor, to induce them to produce
more by the prospect of sure markets, to awaken desires, to
create wants, to force local authorities to respect our merchants, and thus to teach some moderation in their demands
from such of their officials as might treat with French subjects. Some kinds of European goods would soon make their
way among the mass of the people. The comparative severity of the cold season has already forced the Laotians to
use textile fabrics, of which the greater part, exported from
English manufacturers, are introduced by way of Bangkok.
The taste for brilliant colours in cloth is pretty general, and
they are, perhaps, the one luxury which may become common.
Watches and arms are sought for by the rich; and in exchange for such gifts we obtained every possible service
from the authorities. The mandarins transform their houses
into museums, where they show off with pride the refuse of
our coarser manufactures, and think the more of them the
more they have cost.

On the other hand, the timid and gentle nature of these
people, so easily alarmed, would make it necessary to keep
up a constant or periodical watchfulness. Among our fel-
low-countrymen who come to seek fortune among strangers,
there are, doubtless, many honourable men, whom it would
be very unjust to include in the sweeping and summary
condemnation too often pronounced against the whole class.
But it cannot be concealed, that, when access is easy to
a country like Laos, one will meet, among the Europeans
who come to it, men ready, if they find themselves free
from control, to lay aside the peaceful ways of the honest
trader for the successful tricks of the adventurer. This
would be a real calamity; but the governor of Cochin-China
might prevent it by organising an annual inspection in the
lower part of the river, or perhaps by placing one of his
officers at one of the important places of Lower Laos — Bassac, for instance. Not only would the advice of one of those
intelligent men, to whom our colony owes, in part, its pro-

sperity, be a great help to the native authorities; the instant
repression of fraud and violence which he could enforce
would maintain the national rights we could claim.   Complaints which reach the governor of Cochin-China, after a
long interval, through the king of Siam, will never do much.
The first difficulties we met in the village of Stung-Treng
rose from the remembrance of recent acts of brigandage
by a Frenchman who wished to make a rapid fortune.   The
mandarin of Stung-Treng tried to stop his career, and thus
put an end to his depredations; but this strange trader
having complained, on his return, the admiral then at the
head of our colony, misled by a false story, thought it his
duty to address strong remonstrances to the court of Bangkok.   This mistake must needs be repeated, till some official
agent judges things on the spot.   We cannot, indeed, without
letting our prestige suffer, allow the testimony of a Siamese
functionary to prevail against a European, without a word
on the other side.   These considerations should, I would
hope, be strong enough to remove the objections which the
king of Siam, who is always suspicious, would not fail to
raise against an innovation as beneficial to his own subjects
as to ours.   The young prince who has lately succeeded his
father on the throne is beginning, they say, to feel the cost
of English friendship, and to show a tendency towards us;
so that the moment seems favourable for our obtaining a
concession, which we may be able to make him see in its
true light.   Beyond Ubone our political and commercial
interests seem less directly affected.   That place, itself, has
frequent connection with Bangkok, by way of Korat—a vast
entrepôt at about fifteen degrees of latitude, where a great
many Chinese have settled, who go out from it in all directions through the Siamese territories, and carry the English
cotton-checks through every part of Middle Laos.

We had employed our time at Bassac to the best advantage during our forced stay, which proved to be the cause
of great part of our future sufferings.   Our journey on the
Attopée and the other excursions in the interior had no doubt
added to the useful information obtained; but they had, in
part, consumed our resources, without advancing our great
end.   Every day lost of the season favourable for travelling

was like losing a friend, whose place was soon to be taken
by a terrible enemy.   While the wish to avoid a second rainy
season in Laos was a spur to urge us forward, our impatience
beat itself vainly against the opposing ways of the natives,
whose indolence imposed on us the most provoking delays.
It was, moreover, necessary to advance slowly, to give time
to our colleague, who had gone to Cambodgia after the courier we expected, to overtake us again.

We had left the great river for more than a month, and
we wished, in returning to it and following its course again,
to get to the village of Khemarat, and thus cut off the peninsula formed by the Mekong and the Ubone. It was, therefore, necessary to organise a land journey. Our letter from
Siam gave us no right to ask for gratuitous forced labour.
They simply invited the authorities to assist us by what help
might be needed to accomplish our ends. Up to this time
they had done more than was strictly required of them, and
had of their own accord, and very willingly, supplied us with
means of transport. At Ubone, M. de Lagrée was anxious
that the commission should do all its own work; but the
natives refused to hire out their own shoulders, as well as
the backs of their beasts. They seemed almost indifferent
to an increase of wages we proposed, doubting, perhaps, if
our promises could be trusted. For men who called themselves great mandarins to offer money was contrary to the
nature of things. Our repeated and pressing appeals awoke
no reply. If distrust of us had anything to do with this
annoyance, we have, at least had good reason to feel, since
then, that the laziness of the Laotians had quite as much
share in it. Even Chinese merchants, themselves, have told
us that they often succeeded in hiring porters only by heavily bribing the governors of the province, who forthwith
use the means of constraint at their disposal, and thus assist
commerce at the cost of personal freedom. This simple fact
throws a strong light on the rudimentary civilisation of these
parts. We had to end by going to the king once more, who
could extricate us from our difficulty, to the great gain of
our exchequer. We had in vain attempted to make contracts of service; but at a word from his majesty, fifteen
buffalo- and ox-wagons, fifty men, and six elephants, ga-

thered one morning, as if by enchantment, round our hut.
Despotism has its advantages, when the despot is in a good
mood.

On leaving Ubone, we followed a sandy road, like the
streets of the village itself. The wagons sank to the axles
in this burning dust, and we had nothing, when we alighted
at the hours of halting, but nauseous and brackish water.
We found the collection of salt going on over all the country. It is very abundant, and is obtained from different
sources. The water evaporates, and the salt is deposited
in basins of common clay, lined with resin. To ascertain
the saltness of the liquid, the natives have contrived a
ball made of earth and resin, which sinks in fresh water, but
swims in salt. Though they have no other test but this
primitive instrument, their trained eye hardly ever deceives
them.

We soon came on the forest; but it was wretched and stunted, resembling copses, interspersed with immense glades,
most often uncultivated. The roots, which strove to find
the required juices in the earth, showed everywhere the cor-
rosive effect of the salt: the trunks were miserable, and the
branches knotty. There was nothing like greenness; everything was dry, withered, burned up. A thick coat of white
dust covered the leaves of the trees; and the elephants, which
commonly feed as they go, could glean nothing but here and
there, at wide intervals, some creeper, still green, or some
hidden root which they bared with their foot. It is a time
of hunger for all nature, which seems to sigh for the rains.
Some thinly-sown trees—real burning bushes—were covered
with flaming flowers, like leaves of red-hot metal; their very
branches were twisted convulsively.

The having men assigned us had the advantage of being
very economical; but it had, also, the serious disadvantage,
that they would never, on any account, pass the often very
circumscribed limits of the province to which they belonged.
It was thus necessary to change both men and beasts on the
frontier of each new province we entered. It is no use striving against this custom, which is the cause of great delays.
The porters laid down their loads, and ran off into the woods.
When we left the territory of Ubone, we dismissed the men

allotted us by the king; and M. de Lagrée, who had got us
every where a reputation for generosity, established it in this
instance by a liberal distribution of brass wire. The petty
mandarins who accompanied us begged that we would hand
them the whole present, which they engaged to distribute
themselves, or to get the king to distribute; but the crowd
of unhappy porters seemed very pleased when they saw M.
de Lagrée reject this perfidious advice. Not forgetting the
rank of each, we made a democratic division. The mandarins devoured their rage. They had lost about a hundred
francs of illegitimate profit. As to the fellow who had for
his duty to attend to our personal wants on the road, he
managed matters in another way. He simply pocketed all
the money we had given him to buy food in the different
villages where we had stayed. The food was provided, and
we were left ignorant that it had been exacted under the
name of presents. It is the custom, always the custom; and
what can you say? It soon becomes tiresome to play the
reformer. Elsewhere customs temper the rigour of the law;
here, in Laos, laws are needed to soften the barbarism of
customs.

The roads practicable for wagons are scarce, and extend
only a short distance from the chief centres; and we, therefore, replaced our conveyances, at a forced relay we made at
Amnach, by porters, who would not carry more than six or
seven kilogrammes apiece; so that we started from the village where our caravan re-formed itself thus, with a great
part of the healthy male population in our train. All the
villages through which we passed were bound to provision
our whole company, and, this being the case, they had no
pity for the unfortunates so suddenly subjected to so heavy
an imposition. As we got to the river, the country was less
desolate. There could be nothing more sad than the look
of immense plains covered with the straw of rice trampled
down by troops of buffaloes attracted by the salt. The great
forest reappeared at last, thin, but still green. Fires had
made gaps here and there, that looked like great spots of
ink; but the fresh colours of the young bamboos, which the
fire had spared, looked only so much the brighter by contrast.
Our elephants gave themselves a thorough feast. We slept

under huts of leaves built each night near some pool of stagnant water, thick, and of all colours on the surface, thinking ourselves well off if we reached one. It is the great point at this season; and two months later, when the sun will have dried up what moisture was left in the ground, it will be a still more serious matter. It is the fate of the people of these countries, at least when they are travelling, to be flooded for one half the year, and for the other to die of thirst.

We reached Khemarat at last, where M. Delaporte awaited us. He had got to it by the Mekong, of which he had made a chart, from this point to the mouth of the Ubone. The river presents phenomena more remarkable here than at any other part of its course. It roars and boils in a bed only sixty metres across, worn out in the rock to such a depth, that we found no bottom at a hundred metres. Nothing can express the horror of this spot, where the yellow waters twist over and over through the long narrow pass, breaking against the rock with a fearful noise, and forming whirlpools which no boat dare face. Man has fled from the banks; great trees hang over the abyss on both sides, into which their weight often drags them down. There is neither village nor even a solitary hut to be seen. Some daring fishermen had made a shelter for themselves in the clefts of the rocks, from which they have scarcely time to flee at the approach of the rains, so rapidly do the waters rise. At their full height, the increased volume is more than fifteen metres in depth.

We were well received at Khemarat. The governor was just dead, and his substitute for the time—an imbecile old man—seemed to have a kind of veneration for us. The people are very simple, and fancied that M. Delaporte's observations, made to determine the geographical position of the village, were some extraordinary freak of his for reading in the sun. They consulted us about the future; and the old mandarin, who was about to start for Bangkok, persisted in asking us to tell him what hour would be the luckiest for him to set out. We advised him to start after having made a good dinner.

Grand tufted trees surrounded and sheltered our hut at Khemarat. To come on a fine river, and to find mangoes and tamarinds in flower, after the dusty plains of Ubone, was like reaching a fine oasis after a weary march in the desert. The people, like the authorities, lavished their sympathy on us, and information was given us freely. We gathered there some exact data on the political state and the administration of government among the Siamese Laotians. The organisation is the same in every province; so that a sketch of it in one will suffice.

The province of Khemarat, one of the smallest of Middle Laos, has about 20,000 registered inhabitants. It is governed by six high functionaries, who live in the chief place, and take rank under the governor, who is nominated, like them, by the king of Siam. These great personages receive no appointments, and have no privilege but the right to the free service of a certain number of forced labourers; yet they have a hundred extra legal ways of bringing money to their chest, and neglect none of them. At the bottom of the scale come the petty mandarins, who are the heads of villages. These render justice in the first instance, and their power, in civil affairs at least, is unlimited. There is an appeal from their decisions to two tribunals, in the chief place, successively; and if this does not satisfy the litigants they can appeal farther, to Bangkok, which is the fourth and ultimate step in jurisdiction. The highest magistrate of the province alone has the power of condemning to death; but it is still necessary, before the execution, to give information to the central government. It cannot be denied, that all this complication of protecting forms secure certain guarantees for the parties concerned; but, unfortunately, the general corruption destroys in this, as in every thing, the effect of good institutions. The venality of the Laotian functionaries of every rank and kind is carried to the extreme; and the judges, not content with their legal if not legitimate, source of revenue from the fines they inflict, know no such convincing arguments as presents received in advance.

Audiences are given, with a degree of solemnity, in a kind of shed, which serves for a council-chamber as well. I was present at the trial of a woman taken in the very act of adultery. The two offenders were tied one at each end of the same bar, and forced to look each other in the face, striking two sonorous bamboos together, meanwhile, to attract public attention. The husband, never dreaming but that the Frenchmen were much amused by his position, looked very well pleased; indeed, seemed to enjoy it. As the facts could not be denied, the woman was condemned to pay a fine of seventeen ticals, something less than sixty francs, and her paramour twenty-nine ticals, or about ninety-six francs. In such a case the husband may keep or divorce his wife, as he pleases. If he chooses to divorce her, he cannot take her again for ten years; but the fine levied on her is paid to him, while the judges pocket that inflicted on the man. In the affair at which we were present the husband lost no time in getting rid of her; and I understood very soon the cause of his satisfaction. He had given four ticals and a buffalo to her family for her; but he had had her for several years. He now regained his freedom—the right to marry again, and the means of meeting the cost. What good fortune in a climate where beauty withers so soon!

All cases are not so favourable, however. It may happen, for instance, that the woman cannot pay. If she cannot, she gets two blows of a rattan for every tical of fine, which never exceeds forty ticals. Hence, at Laos, any lady may please her fancy, provided she do not belong to a mandarin, for a little less than a hundred francs. The sins of a husband are never interfered with by the law; so that a wife has nothing for it but to shut her eyes, or to study thrift in order to avenge herself. Formerly the punishment was more severe; for a woman convicted of adultery lost her freedom, and became her husband's slave. On this point the law of the ancient kingdom of Tonkin was even more rigorous still: a husband who surprised his wife in the act was authorised, not, indeed, to kill her with his own hands, as is in some measure the case with ourselves, but to cut off her hair, and lead her in that state before the mandarin, who caused her to be thrown to an elephant which was specially trained to be the public executioner; and it, 'lifting her up with its trunk, squeezed her so dreadfully, and dashed her to the ground with such violence, that it stifled her, and made her die in inconceivable torments. If, after all, it saw signs of life in her, it stamped on her with its feet, till she was crushed and broken in pieces.' In Cambodgia the elephant is still employed as executioner for high offences. I have ridden one which, a few days before, had run its tusks through the body of a state prisoner, who had been tied to the trunk of a tree.

The woman first married to a man has, alone, the rights and rank of lawful wife; but this restriction does not make polygamy any the less flourishing. 'As amongst ourselves,' says an old traveller, rather wanting in courtesy, 'one likes to keep dogs, another to keep horses, and still others to keep wild creatures; the Laotians have a troop of wives, some more, some fewer, as they are able, not for the mere gratification of lust, but from an ambitious affectation of greatness.'

Property in land does not exist. As to movable property, if it have often to submit to wrongs from all-powerful officials, the principle is not the less sacred. The husband and wife have distinct possessions of flocks, canoes, or nets, which they can dispose of as they please; but they are mutually responsible to the community. If the husband run away, to escape some obligation—such as the tax or forced labour—the magistrate can seize even the person and the goods of his wife. The tax which every registered inhabitant is bound to pay to Siam is, however, no more than a personal one, which is far from heavy, and is payable sometimes in kind. We saw an instance of this at Attopée, whence so much gold, gathered from the sands of the river, is sent each year to Bangkok, instead of coin, for the tax.

At Khemarat we took again to the river; for in spite of their inconveniences, canoes are certainly the most agreeable mode of transport in these countries. One's bones are broken by the jerking march of an elephant; a buffalo-wagon creeps along at a pace deplorably slow; the ox-wagon, on the other hand, is a narrow and light affair, on an axle that creaks continually, and though it is dragged along quickly by its hump-backed team, and passes over every obstacle, it, gives one a great many violent shocks, and not a few up-settings. The canoes, alone, let you take rest. We had ten, with crews of sixty men, in all. We entered a labyrinth of islets, banks of sand, and rocks, and came to a large island which divided the river in two. The arm we ascended sub-divided itself, as well, into several smaller arms, like torrents ploughing an immense bank of sandstone. This bank was grown over by creeping plants, small and dark in the leaf, thick and twisted in the stem. Other shrubs, of a green that is almost black, bent by the rush of the waters, rise here and there over the vast sandstone bed. The branches, stretched out as if to pray or curse, seem bowed under a kind of cala-mity. As to the Mekong, it has disappeared. Our canoes entered a narrow passage, ten metres broad, where we were stunned by the noise of the waters, and this stream, shut in between two walls of rock, was all we could discover of a river which we had seen more than a league across lower down. Beyond these rapids, the Mekong spreads itself out anew in a channel apparently free from obstructions. But our canoes struck not the less on shoals, which often forced our men to take to the water. Farther on, the sandbanks, the islands, and the islets reappeared, on which everything was growing and flowering in haste, for the rising flood would soon submerge all. The landscape was at once solemn and imposing. Vapours of milky whiteness stretched over the sky and the waters. Nature seemed sleeping, and as if wrapped in a light veil. It attracts one, and absorbs him, dreamily, in spite of himself; ennui invades you at first, then follows an utter indifference. Under the all-powerful con-straint of influences so fatal to human personality, thought dies away by degrees like a flame in a vacuum. The East is the true land of Pantheism, and one must have been there to realise the indefinable sensations which almost make the Nirvana of the Bouddhists comprehensible.

Storms sometimes disturbed the implacable serenity of the heavens. They snatched nature from its leaden coffin; they were like grand bursts of life, of which we were a part. One night, I remember, I listened in transport to the noise of the thunder, and the gleams of the lightning brought a deep and inexpressible joy; but the wind roughened the river, and our boats, dashed rudely on the banks, filled in a moment. The Laotians exerted themselves, without resting, to get out the water, and wiped us as dry as possible, with the care of

benevolent old women. These brave people took no end of
trouble with us, whether from the thought of their responsibility, or from natural kindness: perhaps from both motives,
for they spare nothing to make any one confided to them
comfortable. When we reached a village, a *Simien*, or secretary, came to register our luggage, and the very least of our
packages was guarded as if it had been a casket of jewels.
At Ubone one of these scribes, posted, unknown to us, in
our dining-room, took note of the dishes that seemed to
please us, to let the king know them. In one of our excursions, a wagon having upset, a box of pins opened, and the
contents were scattered on the sand. We had to wait till
the last pin was picked up.

I shall not weary the reader with giving all the stations
of our route. We sailed most part of the day, and slept at
night in our canoes, or in a hut of bamboos. I had, at times,
for courtesy, to land, and go to see wonders related to me
by my head rower, as found in some of the villages on the
bank; but curiosity, often deceived, died at last for want of
food. There are no other public buildings but pagodas, and
they are all alike in general construction and in decoration.
They are made of brick, and thatched, and contain one or
more gilded statues of Bouddha, standing, or with his legs
folded under him; the countenance grave—a little sancti-
monious, perhaps—and hanging ears. I noticed, however,
in a village not far from Khemarat, a statue which differed
altogether from the type uniformly adopted by the priestly
sculptors of Cambodgia, Siam, and Laos. It is in a niche of
grotto-work: heads of monsters peer from all the holes;
and, on the two sides, two gilt dragons rise towards heaven,
from the red base of the recess, in the style of our adoring
angels. The god, himself, has caught some oddities from
this surrounding. His round eyes stick out of their sockets,
and his face is like that of a puffed-out frog's. The outside
of the pagoda is ornamented in a very fantastic way. I had
often seen gables, incrusted with glass, glittering in the
sun; but, in this case, the building was decorated by a set of
the finest Chinese porcelain. The architect has bedded blue
plates in the thatch, and run a garland of rose-coloured
saucers round the wall. I could even distinguish European

washing-basins and water-glasses in the place of honour. Chinese influence begins to make itself felt in other ways, also, in Laotian art, if such a grand word can be used in this connection. The frescoes on the walls of the sanctuaries are generally by Chinese artists. The subject of these gross paintings is almost everywhere the same: first, the picture, coarse, very coarse, of the cardinal sin of the Laotians; then, below, the representation of the punishments which await the impure of both sexes in the other world, which are always inflicted on the parts that have transgressed. The lesson is a thoroughly moral one, but it is a question if it serve its purpose. I have been led to doubt it very much, in seeing the rolling eyes of the young bonzes as they ran over these compositions, in which free reins seem to have been given to an imagination as lascivious as that of some Jules Romain. One is surprised to see European ships, with their crew on the deck, by the side of these pious allegories, in the middle of blue, green, red, and yellow temples and palaces. In one subject of this kind it seemed as if the artist had been most struck by the chimneys of a steamboat, and by the stove-pipe hats, which have made the round of the world.

The rounded tops of the high palms, and the far-reaching perfumes of the ivory-like flowers of the cabbage-palms, which are sure signs of a village being close, announced from a distance the chief place of the province of Banmuk, where a complete establishment, prepared on the banks of the river, awaited us. The Laotians can do wonders with wood, especially with bamboo. They improvise a hut with a marvellous sense of the wants of their hosts. The partitions are always made of a double trellis of bamboo slips, between which is placed the native tapestry, large leaves; and the whole is made firm by bands of rattan, so that we can change the interior arrangements at our pleasure, on our arrival, all that is needed being to untie some knots.

We are still in one of those kingdoms created by Siamese policy for the benefit of the deposed princes of Vien-Chan —a convenient way to get rid of pretenders who might be dangerous. The members of the royal family declare themselves well satisfied with their bargain in Laos, for

nothing is needed to make them happy but a title, a parasol, a box of betel, and a gold spittoon. Phnom, where we
arrived three days after leaving Banmuk, is not a chief
place of the province, and would have no importance but
for its being a religious centre, to which pilgrims gather. A
long narrow avenue, perpendicular to the river, and paved
with brick, stretches under palm-trees, leading to a pagoda,
which is a huge rectangular affair, surrounded by a gallery
supported by red pillars, set with decorations in gold, with
a bundle of long, sharp leaves, like Arab daggers, with the
points bent back, for capitals. Above the doors and windows
are ornaments in pyramid shape on the wall, in the Siamese
taste—a kind of royal parasols, of several stories, topped by
an interminable pointed cap, like that which our astrological
magicians are made to wear. But the most remarkable
decoration is that of a sham door. Two personages equally
begilt stand out in relief on a red ground, between elegant
garlands of flowers and gilt leaves. They are stiffly done,
as usual, yet one may perhaps make out a kind of smile on
their gross features and flat lips. They are supported by
two griffons, or monsters of some sort, who are performing
high above the ground some confused dance. They are
boldly designed; their hands are thrown about furiously,
and their limbs are in extraordinary postures; but the proportions are good, and the whole has truth, force, movement,
and life.

The inside of the pagoda is sad. Some licentious pictures
here and there pollute the walls, from which the thatch is
falling in handfuls. The roof deserves notice, its painted
beams forming compartments, in the centre of which are
tufts of gilt foliage, which look like a large bearded root, as
if the plant were pushing upwards.

Behind the pagoda is a fantastic pyramid, which begins
in a kind of enormous cube, on which, separated from one
another by cornices, are three rectangular masses, each less
high than the other. The architect has set a second pyramid
on this base, reproducing, at first, the forms below then
passing insensibly from square to round, substituting undu-
lating lines for the salient angles, and finishing off a top in
a sharp point. This group of monuments arrests the eye,

Plate 10 *A musical night in Laos (Drawing by Janet Lange, based on a drawing by L. Delaporte)*

Plate 11 *Annamites emigrated to Lakon (Drawing by Janet Lange, based on a drawing by L. Delaporte).*

unused to grand proportions and startling colours, for banners, standards, and rags of cloth of every colour, float in the air. The sun makes the gold sparkle, and the glass, imbedded in the walls among the red bricks, shines brilliantly. But all this, though striking, is not worth much, after all, for the pyramid, having been often rebuilt, is no longer what it was formerly. One is arrested by strange irregularities, and if it were not for the natural craving to admire something, one cares not what, in a country where all the huts are built alike, this mass of bricks and thatch, in which the eye meets hardly a detail worth noticing, would be passed without stopping. Besides, the gilding on the pyramid is mostly gone, and would be so entirely, but for the piety of the faithful, who stick on little leaves of gold, wherever fancy strikes them, as offerings, or in fulfilment of vows. They come in pilgrimage from all Laos to Phnom, the more devoted making a retreat of some days during their stay, and wearing during the time the saffron gown of the bonzes. We met rafts of male and female bonzes on their way to this holy place, beguiling the weary slowness of the sail by chants and prayers, and other exercises made in common. Our Laotian interpreter, who had often appeared to me to have lost all his faith, could not resist the pious influence of this monument, which he had visited before. In a fit of devotion he even went so far as to make an offering of the half of the upper joint of his forefinger to Bouddha. The attendants of the pagoda at Phnom perform operations of this kind very cleverly, with the help of a chopper and a foot-rule, and measure the zeal of the pilgrims by the extent of the sacrifice. It is strange to find in Middle Laos, as a product of Bouddhism, the aberration of mind which leads men to self-mutilation. We had reason, too often, to regret, in the sequel, that our interpreter, instead of confining himself to losing his finger, had not followed the example of Origen, and gone farther; it would have saved us from troubles in which his failings involved us.

The river continued to fall. Huge sandbanks, like stranded monsters, showed their high backs. We saw before us a forest of mountains, made a dark leaden colour, in the distance, by thick mists, which rolled hither and thither under a black

I

sky, at times in indescribable confusion. They were the
mountains of Lakhon, which were in front of our encampment during our stay in this new province. The chain
commences in the south-east, in two or three soft, slow-
rising, gentle undulations, which trend northwards, and form
a vapoury background to the landscape. From them, at once
united and distinct, rise five masses, with rugged crests,
rough, and cut into shady hollows on the sides; a faint pale
aureola, from the sun on the mists, rising over the summits
and sharp outlines. Looking to the north, an immense curved
line shows itself, growing ever greater, opening like the
arch of a gigantic bridge, and binding this first group to a
second, more complicated, each peak of which has a form
of its own, and does, in some sort, as it pleases, without
troubling itself about its neighbour. The most remarkable
thing about these mountains is the kind of life they seem
to possess. It shows itself in an incredible confusion. The
angles are thrown fantastically by some mad geometer,
who could be no other than fierce subterranean fire. A
dome raises its head curiously above the leaning shoulder
of a round hill, and a pyramid reverses itself, as if to the
music of some wild orchestra. Seen nearer, and in detail,
these mountains are in keeping with all that the imagination
most in love with the fantastic, which had been attracted
by their more distant forms, could dream. Valleys, gorges,
sombre gaps, walls cut perpendicularly, rough, or polished
by water, cavities festooned with hanging stalactites, and
notched like gothic sculptures—make up a strange sight,
which cannot fail to excite admiration.

The inhabitants find in them an inexhaustible mine of
limestone. They split the stones with fire, burn them on
the spot, and then carry them to the neighbouring villages
by water. The kilns, dug in the steep banks of the river,
somewhat resemble those we often see in France. They
consist of a deep furnace, communicating with a vast open
kiln, into which they throw the stones. If its salt be the
wealth of the province of Ubone, lime is an equal blessing
to that of Lakhon; for not only do the pagodas absorb an
enormous quantity, it is an object of the first necessity to
every Laotian. With the leaf of the betel, and the nut of

the cabbage-palm, it is an essential part of that abominable quid, which makes the mouth look bloody, broadens the lips, lays bare and blackens the teeth, and makes the women hideous. The natives often add tobacco, and the bark of a kind of tree which is the object of a great commerce.

A considerable part of the village of Lakhon, near the dwelling of the governor, had just been burned. The leaves of the trees were scorched, the trunks calcined, and the look of the tall palms, in particular, was almost melancholy. This great gap in the middle of the flowers and verdure made me feel a kind of sadness. It seemed as if winter had come all at once, in its severity, over one part of the woods, leaving their shadows and mysteries to the rest. But this feeling did not last. The ruined quarter had become a vast work-yard, full of happy activity; bands of children, rejoiced at the unaccustomed stir, adding to the noise. In a French village, such a disaster would have been irreparable; but in Laos, where living is easy, it hardly seemed to be thought of. Farther off, a great number of new huts had risen, by the industry of Annamite immigrants, who, of course, fraternised with our escort. Indeed, it was not without a vivid pleasure we ourselves unexpectedly encountered people like those who fill the streets of Saïgon. Men, women, and children came round us familiarly, their eyes dilated with curiosity, and no trace of ill-will or anger on their faces. Yet they had fled from their country to escape defending it. Our invasion having forced Tu-duc to raise extraordinary levies, many of his subjects thought it prudent to put the breadth of a mountain between them and his recruiting sergeants. Those settled at Lakhon are from a province above Hué, not more than thirty-five or forty leagues off. Except Hathen, our next station, which is not more than thirty marine leagues from the gulf of Tonkin, Lakhon was the nearest point to the Annamite empire at which we stopped. The general course of the Mekong towards the west, already very perceptible since we left Bassac, took us much farther off from this time, by its still more pronounced course in that direction. At the sight of this simple village, which was as busy as an ant-hill, one could not but hope that Annamite emigration would be still more developed in Laos; for the Annamites

would be like leaven in heavy dough, among the Laotians.
Essentially similar in both their good and bad points, they
would be the most useful, and the leading instrument of our
policy in these countries.

The chief village of the province of Huthen offers nothing
special, but it, nevertheless, holds a pleasant place in our
memory. One day, the 6th of March 1867, I was lying
stretched out in one of these wooden turrets, commonly built
on the top of the river-banks, near the pagodas, where the
bonzes while away the time not devoted to the repetition
of prayers, in seeing the waters flow past. At my feet, the
river, broad and smooth as a huge mirror of steel, sent back
a thousand lights from the rays of the sun beaming on it.
A sandbank, dotted with black by the buffaloes creeping
slowly over it to the water, to escape the heat, linked it to
the opposite bank. The sky was like a metal basin heated
to whiteness, and the reflection from the landscape burned
the eyes. My thoughts, in a kind of half-sleep, turned, as
always, to France, when joyful cries rose suddenly to tell me
that we were going to hear from it. M. Garnier had arrived.
He had found part of the post at Pnom-Penh; the other,
which had been forwarded by Bangkok, was probably lost
in the forests. We had, at last, got the passports signed
by Prince Kong, regent of the Celestial Empire, and could
henceforth hope to be able to get into it. We learned, at
the same time, that cannon had roared in Europe, that Germany was in confusion, that public opinion was excited in
France. From the tone of the journals, and the prophecies
in our private letters, a near and terrible war, in which our
country must needs take part, seemed, to our minds, inevitable. To-day these prophecies make us smile, but they kept
a sad hold on our minds at the time; and it was with this
heavy load on our hearts we set about starting afresh for
remote regions, where we had no longer the hope of any
post reaching us. We never failed to send letters by traders
descending the river, or mandarins going to Bangkok; and
we have since learned that they all reached their address,
so great is the respect of the Laotians for anything confided
to them, especially letters. As to ourselves, not knowing
beforehand the places we should reach, or even the way we

should have to go, we felt that we could not hear anything, for long, of the questions debated in Europe. I never felt more keenly the extent of the sacrifice I had undertaken, in any other incident of a journey which proved so full of trials. Our family letters, read, re-read, and commented upon, rekindled our courage. The latest were of the date of September 1866. We were in March 1867, and we were to receive no more till the end of June, in the next year.

Saïabury and Phon-Pissai offer nothing of interest. Between these two centres of the province, or Muongs, as the natives call them, the banks of the Mekong are almost deserted: the great forest comes down to the water's edge on both sides; huge trees lie fallen, here and there, and rest on the cliffs, which have given way below them; the waters fret their roots, and they hold on to the land by their branches, to be swept away, however, when the river rises.

While waiting for the daily rice, which was cooked on the bank, we used to push into the thick tangled woods, as chance led us. We admired the wonderful vegetation, with its hundred-feet-high shafts, linked one to the other by waving creepers encircling them, and hanging from the masses of foliage. We got into the habit of these strolls, walking about, unarmed, under these dark arches of green, without thinking of the terrible enemies that might lie hidden in the bamboos or the jungle. One evening, however, one of us saw a tiger bound out, and stop within twenty paces of him. The ferocious eye of the brute, no doubt, frightened our friend; but his white skin, long beard, and fixed stare troubled the beast as much, and he stood still and let his foe regain the canoes. We snatched up our rifles; but our pursuit was unsuccessful, in spite of its tracks deeply bedded on the moist ground, and the precise directions of our comrade. Terrified apes growled at us from the tops of the trees, and peppered us with whatever they could break off; but it was rather ungrateful of them; for, if the natives were to be believed, the tiger we had just put to flight had been on the watch for them. The plan followed by these brutes is curious. When they see the monkeys sporting on the branches, they crawl through the grass to the tree, give it a sudden blow with their shoulder, as children do to get down apples or nuts, and the poor creatures, which the blow shakes down, are devoured forthwith. The Laotians feeling ill at ease after this incident, notwithstanding our presence, we allowed them to put part of the river between them and these nightly visitors, and they accordingly betook themselves to an island to sleep.

After a long interval of wilderness, the presence of man was once more indicated by an attempt at a settlement. A piece of the forest had been felled, the trees, cut down about six feet above the ground, lying entangled with each other as they had fallen. Banana plants had taken root alongside; chickens, pigs, and dogs wandered through the chaos; and the settlers, crouched under their shanties, seemed waiting for the village to build itself. I could not keep from contrasting the scene with one which M. Ampère gives, in his *Promenades en Amérique*, of a town in the Union, I believe Chicago, in its first beginnings. At the time when that clever traveller visited it, the forest was hardly yet cleared from the spot, and the future citizens were making use of the trees to build their dwellings; but Chicago is to-day an important town of Illinois, with two hundred thousand inhabitants! Asia, the ancient cradle of the world, produces only tyrants and slaves. Would that the races which, springing from it, have been developed under less enervating skies, could give a little of such youthfulness to the ancient nurse of their fathers!

Nong-Caï, the province next Vien-Chan, the ancient capital of the kingdom, has gained in importance since the ruin of the latter. The governor has given proof of some spirit, having, for example, excused himself from attending the funeral ceremonies of the second king of Siam, at Bangkok. He came to see us, splendidly dressed in a silk langouti, and a vest of the same stuff, braided with gold. He had a numerous suite; a magnificent parasol shaded him from the sun, and he had spittoons, ewers, and betel-boxes in silver-gilt; this last feature marking him as only a little less than a king. We returned his visit at once. His palace, though of wood, has a striking appearance, fine pillars supporting the timber work. The vast apartment in which he receives is decorated with Chinese pictures. At our entrance the band played an air, which must be the national one, for I have never heard it but in Laos. His excellency, seated at a table, the first we had seen in the country, invited us to do the same, and we began a friendly conversation, through the interpreter.

Behind the village is an immense plain, over which palm-trees have grown, at random. They have a look altogether their own; more poetical and more eastern than the graceful cabbage-palm, or the somewhat heavy cocoa. Their crest seems almost too weighty for them, and their trunk is often bent. The wind makes a rustle in their leaves, as if they were parchment crumpled in the hand. In this plain stands the chief pagoda, which is approached by a long road, paved with wood. We were there on a feast-day. The crowd flooded the space before it and the porches; the blue pantaloons of Chinese mingling with the fantastic langoutis and many-coloured scarves of the Laotians. The faithful and the curious pressed into the courtyard and the very narrow ground of the sanctuary, where bonzes read prayers, amidst offerings arranged round them with some taste, decorating the temple and sharpening the appetite. Scarlet hangings flowed from the pillars, and in the warm shade, amidst flowers and perfumes, were young girls with languishing eyes and smiles that might have turned one's head. Every person was speaking, smoking, or laughing loudly. None were sedate, nor even attentive, except three young priests, who threw libertine glances under the scarves of the young women kneeling before them.

We had retained the Frenchman who acted as Siamese interpreter, as far as Nong-Caï. He might still have been of use, for long, but his misconduct forced M. de Lagrée to dismiss him. We were getting on farther, and so much the more was it necessary to tighten the bonds of discipline. We had already repeatedly noticed a sudden and inexplicable change in the feelings of the people and the authorities, which turned out at last to be traceable to the theft of some dish, perhaps, or the violation of some girl. Profiting by his knowledge of the language, our interpreter introduced himself to families, and abused our rank as mandarins, to commit offences, of which the victims were afraid to com-

plain. The unhappy man, thrown into Bangkok at the age
of eleven, without relations or friends, had unfortunately
fallen into the hands of many passing adventurers, till he
had learned to be the instrument of all their pleasures, and
the accomplice in their frauds. Retaining the frank and
ready intelligence of his race, he had borrowed craft and
pliancy from the Asiatic air in which he had lived, and a
power of lying which I never saw equalled in my life. I
used to shudder, when at times I let my thoughts down
into the abysses of such a degraded nature, in which good
advice sank like stones in the deep sea. The slave-trade
seemed to hold the first place in the favourite dreams that
crossed the brain of this man. He intended to return to
Laos to follow it, and did not hesitate to tell us so. He
looked on it as a sure way to satisfy his three dominant
passions—the love of adventures, the love of money, and
the craving for debauchery. I have heard a man of experience say, that to learn honesty in the position of an
interpreter it was necessary to be one thrice ; and if this
be true, the relief afforded us when the governor of Nong-
Caï offered to conduct our man back to Bangkok, under a
sufficient guard, may be judged. Each member of the expedition set forthwith to work to learn as much of the language as was necessary ; and the result was astonishing,
from the same reason as forces a man thrown into the water
to learn quickly to swim. M. de Lagrée still, however, kept
the old bonze of Cambodgia, Laotian by birth, who had cut
off his finger at Phnom, to facilitate his intercourse with the
native authorities.

The governor of Nong-Caï put his private canoe at the
service of the chief of the expedition. It was finely modelled
and gilt profusely, and had a crew of eight rowers, in jackets
of red wool, with képis with large shades, and of enormous
height, for head-gear. We each took possession of a less
elegant canoe, and reached, on April the 2d, a point where
the Mekong spreads out like an enormous fan. Our rowers
at once stopped, telling us we had got to Vien-Chan; and we
landed, no little astonished, for we could see nothing on the
banks but dense forests. Vien-Chan was the name, among all
those with which I had charged my memory before start-

ing, round which most interest had gathered. It has often
occurred in these pages already; for we had found the descendants of the royal family, which had formerly reigned
over the capital whose ruins we were about to explore, scattered all over Laos. What it had been at its best may be
judged from the fact that Van Diemen, the governor of the
Dutch Indies, thought it worth while to send an ambassador
to it in the first half of the seventeenth century.

Scaling the steep bank by the help of a bamboo ladder,
we found ourselves among the prickly bushes, which always
grow thickly among ruins, as if they were a veil drawn
by nature over the weakness of man and the vanity of his
works. A guide, bent to the ground by his sad recollections
and the weight of years, guided us with much emotion as
we hurried on. He had seen Vien-Chan, his birthplace, in
its glory. The soil was strewn with bricks, and we soon
came upon the wall of the town. It is high, and very broad,
with ornaments above it in the shape of a heart, set side by
side, so as to make embrasures. A huge post, on which the
principal gate hung, still stands. The wall, which runs down
to the river, stretches in angles and recesses through the
bamboos. Heaps of bricks, lying here and there, are probably
the remains of bastions. After long and anxious search we
found that the town had no other monuments remaining but
the king's palace, some pagodas, and the libraries for the
sacred books; but there were so many even of these, that we
gave up the attempt to count them. They seemed all to
have been built on the same plan, and to have been decorated
in the same style—the proportions alone were different. The
pagoda of Phâ-kéo was one of the largest and finest. The
trees which half hid it, and the creepers which bound its
pillars together, and spread a mysterious shadow over the
ruins, made one feel something of that awe which filled men
of old at the threshold of a sacred wood. The enclosure of
the pagoda was of sun-dried brick. Grand staircases led up
to its platform. A contorted dragon stretched along the
balusters, lifting its head threateningly from its thrown-back
neck. The columns of the gallery are graceful, slender, light,
without a base, but ending in a capital of long, sharp leaves,
bent back, and, as it were, crushed by the weight above. Here

and there they still showed signs of gilding. The three doors
of the façade and the side-windows are richly chased with
ornaments, like those I had seen at Phnom. The whole outside of this building, which was of considerable size, was
gilt. It has no roof, and the colossal statue of Bouddha,
which still sits over the forsaken altar, is exposed to all the
injuries of the weather. At the side of the temple is a library,
built in the same style, but smaller. The artists had run
lozenge ornaments along the black base of the walls, which
looked not unlike the tatters of paper sticking to the street-
hoardings in Paris.

Phâ-kéo—for the natives have religiously preserved the
name of destroyed temples—was the pagoda of the palace;
but that building itself is no more than a mass of ruins
spread over a considerable space. From what we could see,
and from the information given by some who had known it
when standing, its plan was very little different from that of
the pagodas. It was a rectangular building, surrounded by
a gallery supported on pillars. Another pagoda, called Si-
saket, stands in an inner court, round which a cloister runs,
along which are placed some statues of Bouddha, sitting.
Their head-dress, raised to a point, is like the helmets of our
old knights, and, but for the placid face of the god,[1] one might
think himself in some military museum.

The walls of the cloister, and those of the pagoda itself,
are pierced with thousands of little niches, regularly built,
in each of which squats a miniature Bouddha. We calcu-
lated that there must be twenty thousand of these little
images. It is a veritable pigeon-house of gods. Si-saket is
the best-preserved of the temples, and still contains a great
many objects employed in the ceremonies of worship. I admired, among other things, a little carving in wood. It is a
kind of screen, with a light bar still attached to it, for holding the tapers lighted before the altar. It has a gilt frame,
on which fantastic figures mingle their allegorical shapes.
Two serpents are twisted together, and from their twin-
ings rise two arms, which support the taper-stand. In the

---

[1] This expression is hardly correct, for Bouddha never spoke of himself as more than a man who preached perfection; but, in spite of the
orthodox doctrine, the people at large in reality worship him as a god.

empty space in the middle of the screen, a kind of lyre,
which blends its gilding with light seen through it, has the
happiest effect. There is also a chair of cement, gilt, preserved in another pagoda. From a sculptured seat, ornamented with lions having human heads, centaurs of a new
kind, there spring light arches, which bear up the roof.
The place where the bonze stood to read prayers is marked
by elegant little pillars. Innumerable pyramids are hidden
in the forest, which, after first half throwing them down,
keeps them from falling farther by the trees. The natural vegetation harmonises admirably with this vegetation in stone
—the gray tints of the cement giving it the air of granite
darkened by the moist atmosphere. Thousands of kilogrammes of copper and bronze run into figures of Bouddha,
heaps of bricks, no-end of pagodas, and, amidst all this, the
traces of only one secular human habitation—the palace of
the king—was the sum of what I saw in a ramble of some
hours in the ruins of Vien-Chan. The inhabitants lived in
huts, like the Khmers; but one must not recall, in looking
at these ruins, which, after all, are very mediocre—the recollections of the grand Cambodgian architecture of Angcor and
Vat-Phou, else he will think there is nothing at all worth noticing in Laos. When the Siamese general drove out the
king, this town was still flourishing; to-day, forty years later,
everything is destroyed—*etiam periere ruinæ*.

A great highway, broad, straight, and planted with old
trees, runs up to the chief gate, crossing marshy meadows,
which formerly were ditches. It leads to a sandy road
covered with a growth of bamboos. Every instant vestiges
of walls show where a pagoda stood, and small pyramids
abound. The unhappy Laotian who accompanied us trembled to lead strangers into these holy places, often bowed,
sometimes prostrated himself, exhausting his strength in
marks of respect to the guardian spirits of the ruins. He
gave a look of horror when he saw me making for a niche
covered with bushes. 'A spirit lives there,' said he, 'Tepada;
he demands every one who draws near him to creep, and
will stand no trifling on this point.' No misfortune having
happened, I kept on to a monument which seemed to have
been the chief work of this Laotian architecture, but was now

stripped of grandeur as well as ruined, though one could not
deny it a certain air of elegance. This monument had been
spared by the Siamese. The two outer enclosures show nothing particular; but there is a garland of bulging ornaments over the cornice of the third court, like the petals of
a gigantic lotus on the point of opening. Heavy pediments,
covered with inscriptions, support twenty slender spires.
Resting on these supports, as on buttresses, the mass on
which the pyramid lies begins to develop its lines, and the
pyramid itself shoots up from a sheaf of large leaves, like the
stalk of a plant. It has the traditional form, and ends in a
point. Formerly, it glittered with gold laid on a covering of
lead, of which some scraps still remain. The cement is in
good preservation everywhere. It has a uniformly dull appearance, which is deceptive, and leads one for a moment to
think the building must be of high antiquity; but from an
inscription on a stone in it, it does not go back farther than
the seventeenth century. Without going into detail, which
would be easy enough, I may say that, as a whole, the building pleased me. Its fine points and graceful spires rise from
the pleasing ground of a wood of palm-trees, which cast their
shadows over scattered huts of the natives. The inmates
came offering us rice, honey which might have made the bees
of Hymettus jealous, and bowls of palm-wine, an unfermented
and sweet-tasting drink, which flows from incisions in the
palm, like blood from a wound. This hearty and sponta-
neous hospitality pleased us more than if we had had the
grand reception given, two centuries before, to our predecessors the Dutch—companions of Van Vusthorf, from whom
I shall borrow presently some curious details as to the official ceremonies to which their embassy gave rise. I drew
little pleasure from these ruins of Vien-Chan. The temples
and the palace have left nothing to be seen under their
ruined gilding but badly-joined bricks. It is a stage deserted
by the actors, which Time, that great destroyer, despoils day
by day of its last ornaments. Besides, a civilisation which
found room only for bonzes, mandarins, and kings, is hardly
worth the study. As to the architecture it produced, the
type may be seen to-day in most of the pagodas of Bangkok.
One of these, that specially set apart for the devotions of

the king of Siam, contains the famous emerald statue which Pha-tajac carried off from Vien-Chan in 1777. It is a cubit in height; and, according to M. Pallegoix, the English value it at more than a million francs.

In the different contributions of the various geographers who have tried to draw up a map of Indo-China, from the laborious collation of hints given by a few travellers, and details wormed out of the natives themselves, it is, as a rule, impossible to recognise Vien-Chan, under the double veil of vague topographical details, and of the false spelling, which does not always reproduce the sound of the local pronunciation. To this, no doubt, is owing the uncertainty that has long reigned as to the true geographical position of that town. Crawfurd calls it Lang-Chang, and says that it is situated in 15° 15′ of north latitude; Low and Berghaus give it the names of Lanchang and Lantschang; Macleod places it in 17° 48′ of south latitude, which is somewhat near the true position, but the indefatigable English explorer confounds it with Muong-luan-Praban, a distinct kingdom, through which we passed soon after. Marini, in his history of Laos, calls the inhabitants of this country the Langians, and gives the name of Langione to their principal town, which, he says, is situated in the eighteenth degree of latitude. He makes only a slight mistake in fixing the place thus, and his book furnishes the most exact information respecting this kingdom, which he attempted to evangelise. He saw the places, the men, and the things. At the same time as Father Marini travelled in these regions, the Dutch embassy took place, to try to arrange relations with the chief king of Laos. Since then no European has penetrated so far.

These Dutchmen took eleven weeks to ascend the Mekong, from the frontier of Cambodgia to Vien-Chan, which they call Winkyan. They used the same narrow canoes as we, and surmounted the same obstacles in the same way. One even asks himself, in reading the journal of their voyage over again at this day, how any person could ever have had any hope of the river proving navigable. Where we found nothing but ruins, Gerard van Vusthorf and his companions found a flourishing town. Dubois gives the following account of their reception by the king: 'As they approached the capital, some officials came to demand from the chief of the embassy a sight of his letters of credence, before they could be sent forward. These letters having been examined and found in proper form, three large canoes, with a crew of forty rowers each, were sent to carry the ambassador and his suite to their destination.

'They put the letters on a gold dish set under a magnificent canopy, and the Dutchmen placed themselves behind them. A mandarin was ordered to conduct them to the lodgings prepared for them by the king; and then, they were saluted by another mandarin, in the name of the prince, who caused refreshments and some gifts to be offered them. There was no delay in fixing the day of the audience, to which the ambassador was conducted with much pomp. An elephant carried the letter of the governor-general in a golden vessel, and five other elephants bore the ambassador and his people. They passed before the palace of the king, through a double line of soldiers, and at last reached one of the gates of the town, with walls of red stones, surrounded by a broad dry ditch, filled with undergrowth. After a quarter of a league's farther march, the Dutchmen descended from their elephants, and entered the tents pitched for them, while they awaited the orders of the king. The plain was covered with officers and soldiers on elephants or horses, and all encamped under canvas. After an hour, the king appeared on an elephant, coming from the town with a guard of three thousand soldiers, some armed with muskets, the rest with pikes. A train of several elephants followed, all ridden by armed officers; next, came a troop of players on instruments; then, some hundreds of soldiers. The king, who was saluted by the Dutchmen as he passed their tents, did not seem, to them, over twenty-two. After a short time the women defiled, on sixteen elephants.[2] As soon as the two cortéges were out of sight of the camp, every one reëntered his tent, where the king caused the Dutchmen to dine.

[2] According to Marini, the name of Langione means a thousand elephants. Laos is certainly one of the countries where you meet most of these animals. A Laotian told Crawfurd that they used them even to carry ladies. This shows clearly that they did not know what to do with them else.

'At four in the afternoon the ambassador was led to the audience, across a large open space in a square court surrounded by walls, with a number of embrasures, and a great pyramid coated with plates of gold, about a thousand pounds in weight, in the middle of it. This monument was looked on as a god, and all the Laotians paid their adorations to it. The presents of the Dutch were brought in, and laid fifteen paces from the prince. They, then, presently, led the ambassador into a temple, where they found the king amidst all his nobles. The customary homage was then offered, the ambassador holding a taper in each hand, and striking the ground three times with his forehead. After the compliments usual on such occasions, the king presented him with a golden basin, and some robes, and gave other gifts to the various members of his suite.

'The spectacle of a mock battle was then shown, and a kind of ball, ending with a fire of artillery, was given. They passed that night in the town, which was an unprecedented thing, and in the morning were led back, on four elephants, to their lodgings. After that day, the ambassador was taken several times to court, and they did their best to provide all imaginable amusements for him. After having stayed two months at Winkyan, he set out again for Cambodgia, which he reached only after fifteen weeks, much satisfied with the success of his mission.'[3]

' If the finances of the kingdom allowed the sovereign to exhibit such pomp on solemn occasions, his army seemed able to command the respect of his ambitious neighbours. The country was so populous, that 500,000 men were returned, in a military census, as fit to bear arms, exclusive of the old—' who were so numerous and so robust, that even of those of a hundred years of age,' a very considerable army might have been formed, if there had been need. These figures, in spite of their evident exaggeration, prove that the population of the kingdom was then large; but it had not always been so. When the sovereigns of China, after effecting the union of their vast empire, thought of laying a yoke, of which the effects still remain, on all their neighbours, the

[3] *Vie des Gouverneurs-généraux aux Indes Orientales.* La Haye, 1763.

Laotians at first escaped the invasions of these insatiable conquerors no more than the people of Tonkin, the Siamese, or the Cambodgians. Dispersed along the banks of the Mekong, with no central point to which to rally and combine their strength, they gave only a feeble resistance; but they gradually drew together, and ultimately formed a kind of republic.

This organisation, so favourable to the development of the virtues which make or save a country, seems to have lasted till the fifth or sixth century of our era, and enabled the Laotians to drive out the Chinese. At that time the state became monarchical, and, perhaps, the origin of Vien-Chan, which was destined, later, to become the brilliant capital of the most powerful Laotian kingdom, is to be referred to that time. If the old writer, from whom I have obtained these facts, can be trusted, the people of Siam came to Laos to help the Laotians 'to people their kingdom,' and settled in it permanently, from the fertility of the soil and the mildness of the climate. Of a lazy and slothful nature, at once incapable and unworthy to preserve a republican form of government, the Laotians felt the need of intrusting a single person with the sole responsibility of power; but they could not agree on a sovereign, through ambition, fear, and envy. The Siamese, who are clever people, took care, during these struggles, to divide the electors, and neglected nothing to corrupt them. To the ambitious they promised the government of a province, and made gilded pyramids and pagodas glitter in the eyes of the devout. These schemes succeeded, and the name of a member of the royal family of Siam came from the urn in which, at the same time, the liberty of the country was buried. 'It is believed,' adds Marini, 'that though it is more than a thousand years since that time, the kings of Laos are descended from that stock, since they retain the Siamese idiom and their style of dress.'

Though this assertion is probably a tradition obtained on the spot, it seems hardly possible to regard it seriously. The analogy of customs, of manners, and, above all, of languages, which exists between the Siamese and the Laotians, indicates a common origin; but is it not equally allowable, from it, to suppose, that the Siamese came from Laos? Some savants have thought so. It is hard to believe that the action of a royal family, however powerful we may suppose it, could, in all these things, have produced the results Marini attributes to it. But however it be, that young dynasty, which soon became despotic at home, freed Laos from all foreign subjection. It was even able to force respect for its territory on China, and to lend a helping hand, many times, to its enemies. During the war which the emperor Tching-tsou-wen-ti waged against Tonkin, at the beginning of the fifteenth century, the Laotians openly gave asylum to the conquered. The Chinese general had hardly beaten and dispersed the enemy, before other rebels, supported by the prince of Laos, continued the struggle. Tching-ki-Kouang, their chief, himself, sought refuge in the Laotian territory. The Chinese general demanded that this dangerous rebel should be delivered up to him; and the king, fearing an invasion from two Chinese armies, which were massed on the frontiers of Tonkin and Yunan, drove him from his states, outside the limits of which the unfortunate man was taken prisoner.

The Chinese were not the only adversaries of the king of Laos. The ambition of the king of Burmah, rather excited than satisfied by the conquest of Pegou, soon turned towards Laos, of which he made himself master. Adopting a custom of wholesale deportation, still in use in these countries,[4] he forced a great many Laotians to settle in Pegou, to people his new conquest; but they formed a vast conspiracy, and exterminated the Pegouans, everywhere, at the same time. The old slaves, become masters, reëntered Vien-Chan in arms, and made a fresh carnage of their conquerors, whom they surprised while defenceless. The conquest of this part of Laos, and the annihilation of its brilliant capital, was reserved neither for the Chinese nor the Burmans. The people who had triumphed over these terrible enemies became ultimately tributary to Siam, but at what date is not known exactly. Perhaps it was the result of the war of 1777. It extended, however, only to the payment of tribute, not the cession of territorial rights.

[4] At the end of last century, when the king of Siam made himself master of Battambang on the Cambodgia, he drove out all the inhabitants, and replaced them by others.

K

The Annamites, on their side, spread themselves along the Mekong valley. The left bank belonged to them, without dispute, at the commencement of this century, from the sixteenth degree of north latitude to the seventeenth degree, so far as that, within these limits, the provinces situated between the Mekong and the great chain of mountains which ends at Cape Jacques were under the Annamite empire, and paid tribute to its sovereign.

M. de Lagrée having been specially charged by Admiral de La Grandière to determine the boundaries of that empire, and to ascertain as much as possible respecting the provinces to which they raised pretensions, had made persevering, but unsuccessful, inquiries on these points during our visit to Attopée, yet he had found higher up, on exploring alone the basin of an affluent of the Mekong, the Se-Banghien, incontestable proofs of the political and administrative authority of the king of Annam over this part of Laos. Hence, if in the course of years and events, France should find herself heir to the claims of a government, which circumstances of themselves will one day force her either to protect or destroy, she would not want titles to establish her domination over these vast deserts, which European genius alone can make fruitful.

However it may be, the king of Vien-Chan had not to protect himself against these eastern neighbours, the cloud laden with disaster, of which we ourselves saw the fearful extent, burst on this unhappy prince and his subjects, came from the south-west. At the close of 1827, events, with the details of which I am not acquainted, caused a rupture between the court of Bangkok and Laos, and it was followed by a war of extermination. From accounts which, though, perhaps, not minutely, are yet essentially, correct, it appears that an omission, either in the ceremonial of homage, or in the payment of the amount of tribute due to the king of Siam, was followed by the sending an army to Laos, with orders to annihilate the unfortunate people—orders fulfilled with a completeness and cruelty which we, with our manners, can hardly comprehend. The Laotians were exterminated, or carried off *en masse*, and their capital rased to the ground, as Jerusalem once was by the Roman armies. Chao-ko

un,[5] a general whose name still fills these countries, put the
seal by this horrible transaction to a military renown, gained
at the cost of Cambodgia, in the wars to the principal events
of which I have already referred.[6] I saw at Houdon, before
the ancient palace of Norodom, the huge statue of this mur-
derer of nations, which, by an insolent requirement of the
Siamese, abolished only by the French protectorate, the Cambodgians had to salute humbly, as often as they passed
—an ignominy to which this troop of slaves submitted without ever feeling a sentiment of noble resistance; so completely is force, even in its most hideous excesses, accepted
among these nations as the only legitimate power.

The king of Vien-Chan, and several princes of his family,
having succeeded in escaping the vigilance of the enemy,
sought refuge in Hué; but the fierce Minh-man, who then
reigned over Annam, far from protecting the fugitives, as
they had hoped, sent the fallen king to Bangkok, in accordance with a secret agreement made with Siam; and there
the poor wretch, shut up, they say, in an iron cage along
with the instruments of torture, with which they agonised
him day by day, soon died, leaving the last survivors of his
race so utterly abased, that the conqueror could no longer
find any pretext for offence with them.

Thus a flourishing capital has been annihilated in our
own days, and an entire people has, in some sort, disappeared, without Europe ever having suspected such scenes
of desolation—without even a solitary echo of this long cry
of despair having reached her. When I, hereafter, cross
vast fields of massacre in the Chinese empire, I shall have to
lift the veil from scenes not less bloody and not less unknown,—scenes which show human life running in bloody
streams, without leaving either trace or remembrance, like
the waters of a great flood lost in the sands. If the revolutions and wars which turn Christian Europe upside down are
sometimes followed by beneficial changes; if it be possible

[5] The word Chao-koun means a high rank in the military hierarchy;
but the terror of the Laotians has made a proper name of it; so that when
you speak of Chao-koun, without anything more, they think with trembling
of their executioner.
[6] See the Introduction.

to connect them with some philosophical doctrine, or some
grand social interest, the calamities which the Bouddhist and
Mussulman populations of Asia endure remain always barren
sorrows, and disasters that have no compensation.   Nothing
ever springs from these torrents of blood; for the conquerors
are destroying angels for these unfortunate peoples, and
their armies clouds of locusts, exhausting for many generations the countries on which they alight.

CHAPTER IV.

THE KINGDOM OF LUANG-PRABAN. EXCEPTIONAL POSITION OF
THE KING OF THIS COUNTRY TOWARDS THE COURT OF BANG-
KOK. HELP WHICH HE RENDERED THE COMMISSION. TOMB
OF HENRI MOUHOT. SPRING FEASTS.

THERE would be a great risk of deceiving oneself, if the degree of civilisation in any people were always measured by
the development of architecture among them. Of all the
monuments of Europe, those most worthy of admiration belong to ages which many writers of the day call barbarous;
for the generations of the middle ages, kindled to enthusiasm
by their faith, and by enthusiasm to genius, have left as a
record of their lives those noble cathedrals which we imitate
without the ability to equal.

The traveller who seeks to restore the history of nations
that have disappeared, must not, however, be hindered from
interrogating the ruins buried in the sands of the desert, or
under the soil of the forest. These ruins become, often, a
fruitful source of precious information, in the absence of
written annals, or even of tradition. It was in this way
that, in exploring the wreck of Vien-Chan, the ancient Laotian metropolis, we came on characteristic traits of the
government which had had its seat in this ruined town.
Temples and a palace were what might be called the symbolic columns of this strange social edifice; and I must
add, that these pagodas and that royal dwelling had no real
grandeur. While the old Cambodgians brought the enormous blocks of stone, which they knew how to build up and
sculpture with inexhaustible art, from a distance of nearly
ten leagues, the Laotians built walls of brick, badly put
together with plaster, covered with gross pictures, which

could not stand the dampness of the climate for any length
of time, for ornament. The one seem to have had no faith
in their future; the others to have counted on centuries of
power for their country. Cambodgia has been, in fact, to all
appearance, the first nation firmly organised in Indo-China:
it played a preponderating part for long; and its name, which
is often quoted in the sacred books, is still the object of the
veneration of Bouddhists even in countries the farthest from
its frontiers. I must not return to this subject, of which I
have spoken already; but, before leaving Vien - Chan, the
most important political centre of the old independent Laos,
it is fitting to ask, what could be the origin of this Laotian
people, whose settlement in the Mekong valley seems to have
been comparatively recent? From what point of the horizon
did those invaders come, who are still at times forced to
struggle with savage tribes, driven back, but not destroyed?
The resemblance which I have noticed between the Laotian
and Siamese languages — a resemblance which cannot be
ascribed to conquest—permits the inference that the two
races are branches from the same trunk; but where did the
tree grow? what country must we assign as cradle to those
men, who, after having expelled the first occupants of the
Meïnam and Mekong valleys, ended by mutual slaughter in
fratricidal strife? The ignorance of the Laotians, the almost
total loss of their traditions, and, lastly, the necessities of
our journey, which had geographical aims more than any
other, made the elucidation of this problem impossible; and
we can only answer these questions by pure hypothesis.
The most probable, and the only one, besides, which, so far
as I can see, is supported by the vague indications received
from the mouths of the natives, makes their ancestors the
descendants of the kingdom of Xieng-Maï, tributary at this
time to Bangkok. Before establishing themselves at this
place, and founding a state there, did they come from Thibet,
along the valley of one of the great rivers which flow between the Brahmapoutra and the Yang-tse-kiang? Did
they come from the west? or are they, rather, the result of
two different races, which in early ages met, became allied,
and became one? It would be unwise to decide the question. It will be only by a more thorough study, and by the

comparison of the languages, that some sparks will one day be struck into the bosom of this profound night.

None of us could commit himself to this serious undertaking; and, therefore, it is better to be silent, at the risk of appearing incomplete, than to run the danger of misleading the investigations of men especially devoted to such subjects, by a display of artificial learning and improvised science. Indo-China is, besides, the most fruitful field which the savants who seek to discover the lost sources of that grand stream, whose waves are nations, and to make out, in some sort, the genealogy of humanity, can ever explore. Like the deep bays dug out on our shores, where opposing currents dash against each other with violent and continuous agitation, this part of the world seems to have been the point where peoples of different origins, whom constant wars have thrown together, without having absolutely confounded one with the other, have met. Those bloody struggles, which became, at times, in Europe, the powerful agents of civilisation, have only served, in these sad countries, to make the passions fiercer, and the hatreds more bitter: no fruitful germ has ever sprung on this soil, watered with so much blood.

The Burmans and the Siamese, like the Annamites and the Cambodgians, were irreconcilable neighbours. A long peace was impossible between these nations, thrown into juxtaposition by the accidents of emigration; and European intervention, though denounced at first by a patriotic instinct, rooted even in the heart of savages, will, for certain, be one day acknowledged a benefit by the populations to which it secures repose and stability. It is to be always noted, that if some races cannot coexist, from incompatibilities in a sense organic, others, kept apart only by the ambition of princes, will probably come to blend and lose themselves in each other. Between the Annamites, with their harshly-accentuated language, the ideographic characters of their writing, and their exclusively Chinese civilisation, and the Cambodgians, who differ not less in their idiom than in their national character, there is an abyss. If these last had not, at the nick of time, been put under the protectorate of France, they would now, like the greater part of the Lao-

tians, have been absorbed in the Siamese monarchy, toward
which, it must be remembered, they are drawn by man
affinities.

The laws, the manners, and the faiths, seem to be the sam
in these three countries, moulded by a uniform civilisatio
Besides, with the system of government which prevails in th
East, it is a question whether it would be better for the sul-
jects to form independent kingdoms rather than to restor
a centralised empire; perhaps, it is even more dangerous to
have to do with a king than with a simple prefect. Howev
this be, the Laotians, to whom the ruins of their capital reca
the darkest pages of their contemporary history, have lo
seemingly for ever, the least desire for insurrection.   W
knew that it was not thus in the part of this vast countr
which we had yet to visit, and we hoped to find in Southern
Laos signs of independence, and traces of vitality. The sight
of the general decay of the people, among whom we had had
to live for the time, began to depress us, and we hastened t
reach Luang-Praban, the first kingdom of the valley of tl
Mekong which could be regarded as a simple tributary
Siam, and not as a province making an integral part of that
ambitious monarchy.

We left Vien-Chan in the afternoon of the 5th April 1867.
After leaving it, the look of the country changes.   The river
buries itself between hills which soon become mountains, and
push their rocks into the waters, like rugged roots.   The
narrow bed of the Mekong was literally choked with them.
In spite of the smallness and extreme lightness of our canoes,
we had to halt for guides to take us beyond the dangerous
parts.   The current soon becomes so strong, and the steep
masses of rock are so difficult to turn, that we had to abandon boat-hooks and paddles, and yoke ourselves to enormous
ropes of rattan. The Laotians, mounted on the blocks of red
sandstone, rising out of the water, had to catch with one
hand at the clefts of these ragged masses, and drag the
canoes towards them, with savage cries, with the other.
With their cables, and their long iron poles, they might have
been taken for those sea-robbers, who, in the fifteenth century, lived prosperously, in Brittany, on the produce of shipwrecks. When a point, round which the water boiled, had to

be doubled, or the other bank had to be reached through whirlpools, the captain of our canoes never failed to address resounding prayers to heaven.

For several days' sail the banks of the Mekong were nearly deserted. It is only very rarely that huts, built in less time than it takes to pitch a tent, reminded us that men lived in these forests. The inhabitants of these fragile dwellings escape in good measure from forced labour, by the difficulty of reaching them; so that it was not without trouble we got them to lend a hand and help our crews, who were exhausted by fatigue. They grounded their unwillingness, mostly, on their wish for our safety, the river being, as they said, impracticable at this season of the year.

We were forced to confess that these brave people were not altogether wrong. The rocks grew thicker, and the waters rushing against them furiously, it soon became clear that we could not advance farther without peril. We, therefore, unloaded our canoes, and seeing some traders who were passing very opportunely, the petty mandarin appointed to conduct us forced them to lay their goods on the ground, and to carry our baggage. They had to do so for several kilometres; but when we wished to pay them for their services, they could not understand such liberality, being too much accustomed to violence to expect anything like justice.

It was April, when the waters are at the lowest. The Mekong was only a couple of torrent-like streams, of immense depth. The part of its bed left dry was a curious sight. Most of the rocks by which it is fretted are of bright colours, so that it looked, sometimes, as if we were walking between walls of polished marble. A little torrent, running over a blue-and-white bottom, made a delicious natural mosaic, which seemed formed of lapis-lazuli and alabaster. We encamped, at last, on the sand, in improvised huts. From the top of the rock, from which the national colours floated, we had at our feet one of the greatest rivers of Asia reduced to two arms, narrower than those of the Seine, round the island of St. Louis; but when we threw the lead, there was no bottom.

Our cabins of leaves were in the midst of a vast arena, surrounded by an amphitheatre of hills. Wild beasts called and answered each other round us. We heard the hoarse cry of stags, and, also, towards night, the sharper voice of the tiger; an invisible enemy, against which the Laotians protected themselves by raising a small chapel to Bouddha on the edge of the forest. These poor creatures, who, if we can believe some commentators, were aspiring to annihilation, as the highest felicity promised by their faith, held on to life; held on to it, like the most wretched of our peasants, and like them, when they thought themselves in danger, tried to protect it by an act of faith and a fervent prayer.

If the lightest canoes stop at some of the dangerous places in ascending the river, it is very different when they go down. A skilful pilot then abandons himself to the current, and directs his skiff, which is carried forward with a giddy swiftness, by a bold stroke of the paddle. Even great covered rafts, some of them twenty metres in length, are trusted to this perilous voyage; and although they have barely room to turn in the sharp bends, where the river is hardly forty metres across, shipwrecks are rare. I visited one of these merchant vessels, loaded with ivory and bales of cotton, which is cultivated in all this region on a large scale, in spite of the fewness of the villages.

The debilitating influences of the climate had very much weakened our ardour in hunting, and our table suffered correspondingly. We encamped as seldom, and for as short a time as possible, at a distance from villages, to escape the pain of hearing, with an empty stomach, hypothetical roasts belling out in the thickets round us. The chief place of the next province was Sien-Kan, which we reached on foot, marching all day over the burning sand, without any shelter from the heat of the sun. The heat was so great, that even the natives could not pass a pool of water without plunging their heads into it. My ears were ringing. I looked about without seeing, and entirely lost command of myself; my limbs went like a machine wound up, and without consciously receiving any impulse from the brain. The path plunged at last into a forest of bamboos; but our guide persisted in marching behind us, and if we ultimately reached Sien-Kan, it was thanks to the river, which, moaning in the distance, directed our march.

Sien-Kan,—called, also, Muong-Maï, New Muong, in contrast to Muong-Cao, Old Muong—is the chief place, but is as destitute of anything distinctive as it is of importance. Though the governor was away, on a visit to one of his confrères on the borders of the Meïnam, we were well received. They expected us, and our dwelling, which was made ready beforehand, was constructed on the model of those we had occupied before. The voyage lost, each day, in my eyes, something of the charms with which my imagination had pleased itself with surrounding it. Illusion was no longer possible. As long as we were in a Siamese country, the most trivial adventure was not to be hoped for. There would have been more chance of one in crossing the Abruzzi.

At Sien-Kan a lively sensation was, however, in store for us. Some wandering merchants put up close to us. In these countries, where there is no press, these traders are peripatetic newsmongers, and supply their customers with gossip as well as cotton checks, talking all the time they are selling. Very soon the most astounding and most depressing news flew from their shops, and came to overwhelm us. The English were at Luang-Praban; they came from the kingdom of Xieng-Maï, and consisted of a company of explorers made up of several officers and a numerous escort. A general who sees his combinations destroyed, and a battle of which he felt sure lost by a manœuvre of the enemy; an artist who sees his own conception in the picture of a rival, —are not more cruelly heart-struck than we were by the announcement of an event which would take the glory from our enterprise, and deprive us of all the honour. We left Sien-Kan under the painful influence of these rumours, thinking of the sad figure we should make before our rivals; we, who had started a year ago, and yet were distanced by them. Material difficulties came, besides, to help to cloud our brows. We could not get canoes enough, and had to go two by two in these narrow prisons.

A Laotian informed us, in passing, that the English had left Luang-Praban, that they were rapidly descending the river, and that we should soon see their rafts. Then they had not continued their voyage beyond Luang-Praban? Excellent news! But they were descending the Mekong—sad counterpoise! They will, on their return, publish their observations. We shall be almost lost. It was none the less necesssary to dissimulate, and to prepare to receive them. Our hencoop is emptied by slaughter; a peacock is roasted on the brazier: we are about to renew over a dinner hypocritical demonstrations of cordial alliance. O nature, virgin and wild, what profanation! If some Alcestis had fled from men on these desert banks, he would throw himself into one of the whirlpools of the river, as he listened to us. For myself, who cherish no professional hateful jealousy against England, I shared, from duty, in the general vexation; but I could not help laughing in my beard. Lunettes are levelled; a raft appears in the distance, gliding carelessly over the waters; good eyes see Englishmen clearly, and they are pointing their fingers at us. The raft approaches. It hails us. It is a splendid floating house, with a verandah before and behind, its height enormous, its proportions magnificent. What luxury! what comfort! An Englishman is seen making his toilet. For myself, though short-sighted, I continue to see nothing but Siamese crouching and smoking their cigarettes. The most ill at ease smooth their faces, and wait in the sun. Still, no one shows himself, except an officer—of the king of Siam. He announces that the English follow close behind; that there are three of them; and that they are busy with the geography of the country. Smiles turn to grimaces. A second raft is on the horizon, and there is fresh anxiety. Keen eyes distinctly see the French flag floating from the top of their vessel. It is from courtesy; but courtesy is easy to those who have won. O surprise! The French colours are Dutch, identical with ours, as every one knows, except in the order in which they are arranged. The raft keeps the middle of the stream, passes openly before us, and no European answers our signals. It is evidently a crafty, diabolical ruse of British insolence; just like them! Concentrated wrath succeeds disappointment. At the moment the raft is about to disappear in a bend of the river, it steers to the bank, and stops. A card is brought us from 'M. X—, land-surveyor and architect of his Siamese majesty's government.' M. de Lagrée sends his second offi-

Plate 12 *Passage through a rapid (Drawing by Th. Weber, based on a sketch by L. Delaporte)*

Plate 13 *Burmese traders selling goods to Laotian women at the gate of a temple in Muong Mai (Drawing by Émile Bayard, based on a sketch by L. Delaporte).*

cer, who finds, instead of an Englishman, a Batavian in the service of Siam, flanked by two mulatto servants. The poor devil seemed to have only the one thought, of escaping the rains, which, according to him, spare no European in these quarters. He showed his wonder to see that we were ready to face them. The information he had gathered on the way, about us, repaid for the annoyance which the popular rumours about him had caused us. Applying the same rule to both expeditions, Fame had given proof of an impartial exaggeration on both sides. If she had seen in a single wretched creature several English officers, and in two half negroes a numerous escort, her hundred voices had announced that we were sixty instead of six, and that the Annamites in our suite formed a veritable army. The Siamese agent had been thoroughly frightened at these reports, and trembled to meet us, I can hardly see why. He had formed a resolution to take advantage of the current of the river to burn our camp, and only laid it aside when he saw the peaceful look of our little group. Nothing was left but to laugh as we thought of the fable of the floating sticks.

The king of Siam, whose attention had probably been drawn to these countries by our expedition, wished to know exactly about his kingdom. To satisfy this legitimate curiosity, he had sent a European, provided with chronometers, with a quadrant and compass, and ordered him to note the topography of the provinces bordering the Meïnam and the Mekong. This trader had a thousand francs a month for his work, and travelled as a mandarin. He had left the banks of the Meïnam at Utharadit, in about 17° of north latitude, and had ascended by land to twenty leagues beyond Luang-Praban. He had only stopped from regard for the Siamese functionary who was with him, who had been near having his head taken off within the bounds of a province that had succeeded in shaking off the Siamese yoke. After long months passed in the most perfect security, with no other incidents than our daily halt, with none of those perils that inflame the imagination, sicknesses weaken instead of rousing courage; and I saw with joy, in a near, though yet dim, future, a different existence.

The passport drawn up at the chancellery of Bangkok,

which had opened every door to us, and made everything so easy, would soon be useless, or even dangerous. We were about, at last, to see countries where they cut off Siamese heads. I may deserve to be accused of ingratitude, but I confess I was delighted by the prospect. Already, it is true, the aspect of nature was greatly changed, but it had been so very imperceptibly. The mist, accustoming us to rapid changes of view, had made us impatient of those slow transformations, which come on almost insensibly, and are prepared for and almost anticipated. A mountain, which would have captivated us if it had been seen on a sudden, left us unmoved, because it came only after a range of hills.

The people had nothing about them to disturb us; and I soon found, that in Laos, as in Europe, ennui is the child of uniformity. But since leaving Vien-Chan, we felt some pride in having before us a region that had never been explored; for the Dutch ambassador sent in the seventeenth century to the king of Laos had not gone beyond the capital, where the sovereign resided. The river alone continued to interest us by its caprices. The changing aspect of its bed; the colour of its waters, here impetuous, troubled, and crowned with foam; there calm and almost transparent; its windings to get round obstructions; the effort it made to throw them over: everything, in this, was fresh or imposing.

At the eighteenth degree the Mekong makes a bend which is not on any map, and it does not turn to the north again, till after having inclined for nearly two hundred miles to the west. The village of Paclaï, which marks the end of this bend, was the point farthest from Bangkok, at which we had rested since leaving Crachè. The caravans coming from the upper parts of the river land there, to go on to the capital of the kingdom of Siam; and the merchants going to Luang-Praban, or the higher provinces, in the same way embark there. This poor village would soon grow, if commerce were any way active; but it is still in an embryo state. Every one supports himself only, and Paclaï sees more functionaries passing on the way to Bangkok, or returning, than bales of silk or cotton. M. Mouhot, our scientific compatriot, came to Paclaï, to look at the river before continuing a journey which death speedily closed. A portrait of this unfor-

tunate naturalist, which we showed the head man of the
village, reminded him of some sharp suffering caused by
toilet-vinegar given him by the traveller as an excellent
remedy for something or other, but which the too-credulous
client had rubbed into his eyes.

Magnificent forests closely hemmed in the village of Paclaï; streams of quick-flowing water ran under the trees;
the birds were not contented, as in Cambodgia and Lower
Laos, with showing-off their bright plumage, but had turned
musical, and began to sing. They seemed by their concerts
to link themselves with the rejoicings which the festival of
spring brings back each year at that season. When the time
of celebration comes, the girls saturate their hair with an
extra quantity of hog's lard and castor-oil, and walk about
in gala dresses, with fragrant flowers in their hands, and a
red scarf on their bosoms, intended less to hide their breasts
than to set off the yellow saffron tint with which they dye
their skin. Such manifestations were needed to remind us
that it was spring, because in those regions, so dear to the
sun, growth is so rapid, that there is no hint of the months
from the slow advance of vegetation, which in our temperate
climate raises the sap in the trees by unperceived advances,
and gives such a charm to spring. It is a sort of magic, which
one enjoys with the eye, but in which the rest of his nature
has no part. The earth elsewhere seems to be conscious of
the transformation; it shakes off its winding-sheet of hoar-
frost, and makes a visible effort to escape from its tomb.
Here, on the contrary, it seems to yield passively to secret
influences. It is not a Lazarus raised from the dead,—
coming from darkness to live again in the light, and feeling
the new life with a double intensity; it is an odalisque, who
awakes, turns herself gently towards her mirror, and puts
flowers in her hair.

At Paclaï the river is calm, and pretty broad, and is
bedded between two straight banks of rock like the sides of
a canal. But for its depth, it might seem dug out by human
hands; at least, this is the impression it makes on a traveller
who sees it in April, the last month of the dry season, for its
appearance changes completely during the rains. The bed,
filled by the river when it is at its height, is fringed with

white sand, and is on a level with the trees of the forest; that which contents it when it is low—that is, sixteen or nineteen metres beneath the high-water mark—is through rock, and is largely strewn with huge stones. At a little distance from the village are the ruins of a large fishery establishment, looking like the wreck of a great town that had been built of bamboos. Besides the sources of wealth on its banks, the river contains in its slimy waters many kinds of fish, which form a large part of the food of the Laotians, who, indolent and hating work, prefer fishing to farming, and leave their rice-ground when evening comes, to visit the nets set in the morning in favourable places, or cast lines, which the current carries along at the same rate as it bears on their boats. We bought for a tikal—a Siamese coin worth a little more than three francs—a fish a metre and a half long, and as fat as a fed pig, with flesh of the colour and consistency of beef. The capture of one of these monsters is a piece of good fortune for a family. It is cut into strips and smoked, and supports them for long.

We left Paclaï, on the 19th of April, for the capital of the kingdom of Luang-Praban, to which that poor village belongs. The hills grow higher, come nearer, and hem-in the river, from which a belt of gray and rugged rocks separates them, and they are covered with fine vegetation. The white trunks of some kinds of huge trees stand out from the green, like marble pillars. A sharp bend of the river shut it in before us like a lake; and at the back of the picture a high mountain showed its steep outlines through a veil of blue vapours, which seem to shiver in the cold.

The great charm of scenes of this kind is the brightness of the light. The memory carries away from these regions, which are characterised by a kind of monotonous grandeur more than by anything else, only a recollection of so many landscapes flooded with light, a corner of the forest, or the peak of a mountain. When you get back to northern regions, you have only to shut your eyes to bring back the dazzling and luminous perspectives; so wondrously do the tropics fill one with their beams. The whole external world, so little varied, so calm, so full of transparency and grandeur, influenced me without my knowing it. I slighted enjoyments which dulled my faculties. My sensations destroyed the power of reflecting, and I felt myself on the slope which leads up gifted souls to a state of dreamy contemplation, but leads others to the verge of idiocy. I hardly know to which of these two results these fatal moods would have urged me, had they continued long enough; but I am very grateful to-day to the Laotians of my canoe, who were never very long in recalling me to reality. They were in the habit of piling up their inevitable sacks into a barrier far from fragrant, between me and the landscape. These bags contained an extra langouti, a little basket of rice, a box with the various elements of their quids, not to speak of the rotten fish and other ingredients, which, joined to the odour of the natives themselves, would have moved the most callous heart. My attention was, moreover, at times drawn off to the difficulties of the navigation.

This becomes once more dangerous at a short distance from Paclaï. Sharp rocks rise in the waters like needles, and we had to get past them by a method already familiar to us—hauling ourselves on by a rattan cable. We entered a gorge where mountains, softly lighted, rose in a second row behind the hills, reproducing their tossed and tumbled shapes as if they had been their magnified shadows. The colours of the sky all at once changed, the tints became deeper, the water turned a strange hue like withered leaves, the wind blew hard through the defile, the thunder echoed, and the hail came down furiously. The hailstones, which were as large as musket-bullets, rattled against our leaf roofs; the Laotian crew sheltered itself as it best could: and our Annamites, to whom this phenomenon was quite new, thought it was raining pebbles on their heads. The wild elephants, frightened, marched at random through the forest on the river-bank, crashing the bamboos under their feet. with a noise like that of bursting petards. The sky, the earth, and the water were alike full of noise, and Nature seemed to me more beautiful in these sudden outbreaks than in her gloomy tranquillity.

We chose for our resting-place, that day, a little village cowering in a fold of soil between two mountains. A river rolls its limpid waters, now swollen by the storm, by its side

L

over a bed of flints. It is of recent erection, as may be seen from the age of the valuable trees, which the Laotians take care always to plant even before building their dwellings. The poor people had been stripped bare of almost everything by the escort of the Dutch geographer we had met. The Siamese mandarin who commanded it had plundered all along his route, in accordance with the hateful custom which raises spoliation to a principle, and transforms the functionaries of the court of Bangkok into brigands. They are not authorised, it is true, to exact more than some specified things and services gratuitously, and these they can only demand so far as they are needful for their travelling requirements; but they know that they need fear no censure, and they hide under a kind of seventy-fifth article—a legislative arrangement by which Eastern mandarinism puts everything to rights for itself. I was thankful that the terms of our passport, in compliance with our personal wish, obliged us to pay for men, boats, and provisions. It caused us to be less thought of; but it will be a pleasant recollection in connection with us, and when favourable circumstances come, it may bear good fruit.

For some time we met no more great affluents, but numerous streams, and many brooks or torrents which fall from the mountains. We had finally left the plains, and henceforth sailed through the midst of hills and bluffs. Our canoes coasted along enormous rocks. We one day came upon corpses in rush mats, at the turning of a promontory. They were in a cleft, where the water had, perhaps, landed them, to bear them off after a time, or, perhaps, they were put there by the hands of the living. However fine such a tomb may be, it is sad, when one feels oneself dying, not to be able to reckon on a little earth near the hut where one has lived. Of the three elements to which man commits his remains, water, always changing and oblivious by its nature, seems the least worthy of this mournful trust. The earth grows green again above us, the fire leaves ashes for our family to venerate. Though they surround mortal agony and burial with a crowd of noisy ceremonies, the Laotians do not look on death as we do. That grand mystery terrifies them; but that which they dread, above all, is lest the ghost should revisit them. This danger seems less if they annihilate or banish the body.

Masses of black shining rocks, which seemed as if they had been varnished, encumbered the river once more so much, as to leave it only a narrow passage, through which it darted, writhing. We had, therefore, once more to unload our canoes, taking off even the light rounded roofs, which it would not have been safe to have left on them. In spite of these precautions, one of them filled while they were dragging it along, and we saw nothing but the captain, erect and impassive, notwithstanding the danger, his paddle in his hand, and seeming to walk on the waves. When the specially dangerous spots were thus passed, the flotilla resumed its way. It needed all the strength and dexterity of our boatmen not to be swept away in doubling some points, where they had nothing by which to hold on, and a terrible current bore down on them, with a smooth wall over their head and an abyss at their feet. As they knew they were responsible for our lives, they threw an ardour into their task, demanded for their self-preservation. They could not drown such great mandarins as we with impunity.

From Nong-Caï the villages are thinly scattered, but the country grows more populous as you approach Luang-Praban—a town famous through all Laos, but whose size, in contradiction to the laws of perspective, grows less as we get near it. The Mekong is clear at last, for some time, of the rocks which till then obstruct it: the outlines of the mountains lose their rigidity, the hills are covered with a rich and more varied vegetation, and the river flows round them in soft bends. Free from obstacles, it spreads out into a broader bed, and forms a vast sheet of calm water before the town.

Luang-Praban makes itself known by the top of a gilt pyramid rising from amidst the trees, as our towns in Europe are announced from a distance by the steeples of churches. Boats are drawn up on the bank; nets by the hundred, hung from stakes, dry in the sun; immense rafts are being put together; others, smaller, in great numbers, float at anchor from long cables. We saw at once in this mean town, which lives by the river, signs of activity; a sight so new to us, that we stopped to enjoy it: then, to let the authorities know we had come, we struck our bronze gong with extra force, as is the way with mandarins. We waited a long time; the curious gathered in groups round us, but no official presented himself to receive or direct us. M. de Lagrée determined, at last, to march into the town, at a venture, with all the military following he could muster. On this, some stir showed itself in the crowd, and we saw a functionary, important so far as stoutness went, but mean in rank, running towards us. He told us, what was hardly likely, that we were not expected, and that nothing had been prepared for receiving us; and added, that the king not liking us to occupy the caravanserai near the palace, it would be necessary, for the time at least, to content ourselves with the small, black, and squalid house which he pointed out. If the tone of this chamberlain was courteous, his language was imperative. M. de Lagrée consented to make use of a slovenly and dilapidated lodging, but he announced his intention to see the king next day, and have an explanation. It was necessary to accede to the usual ceremonies. His majesty would not rise to receive us on our entering the throne-room; he wished to force us to remain sitting on the ground in his presence, and we were with difficulty allowed to dispense with striking our foreheads on it, and crawling towards him, like the natives.

M. de Lagrée having energetically resisted these pretensions, the plenipotentiary of the king yielded on all these points, and we had the honour of being received on the afternoon of May 1st, 1867, by the sovereign of Luang-Praban, who condescended to take three steps forward, and to suffer us to shake hands with him. His throne was a sofa of gilt wood, incrusted below with glass; and on this he squatted, chewing his betel, while we took our place on benches. He was an old man with a wrinkled face, and so high an idea of his dignity, that it hardly allowed him to open his mouth. He scarcely replied to our questions, and took care never to speak to us directly. The lords of the court and the body-guards knelt on both sides down the whole length of the hall, holding their sabres and muskets in their hands with the martial air of sacristans who carry the candles on a procession-day. The king con-

sented to examine the presents M. de Lagrée offered him, and
we retired, not without once more grasping the royal hand.

It was easy to see, by the stiffness of this reception, that
we had to do with a man in whose eyes the Siamese letters
were not a sufficient guarantee. We had been told that he
was tenacious in exhibiting this quasi-independence, and
that he wished to know us before displaying his sentiments.
He authorised us, however, to stay in his town, and even
invited us to mark out the site for our lodging, which he
proposed to erect at his own cost. We chose a spot consecrated by the ruins of a pagoda, which gave rise to countless stipulations. We had to agree not to kill anything in
the enclosure of our camp, not to profane the soil by traces
of our humanity; to live, in short, like pure spirits; promises
more easy to make than to perform. Our bamboo huts were
soon ready; a splendid banyan, the sacred tree, *par excel-
lence*, stretching its great arms over them.

We had at last come to a collection of houses and people
meriting the name of a town. We had seen nothing like it
since leaving Pnom-Penh. Without going the length of
Mgr. Pallegoix, who sets down the population at eighty thousand, I am inclined to think M. Mouhot's estimate of seven
or eight thousand a little under the mark. From the top of
a knoll which serves for base to an elegant pyramid, you
overlook a plain covered with thatched roofs, shaded by a
forest of cocoa-trees. From this point, from which the eye
embraces at once the whole panorama of the town, one
hears the confused hum which rises from all centres of human
activity, resembling, according to its intensity, the dull sound
of waves dying on the beach; or, it may be, the hoarse roar
of billows dashed upon the rocks by the storm. To the ear
of the traveller, tired with vast solitudes, this confused murmur, in which all articulate words are lost, is a delicious harmony. The town of Luang-Praban, which is traversed for
all its length by a great artery, parallel with the river, stretches
along the two sides of a hill, bathed on one side by the Mekong, on the other, by the Nam-Kan. This little river throws
itself into the great one by a sharp turn at the north-west
end of the town. The side towards the Nam-Kan is not less
peopled than that towards the Mekong. A crowd of filthy

lanes abut on the principal street; some slope rapidly, or are made into stairs, and paved with brick, or even with blocks of rough marble, polished by the feet of the people. Macadamising is not altogether unknown. It is strange that the Laotians have so wholly neglected to take advantage of the inexhaustible quarries of marble they have at hand, that when they have wished to use some in ornamenting, for example, the space before a pagoda, they should have thought of bringing it from Bangkok, to which, if we can credit a mandarin, who flattered himself that in giving us this detail he would excite our admiration, it had previously been brought from China.

Luang-Praban forms a kind of rectangle, which is bounded on three sides by running water. The fourth is shut in by a wall with five gates, which extends from the Nam-Kan to the Mekong. At the point where this wall, hardly visible under the growth which buries it, joins the great river, a little sanctuary, on the very bank, white, with a round roof, attracts attention : it protects the footprints of Bouddha, impressed on a rock. We had seen at Angcor, on Mount Bakheng, and at different other places in Laos, hollows somewhat like a foot, in which the faithful fancied they saw footsteps left on the rock by the great reformer of the creed of India—the venerated founder of their religion. The Siamese have discovered phenomena of the same kind, and Mount Phrâbat is a place of pilgrimage to the inhabitants of Bangkok. One can readily understand how an apostle claiming to be inspired, and preaching a positive religion, should seek to secure success by miracles: the power to work them would assuredly be the best of warrants, given by God himself, to the representative he had chosen; but if Bouddha appeared on earth only to show men the way to annihilation, it is hard to see whence he could derive the power to change the laws of nature; how, for example, he could dig out a deep hollow in a rock by simply setting his foot on it. I know very well that we have no right to lay on Bouddha, himself, the responsibility of these simple credulities; but they exist, and are common, and, fantastic contradiction, the faith of the people has become so distorted, that they acknowledge a god in him who was, beyond all men, an atheistic philosopher! I respect the grave intellects, and eminent writers, who, of late years, have expounded the theory of Bouddhism from this point of view, too much, to dispute their conclusions. I grant that the torch of analysis, borne with a firm hand into the deepest obscurities of the Bouddhist doctrine, has revealed a throne raised to annihilation at the bottom of the abyss; but I do not think there is a single Bouddhist in Laos, who would picture its extreme consequences thus, in giving an exact statement of his belief. In any case, even supposing Bouddha really considered life as the supreme evil, such an idea could not rise except in the heart of a man profoundly moved by the miseries of his brethren; a dogma so depressing must have needed a soil watered with blood to develop it; and, in this light, Indo-China was a region especially well prepared for it.

However it may be, the legendary foot of Charlemagne was only a miniature alongside the foot of the god, whose steps remind one of the famous cat of Perrault. From the river-bank where he left the mark of one of his feet, the heavenly traveller, in visiting Luang-Praban, set down the other on the top of a little knoll, adorned now, in memory of the fact, with an elegant pavilion supported on ten pillars. The roof is covered with coloured tiles, and edged with bells which tinkle in the wind: the sacred footstep is in a grotto, at its side, and is covered with leaves of gold. From this picturesque spot, which is reached by a very steep stair, the view is magnificent. On one hand, stretch the great river and the mountains which border it; a gap in the mass of the first range lets the eye lose itself over distant undulations bathed in mist; nearer, you see the thatched roofs of the houses, and the tiles of the pagodas, the trees with waving plumes, and the tops of some pyramids; on the other side, the eye ranges along the valley of the Nam-Kan, which runs at the foot of the bluff, separating a great faubourg, planted, like the rest, with cocoas and palms, from the town.

It was on the banks of the Nam-Kan, not far from the village of Ban-Napao, that the king of Luang-Praban caused the body of M. Mouhot, who had come there six years before, and had died of fever, to be buried. This traveller had made himself beloved by the natives, who still hold his memory in respect; and the king himself paid a last homage to it, by furnishing, at his own cost, the material for a modest monument, which we raised over the tomb of our brave countryman. Admiral de La Grandière had specially charged M. de Lagrée with this sad duty. He felt that France, summoned to resume in Indo-China the place she had lost in India, owed recognition and regret to the hardy explorer, to whom she had granted neither help nor encouragement when they could have been of use. Leaving London in a merchant vessel, in April 1858, with some slight assistance from an English learned society, Henri Mouhot had resolved, after a sufficient stay at Bangkok, to explore the basin of the Meïnam and part of that of the Mekong. Having reached Luang-Praban, he conceived the project of attempting, by the ascent of this latter river, the work which a near future reserved for other Frenchmen to accomplish, who have been happier than he, because they could support and encourage each other. Such an enterprise was beyond the power of any single man. M. Mouhot died in the midst of a vast forest, leaving, in the hut where his lonely agony sought shelter, a journal continued almost without a break to the day of his death, the last page of it, written with a hand already cold, containing a touching expression of his sorrows, tempered by religious confidence.

The pagodas are numerous at Luang-Praban, and there is some variety in the architecture. Each has a bonzery, and the yellow dress abounds in the streets. They are well supported; sometimes decorated richly, and not without taste. In one I admired an altar incrusted with blue glass, in imitation of enamel: on the blue ground, pleasantly lighted by the soft rays of evening, a rose in relief, full blown, with gilt petals, spread itself. In another pagoda, which rested on magnificent columns of wood, and was nearly circular, two of the most beautiful elephant tusks that could be imagined, have been placed near the principal statue. The chord of the arc formed by these huge weapons of defence is a metre and seventy-six centimetres across. As a rule, gilding and vermilion are lavished on the ceilings and the pillars, and the altar is heaped up with so many statuettes and ornaments, that it might be taken for a shopkeeper's display.

The services seemed regularly observed, and I was often present at the evening ones in the pagoda nearest our camp. The faithful, on their knees before a great statue of Bouddha, listened, with the attitude of meditation, to the prayers read by a bonze, giving the responses, themselves, at long intervals. Lighted tapers illuminated the building; sweet-smelling canes burned at the feet of the god; and a charming lace-work of flowers, woven each day by the women and children, a perfumed and beautiful drapery, hung before the altar. The ceremony ended commonly with some notes of music: the women beat a small bronze timbrel; then went out to the porch, laid flowers on some sacred stones, and watered them, as they murmured their prayers. Not seldom they mingled grains of rice with the flowers; and I noticed that the poultry of the neighbourhood, into whom, perhaps, the soul of some bonzes, dead in a state of sin, had passed, had retained from their former existence a very exact remembrance of the hour of the offering. Besides the daily offices, the Laotians have also periodical fêtes, at some of which we had already been present. Those of spring, which we had seen begin at Paclaï, were celebrated at Luang-Praban with a noisy solemnity, in keeping with the size of the town and the number of the population. Naturally, young people take the greatest part in them. During the day, while the overpowering heat lasts, all is dull, for the Laotians themselves suffer by the sun; but hardly has this redoutable foe to pleasure disappeared behind the mountains of the right bank of the Mekong, than the air is full of din, from bursts of laughter, and wild songs, to which the dogs add their voices. I had the curiosity to look on from a distance at these nocturnal rejoicings. The white light of the moon threw silver tints on the porticoes of the pagodas, on the pyramids, on the thatched roofs; the cocoas; the palms, and the light leaves of the clumps of bamboos defined themselves sharply against the clear sky; and though no perceptible air came to stir the atmosphere, the whole trembled before me like a dream, without my being able to seize the moving outlines of this magic picture. The nights are beautiful in the East, and the East is beautiful only at night; both men and things gain by being seen in an uncertain light; the landscape loses its monotony, and the civilisation of the spot its grossness.

Under the dim vault formed in the distance by the great trees, a shrill and piercing voice, all at once, sent up into the air some extraordinary notes, to which a whole chorus of women, walking very quickly, and soon coming up to where I stood, answered in a more serious tone. My curiosity was keenly excited; I was as astonished as an ancient barbarian would have been who had met in the streets of Eleusis a procession of matrons marching towards the temple of Ceres. I resolved to be initiated into the mysteries. The solo began again, and was followed by sharp, discordant cries, as if twenty angry women were stamping and shrieking, in competition, at the top of their lungs, without thinking of the measure, only caring that they should end at the same time. So far as the vocal music went, this was all the concert. Young girls were the attraction. They escorted a great pyramid of flowers, which was laid under a canopy in the porch of the pagoda by the men who carried it. An old bonze, with his face hidden by a plume of feathers, said some prayers, and then the crowd broke up. Young girls and young men, their religious duty finished, mingled together; and I went away, for it was easy to see that the presence of a stranger checked their freedom. The Bouddhist priest was about to be displaced by the eternal minister of the one worship universally practised in the world, and I regained my chamber, not without sadness. It was the first year which had had no spring for me. I met other bands; some went to the pagodas with the same solemnity; others did not seem to trouble themselves with the sacred character of the fête. Young men, the worse for wine, chanted a Laotian bolero, or blew sounds out of reeds tied together. Farther off, two violins of two strings, a guitar, a flute, and cymbals handled like castanets, performed a very simple, very original, and very lively air. The dandies who gave this concert in the moonlight had a love rendezvous as well. It was just as in France, where those who would on no account go to a midnight mass, will on no account stay from a midnight party. All these young Laotians, dressed in a light cloak thrown over the shoulders, and a large langouti which looked like huge hose, had the confident and swaggering walk of our grand seigneurs of former times, in pursuit of rich heiresses.

A gambling-house stood near our hut, and men and women gave themselves noisily up to their passion, in it: a mat stood for the green table, and ticals for louis. The players, who prepare themselves by libations of rice brandy for the sensations of the gambling-house, have a burning eye and a shrivelled figure; the women, especially, are hideous: many, who are no longer young, have enormous goîtres, and these monstrous tumours hang down on their bosoms, so that one hardly knows whether they have three breasts, or three goîtres. The use of opium seems more common in Luang-Prabän than in Lower Laos. The Chinese no longer come there, but they have for long sent numerous caravans. These, like a wave charged with ooze, which leaves its abomination on the bank as it retires, have inoculated the population with part of their vices. These indefatigable traders, who formerly came down from Yunan to the number of two or three hundred a year, have given up a journey, which has become too dangerous since the revolt of the Mussulmans from the emperor of China. They are replaced by Burman pedlars, who supply the place with cotton and woollen goods, and with a small number of other European articles sought after by the natives. These Burmese may be recognised by their features, which are more open and more intelligent than those of the Laotians, and by a turban smartly put on on one side of the head. They have their thighs, their stomach, and often their chests, covered with tattooing, generally blue, but sometimes red—fantastic arabesques, which destroy the colour of the skin, and, at a little way off, have almost the look of swaddling-bands.

At Luang-Prabän the Laotians have adopted the same custom, whence, probably, has come the name of Black-bellied Laos, which is given them by ancient geographers. One must go to the market to judge the variety of costumes and types. At a glance at this mixed population, the least skilful of anthropologists would see beforehand the inextricable confusion of races and languages, which he will meet at a short distance from Luang-Prabän. Numbers of savages, who have submitted to the king, come every morning to the town to

sell or bu . They live in the mountains. Their dress is
extremely simple; so much so in some cases, that it could
hardly be lessened. Their hair, plaited over the head, and
cut horizontally along the forehead, sticks out freely behind,
and is sometimes done up into a chignon. Others, more
elegant, wear a blue vest set off with white edging. All
have the lobe of the ear perforated by a hole that measures,
sometimes, a centimetre across, in which they put an ornament of wood or metal; the women using a great bodkin of
silver, with the head gilt, in this way.

The costume of these good ladies consists of a vest and
jupon of blue cotton check, edged with white; and they have
a piece of some cloth on their head, of the same colour, encircling and mingling with their black hair. Their little
scared figures contrast agreeably with the masculine features of many of the Laotian women, who display a de-
formed throat without shame. Their savage sisters have
more modesty or more of the coquette. It is only through
their tight-fitting vest the eye can follow over their bosoms
the often graceful outlines of their hidden charms. The
Laotians, who are very proud of their half-civilisation, look
on the savages as much inferior to themselves, and, indeed,
as almost contemptible. Every group of three miserable huts
of theirs has a name of its own, known in the neighbourhood; but he most important village of the people, who may
be regarded as the original owners of the country, is called
by the common and scornful name of Ban-Kas—a kraal of
savages. The stranger refuses to accept this estimate formed
by a perverted pride. The savages are hard workers, and
the finest fields of rice and noblest herds of cattle I have
seen have been in their parts of the country. They are all
shy at first but they are easily brought to be familiar. How
often have I, in my walks, had to ask these children of the
woods for shelter from the sun, or water to quench my thirst,
or a mat on which to forget my fatigue! They did not understand my words, but divined, with the quick instinct of
hospitality the wants which brought me among them, and
hastened to satisfy them. I have enjoyed positive feasts in
these huts where the bamboo, worked in a hundred ways,
spread all the luxury before me it could display; and I cannot

recall without gratitude the recollection of a collation made
up of sticky rice, smoked iguana legs, and pepper, which a
savage, some sixty years of age, whom I met in the forest, to
whom my long beard caused astonishment rather than fear,
offered me one day. This good old man spoke a harsh and
sonorous language, in which the *r* abounded, in contrast with
the Laotian, in which that letter seems little used. He took
as much pleasure in showing me his cabin, and his fields of
maize and rice, as any civilised proprietor could. The plains
having become rare, it was necessary to grow rice on the
hills, and, by the force of circumstances, the management of
the rice-plantations of the forest have been brought to high
perfection. The agriculturists of the neighbourhood of Luang-Praban avail themselves of the numerous springs which
escape from the rocks, to irrigate their grounds, and even
seem, where necessary, to dig little canals for leading the
water where it is required—a thing unheard of in Lower
Laos. The cultivated spots on the slopes of the mountains
are scattered with a freedom possible to a people not very
numerous, and enjoying an immense extent of unoccupied
land. They burn the trees, and cut away the stumps, as far
as they can, without pulling out the roots, and plant the rice
on the round tops of the knolls, or on the steep slopes, without an attempt at levelling the surface. Hence, after a short
time, the roots spring again, and invade the rice-grounds. If
they were to dig the ground deep, they would avoid this inconvenience; but, then, the diluvian rains would carry off all
the soil, no longer kept in its place by the roots, into the
valleys, sweeping it away in its rush. In the month of May,
during our stay at Luang-Praban, the fields were only prepared for planting, and looked, from a distance, like scars
on the hill-sides, or like stains on the green robe which
covered them. The obstacles which nature offers to the toil
of man have always the result of developing his energy and
activity. Though the labourer has to water the ground with
his sweat to make it fertile, he not only secures a living by
doing so, but has, without his knowing it, and, as it were, into
the bargain, acquired manly qualities, which make it impossible for him to remain long a slave. Agriculture exacts
more labour in the mountains of Luang-Praban than in the

fertile plains of Lower Laos; and the people, though they
have not reached that insolent rudeness we soon after found
among the tributaries of Burmah, have no longer the stolid
features and the indolent ways of the people of Ubone and
Bassac.

In the capital a wonderful animation prevailed every
morning in the market. I liked to go through the close
crowd, to look at the singular eatables piled on the tables;
but especially to watch the buyers and sellers. On the two
sides of the street, under the shelter of the low houses, the
sellers, of both sexes, crouched on mats or on large leaves
of banana, waited for their customers without importuning
with wearisome invitations, as is the case in our provincial
markets in Europe. The housewives go about in peace;
there are no cries or disputes; the whole goes on gravely,
almost in silence. Everything may be found that is needed
for living—that is, for Laotian living—in its modest sense.
I have not to do here with the names of the different delicacies which tempt the curiosity of the passers-by, or
solicit their appetites; I omit, purposely, the ragouts, all
ready; the savoury drinks, consumed on the spot; for a
smell rises from one and all that won't let me think of
stopping. The Burmese offer the public English stuffs,
cotton checks, printed calicoes, woollen fabrics, buttons, and
needles; the inhabitants of the kingdom of Xieng-Maï bring
lacker boxes, gargoulettes, and parasols; and natives sell fish,
buffalo-meat and pork—often that of beasts which have died
of disease—rice, salt, Chinese nettles, silk, and cotton. There
are, besides, tobacco-shops, where you find cigarettes and
pipes of different models. All the world smokes, men,
women, and children. The children, indeed, while still at
the breast, draw puffs of smoke through the pipe-shanks,
mixing it in some sort in their mouth with their mother's
milk. However, these appearances of a commercial life
must not be allowed to deceive one, and the traveller,
anxious to see such, must guard against first impressions.
There is hardly anything at Luang-Praban but a retail
trade, and this has itself already suffered considerably from
the revolt of Yunan, which has made intercourse with the
Celestial Empire impossible.

It will, perhaps, be remembered that at Stung-Treng, our first station in Laos, we received from the natives, in exchange for the Siamese tikal, so many little bars of iron, varying commonly from seven to ten to a tikal. On leaving Bassac the bar of iron was exchanged for one of copper, lighter and more convenient; at Phon-Pissaï, copper money entirely disappeared. We found the only money current at Luang-Praban was in the shape of little white shells, strung together like the sapecks of Cochin-China. Twenty-five of these strings are worth a tikal. This piece of silver, which reigned alone with its subdivisions in all Lower Laos, finds a redoubtable rival in the market at Luang-Praban, in the English rupee, which has a fictitious value equal to that of a tikal, although the latter shows an intrinsic difference in its favour of about 93c. This anomaly comes, no doubt, from the frequent and direct intercourse of the Burman traders with this country, and would probably cease with the first experiment of speculation in exchange. As to the Mexican dollars, of which we had brought a number, it was very difficult to know how to value them. The exchanges in the market—for there are exchange offices—persisted in refusing them, and we had to find out a good-natured person, who wished them as curiosities, before we could get rid of them. Several great people bought them to hang from their children's necks, who then found themselves dressed in this piece of money, and a kind of silver heart hung by a string tied round their loins, and serving the same end to modesty as the vine-leaves do in Europe. A tax-gatherer passes through at the close of the market, and levies so many shells from each booth as the king's right; for in Laos there is no difference between the king, the state, the town, and public and private property. Yet, however great the power of the sovereign may be, established usages impose bounds on it, and it meets a kind of control in the assembly of the chief functionaries who form the royal council—known by the native name of *Séna*. These functionaries being nominated by the king, and being very proud of the honour, can exercise only a delusive check; but after having passed through a country which the sun might make so rich, and despotism has made so poor, one clings to these shadows of guardian institutions, and offers ardent prayers that the phantoms may take a body, and drag the land at last from the rut in which it will otherwise perish. The second king, who, at Luang-Praban, as at Bangkok, sits below the first, has only a title, with no real power. It was he who had gone to be present at the funeral ceremonies of the second king of Siam. The first king did not deign to trouble himself about the ceremony, at which all the governors of the Siamese provinces had received orders to be present, to add to the splendour. He contents himself with sending his annual tribute, and will not allow the interference of the agents of Bangkok in the affairs of his kingdom in any way. His predecessors had been in the habit of sending gifts to the *Son of Heaven* as well; but he profited by the revolt of Yunan to put an end to the practice, which was simply a voluntary homage, though it had, no doubt, at one time been a tribute. The ambassadors who go from Luang-Praban to Pekin take not less than three years to make the whole journey.

There is reason to believe that this vassalage of the king to Bangkok would very soon change to total independence, if his own interest did not prompt him to keep on good terms with a sovereign who, if necessary, might be a powerful ally. The boundaries of the kingdom of Luang-Praban are, on the south, the district of Sien-Kan; on the west, the important Siamese province of Muong-Nan; from west to north-east, a number of principalities tributary to Burmah or to China, now one, now the other; on the north-east, Yunan; and from north-east to south-east, Tonkin.

On the side of Tonkin, there have been frequent disputes respecting the frontiers between the emperor of Annam and the king of Luang-Praban. Some Siamese soldiers were still in the capital, left behind from the small army which had come, a few years before, to aid the king to take possession of the countries bounded by Tonkin, which were laid claim to by the Annamites. From these ambitious rivalries, which spring from near neighbourhood, there is constant hostility between the Laotians and the Tonkinese. The route of commerce, which formerly united the two peoples, is nowadays wholly deserted by traders, and travelled only by soldiers. On both sides, they slaughter each other with equal remorselessness, so that a barrier of heads cut off rises each day higher between these unhappy populations, condemned to the scourge of unceasing war. Victory in the last campaign remained with the king of Luang-Praban; but it may desert his flag, and the two sides may know, in turn, the barbarous joys of triumph, and the horrors of defeat; and thus hatred will only become more intense, and reconciliation more impossible. It is, therefore, to be hoped that some new influence may bring a remedy for a state of things that remains without result, imposing peace on the princes, and healing the wounds of the peoples. If I were asked whence this help could come, I would repeat what I have already said of Cambodgia in the beginning of this book. The part which France has played, under the guidance of an intelligent and far-seeing governor, in the extremity of the valley of the Mekong, is not without some analogy to what seems reserved, at the twentieth degree of north latitude, to the successors of Admiral de La Grandière. In the delta of the great river we cleverly interposed between the Siamese and the Annamites, under cover of the Cambodgians; and they are the same enemies we find face to face as far up as Tonkin. 'The kingdom of Luang-Praban has, no doubt, more life than that' of Cambodgia, but it is not less excited and sustained by the Siamese in all its enterprises against the empire of Annam—that old enemy of the court of Bangkok. I know well that we are not established at Tonkin as we are in Lower Cochin-China; I am, moreover, far from being convinced that it would be a real advantage to us to take immediate possession of the direct government of this country; but it is necessary that the emperor Tu Duc should consent to tolerate our presence in it, to protect attempts at any agricultural, industrial, or commercial establishments which may be made by our compatriots. When the voice of the governor of Cochin-China plays a greater part in the councils of Hué, it will not be long before it makes itself heard also at Luang-Praban. If, as there is some reason to believe, there are some unsubdued tribes of savages, who have revolted from vassalage, and are exasperated by hideous outrages, their misfortunes perpetuating their barbarism—in the region occupied by those of their race who

M

have submitted to one or other of the neighbouring nations, they will never be an insurmountable obstacle to the revival of intercourse. When these men are no longer tracked like wild beasts, and sold in the markets, they will at once cease to be ferocious.

The port of Bangkok may be considered the one outlet, at this time, of the commerce of these countries. This commerce, as we have seen, is yet in its infancy, vegetating in the thick political atmosphere which surrounds it; but it will grow under a new régime, which will guarantee liberty and security—the two conditions everywhere essential to the development of public wealth. The town of Luang-Praban is not more than seventy leagues from the gulf of Tonkin; and thus it is rather on that side than to the capital of the kingdom of Siam, which is still farther off, that the rude labourers of these mountains seem designed by nature to export their produce, and to receive the imports which industrial Europe could send them. We shall not have long to wait for more full enlightenment on this question, and those connected with it. A short time after the return of the expedition commanded by M. de Lagrée, two energetic and enterprising officers—MM. d'Arfeuille and Reyna d reascended the Mekong to Luang-Praban, to cross from that town by land to the town of Hué, and thus pass obliquely through the Indo-Chinese peninsula. If this perilous journey be successful, it cannot fail to be richer in results, as regards our Annamite colony, than even the expedition in which I was called to take a part, which had a more general aim.[1] I shall soon have to cross and describe the Chinese province of Yunan, by which the great empire touches Tonkin. I shall sail on the river, which falls into the sea near the capital of the latter kingdom, and will then be led, in the course of my narrative, to state more fully the end which France should seek to attain in that country; but before reaching the fair plain of Yuen-kiang, where the Sonkoï flows with brimming banks, what mountains must we yet pass, what struggles must we have with the ill-will of the natives, to what miseries must we submit, what sufferings endure!

[1] Less fortunate than we, these two explorers were forced to return to Saïgon after some months.

The rainy season had begun; and at that time, when even the Laotians almost entirely give up travelling, fate required that we should set off to penetrate a region which the rudeness of nature, and that of man, make specially inhospitable. The rebels of Cambodgia, who, shortly after our starting, had pursued, but failed to overtake, us, had, without knowing it, prepared trials for us, the sight of which would, without doubt, have glutted their hatred and vengeance. By hindering the post, which had started from Saïgon to catch us, from coming by the direct way of the river, they had forced M. de Lagrée to send after it, and to wait for it. The fine weather had passed away in these wretched delays, and our task, no less than our funds, so much reduced already, made the delay most hurtful.

Our regular life, and the discipline of the men of our escort, had excited the esteem of the king of Luang-Praban, and conciliated his good-will. Yet he did not hide the feeling, but owned it openly to M. de Lagrée, that though he liked to have us with him, our farther progress was very disagreeable. According to information that reached him, the gravity of which he purposely exaggerated, rivers of blood flowed on his frontiers. He said he was at war with his neighbours, little independent sovereigns, who were tearing each other in pieces. As commonly happens in times of political confusion, brigandage had been organised on a great scale, and bands of savages, of Chinese, of Laotians, and of Burmese, plundered all travellers alike impartially who were rash enough to pass through these parts. In such a state of affairs, the king hesitated to provide us with means of transport, in some measure to escape from the responsibility of an affair, which he thought would turn out very badly for us; but much more from fear of seeing his horses, boats, men, and, especially, his elephants, fall into the hands of his enemies. On the other hand, we learned from reports gathered by our interpreter, that the emperor of China had begged the king of Luang-Praban not to let any Europeans pass, who might be trying to reach China by the valley of the Mekong. This appeared quite in keeping with the well-known habits of Chinese diplomacy. If we succeeded in setting foot on Chinese territory, the government would become responsible for the conduct of its functionaries towards the foreign mandarins, who came furnished with regular passports issued by itself. It would, therefore, have been a clever stroke, if not very honourable, to get a prince long tributary to the great empire, and still under the shadow of its venerable prestige, to consent to detain us in his state. It was possible that the king, playing a double game, would dissimulate as to the real motives for opposing our starting; but it was also no less possible that his fears had a very serious foundation. Our hut, open to all comers, was the rendezvous of the quidnuncs and the idlers; the mandarins and the bonzes were a great deal with our chief, and all agreed in drawing a terrible picture of the neighbouring countries. We had to appear very resolved, while all the time trying to find out the truth amidst the haze of exaggeration—an ungrateful task, which left us commonly in cruel perplexity.

M. de Lagrée devoted himself to it with an admirable perseverance. His days were entirely filled with minute interrogatories, in which he showed, at once, the patience of a savant pursuing a difficult problem, and the sagacity of an examining magistrate. Up to Luang-Praban his laborious inquiries had had for their end, almost exclusively, the collection of all kinds of information likely to help our labours, but from that point they bore directly on the very success of our enterprise. Henceforth he sought not only to obtain precise facts as to the geographical position of places we were not able to visit, or to recover some half-forgotten recollections from the treacherous memory of old men and bonzes; but rather to learn, if it would be possible for us to get to China, or whether we should need to go back. Dreading the enthusiasm, which leaves the resources of the mind unmanned and dissipated when it passes off, M. de Lagrée was readier to communicate his fears and doubts, than his hopes, to us. He retained, besides, from his military habits, the liking for command, and formed his resolutions as the result of solitary thought; so that if his companions sometimes had reason to regret his silence at critical moments, it no less becomes them to acknowledge that all the honour of success is due to him alone, since he would have had to bear all the weight of failure.

As it was impossible to trust to the information he collected at Luang-Praban, M. de Lagrée determined to go on to the scene of the events itself. The difficulties in our way which had been intimated determined us to reduce our baggage as much as possible. We intrusted some arms, some ammunition, and a quantity of clothing, to the keeping of the king. This step secured us resources, in case we were forced to beat a retreat, and leave our stores behind us, and at the same time lightened our little column; which was a great matter in a country where the means of transport were so limited and expensive. We resolved to distribute among the crowd whatever seemed not absolutely indispensable; and no sooner was this known than we were fairly invaded. The greatest personages contended for the leavings of our wardrobe; even the women became bold, and offered anything for a white chemise; and nothing remained for us, in the end, but to throw our handkerchiefs to the best-looking. They made the most sinister predictions, and pressed us to come back again at the first attempt of the brigands to cut our throats, for it was certain that the attempt would be made. These sympathetic manifestations were sincere, for we had become popular by the simple process of paying our debts in the market, showing ourselves in the pagodas, and respecting the laws, the faith, and the prejudices of the people. This is the whole secret of winning over savages, and European travellers could not keep it too well in mind. They may feel sadness and pity in coming in contact with infant races, but should never show contempt. It rests with them to open and make easy the way for those who follow them, or to multiply their difficulties a hundredfold. Let them, then, reject the suggestions of a pride, which their bearing does not always justify.

CHAPTER V.

ENTRY INTO THE BURMAN TERRITORY. BAD FEELING OF THE
AUTHORITIES. THE RAINY SEASON. MUONG-LINE. SIEN-TONG.
MUONG YOU AND SIEN-HONG. FRONTIER OF CHINA.

THE town of Luang-Praban had been to us what an oasis is
to a caravan wearied by a long march. We had stayed there
a month, in the midst of comparative abundance. To pass
the night under one roof, and to sit twice a day at the same
table, were pleasures which we had enjoyed there for the
first time since leaving Bassac. A wandering life is contrary
to man's nature, which attaches itself to places by a thousand
invisible ties, as the tree binds itself to the soil by its roots.
Even the races who live under tents pitched each night, to
be struck in the morning, make a native country of the desert,
whose every spring they know, or of the forest, every old
tree of which they reverence. To march on steadily, to know
that you will never see the ground you are treading again,
or the men with whom you exchange friendly words, is to
turn Wandering Jew, and causes an insurmountable sadness,
making you think, without the power of helping it, of that
immortal type of the unfortunate and accursed. We had, it
is true, the hope of aiding Science, and adding by our researches to the facts with which she works, and this ambition acted on us, without doubt, like that which urged the
knight from his castle to redress wrongs, or to follow the
track of amorous dreams ; but we had in our hearts, beyond
all things else, an image bright as the star of the Kings—the
image of France, to which each step was now, henceforth, to
bring us nearer. The idea of dying far from her, and of lying
in a lonely grave—a sad thought, which thrust itself on me at

the beginning of the journey—had ceased to cross my mind; the past guaranteed the future. We were, besides, leaving the boundaries of Laos, of evil name, and that calumniated Minotaur had devoured nobody. The objections of the king of Luang-Praban to our departure might, without doubt, have their source in some political motive; but the sympathetic manifestations of the people were so pure, and so free from all suspicion of that sort, that it was impossible for the most distrustful to see anything in them but the signs of an anxiety rising from sincere interest in us. We were moved with it, without being intimidated; and on the 25th May 1867 went on board our canoes, full of ardour and confidence, and almost glad at the sacrifices which reduced the personal baggage of each of us to one package. The Commandant de Lagrée, alone, was engrossed by his reflections, seeing a sombre cloud on the horizon, and feeling that he was the Œdipus whose words would decide the fate of all his companions.

The Mekong, which slackens its speed, and spreads itself out before Luang-Praban in a bed free from any obstructions, resumes its headlong course and its troubled look not far from the town. A colossal statue of Bouddha, seated at the mouth of a cavern, seems to gaze impassively at the gliding waves, the image of the life whose constant changes saddened the great teacher, and drove him to place eternal happiness in eternal stability. The cavern is transformed into a pagoda; but the bonzes have had the bad taste to scrape the stalactites which adorn the arch and the walls. Farther on, in the bosom of a vast perpendicular rock, which plunges into the water, a second grotto is also consecrated to worship. It is adorned by a notched balcony, reached by a brick staircase, the lower steps of which are washed by the water. Opposite this picturesque temple, the gate of which looks, at a distance, like a rent in the rock, the Mekong receives a considerable affluent on its left bank. The Nam-Hou, before losing itself in the great river, runs through a vast verdant prairie, bounded by a vertical wall of at least three hundred metres, which seems as if it had been cut out. To show the height of an extraordinary rise of the waters, the inhabitants had drawn a red line, which was nineteen

metres over our heads. We looked at this river, which seems
to come from the north-east. with some curiosity; for M. de
Lagrée had resolved to get into China by this stream, if he
did not succeed in doing so by the Mekong.

We were told that there was a mountain, which vomited
fire, to use the words of the natives, at a short distance from
the village of Tanoun. We had already met extinct vol-
canoes, notably in the basin of the Se-Hon, on our way to
Attopée; but it was the first time that we had been told of
a crater in activity, and it was a fact of too much importance
not to take steps to examine its correctness. While the other
members of the commission continued their voyage in the
canoes, Dr. Joubert and I set off on foot, with guides, and
struck towards the south-east. After a walk of about thirty
kilometres, along the side of mountains or through the gorges
of mountain streams, we saw, from the top of Pou-Din-Deng
(the Mountain of Red Earth), a large village surrounded by
vast rice-grounds, and standing in the middle of an immense
plain, like the basin of an ancient lake. It is the village of
Muong-Luoc. We were near the source of one of the arms,
into which the Meïnam separates at its rise. The Mekong,
forming a new bend to the east above Luang-Praban, comes
very close to this river, from which it is only about eight
leagues off; but there is no communication between them.
It has been thought that, farther down, these two streams,
disappearing, in some sense, amidst the inundation which
covered the country, mingled their waters during the rainy
season. It is a very natural exaggeration in the lower parts
of their course; but at the height where we were in this
mountainous region, the two basins, clearly defined, remain
absolutely distinct. The opinion expressed by Martini, and
more recently reproduced by Vincendon Desmoulin, that the
two rivers unite in Laos, must be finally abandoned.

The head man of Muong-Luoc showed himself very
friendly and hearty, and had gathered to his house all the
high society of Muong, to see two curious creatures with
long beards and pale faces. As to himself, he already knew
some specimens of this singular race; for he had been to
Bangkok, where he had met European women, with their
hair tied up behind the head, and long, standing-out dresses,

the ⟨ ⟩ry recollection of which made him, even yet, almost
die w th laughter. He had among his concubines a young
sava⟨ ⟩ of a very light colour, with a burning black eye,
whic⟨ ⟩ would have seemed in its right place in an Andalu-
sian ⟨ ⟩sada rather than in a Laotian hut. The conversation ⟨ ⟩is very animated, though there was no interpreter,
and ⟨ ⟩ filled with blunders and all kinds of cock-and-bull
nons⟨ ⟩se. Tigers being very numerous in this region, the
gove⟨ ⟩or wanted to give us an escort, of ten men, to take us
to th⟨ ⟩ volcano, and pushed his prudence so far as to cause
our h⟨ ⟩, which stood a little out of the village, to be sur-
round⟨ ⟩l, through the night, by an army of watchmen, who
smoke⟨ ⟩ and chatted till morning, and chased away sleep
much ⟨ ⟩ore surely than the fear of the most terrible flesh-
eater ⟨ ⟩uld have done.

We sought in vain for the streams of lava, the canopy of
smoke, and all the features of desolation, which the word
volcano raises in the mind. We saw nothing but a depression of the ground on the top of a low wooded hill. The
earth i⟨ ⟩ chapped, and has given way, as if the fire were consuming it within. Vapours rose in the air through numerous
crevices, exhaling a smell of sulphur and of pit-coal. At
some places yellow flakes of sulphur, crystallised, covered the
soil. By day no flames could be seen; but I can suppose
that they appear at night, as happens at Vesuvius, which,
even when not in eruption, shows its flaming summit in the
splendour of the Neapolitan nights. The subterranean fire
spreads little by little, and burns the roots of the great trees,
whose skeletons mark its progress. The two hills where
these solfaterras are found are near each other, and are called
Pou-faï-gnaï and Pou-faï-noï — the Great and Little Fire
Mount in.

Having noticed a great many elephants in the plain of
M'uong Luoc, we asked the governor for the loan of two, to
take u⟨ ⟩ back to the Mekong; but the Laotian very kindly
wished to keep us by him, and persisted in not acknowledg-
ing our reasons for hastening our return. Putting any value
on time is an infirmity these people cannot understand. 'I
hardly like to give you elephants,' said he, joking; 'they go
so slowly that they will weary you, and you will leave them

behind, and run like hares. Is there something in your legs
that makes you able to do it?' He ended, however, by ac-
ceding to our wish; and seated on the backs of our huge
beasts, our heads brushing through leaves of trees dripping
with rain, we took eleven hours, by paths in which two men
could not walk abreast, to cross the chain of mountains which
separates the infant Meïnam from the Mekong, already a
grand and powerful stream.

At Tauoun we took to the canoes again, to rejoin the
expedition. The inhabitants of the village of Paegnio, where
we had to pass the night, surrounded us in their curiosity,
and overwhelmed us with questions about the 'mountains of
fire.' They are three days off, and are thus a perfect mystery,
for no one has taken the trouble to visit them. The kind of
aureola which the imaginary flames of the volcano set on
our brows, and the generosity with which we let the housewives cut the mother-o'-pearl buttons from our clothes, got
us an excellent reception in the village. Though they had
a caravanserai for travellers, they allowed us to spread our
mats in a wooden pagoda, a kind of public-house room closed
in, such as we had not occupied till then. In truth, the *salas*
where we commonly lodged, and even the huts built expressly for us, were always made of a trellis of bamboo, which
often intercepted the light of day, but hardly kept out either
the wind or the rain. A little gilt statue of Bouddha, up-
right and stiff like our saints of the middle ages, shone in
the gloom; and I slept that night, to dream of the wonderful
fortune of Siddârtha, the young prince who, for having preferred the austere life of an ascetic to the seductions of
power, attained the rank of Bouddha, and receives still, after
twenty-five centuries, the worship of a fourth part of the
human race.

M. de Lagrée had stopped at Sien-Khong, a large village,
from which war had driven away the inhabitants, who were
just beginning to come back, to gather behind a vast enclosure of brick. It is a chief place of the district, depending
on Muong-Nan, and the last important centre of Lao on the
right bank of the Mekong, where the authority of Siam is
still acknowledged. The kingdom of Xieng-Maï, a vassal of
Bangkok, almost touches the river by its province of Xieng-

Plate 14 *View of the Nam Kan or the river of Luang Prabang (Drawing by E. Tournois, based on a sketch by L. Delaporte)*

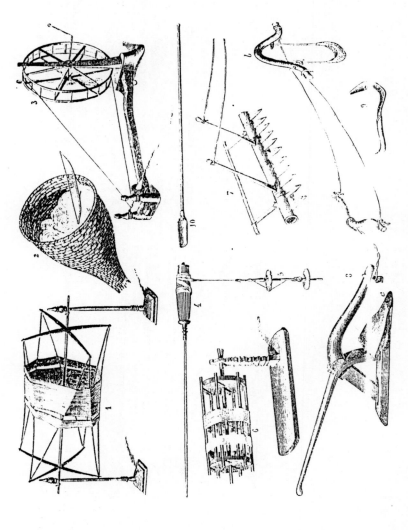

Plate 15 *Utensils used in agriculture and textile production in Laos (Drawings by B. Bonnafoux, based on sketches by L. Delaporte). 1. A reel for spinning cotton; 2. A basket and an arc serving for carding cotton; 3. Spinning wheel; 4 & 5. Distaff and spindle for hemp; 6. A reel for spinning silk; 7. A harrow (1.30 meter in length); 8. A wooden plough (1.80 meter in length), c: iron blade, b: line and yoke for a buffalo; 9. A sickle (20 centimeters in length); 10. A hoe.*

Haï, but it possesses only one town, recently destroyed, on the banks of the Mekong, Xieng-Sen, whose ruins, which have no interest for travellers, are already buried in the rank vegetation.

We had reached the frontier of Burmese Laos, as might easily be seen in the scared looks of the Siamese functionaries, who trembled lest they should be carried off by their neighbour, the Laotian king of Sien-Tong, the implacable enemy of their master. The time had now come for our hiding our letters from Siam; but we should have been able to show passports from the Burmese government. When Admiral de La Grandière applied to the emperor of Burmah for these papers through the Catholic bishop, for France has no official representative at Ava, the empire was passing through a crisis, which ended in one of those revolutions of the palace so common in these countries, and it had for the moment paralysed all the influence of the missionaries. Deprived of those safe-conducts, which make the mandarins responsible for any hurt that may befall strangers in their respective districts, we had everything to fear from the Laotians tributary to Burmah, if the Burmese, along with their yoke, had succeeded in transferring to them their hatreds. Every one knows the result of the strife between the East India Company and the Burmese sovereigns. That long war, the origin of which I shall presently state, gave Tennaserim, Pegou, and the Aracan country to England, thus taking from the Burmese the possession of the lower course of the Irawady, and at the same time shutting them out from all access to the Bay of Bengal and the Indian Ocean.

Neighbours so turbulent and ambitious as the Burmese could not be long in furnishing the English with one of those complaints which serve too often as a pretext for a rupture, and enable it to punish the most insignificant violation of international law by the annexation of a territory. They went farther, and by a series of deliberate provocations rendered inevitable a war, in which they may be said to have taken the initiative. Full of confidence in his army, and, like all Orientals, of contempt for foreigners, who had given ground for suspecting their good faith ever since the war which Alom-prah the Great waged against the Pegouans,

the son of that monarch bore with impatience the sight of
the extension of the British empire in India.   Up to the close
of the eighteenth century the king of Siam, whose dominions
extended to the peninsula of Malacca, had been the enemy,
always beaten and always hated, against whom the Burmese
had vented their warlike passions and thirst of conquest;
but after the cession of Tennaserim, Minder-Aghee-prah
turned his thoughts to the west, and endeavoured an alliance
with the Mahrattas, to ruin the edifice raised on his frontiers
by those Europeans, whom his victorious father had treated
with as much insolence as cruelty.   Lord Hastings, then
governor-general of India, shut his eyes on this complicity,
the proofs of which thrust themselves on him; and the emperor of Burmah, emboldened by an act of prudence which he
took for weakness, determined to place a claimant hostile to
England, on the throne of Katchar, a principality bordering
on Assam.   This daring intervention took place in 1824; and
before the close of that year, it was punished by the occupation of Tavoy, Mergui, Martaban, and Rangoon.   The loss of
all his ports was not compensated by the defeat inflicted on
the English at Tchittagong, by the general-in-chief Bandoola,
who was soon after recalled from the frontier, to defend the
very capital of his country, and perished by the bursting of
a shell.   The Burmese troops, utterly defeated at Sillhet, driven from Assam and from Aracan, were forced, at the close
of the year 1825, in spite of their courage, to demand a truce
from Sir Archibald Campbell, who had almost reached Patu-
nagah in his ascent of the Irawady.   The convention signed
in January 1826, by the plenipotentiaries of the two countries, was not ratified by the emperor of the Burmese, on
whose pride the conquerors wished to impose hard and
humiliating conditions, which were not finally accepted
till after two more battles, in which the superiority of European arms triumphed over the undisciplined heroism of the
Burmese.   The treaty of Yandabo laid the foundations of the
English power in Burmah, and it has since developed itself,
till the Burman empire is, to-day, surrounded by a vast circle
of conquered territories, extending from Moulmein, in the
Gulf of Martaban, to Sodiva on the Brahmapoutra, at the
point where that great river, leaving Thibet, bends sharply

to the west, and throws itself at a right angle into the Bay of Bengal.

Patriotism has survived the conquest, and hatred has become only the keener for its impotence. It is driven back to the heart of the conquered, as their nationality itself has been concentrated by the force of arms round the cradle of its ancient greatness. Realising, too late, that they were unable, from their own resources, to expel the English, they have tried to oppose them successfully by the help of Europeans; but the attempts have been vain, and none of them have remained unavenged. France has had nothing to do with them, though Frenchmen may have taken part in them. We had a hope that the memory of D'Orgoni, the last and most famous of those of our countrymen who put their intelligence and courage at the disposal of the Burmese emperor, would have aided our passage through the vassals of that sovereign; but, on the other hand, was there not reason to fear that princes distant more than a month's march from Ava might be unable to see any difference between the various European nationalities, and be ready to treat us as enemies? We were reduced to conjectures on this point, and did not even know the nature of the political rule imposed on the Laotian populations by the Burmese government. The mandarin chief of the village of Sien-Kong, where the most cruel uncertainty prolonged our stay, consented, at last, not without difficulty, to conduct us to the limits of his territory; but would the king of Sien-Kong, his neighbour, let us go farther? M. de Lagrée had sent him magnificent presents, and a letter in the Oriental style, with as many words, and as little in them as possible. If he were absolute master, he would, probably, refuse to let us pass; but if he were dependent on Ava, perhaps he would fear to compromise himself. But it would take forty days to get instructions from the capital, and we should be with him when he received our letter. We had to supply the want of exact information by guesses of this kind.

At a little distance from Sien-Kong the mountains retreat from the river, which winds along through a magnificent plain, in the centre of which the town of Xieng-Sen has been built within the last fifty years. We were sailing in

the waters of the kingdom of Xieng-Maï, a tributary of Siam,
like that of Luang-Praban, but we avoided any landing. The
disputes to which the use of teak-wood, by the English, had
given rise, might have caused some ill-feeling in the authori-
ties towards Europeans, and M. de Lagrée thought it inexpedient to expose himself to the risk. Besides, he had promised the king of Luang-Praban, who was on very friendly
terms with his neighbour of Xieng-Maï, that he would not
set foot on his territory. The valuable tree, the durabil-
ity of the wood of which, according to M. Reinaud,[1] was
already known and appreciated in the time of the Romans,
is found for the first time, in any abundance, on the banks of
the river at Sien-Kong, our last station; but it is stunted
there, and badly cared for by the inhabitants. In the plain
of Xieng-Sen, on the contrary, it formed magnificent forests
on both sides of the Mekong, which here ends its second
bend to the west, turning now directly north. From the
enormous quantity of water which this great river already
pours along, we could see that the sources must still be very
distant. It looked very probable that, like the great rivers
of China and India, it took its rise somewhere in the table-
land of Thibet—that immense reservoir, which sends, so to
speak, the colossal tribute of its waters into three different
oceans. If it flowed out of a lake, as the *savants* of the country told us in Cambodgia, that lake must be beyond Yunan,
or, perhaps, it contributed only an affluent of secondary importance to the river. This last hypothesis, as we shall see
farther on, is correct. We amused ourselves with these conjectures, now, when we were about finally to abandon the
route of the Mekong, which had become impracticable, and
prepare for the painful marches and all the miseries of a
land-journey in the depth of the rainy season.

We installed ourselves in a caravanserai on the banks,
and sent back our canoes. It was burning our boats; for to
reach even Muong-Line, the nearest of all the villages dependent on Sien-Tong, means of transport were needed, and

[1] Dr. Sprenger, who has lived long in India, having some years since
visited the palace of Chosroes at Ctesiphon, found that the wood-work
was of teak. (*Relations politiques et commerciales de l'Empire Romain, avec
l'Asie Orientale,* par M. Reinaud, de l'Institut, p. 171, note.)

we did not yet know if it would be possible for us to procure
them. We did not even know whether the mandarin of the
Muong-Line would not give his soldiers orders to expel us, as
soon as he heard of our arrival in his district. M. de Lagrée
hastened to send him a message, demanding authority to
wait with him till his superior, the king of Sien-Tong, had
answered our letter. We were, in truth, very much in danger of dying of hunger in our bamboo hut, built between the
stream and the forest. Hunting was hardly any easier than
fishing, for the rain fell in torrents. At last, after two days'
anxious waiting, a strange noise was heard from the woods,
and each of us pricked up his ears, and sought to pierce
the gloom of the trees. The first ox that emerged from the
path, with a double seat on its hump, was received with
transports of joy; it was, to us, what the dove and his branch
of olive had been to Noah. The chief of Muong-Line had
sent us sixteen pack-oxen. We put our baggage on their
backs without a moment's delay, and set out in such a down-
fall of rain as raised the level of the river perceptibly in two
hours. Our caravan presented a picturesque sight in the
narrow path in the forest. The little humped oxen followed
each other, obeying their own whims much more than the
voice of their drivers. Subaltern mandarins escorted us, with
a long musket on their shoulders, their heads covered with
broad-brimmed hats of banana fibre, ending in a point. Their
bronze colour, their moustaches, and their determined air,
reminded us of Calabrian brigands. All went well so long
as the road, winding through the plain, led us along the river,
under the great trees; but our difficulties began when we
reached a steep hill, which it was necessary to cross.

The rain had effaced all trace of path on the side of the
mountain, and the soil was so slippery, that we could only
advance by catching hold of the bare roots of the trees, the
creepers, and hanging branches. As for the oxen, they fell
at each step, rolling one over the other; and, though they
made the greatest exertions, some of them, after continued
efforts, were obliged to give up the attempt, the men divid-
ing their burden amongst themselves. The remainder of the
way was in keeping with the commencement. After having
followed the ridge of the mountains, marching several hours

in a torrent of rain, in the midst of a splendid vegetation of palm-trees, sicas, and tree-ferns, we at last reached the borders of the river of Muong-Line, which we crossed at a ford, the water reaching up to our shoulders. Some huts, one of which had been prepared for us, were presently seen in a grassy plain, surrounded by mountains. It was four o'clock in the afternoon; we had been walking, with difficulty, since the morning, under a veritable deluge, and the oxen which carried our provision of rice were behind, so that we had to wait wearily for them; and nearly all of us caught a touch of fever.

Such was our first stage in Burman Laos. The houses differed from those of Siamese Laos, by being raised higher above the ground, and by the length of roof, which descends in such a fashion as completely to hide the house. The one we inhabited resembled a stack of straw on trestles. Underneath, the pigs sleep at their ease, and the oxen find a commodious shelter. These last wander amid the fat pasturages in large herds, but notwithstanding their great abundance, we could not succeed in procuring one. A more substantial food than boiled rice and consumptive fowls was, however, necessary; but M. de Lagrée, finding his funds much reduced already, thought, with reason, that it would be imprudent to throw away sixty francs—the relatively exorbitant price asked for an ox—at a time, on food. The asking a price so much beyond us, for these precious animals, is explained by the value of the services they render the natives. The river ceasing to be of use, the transport by land becomes ruinous, even for short distances; but when the journey has to be somewhat long, and there are any risk to run, as nearly always occur in these perpetually troubled regions, the proprietors of oxen raise their prices still higher. We were obliged to submit to them; for we were not authorised to demand, as in Siamese Laos, the coöperation of the mandarins, who raise, or lower, the price of transport according to their interests or their caprices.

The village of Muong-Line occupies the centre of a plain, of many miles in circumference, which the rain speedily converts into an immense swamp. We missed the river: we were accustomed to see it animate our encampments, and, in

whose course we often ascended in thought, seeking to solve
the mystery of its source, and whose rapid waters, which,
before losing themselves in the sea, would bathe and fertilise
a land, now French, we often watched as they glided past.
Notwithstanding the small number of its inhabitants, the
village has a daily market.   It was at Luang-Praban, for
the first time since leaving Cambodgia, that we came across
this periodical or permanent public sale of the necessaries of
life; a notable institution, of which it is necessary to be deprived, in order to appreciate the value.   The market of
Muong-Line was not of great importance.   Vegetables and
fruit were sold in it, and some peaches, which, though small
and green, we found delicious, when eaten with eyes shut,
and hearts thinking of France.   They also sold cotton stuffs
of all sorts, of English manufacture.

These last articles are intended expressly for the country,
Burman characters and designs being woven into the cloth.
The most important house in the market is that of the black-
smith, who is at the same time goldsmith, and manufacturer
of money.   These three professions, exercised by the same
mechanic, very closely resemble each other in this country,
where coined money does not circulate.   The tikal, and its
subdivisions, ceasing to have the current price, we were compelled to have our Siamese silver melted in a crucible, which
gives it the form of a macaroon.   For daily transactions of
small importance they cut off at hazard pieces of unequal
value, which are appraised, at a glance, by the interested
parties.   They make use of scales in more serious transactions; for, in default of a uniform money, the standard of
value is fixed by weight in silver.

When one passes from Cambodgia to Siamese Laos, the
transition is scarcely perceptible, and this the rather, that, for
the men at least, the costume remains the same.   Here it is
quite otherwise; the change is sudden, and the contrast
striking.   The Siamese tuft of hair is replaced by a chignon,
which gathers the whole of the hair on the top of the head,
a turban, of various colours, leaving only the tip of it visible.
The langouti also gives way to wide trousers, which reach
the ankle.   Smoking, even by children, is still more general
amongst these tributaries of Burmah.

N

The women, more sensitive to the cold, or more modest, wear a tight vest, crossing over the chest, of blue or white cotton, sometimes of silk, dyed in different and very rich colours. Besides this, they wear a petticoat, in horizontal stripes of blue, yellow, and red. Their head-dress is composed of stuffs of all shades, rolled as a turban round the hair, or arranged after the fashion of the Neapolitan peasants, and kept in its place by silver pins, the large heads of which, with bracelets of the same metal, constitute the principal ornaments of a Siamese belle. To these details of costume I would add a general remark on the language, which is the clothing of thought. We are still in Laos, and they always speak Laotian; but this language is employed with modifications, which affect, especially, the pronunciation of the words and the construction of sentences. There are, as yet, but a small number of new expressions. The shades of difference, which do not appear to alter the foundation of the language, upset the slight knowledge we have acquired by superficial study, but do not embarrass our interpreter, who maintains long conversations in a new dialect, M. de Lagrée, since our starting, having forced him to carry them on with the natives, in order to obtain from them useful information. But it was no longer thus with the savages, whose number and importance increased at each of our stations till our entry into China. They speak a language absolutely unintelligible to him, and live grouped in tribes amongst the mountains, where their villages present a peculiar appearance. Like the Laotians, the greater number have adopted Bouddhism, with a strong mixture of superstition; but while the former erect pagodas, the others have no temples, and practise no outward worship. They have not the timid air of the other aborigines scattered through the valley of the Mekong; they carry their heads high in the midst of the Laos-Lus;[2] and it is because they like it, and not because

[2] The inhabitants of the northern part of Laos have many different names; they are called indifferently Lus, Thaï, or Shans. In certain parts of this vast region they give themselves other appellations, as will be seen, for example, at Sien-Tong. By the side of these the savages are grouped in tribes, which in the same way bear different names. Are their names of as little importance as those of the Laos-Lus, or can ethno-

they are forced, that they live on the hills. They appear to consent to give up their land rather than yield to masters. They are remarkable for their distinct physical type, for the comparative whiteness of their skin, and for their picturesque costumes, of which I can vouch for the endless variety. I shall content myself with noticing briefly the most striking.

At Muong-Line, and the next station, we received visits from female savages, who wore on their heads semicircles of straw, of different colours, intermixed with ornaments of glass and silver, which, falling from the forehead, back, form a long veil, such as used to be worn in France, the lower end of it being kept in right shape by a huge comb covered with cloth. They also wore earrings, of glass beads or hollow silver, which fall over the shoulders, and ornaments of the same description decorated their neck and chest; their arms, also, were loaded with bracelets. They could not make a movement, without the whole of these decorations producing a strange tinkling. Their short vests were of a dark colour, as also their plaited petticoats, which only reached the knee. Their calves, well developed by mountain roads, were imprisoned in gaiters of dark blue cotton. To complete the description of this costume, must be added a small cloak of leaves over the shoulders, and a wooden pipe in the mouth. The dress of the men of the same tribe was more simple, with much less ornament. They wore a turban, a vest, large trousers, and round the neck a simple collar of silver. They have regular features, with large black eyes and moustaches.

The exigences of a similar life, in the same district, and under the same climate, have given rise to very similar habits and customs among the Laotians, and the numerous savage tribes mixed with them. One can draw no conclusions as to the diversity of races from the variety of the costumes, since, even in France, we see they vary so much in the different departments. There remains, therefore, only the language. Men versed in the science, so interesting and so new, of philological palæontology, would

graphy make use of them? It seems probable, though I cannot take upon me to give a positive opinion.

find, no doubt, a source of fruitful study, if not of satis-
factory conclusions, in the documents on this subject collected by M. de Lagrée, who, alone, could gather them, he
being the only one of us then able to communicate, through
the Cambodgian interpreter, with the Burmese Laotians, and,
through them with the greater part of the savage tribes.
But such documents could not find place in a work of this
nature. I shall confine myself to a general observation,
which has already been made on the subject of Indo-China
as a whole, but which applies, in a special manner, to the
northern portion of that vast peninsula. The nearer one
approaches the gigantic mountains, which compose what
might be termed the backbone of the Asiatic continent, it
would seem that the ethnographical problem becomes more
complicated and insoluble.

From the gorges of the Himalayas, as though from the
sides of a great Tower of Babel, have issued multitudes of emigrants, speaking all languages, and following at hazard the
valleys of the rivers. If many tribes have descended even
to the shores of the sea, to form nations there, others, more
numerous still, unable to break away, have remained wander-
ers round their cradle in the west of China, and the north of
Tonkin, Laos, and Burmah. As far as we had reached, the
Laotians still formed an organised nationality — compact
and comparatively powerful. Though we had heard of the
yoke imposed on them by the Burmans, we had not, as yet,
seen any signs of it; but they were soon to appear. We
had been some days at Muong-Line, inhaling the miasma
from the inundated rice-fields; and the chief of the village,
a mandarin of an inferior order, had not yet paid a visit to
M. de Lagrée. Fearing to compromise his responsibility, he
waited for the king of Sien-Tong to indicate his line of conduct. This reserve, the motives of which we easily discerned,
began to make us uneasy. At last he presented himself in
great pomp, dressed in striped yellow and black silk drawers,
like a salamander; a large white calico dressing-gown, reaching below his knees, half hiding his thin calves, which were
tatooed all over; and a turban of green silk on his head.
He was old and infirm, his heavy prominent eyelids over-
shadowing his dull eyes. He brought a favourable reply from

the king. The council of Sien-Tong had taken four days to
deliberate on our simple demand for a pass. The Burman
mandarin sent from Ava to watch the king, as we have seen
some governors of provinces watched by the court of Bangkok, had, we were told, assisted at this council.

Thus we learnt that authority is divided in the Laotian countries, tributary to Ava, between a native sovereign
and a Burman mandarin, and that these two authorities,
after long debates, had agreed to let us pass. At least,
this was the meaning we put on the obscure words of the
message, and the verbose details of the messenger. We
prepared to start at once; but lost two hours in collecting
and loading the oxen, and meanwhile the rain had changed
a brook we had to cross into a torrent. It was necessary to
choose the moment when the stream became again fordable,
which was not till the following day. It was with limbs
bending under me, and as though intoxicated by two grains
of quinine, that I started with my companions. An officer
attacked with ulcers in his feet was carried in a hammock
by our Annamites, for the Laotians had refused to charge
themselves with this burden.

Sickness of any kind inspires them with a superstitious
terror: as we approached the villages, the inhabitants compelled us, by their cries and expressive gestures, to take the
hammock another road. Both oxen and men carried our
baggage, but these last measured the weight by their own
convenience, not by ours. The state of our funds, which
suffered sorely at every station, prevented us from hiring
more beasts or men. The natives would do nothing but
what they pleased, and were not afraid of our threats, for
our prestige had vanished. Any act of violence, however
justifiable, would not have been without peril. The inhabitants of this part of the country were more high-spirited, and
more to be feared, than the timid Laotians of the south, who
could be taxed and loaded at will. This independent self-
respect, which we were happy to meet with again, consoled
us a little, when we saw a porter, wishing to rest himself,
throw his load on the ground, at the risk of breaking it, and
receive our remonstrances with an insolent laugh.

On leaving Muong-Line, we had to traverse interminable

rice-fields, over which the plough had just passed. It was a
sea of sticky mud, which, at each step, emitted fetid ema-
nations. In the paths through the forest, walking was
still more painful; we sank up to our knees in moist clay.
Leeches, lying in wait on the leaves, rushed down on their
prey; and if we stopped to free one of our legs from these
famished parasites, the other was immediately attacked.

These annelids have such an acute sense of sight, smell,
or hearing, that at the slightest halt we each became the
centre of attraction to a black and rapacious crowd, which
crawled towards us over all obstacles. At the end of seven
horrid hours' march we reached the village of Paléo, covered
with mud, shivering, and worn out with fatigue and hunger.
As it had suited the bearers of our breakfast to stop and
rest frequently on the journey, and take their own food, we
had to wait for them until the evening, devouring our anger;
an aliment not very substantial. We had hitherto been spoilt,
and some of us were sorry enough at the thought that our
mandarinism was no longer of any account.

The pagoda, where we encamped, was a great shed, the
straw roof of which, supported on posts, scarcely protected
us from the rain. We were present at the offerings made,
each morning, by the women to the little statue of Bouddha. The bonzes came every evening, to take away whatever had been placed on the altar. These men live plenti-
fully on such casual offerings, and their flourishing condition
bears good testimony to the piety of the faithful. Besides
these regular offerings, several times a day devotees bring
flowers or more nourishing objects. They fetch a priest from
a neighbouring monastery, who lights some candles, and re-
cites prayers till they are burnt out, when he takes possession
of the delicacies. Our presence did not seem to annoy these
worshippers of the god, who came in crowds to sell us their
fowls, or rather to exchange them for pieces of red cotton.
The authorities were not over kind, and declared that their
village could not furnish us with the means of transporting
our baggage, greatly diminished as it had been. We were
therefore compelled to reduce it still more, by leaving some
indispensable objects, hoping to be able to replace them in
China. The last remains of our wardrobe helped our larder;

we gave a pair of pantaloons for a duck, and—God forgive
us such simony!—we even exchanged, in the same way, the
medallions and religious images which were destined for
the Christians of the missions, whom we had not, as yet, encountered. St. Antony of Padua went for a pumpkin, St.
Pancras for a basket of potatoes, and St. Gertrude for three
cucumbers.

At Paléo we were joined by a courier, who brought a letter from the king of Sien-Tong to M. de Lagrée. This letter,
of which our interpreter indifferently succeeded in deciphering the characters and making out the sense, was taken, after
mature deliberation, to be a gracious invitation to pass through
the city of Sien-Tong; but M. de Lagrée believed it his duty
to decline the offer, which he considered as an advance inspired at once by politeness and curiosity; for we had already
met with too many troubles, to allow of our lengthening our
journey. This deplorable blunder caused our most cruel
embarrassments. The same reason which had retarded our
departure from Muong-Line detained us at Paléo. The rain,
falling with incredible persistence, kept a river we had to
ford at too high a level. Before quitting the territory of
Sien-Tong, it was necessary to obtain, from the master to
the neighbouring state of Muong-You, the permission to
traverse his territory. From reports, which we afterwards
found to be false, we were led to believe in the independence of this prince, who is, in reality, subordinate to the king
of Sien-Tong.

M. de Lagrée sent his interpreter in advance, charging
him to announce our approaching arrival, in the first village
of this new kingdom, and to dispatch from thence to the
king a letter, accompanied by the customary presents. We
started shortly after, and soon penetrated the forest, where
the night overtook us. Each one made, for himself, a bed of
damp leaves, and went to sleep in the clothes he wore, resigned to endure the water which poured from the sky. We
protected our papers, astronomical instruments, the powder,
and the box containing the sulphate of quinine, as much as
we possibly could, by means of the hard skins which formed
part of the equipment of the oxen. The fires of our encampment went out, notwithstanding the attention of the natives,

who are always uneasy in the neighbourhood of tigers. On
the following day, one of these animals did us the service of
throwing down, before our eyes, a stag of large size, which
was crossing the pathway at a bound. Two shots from carbines, fired in the air by our Annamites, who marched in front,
frightened the terrible hunter, who abandoned his prey to us.
To fire in the air, instead of aiming from the shoulder at a
wild beast, is a manner of proceeding which, doubtless, appears more prudent than heroic; but those who chanced to
find themselves nearest the tiger were Annamites, and, for
men in such circumstances, showed themselves, comparatively, courageous. Their brothers of Cochin-China, surprised by one of these dangerous man-eaters, treat him like
a great mandarin : give him the very respectful title of
grandfather, kneel, and beat the earth with their foreheads,
till they meet the fate of Red Riding Hood, whom her grandmother ate.

The forest ends at the border of immense rice-fields,
which extend as far as the Mekong. The ploughs, with
shares of copper shining like gold, easily open their furrows
in the mire, in which the buffaloes, harnessed to them, sink
up to their chests. It was the plain of Siam-Leap, a small
village, where our interpreter awaited us. He had had
time to speak well of us, and the population flocked to the
pagoda, where we lodged. The women brought us food, and
asked for bits of red cloth instead of money : but when the
piece is used up, our supplies will be, once more, hard to
get. The mandarin of the place, after long hesitation, decided on paying a visit to M. de Lagrée, who expressed his
desire to leave without waiting for the reply of the king of
Muong-You. The timid functionary hesitated, and finished
by declaring that he dared not decide in a matter so grave.
He came, however, on the evening of the 14th of July to
acquaint us, that in two days' time there would be a great
festival at the village, on the occasion of the full moon. The
pagoda which we occupied would be full of people, from sun-
rise to sunset; and he feared that the tumult would annoy
us, and proposed that we should remove to a group of
houses on the borders of the Mekong. This would, he said,
be so much gained on the following stage of our journey;

and should a favourable reply arrive from Muong-You, we should be immediately informed.

M. de Lagrée was on the point of accepting this skilfully presented proposal, which would have been disastrous; for in the desert place, where the crafty mandarin wished to confine us, we should have found no means of living. The increasing exactions of the porters and proprietors of oxen kept us at Siam-Leap. These last demanded three times as much as had been asked of us since our entry into Burman Laos, and refused the hundred francs that we offered them for half a day's march. The time had gone by when we could give what we pleased to bearers, too happy to aid philanthropical mandarins; we had now to submit to burdensome conditions, and were obliged to make formal contracts for hiring, in which we had to take precautions against the bad faith of the natives, who were always ready to falsify the weights, or to deceive as to their value. The Chinese ingot, called *tè*, and the Burman ingot, also called *tè*, do not represent the same quantity of silver; but both are in use; so that these rogues offer you one when they are your debtors, and require the other when they are your creditors. This merciless dealing was accounted for, however, in a certain measure, by the season in which we travelled. I have already said, that the greater number of the dealers suspend their business when the rivers overflow, and the roads are submerged; but as we wished to proceed, a higher price had to be paid for doing so. M. de Lagrée then decided on awaiting, in our pagoda of Siam-Leap, the reply from Muong-You, and we employed all our philosophy to enable us to support the full moon, and the festivals of which it was the occasion.

Children dressed in yellow, and some old frequenters of the sanctuary, to judge by the familiarity with which they treated their god, undressed the little statue of Bouddha, threw water over its head, sponged it with care, and then put on its red shirt again. The cymbals, gongs, and great drums woke us with a start, and the crowd invaded the shed, in which we occupied the smallest possible space. They lighted candles, and burnt old rags and long cotton wicks. The assistants made all sorts of gestures, put their hand to

their forehead, and kissed the ground, and then watered it
with the aid of a bottle, with which every one was supplied.
This did not prevent their chattering, laughing, and smoking; not the slightest respect or meditation, or any sign of
inner religion, appeared on any of their countenances, with
the exception of that of the old bonze, the chief of the
pagoda. He appeared to pray with faith. Besides the
regular services, the time that he did not employ in singing, and instructing the children confided to his care, was
devoted to his beads, which he told on and on with his
fingers. Assisted by his brethren, he recited prayers during
part of the day, and read to the inattentive faithful some
pages of the life of Bouddha. It was a legendary tissue of
marvels. The gifts, placed on a shelf at the foot of the statue
of the god, appeared to me to be of small value : a candle
perhaps, or a ball of rice; but that which was offered to the
bonzes was more substantial. It was a feast as delicate as
their pilgrim flock could contrive, in every form of culinary
skill. The next day, parents, who had need of their children
for the important operation of picking the rice, came to take
them away from the school; lay dresses were laid before
Bouddha, and then five or six little boys were stripped of
their yellow robes, to our great satisfaction, for they made
so many shrill voices the less in the choir that awoke us
each morning. The gravity of all these Eliakims, when they
see they are noticed as they mutter their prayers, is very
comical; for it ceases when there is no one to admire their
fervour.

Notwithstanding the inconvenience of such lodgings, we
were happy to take shelter under the stubble roofs of the
pagodas, and to sleep on their floors of beaten earth. It is in
Laos, as in certain remote places in Europe, where travellers
find repose in the cloisters, and convents take the place of
hotels. Without wishing, by a misplaced comparison, to put
the religion, which has given us our moral grandeur, on a
level with that which has produced the abasement of the
Asiatic races, I may be permitted to note, in this monastic
hospitality, practised 500 years before the Christian era, one
of the first effects of that law of charity which Bouddhism
taught, though without giving it its highest sanction; a

law very imperfect, no doubt, but sufficing to open the temples of Indo-China to travellers, as it used to be appealed to, to open to them the cells of St. Bernard.

We received from Muong-You a favourable answer; but the festival being over, the chief of the village, though he had no longer any motive for getting rid of us, showed us great ill-will. Spending his days in smoking opium, and indifferent to everything, he treated the interpreter charged to arrange for our departure very badly, for he was too inferior a personage for M. de Lagrée to enter into direct communication with. The days glided away, the rain fell in torrents, and this impertinent fellow notified us that, the river having reached already a height to which it had not risen, the preceding year, till two months later, all the roads had disappeared under the waters, and our departure was therefore impossible. He advised us, ironically, to wait till the twelfth month, though we were then only in the eighth. Such a prospect, as being blockaded for four months at Siam-Leap, filled us with consternation. A petty mandarin, touched with pity, and, perhaps, by the desire of making a good business of it, told us of a road, that remained open, across the mountains; a frightful road, it was true, but yet not impracticable. 'Three more days of rain,' he said to us, 'and it will cease to be available by the men with your baggage, for their animals will not be able to pass it.' He offered to arrange our departure for the following day, and asked 300 francs for our porters. It was an urgent case, hesitation was not possible, and M. de Lagrée agreed. During our stay at Siam-Leap, sickness had seized on our companions, like vultures on their prey. Leaving behind us, stretched on the mats of the pagoda, two officers and three men of our escort, unable to rise, we left with aching hearts, taking with us their baggage and their arms. An unencumbered man can pass everywhere.

We followed our guides through a dense forest, for there was no longer a trace of road; and they conducted us by the side of the river Mekong, which I had not seen for more than a month, though we had encamped very near it at Paléo and Siam-Leap. It flows between wooded hills, with a fearful current, sending up a dull roar, and its tumultuous waters

have the colour of red copper. We penetrated, with much
difficulty, through the forest; the Laotians opening a way
through it with their knives when the brushwood was too
thick. Obliged to follow the undulations at the foot of the
hills, we descended into all the ravines, at the bottom of
which ran torrents, at times strong enough to throw us
down; many of them, indeed, swollen by the river damming
back their waters, only fordable at their source, to reach
which we had to make our way through interlacing creepers.

It always rained, and most of us were without shoes.
Our feet were bruised by the stones, pierced by the thorns,
and bleeding from the leeches; the fever paled our cheeks,
and, most fearful symptom of all, our spirits began to sink.
Notwithstanding the stifling closeness of the air, after some
hours walking, in such a state, the cold struck us in crossing
torrents whose waters were ordinarily glacial. What, then,
was our surprise, on entering, for the hundredth time, into
one of these innumerable affluents of the Mekong, to find it
so hot as to be almost painful! We had discovered a sulphur
spring of 86° centigrade, and wished this corner of the forest
the fortune which the first explorers of Gaul or Germany
might have predicted for Bagnères or Ems.

The leeches were a dreadful torment. Countless as the
dead leaves, on which they kept watch, they rushed from
the thickest of the wood, like vampires, and hung on, in
clusters, to the body, which they drained; squeezed themselves even between the toes, quitting their hold only when
glutted, and leaving a poisonous sting in the skin, to turn,
before long, to an ulcer. The natives advised us to fasten
to the end of a cane a plug of damp tobacco. It had a
magical effect. It sufficed to touch the leech, to enjoy, for a
moment, the agreeable spectacle of its agony; but this remedy required constant attention, and was soon abandoned.
Like men forced to remain seated in a nest of ants, we were
obliged to be patient, and let our blood flow till we halted
in the evening, when we each had to stanch his wounds.
When we were compelled to pass a night in the forest, we
avoided setting up our camp amidst the large shrubs, where
the leeches were still more numerous. On the more elevated
places we were less exposed to serve as pasture to these

hideous worms, which, like the ghosts of Slavonic countries, come out from their tombs at midnight, to drink the blood of their victims, without awaking them. Sometimes, to escape them, we stretched our blankets on a narrow piece of sand, a foot above the Mekong, where, before sleeping, we had to place a sentry to watch the stream, that we might not be carried away by any sudden rise of the water. But there, if there were no leeches, the mosquitoes became maddening; and, above all, the impalpable gnats of the forest, against which no mosquito-curtain can protect, and whose bite is fire.

At last, we perceived the five miserable and dilapidated houses, which composed the dismal village of Sop-Yong. They were separated from us by the pretty river of Nam-Yong, which we crossed at its entrance into the Mekong, by means of a raft, made of three planks, badly tied together. The natives use the river so little, that they have nearly lost the art of making canoes.

According to custom, we took possession of the pagoda, furnished with its small altar, but unprovided with bonzes, for they, no longer inspired with the spirit of their master, hardly ever establish themselves among the poor. If they still think life the supreme evil, they no longer despise its pleasures. The women came none the less, bringing their very modest offerings to the god. One of our Annamites— a freethinker, like the rest of his race—placed his bed at the foot of the statue of Bouddha, and conducted himself, in the morning, in such a manner as to distract the pious souls from their meditations. I was never weary of admiring the tolerance of these excellent Bouddhists. We strove never to wound them; we always respected, even in the most urgent circumstances, the enclosure of their pagodas, and never took the life of any animal within it. The demands of the bonzes went no farther, and they readily consented to eat flesh, themselves, in spite of the doctrine of metempsychosis.

The rain never ceased, and the river visibly increased: it rose three metres during our short stay at Sop-Yong. Every moment a piece of the bank gave way with a dull sound, like a subterranean explosion. Our sick companions, whom

we had left at Siam-Leap, rejoined us at last. Their hollow
eyes and pale lips gave them the appearance of walking
corpses. Those of us who were still strong hastened to quit
the village of Sop-Yong, so as not to use up the small amount
of provisions it was able to furnish. Attracted by the hope
of good wages, even the women offered to carry the baggage ; and the caravan, smaller by half, followed first the
valley of the Nam-Yong, which becomes very rapid a hundred metres from its mouth. We left the banks of this
stream, swollen by the rains, and entered a plain, which
might be called a vast savannah. Many ranges of mountains
rose one above the other around us ; some of them wooded
and dark, others burned and bare, like nothing so much as a
leper's skull. The parts of the valley not planted with rice,
formed, for a space of several kilometres, putrid marshes, in
which we sank to the waist. We were not far from Muong-
Yong, where a Burman official resided ; and it behoved us
to present ourselves all together, with all our attendants, before this mandarin, whose feeling towards us was unknown.
It was, therefore, necessary to await at the village of Pass-
ang the arrival of those we had left behind us, amongst
whom was M. de Lagrée himself. We then made as imposing an entry into the chief town of the district, which was to
serve us as a prison for a month, as our bare feet and tattered clothes would permit.

Muong-Yong is an insignificant village. Facing a covered
bridge, by which we arrived, lay a greensward, bordered by
magnificent banyan-trees, and terminating by the enclosure
of the pagoda. An earthern wall, and a ruined monument on
a neighbouring hill, gave evidence that the place had been
inhabited for a long period. It appears, indeed, to have
been the centre of a powerful tribe of aborigines, whom
the Laotians superseded. Whilst the chief of the expedition
— an enthusiastic archæologist, and indefatigable walker,
notwithstanding the fever — went to explore the piles of
bricks concealed under the brushwood, we took quiet possession of a large wooden house, disdaining the *sala*, open
to the wind and the rain. We had scarcely installed ourselves, when two Burmans, armed with sabres, entered, and,
speaking to us with great animation and their hands on

the hilts of their weapons, summoned us, with expressive
gestures, to follow them immediately. They spoke in Burman, and we did not understand a word of their discourse; but, as they seemed impertinent, we simply turned
them out of doors. They were loud in their menaces, and
proceeded to attack our cook, who, in order to hold his
own, was obliged to suspend the execution of a fowl. As
nothing farther occurred, we waited patiently the return of
1. de Lagrée and his interpreter, who was very soon in a
position to furnish us with explanations. Muong-Yong still
belongs to the immense province of Sien-Tong; and Muong-
You, which we had supposed to be a separate kingdom, is
also a portion of it. In the town of Sien-Tong, as we already
knew, a grand Burman mandarin reigns, by the side of the
king, having under his command two of his compatriots,
who fill the same functions, one with the prince of Muong-
You, and the other with the prince of Muong-Yong. It was
to the one who governs this last-named country we owed
all our difficulties.

It was the custom for all strangers of importance to
present themselves at once on their arrival at the sala, where
the Burman comes to meet them in ceremonious state, and
where explanations are exchanged, and papers verified. We
were in ignorance of this custom, and the police were sent
to enlighten us. The reports of these people exasperated
their chief; and the next day, when we wanted to fulfil the
necessary formalities, he received us in a haughty and indignant manner. He examined our papers, amongst which he
vainly looked for a passport from the emperor of Burmah,
and it was with a sarcastic smile that he declared it was his
duty to detain us, until he had received orders from his supe-
ior at Sien-Tong. That prince had, it is true, authorised us
at first to pass; but we had entirely misunderstood a letter
from him, which we took for a polite invitation to pay him
a visit at his capital, and which, it will be remembered,
reached us at Paléo, and our interlocutor told us plainly, that
the desires of a man, who had the honour to direct the affairs
of a province, for the government of Ava, even if they were
expressed discourteously, were orders it would be rash to
evade.

Nevertheless, each present we gave him seemed to
shake our enemy's resolution,—as the stroke of a battering
ram shakes a wall,—and we began to hope that he would
alter his opinion of us, and reduce some part of the three
weeks of detention with which he had threatened us. But
the next day he had returned to his former idea. At the end
of a long discussion, he appeared to have again abandoned
it, but catching at another string to his bow, he told M. de
Lagrée he could not let him leave without announcing our
arrival to his colleague at Muong-You; which was a useless
precaution, as that functionary had already authorised our
entering his territory. We fancied that this decisive observation had terminated the debate; but we did not know our
adversary: he insised that the step he was about to take
was simply conformable to custom, and would only delay us
a few days. We were, therefore, obliged to submit, and wait
for a letter from Muong-You. It arrived at last, but was
most vexatious. 'It is incredible,' it said, 'that, invited to
present yourselves at Sien-Tong, you neglected to do so;
we, therefore, do not admit people, who are so ignorant of
good manners.' He had, however, accepted our presents.
It was evident that these orders had been sent from Sien-
Tong itself. After having granted our request, the suspicious Burman mandarin had, without doubt, reflected;
hence the invitation to visit him, that he might see what we
were like, and sound our intentions, hence, in the end, the
order to stop us. The hour of conjecture was past, and M.
de Lagrée decided immediately on going himself to Sien-
Tong. He asked M. de Thorel, an enthusiastic botanist, who
would have herborised even under the poniards of the Burmans, to accompany him; and he also took a few men, as an
escort. The little box of European articles was not forgotten. We had already sent presents to the king; but, being
ignorant of the existence, and, above all, of the importance,
of the Burman mandarin, nothing had been sent to him; and
this involuntary negligence on our part had certainly contributed to the ill-will he bore us. The daring resolution
M. de Lagrée had come to, obliged us to prolong our sojourn
at Muong-Yong. We availed ourselves of the circumstance,
to endeavour to discover the principal elements of which

the population of Burman Laos is composed, and to make as exact an account as was possible of their respective conditions. Until then, we had gone on, in great measure, at a venture, not knowing the political constitution of these countries, and frequently taking provinces to be kingdoms. By the aid of the information we gained at Muong-Yong we gained a great deal of light on these points.

China, which has hitherto exercised an effective power over these countries, has lost ground on this side. Of the three ancient Laotian kingdoms, where, at this time, the rule of Burmah is supreme, the Celestial Empire, from which Sien-Tong and Muong-Lem have seceded, does not retain at Sien-Hong, as we shall see farther on, even sufficient influence to seat its own candidates on the throne. Not content with the immensity of their dominions, the kings of Siam have always desired more; but, repulsed by the king of Sien-Tong, since 1852 they have left the field open to the Burman emperor. This potentate sends representatives to each of the Laotian sovereigns, who hold the same position as the English residents in India. The chief Burman mandarin, who rules over all the tributary Laotian provinces, resides at Muong-Lem, the most northern of the three ancient Laotian principalities. That of Sien-Tong is the second. Under him, as I have already said, are mandarins of inferior rank, who watch the prince of Muong-Yong, in whose territory we were staying, and the prince of Muong-You, whose acquaintance we were soon to make. It was a sad spectacle to see only the pale shadow of a native king, entirely put behind, whilst the Burman mandarin swaggered in the foreground, making a parade of his military escort, with the brutal insolence of a conqueror. His conduct recalled that of the Siamese mandarin, who occupied Cambodgia before the establishment of the French protectorate. The soldiers, following his example, seized what they chose in the market. The king only retained his right of precedence; and, in consequence, it was to him we paid our first official visit. It was quite different at Sien-Tong: there the native sovereign has not abdicated; he still directs his affairs, and we should have been lost, without his powerful intervention. Supported by him, M. de Lagrée had been able to hold his own against the

ill-will of the mandarin resident, who, pertinaciously calling
us English, refused one day what he had accorded on the
previous one, denied boldly what he had just said, and conducted himself like a man in whose heart hatred had left
no place for good faith.

The king, on the contrary, troubled himself very little
about our nationality, and seemed to find in the bad temper
of his watcher a good reason for treating us as friends. Determined to facilitate our passage, notwithstanding the formal opposition of the Burman, he decided on writing us
the letter, inviting us to visit him, which we had so unfortunately misunderstood. He received MM. de Lagrée and
Thorel with benevolent cordiality, and while the chief of the
expedition and his companion had the freest access to him,
his wife pleased herself in making them appreciate the refinements of Laotian cooking. The Burman, on the contrary,
remained hostile and menacing. Satisfied with the petty
humiliations he was able to inflict on those whom he took
to be his abhorred enemies, this chief did not dare to pro-
voke a conflict, in which the king's energy seemed willing
to accept all risks. The Burman emperor has to be very
circumspect in his treatment of this great tributary, who,
with his troops, has gained a victory over the war-minister
of Siam in person, from whom he took a mortar, several
pieces of cannon, and other trophies, and he is well aware
that the king of Siam would joyfully accept the advantageous position of sovereign protector, which he holds. This
rivalry of influences, and the dualism of authority which
exists, singularly favoured the success of our journey. The
negotiations, so skilfully conducted by M. de Lagrée, secured
our entry into Muong-You; and when there, we were only
separated from China by the small kingdom of Sien-Hong,
which has a government of its own.

This good news took a long time to reach us at Muong-
Yong. It was preceded by a series of contradictory rumours,
which gave us great uneasiness. We had, however, become
completely reconciled to the Burman functionary, who, being
at last entirely satisfied as to our nationality, frequently held
long conversations with us, which were very difficult to carry
on, owing to the absence of any interpreter. At the com-

mencement of our intercourse, this fiery mandarin always came attended by a guard of a dozen poor wretches, armed with all the flint-muskets in his arsenal; but it was not long before he dismissed them, and came alone for an amicable chat with us; his wife also, a nice plump little woman, did not hesitate to pass long hours in our house, at the risk of furnishing some material for local gossip. The explanations we were obliged to give him, on the political divisions of Europe, had contributed more than anything else in effecting this prodigious transformation. When he spoke of the English (*Englit*), his eyes sparkled with rage, and he felt the need of describing, with visible enthusiasm, the power of the sovereign of Ava. The conquerors of the Burmese had formerly pushed their reconnoitering even to these parts. The king of Sien-Tong remembered having seen a European officer, who passed his days in looking about him, and absorbing, with the help of a curious instrument, three times more nourishment than a vigorous Laotian. This officer, with a robust appetite, was no other than the Major M'Leod, who, by his friendly terms with the emperor of Burmah, Tharawady, in 1839, got himself appointed to the post of interim resident to that prince. His explorations in the east of Burmah date back to 1836. He reached Sien-Hong, and came across the Mekong at 22 degrees north latitude. It would, no doubt, have been easy for him, at that time, to have entered China by the road we were going. To do so to-day, it would be enough for the English to obtain from the emperor of Burmah, who is accustomed to the most painful concessions, an imperative letter, addressed to his agents in the Laotian provinces.

But this is not the best road for the flow of merchandise from western China towards India and Europe. Captain Hannay, in ascending the Irawady as far as Bahmo, followed the correct road, which already unites Yunan to the capital of Burmah. It is by this route that the productions of part of this rich province will, one day, descend even to Rangoon. I shall have occasion to notice, farther on, the obstacles which Europeans, who may try to establish regular communications between these two countries will meet;—obstacles which appear to be more owing to man than to nature.

The storm which had threatened us had happily passed over. The Burmans were not the absolute masters of the Laotian populations, which an English traveller has not hesitated to declare superior to them, and their obstinacy had been vanquished by the energy of a native prince. A letter from M. de Lagrée having told us to meet him at Muong-You, we joyfully quitted the damp house, where we had spent thirty days, inhaling fever with the poisonous breeze which passed over the marshes. The Burman mandarin gave us two letters of recommendation, cut with a knife on bamboo sticks; one addressed to his colleague of Muong-You, the other for the chief of the village of Ban-Tap. In this village there is a custom-house, the great end of which is to compel travellers to quit the shortest road, that they may present themselves at the administrative centre of the district; it is less a custom-house, in fact, in the sense we attach to the word, than a direct robbery of the traveller, who is compelled to purchase the good graces of the authorities by presents. This invention of a merciless exchequer was very lucrative when the civil war, which now desolates the country, did not prevent the Chinese from traversing these regions, on their way to Luang-Praban. Thanks to the passport, we were not troubled at Ban-Tap, where we arrived, after a march under a scorching sun, through the beds of streams and of torrents. The roads had begun to get firm on the heights, but all the lower parts were sloughs, where we frequently sank up to our middle. We noticed, however, not without surprise, certain useful public works: that is to say, on the border of a stream, under tufts of bamboos, in a sort of romantic nook, were two benches with backs, and a wooden bridge across a large river, uniting the two sides. We were evidently approaching a civilised country; for, with the exception of the *salas*, constructed in certain villages at the side of the pagodas, we had not seen, in all Laos, any measure taken to facilitate travelling.

We had scarcely arrived at Muong-You, which is forty kilometres from Muong-Yong, till M. de Lagrée rejoined us. He had travelled more than one hundred and fifty miles to reach Sien-Tong, which is on a very high plateau, and could only be reached by scaling a continuous chain of mountains.

This city, which is farther from the Mekong than from the Salween, appears placed on the line which separates the basin of these two rivers, of which the size, thus far inland, seems the same. It must, however, be remembered, that the Salween is not more than one hundred leagues from its mouth, whilst the Mekong, by latitude alone, is more than three hundred from the sea. The valley of Sien-Tong is of immense extent, full of inhabitants, highly cultivated, and the most beautiful one could well see. At this height snow is not unknown, and the temperature, which is sensibly lower, permits a great many European fruits, if not to attain quite the degree of perfection to which they arrive in our climates, at least to form and ripen. The population of the city is sufficiently large to allow of a daily market, in which they slaughter five oxen and a great many pigs. The inhabitants of this region begin to repudiate the title of Laotian; they give themselves the name of Kugn, and call Sien-Tong Muong-Kugn. The ancient maps only know it as Kemalatain. The multiplicity of different names given to the same locality by the races which have successively acquired even a temporary preponderance, is not one of the least difficulties which the future historian of these countries will meet with. The Kugns have a whiter skin than the Burmans descended direct from the Hindoos; but, like them, they cover the lower part of the body with indelible designs, which show some art. What is the origin of tattooing? Has it been borrowed by the Laotians of the north from the aborigines, whom they have supplanted? Have the Burmans themselves adopted a custom which might have been in use with the savages at a remote period, though at this present time it has been almost entirely abandoned by them? This does not seem probable. As far as the Burmans are concerned, tradition is not silent; it explains tattooing in a manner which has, at least, the merit of being piquant. One of their kings, it is said, becoming alarmed by the general corruption of morals, ordered the men to disfigure themselves, and the women not to hide their charms, so that the perverted tastes of his subjects might be attracted to them. M. de Lagrée stayed in several villages inhabited by men whom the Kugns called savages, though they were quite as civilised as themselves. They have large

198 TRAVELS IN INDO-CHINA.

well-constructed houses in general palisaded, markets, and
pagodas. They are not ignorant of agriculture, commerce,
or industrial arts; and, like the Romans, who, when they had
taken a Carthaginian galley, made a fleet from the pattern,
they make themselves excellent flint-muskets, after European
models.

We found that the crown of Muong-You was on the head
of the younger brother of the king of Sien-Tong, who showed
us so much kindness. The day following the arrival of the
chief of the expedition, we commenced our visits of ceremony. We were first conducted to the residence of the
king's brother, who complacently exhibited his delicate white
hands. He held his fan with as much coquetry as a pretty
woman her book of hours at the noonday mass. He was
surrounded by noblemen enveloped in long white robes, bound
round the waist, according to the Burman custom, with a
piece of silk of gaudy colours. These courtiers were as grave
as Roman senators. We avoided speaking to the king's brother of our affairs, and contented ourselves with exchanging
courteous words. From him, we went to pay our respects
to the Burman mandarin. This man, the picture of solemn
foolishness, kept thinking what he should say; let drop a few
words between winks of his eyes, and gave himself great
airs. Happily, his wife served as interpreter, and contrived
to make us forget, by her amiable disposition and grace, the
fatiguing majesty of her spouse. At last, as a termination
of our visits, we went to the king. The palace is situated
on a rounded hill, from whence the view embraces a vast
horizon of mountains. Though it was only constructed in
wood, and covered with thatch, it showed real progress in
architecture. The carpentry was good, the partitions well
joined; there was also, near the palace, a number of sawpits,
which are entirely unknown in southern Laos. A crowd of
mandarins, in respectful attitudes, filled the room into which
we were introduced. The light barely penetrated this spacious apartment, the roof of which is supported by magnificent columns. In a corner of this hall, under an ornamented
canopy, the king was lazily seated on cushions of silk, embroidered with gold. He wore a turban, elegantly arranged
by a woman's hand, its ample folds entirely covering the

head, and hiding the hair. His costume was composed of a
vest and trousers of green satin, with gold ornaments. In
his ears he wore large gold cylinders in the lobes, set off at
one end with diamonds, and with emeralds at the other.
They were a present from the king of Ava. Our host seemed
to have disposed everything for effect; his attitudes were
gracious, but studied. A narrow window, near the throne,
was so arranged, that the sun's rays made the king's dress
sparkle like the wings of a glittering beetle. All the most
precious vases in the palace were grouped near their owner,
and the attendants brought each of us a large box in em-
bossed silver, containing all the materials for the preparation
of a betel quid.

This custom is still in existence here, though less practised than in Lower Laos. The areca nuts, being more rare,
one must be richer to get them to chew. The king of Muong-
You has a white skin, an intelligent, open and pleasing countenance; he never tired of asking us questions, and each of
our words appeared to open before him a new world, full of
strange visions. I realised, on seeing him, what an oriental
prince might be; and the charming fancies, which floated
in my memory as imaginary creations, were now embodied
before me. Unfortunately, there was another side to this elegant picture; for I saw empty bottles of pale ale decorating
the columns of the audience-chamber. This vulgar product
of European industry excites the same infatuation in the
king of Muong-You, which Chinese *craqueles*, for example,
that always look to me to be nothing but crockery dried up
by the kitchen fire—excite in our well-to-do idlers. In a
portion of the room, separated from the throne by lances,
whose heads formed a sort of silver grating, I remarked a
heap of elephants' teeth.

Our royal friend did not hesitate to make use of his people, in order to render his own life agreeable. He carried
them, so to speak, of his own choice, on his back, as the
gentlemen did their forests and mills, on the Field of the
Cloth of Gold. We saw him five times, and always in a
different costume. He passed a whole day with us, insist-
ing on seeing everything. Taking for aim, unknown to the
victim, the figure of a grand mandarin, he made us use a

perfume-sprinkler before the queen, who could not resist the
desire to carry it with her wherever she wished to repeat
the process. The king showed us, in return, several specimens of iron ore, which appeared to be rich; he also confi-
dentially told us, that there was gold in his dominions, but
he did not dare to let us know where it lay. He is obliged
to disclose to the Burman mandarin all the gold-fields that
are discovered, in the same way as all the inhabitants of
his kingdom are compelled to reveal to him findings of a
similar nature. 'It is necessary,' he said to us, 'on the receipt of precise indications, at once to visit the place, and to
have the appearance of putting one's own hand, as though
by chance, on the treasure.'

    We had no time for similar researches. It was our mis-
fortune to remain in places devoid of resources, in the midst
of hostile people, and only to pass through where information of all kinds offered itself to us. For this we had no
remedy; for we were unprovided with passports, and it was
free to the lowest mandarin to retard our progress; and
M. de Lagrée wished to have quitted the territory of Sien-
Tong before the Burman mandarin, who resides near the king,
could receive the orders he had secretly asked for from Ava.
It became necessary, therefore, to resist the friendly persua-
sions of the young sovereign of Muong-You, who wanted to
enjoy a longer intercourse with us. Finding M. de Lagrée
was not to be shaken in his resolution, he placed himself
completely at our service, made porters precede us with our
baggage, whilst he gave the orders to prepare our boats.
The current of the Nam-Loï bore us away. This river, which
is larger than the Seine, and as winding, flows first through
the plain of Muong-You; with pretty houses, sheltered by
plantations of areca-trees, on its banks; but it soon after enters
a region of varied aspect, and closed in by steep mountains.
The rain had almost completely ceased; yet there still remained sufficient humidity in the air to soften the glare
of the sun, and to cast a transparent veil, beneath which the
tints were delightfully softened, over the landscape. We
greatly enjoyed the spectacle, for we did so without fatigue.

    The men who carried our baggage were in waiting for
us at the point where we landed. We slept in an empty

house, open to all the winds, at the foot of the mountains, which we began to ascend on the following day. The pathway was, in general, along their crest; and when, sometimes, it descended into shallow valleys, it was only to rise again soon after to the heights. As far as the eye could see, there was nothing round us but deep undulations: I might have said, immense furrows, like those the tempest hollows on the bosom of the sea. The play of light, with its changing effects, following the clouds which passed under the sun, added to the illusion by giving an apparent motion to the crests of these frozen waves. Numerous paths crossed each other in the mountains. The one we followed, though it was the ordinary road from Muong-Long, was overgrown with shrubs, and while hardly traced out at first, was now wholly neglected. In contrast with this, when we came on a broad road, kept as carefully as the alley of a park, we were told that it led to a village of savages. These little towns, built, and as it were suspended, on the slopes of the hills, are inhabited by a laborious population, who subsist on the rice of the forests, which they irrigate by means of long bamboo pipes, in which they bring all the water it requires. They do not mix with the civilised people of the plain, whose language they do not speak; in short, they keep to themselves, intrenched in their pride, and live on the heights.

After walking for long hours in the mountains, we at last reached the plain; and, as elsewhere, we perceived, grouped along the banks of the streams which traverse it, the habitations of those whom I shall continue to call Laotians. The land was cultivated far round, on every side, the soft velvet-like green of the rice-fields delighting the eye. Numberless villages revealed themselves by the white gables of their pagodas, which were half hidden in clumps of large trees. The valley is traversed by the Nam-Ga, a broad and r-- -- ---er, which we crossed without boats, though we had , resist current strong enough to throw down one of our porters. We directed our march towards a pyramid, the point of which could be seen in the distance on a low hill, at the foot of which lies Muong-Long.

To get into this chief place of the district, we had to go through the market-place, between two ranges of houses,

which lined both sides of the road thickly, and showed that
the village was of some importance.   I will not attempt to
describe our surprise on perceiving a fine stone bridge across
a tributary of the Nam-Ga.   Even in the best days of their
country, when they raised the magnificent monuments of
Angcor and Vat-Phou, the Cambodgians were ignorant of
the art of constructing arches; they could only corbel out
the blocks of stone.   The Chinese are more skilful ; the arch
of the bridge of Muong-Long, built by them, is elegant and
solid, and the parapet is ornamented with sculptured lions,
now thrown down.   The keystone of the arch still projected, on both sides, as a gargoyle.   The Chinese, driven
little by little from the country, are no longer there to keep
up the works by which the Laotians profit, without even
being able to prop up a falling stone, or to raise a tumbling
wall.

With the exception of this bridge and the paved causeway, Muong-Long has a very Laotian appearance.   The
houses, made of the same materials as in Laos, are always
in the same style; the inhabitants wear the same costume—
wide trousers, vest, turban round the head, and a poniard
passed through the waistbelt.   We had barely arrived, before
we were surrounded by a curious crowd ; and sellers besieged our doors.   We distinguished amongst them two
women in long dresses, whose tiny feet were enclosed in
microscopic shoes.   They were Chinese women, real Chinese !   There was no longer any room for doubt.   These
women with mutilated feet, and the stone bridge — were
they not the signs of a different civilisation?   were we not
beyond Laos?   Venus Astarte rising from the Nam-Ga, the
Parthenon appearing all at once behind the bamboos, would
not have charmed our eyes and made our hearts beat more
than this simple bridge, ten metres in length, and these
poor peddling women, with their sun-burnt skin and thin
figures.   Fifteen months of fatigue, privation, and suffering,
were in a moment forgotten.   China! it was the end of our
journey, and it was also the commencement of our return.
Nevertheless, we were not yet there; for though we had
left Burman Laos, we had not in reality put our foot on
Chinese territory.   Muong-Long is the first of the twelve

Muongs which form the kingdom of Sien-Hong, the third state founded by the Laotians of the north, and Sien-Hong has not kept its in dependence, any more than the states of Sien-Tong and Muong-Lem; though, as a tributary to two rival states, it in reality enjoys the privilege of self-government more than either of the others.   We found ourselves at once at the mercy of Burman, Laotian, and Chinese mandarins.   The chief of the village seemed, at first, to be very zealous in our behalf; and, at the request of M. de Lagrée, had the drum beaten to assemble porters for us; but at the moment of our departure, a letter arrived from the king of Sien-Hong to the mandarin of Muong-Long, his inferior, containing, without other explanation, these simple words: 'When the Europeans arrive at Muong-Long, you will desire them to return by the road they came.'

This dreadful blow crushed our enthusiasm, and reminded us that the fight was not yet over; but we were too well accustomed to the tricks of the authorities of this country to fear anything but a tiresome delay.   M. de Lagrée dispatched his interpreter to the king of Sien-Hong, and we awaited his return at Muong-Long.

The market, held in this place, is very considerable. They sell a great deal of cotton, tobacco, and raw silk, cotton stuffs imported through Rangoon, articles in silver and copper, clocks, weights and balances, and edible commodities.   Large restaurants were filled with a noisy and picturesque crowd; a bar-woman offered to all those who presented themselves a bowl of rice, rolled and cut like vermicelli, to which she added salt, allspice, fine herbs, pork cut up very small, with fish-broth, which is made at the side of each table in an immense iron pot, for sauce.   It was very different from those villages of Laos where every one lives in a state of such profound isolation, that with the exception of the pagodas, one never meets a single public establishment.

We had time to visit the monuments of Muong-Long. There are two pyramids in the village, but one is not worthy of description; the other, on the contrary, from its originality, seemed to have left the rut into which religion, the one source of art in these countries, has sunk Laotian architecture.   A round tower like a skittle, supported at the base by eight smaller towers, surmounting niches filled with statues of Iouddha, crowns a low hill a little out of the village. The whole is not without a certain elegance. I cannot comprehend the meaning of these fantastic pyramids, which, being neither tombs nor temples, give accommodation neither for the remains of the dead nor for the prayers of the living.

After some days of forced halt at Muong-Long, the mandarin brought us a letter from Sien-Hong; in which the king of this province, which borders on China, sought to explain the brutal curtness of his first message. To believe him, the Chinese authorities had ordered him to bar the road to travellers wishing to pass the frontier of the empire. This was what we had previously heard said at Luang-Praban. The king of Sien-Hong added, in a confidential manner, that if the orders of the emperor of China did not appear sacred to us, he, for his own part, would not oppose our journey.

Our interpreter had been charged to tell us, that we could not pass anywhere without loading the functionaries with presents of gold and silver. Had this argument been sufficiently strong to produce a decisive impression on the king's mind, and was he unwilling to let a chance escape him of an honest advantage, by making friends, if not with heaven, at least with its son? We could only obtain the key to this enigma by going to Sien-Hong, which place we reached in three days, by roads well laid out, but much travelled and greatly cut up. The oxen, carrying merchandise, had poached furrows in the mud as it began to harden, which might have been drawn by a plough, they were so deep and regular. In haste to attain the goal, which, for three months, had seemed to fly from us, we quickened our steps, and confided our baggage to the porters, whose feet were aching and shoulders swollen. These men will never consent to travel more than thirty kilometres a day, when they are employed a porters, but when charged with a message, on the contrary, they are both rapid and indefatigable couriers. No distance frightens them; and they will carry a letter forty leagues across mountains and forests as easily as, in Europe, one sends an invitation to dinner twenty minutes' distance from his hotel.

Plate 16 A Chinese bridge in Muong Long (Drawing by L. Delaporte, from life.)

Plate 17 *Our first night on Chinese soil (Drawing by Émile Bayard, based on a sketch by L. Delaporte)*

A native, who had no special official character, else, came to meet us, and conducted us to the pagoda destined to serve as our lodgings. Mats were spread on the floor, which was of mortar, and cords were passed from column to column, like those seen in menageries to prevent the public from touching the wild beasts. This precaution was not useless; for a crowd soon collected, and pressed into the sanctuary, impatient to see people who had come so far. At the first glance at the population, it was easy to see that it presented an incredible mixture of types and different races. Some Chinese from Yunan, on the extreme frontier of which we were, wore on their heads black turbans, as wide round as a straw hat with broad brims. As for the authorities, they continued to sulk. According to our interpreter, we were only at Sien-Hong, through his energy and intrepidity. When he first arrived, no one would receive him; and the king having sent him an order to return to Muong-Long, he replied, in the hyperbolical language used in the East, 'I am in your hands; you may kill me, if that will please you; but I have the order of the great French mandarin to remain here; and here I must stay till he come. If you take away the life of your slave, you will expose yourself to serious trouble; for I belong to a master who never abandons his servants. I must also inform you, if you oblige the French to await, at Muong-Long, a reply from China, that they are a very hasty people, and I cannot answer for the consequences that may occur in that small place.'

This discourse, which was not devoid of ability, was carried to the ruling powers, and produced on them a profound impression. The grand council, or *séna*, which, in the kingdoms tributary to Burmah, as at Luang-Praban, assists the sovereign, assembled without loss of time. The king conferred, for the greater part of a night, with the Chinese mandarin, who, in concert with a Burman envoy, watches over the affairs of the country; and this functionary decided at once to start for Muong-La, the first Chinese town of Yunan. They wrote, at the same time, to the governor of Muong-Long, that we were to remain with him, informing him, at the same time, that if we appeared to get angry, he was

authorised to let us go. This was the explanation of what
had seemed so ambiguous. As for the pretended prohibitions, sent us by the Chinese government, we found out, at
a later period, the origin of these rumours. The pro-vicar
of the Catholic mission of Yunan, and the viceroy of that
province, on learning our arrival on the frontier, moved by
a sincere sentiment of sympathetic interest, both wrote to
us, each in his own language, describing the state of the
country, and the dangers of the road, and dissuaded us
from continuing our journey. Though Sien-Hong is a
tributary of China, they can barely read the Chinese characters; and the letter of the viceroy of Yunan, not being understood, and being wrongly interpreted, was considered as a
prohibition from entering the territory. As for the letter of
the missionary, no one being able to decipher it, they deemed
it prudent not to speak of it at all, and we only heard of its
existence indirectly. Removed by only a few days' march
from a town entirely Chinese, and able already to count
on the moral effect of the passports signed by Prince Kong,
it behoved us to show ourselves confident as well as resolute. To avoid violence in word and deed, never to give utter-
ance to any definite menace, but to excite uneasiness—which
is more efficacious the more vague it is—in the timid minds
of the mandarins, whom responsibility invariably frightens,
was a method we frequently found to succeed, and the
application of which had never been more opportune. M. de
Lagrée had recourse to it. When a mandarin came officially
to inquire from him his intentions, he appeared hurt at the
obstacles placed in our way by the act of the king of Sien-
Hong; expressed no desire to see his majesty, and only
demanded to be allowed to leave for Muong-La without
delay, or else to write him the reasons for his detention,
which he would make use of as he should think best. This
conversation threw the counsellors of the crown into a visible
perplexity, which was very amusing to us. They, at last,
decided on making advances to us, inviting us to appear
before the *séna*, in the *sala*, where they transacted business,
after which the king would do us the honour of receiving us
in person.

The principal functionaries, to the number of twelve, were

ranged on each side of the prime-minister, who was enthroned on a bed-side carpet. They were attired with turbans, white vests, and wide trousers, or else in white calico
dressing-gowns, with a great langouti, in Burmese colours,
girt round the waist, and brought over the shoulders. To
the left of the prime-minister was seated the Burman mandarin ; a place to the right, ordinarily occupied by the Chinese
mandarin, was vacant : for, as we knew, he had set out for
Muong-La. M. de Lagrée made the assembly understand
that we only wanted one thing, and that was, to leave as
soon as possible. They then proceeded to the verification
of our papers, which a Chinese read, after the people had
squatted on the ground, for respect. They were found in
order, and they then introduced a subject which appeared to
be still more serious. We were required to enumerate, and
show to the members of council, beforehand, the presents we
intended to offer the king. Our resources, in this respect,
were much diminished; and it was the first time, besides,
that any one had made a demand of the kind, which they
now maintained with such a rude insistance. M. de Lagrée refused to comply with the request. The discussion
lasted two hours, after which, the king having sent word
that he was waiting for us, we directed our steps towards
the palace. Several days had been spent in cleaning the
whole place. The dunghill, which filled the grand court of
honour, had been raked; but there had not been sufficient
time to take it away. We passed between a double row of
ragged men, armed, some with old firelocks, others with
lances and indefinable instruments of war or of the chase.

We recognised in the ranks our baggage-porters, who,
enrolled momentarily in the royal guard, had exchanged
the bamboo of the porter for a warrior's lance. This sight
greatly diminished the impression of respectful terror which
this military display was intended to produce on us. The
palace is a miserable house, in bad condition ; and had
been fitted up with all the hangings the wardrobe had been
able to supply. Some Chinese carpets, ornamented with
embroidery in relief, prevented the daylight from penetrating between the badly-joined bamboos of the walls. On
each side of the platform, which served for throne, crouched

guards, carrying sabres with gilt scabbards, the handle, as
usual, on the ground, and the blade on the shoulder.   The
king, who kept us a long time waiting, at last appeared
from behind a curtain.   He wore an indescribable costume.
His head was covered with a Chinese hat, gilt, and ornamented with little bells; reminding one, if I might be so
disrespectful, of the musical instrument which is the standing accompaniment, in Europe, to the large drum.   A sort
of collar, with many frills, which came down in half circles
on the chest, their upper sides reaching the ears, made his
majesty resemble the classic Punch.   The king is a young
man about twenty years of age, who seems not allowed to
have any will of his own; for a mandarin asks questions,
and gives replies for him.   He has been placed on the throne
by the emperor of Burmah; and wears the small gold chains,
arranged in the form of a St. Andrew's cross, so much sought
after by Burmese nobles, as a mark of honour, and which Major
Burney, the first English resident at the court of Ava, was
gratified with.   The question of our departure was mentioned, and decided favourably.   We left the palace, as we
had entered. to the sound of music; the orchestra consisting
of a guitar and a nasal voice.   A tremendous shower of rain
had dispersed the troops; the artillery alone were at their
posts; three Chinese swivel-guns, stuck into the earth vertically, and charged to the mouth, saluted us as we went off.

The town of Sien-Hong, which in Pali is called Halévi,
has still another name,—Sip-Song-Pana, which carries with
it an allusion to a kind of dodecarchy, of which it is the
centre, and which we have seen begin at Muong-Long.   The
houses, which are very thinly scattered, have all a miserable
appearance, and give one the idea of a vast temporary encampment.   The country has been desolated by war, which
has several times ruined the town; and the inhabitants, at
each new catastrophe, have gathered together on another
part of the plain.   It is to this cause that the difference
of two minutes in the latitude of Sien-Hong, as given by
M'Leod in 1836, and as determined by the expedition of
M. de Lagré in 1867, is due.   There remain of the ancient
town, at six kilometres from the present one, some old gray
bricks, hidden amongst the vegetation, not far from the Nam-

Tap, which is a tributary of the Mekong, and the remains of
a brick wall, separated by a ravine from an elegant and well-
preserved pagoda. A fine garland, in carved wood, runs
below a ceiling supported by columns; between these are
large and well-shaped windows, which fill the interior of the
building with light.

The Mekong, which runs at the foot of the town of Sien-
Hong, carried us, for the last time, on its waters, and we
landed on the left bank of the river, at which we had not
touched since leaving Luang-Praban. We entered upon one
of the most rough and broken countries in the world, the
first mountains which we had to ascend joining on to the
spurs which the Himalayas throw out across Yunan. The
natives looked at us with a mixture of suspicion and curiosity. For the transport of our baggage we could only procure weak and sickly men, taken at hazard from the troop
of emigrants, whom the Mussulman insurrection had chased
from their country. Entire villages are peopled by these
unfortunates, who seem to find it hard to resign themselves
to the cultivation of a strange soil. The march became more
and more painful, as we had to ascend still steeper paths.
At 1200 metres above the level of the sea, we found only
savages, and it was from them we had to ask shelter for
the night. They have no *sala* for travellers; and we had to
content ourselves with a badly-roofed stable, where we were
invaded by myriads of fleas. Sleep, which our great fatigue
so imperatively required, could not triumph over these un-
seen enemies. It was the first time we had suffered such an
annoyance, and we recognised it as a sign that the nation, so
justly reputed to be the dirtiest in the universe, could not be
very far off. In these small villages we had some difficulty
in organising our transport; so much so, that, on several
occasions, we were compelled to employ both women and
children as porters. The most vigorous men took possession
of the lightest boxes, whilst their wives, bending beneath the
load, put a strap, fixed to the heaviest packages, over their
forehead, and walked along like oxen yoked to a heavy
strain.

Little by little the traits which characterise Laos pass
away from the customs, dress, and architecture of this part

P

of the country. The language gradually alters, and melts
into another. The inhabitants of this intermediary zone are,
in reality, neither Laotians nor Chinese; they mix the two
idioms in their speech, and you see touches on their features
taken from both the great neighbouring races. As regards
language, one passes, especially after leaving Luang-Praban,
through a succession of shades, which do not seem to constitute different languages, but rather special dialects. Between the first and last link of the chain the distance appears
considerable; but you receive a totally different impression,
if you have come in contact with the links between.

Cultivation became more general on the mountains; the
houses were small, constructed with mortar, and rested on
the ground, not, as in Laos, on posts. The door is narrow,
and ornamented with bands of red paper, on which were
traced Chinese hieroglyphics in black ink, beseeching the
evil genii to keep themselves at a distance, or recalling to
the passers-by some fine maxims of the moralist Confucius.
These villages, set on knolls, or hidden in hollows, are very
picturesque. We stopped in them twice a day, and even in
the poorest we found a table and benches,—precious furniture, almost unknown in Laos. The streets, the men, the
animals—are all plastered with mud, like the houses themselves, the partition walls of which, made of straw, earth,
and cow-dung, exhale a sickening odour. The buffaloes had
a fine time of it, and were taking their ease: lying in the
mire, they looked on idly at the beasts passing, loaded with
rice; but they, too, have their hard work, for they plough
the furrow, from which the others bear home the harvest
thrashed in the field.

The mountains grew higher, and were covered with vast
forests of pine-trees. This natural ornament completely
changed the aspect of the country, which becomes one of the
most beautiful in the world. Torrents foam down the
gorges, veiled by a curtain of great trees; sometimes, on
a ridge, a field of buckwheat shining in the sun looks as if it
were the beginning of the eternal snows; the strong scent of
the pine-trees was delightful. Forgetting the fatigues of a
toilsome ascent, we wished to mount higher and higher still,
and at last see the Celestial Empire at our feet. We were

close to it; at each step material proofs confirmed our conviction of this: the tombs by the side of the road piously kept up, the altars of stone, inscriptions in Chinese characters, and even a post of soldiers, wearing the tail, with the martial appearance so often described. At last, in the afternoon of the 18th of October 1867, five months after our departure from Luang-Praban, and sixteen months after quitting Saïgon, from the summit of a high mountain, a great plain lay stretched out before our eyes, and at its extremity, on a low hill, was a veritable town, with its white gables, red walls, and brick roofs. We were about to tread the soil which bears one of the most ancient and least-known people in the world; all our hearts beat with emotion, and our eyes were moist with tears; and if I had had to die during the journey, I should have wished to expire there, like Moses on Mount Nebo, embracing with his last look the land of Canaan.

CHAPTER VI.

WESTERN CHINA.

CHINA! This word alone awakens the idea of a people that has triumphed over space by the extent of its empire, and over time by its duration. One feels in the presence of a nation, unchanging alike in its customs and maxims; and which, notwithstanding the revolutions which agitate it, and the invasions it undergoes, opposes to the current of events and idea a sort of colossal petrifaction. Imprisoned in the meshes of an idiom which makes intelligence subordinate to memory. and in a network of institutions which regulate even the attitudes of the body, China has, nevertheless, anticipated Europe in its social life, in science, and in art; but the most fruitful inventions have remained sterile, as though Providence had willed this race should pass abruptly from a premature youth to an irremediable decrepitude. Master of the half of Asia, this people might again assemble armies as numerous as those of Gengis-Khan; but its soldiers fly before a handful of Europeans, after shaking at them, in impotent menaces, the painted monsters whose hideous shapes are to be seen on our screens and hangings. It is a strange country full of contrasts and mysteries, where grandeur is side by side with the grotesque, and where apes, justly proud of the forty centuries of their history, look down on you from the top of a folding screen as if from the summit of a pyramid.

To visit this sphinx in the least-known part of its domain, was the hope which had so long sustained us, and which we were on the point of seeing accomplished. We found ourselves. in fact, on that extreme frontier of China, which, until now, had never been traversed by a European. We had not entered the Celestial Empire by its so easily-accessible coast, where the traveller finds more of Europe than of China itself; we were nearly 2400 miles from the sumptuous hotels of Shanghaï, and from that consular protection which extends to the confines of the habitable world the shadow of one's native country. We arrived drained of resources, without shoes, almost without clothes, in a country where esteem for outward appearance has survived the horrors of a civil war. But whilst fearing to compromise our dignity in the eyes of mandarins, who might judge of our rank by our clothes, we had firmly resolved to make use of the imperative orders of our passports to assure our safety, and to make our persons respected. The letters signed by the regent of the empire had, in reality, clothed us better than the most brilliant official costume would have been able to do, even in the eyes of this most formal of all races. The representatives of the Chinese government did not justify towards us their old reputation of perfidy; from which one may conclude, it was to their want of power, and not to their hostility, that the distress and the perils which the members of the commission had to undergo during the latter part of the journey must be imputed.

It will, perhaps, be remembered, that the Laotian king of Sien-Hong, hesitating to let us continue our route, had sent the Chinese mandarin, in residence with him, to take the instructions of the governor of Muong-La. But the town which lay before our eyes was no other than Muong-La itself; so that the unworthy schemes by which, for a moment, he had hoped to intimidate us, had not succeeded, thanks to the firmness of our attitude. The orders of the emperor of Burmah could no longer affect us; we had slipped through the hands of his agents in Laos, and had crossed over the southern frontier into the province of Yunan, the least-known of the Middle empire. Muong-La is called Seumao by the Chinese; it is also, I believe, the same town that an Englishman proposed to unite to Rangoon by a railway, in order to bring the whole stream of commerce of western China to a port in British India.

After the inauguration of the Suez Canal, and on the eve of the opening of the Mont Cénis Tunnel; in presence, above all, of that colossal enterprise, which has joined New York to

San Francisco, notwithstanding the Rocky Mountains,—one
can assign no limits to the power of man. If the Anglo-
Saxon race should choose, some day, to apply to the execution of such a work the resources it is able to command, and
the perseverance which characterises it, it would, no doubt,
succeed in triumphing over all obstacles; but I am inclined
to think it will be long ere it undertake such an enterprise.
Without enumerating the difficulties of all kinds which it
would be necessary to overcome, before linking together the
mountains of Yunan and the shores of the Gulf of Martaban
by a railway, it suffices to say, that the immense sums which
would be swallowed up in this work would remain a dead
loss, if the order of things inaugurated in 1855 by the revolt
of the Mussulmans prove permanent; for a state, founded on
the triumph of Mahometan fanaticism, would leave such an
enterprise without a future, and without a guarantee. Proofs
will not be wanting in the course of this narrative to support
this assertion. We had scarcely entered China till ruins on
every side saddened us. The scourge of which we had seen
the traces, more particularly in the province of East Laos,
had still more cruelly devastated this part of Yunan, and
deserted or destroyed villages became more numerous the
nearer we approached the town.

Paved roads crossed each other in the rice-fields. We
followed one, which led us over a stone bridge, similar to the
one that had caused us so much pleasure at Muong-Long.
Then we entered the faubourgs. Women crowded to their
doorsteps to see us pass; children escaped from school, followed by their master, still carrying in his hand a long
rod, and wearing spectacles with round glasses; and groups,
formed round the notices stuck up on the walls, left off reading to look at us. Armed guards were in waiting for us;
they saluted us politely, and requested us to follow them.
Our escort, which augmented at each step, soon comprehended the entire population of Scumao. We kept by the
wall of the town; then turning to the right, we arrived, after
ten minutes' walk, at the pagoda where we were to stay.
The narrow court was already invaded, and the soldiers
had some difficulty in making a passage for us through the
tightly-packed ranks of the crowd; they were even on the

roofs. The pagoda, a vast square building, quite open on the side of the interior court, was in a moment filled by the multitude, in spite of the effort of policemen, armed with staves. These officials, finding themselves powerless to keep back this flood let loose, were obliged to give way, at the same time recommending us to look well after our baggage. Accustomed for long months to vast horizons, and solitudes without bounds, I felt myself quite giddy amidst this human ant-nest, crowded into a narrow space.

A movement was, at last, made in the court; the compact mass of the curious opened, and closed again. It was a mandarin, preceded by soldiers in red coats, who came officially to bid us welcome. His turned-up hat was ornamented with a cord and tassels of silk, and surmounted with a blue ball. He bowed gracefully, and informed us we had been expected for some time, and that they had begun to despair of ever seeing us. He ordered rice and pork to be brought to us, and begged to know our wants. Notwithstanding the presence of this functionary, the public pressed closer and closer. The police, with their sticks, kept off the most audacious; and two of our Annamites, placed as sentinels, drove back the curious into the court, so that we might have at least our room to ourselves. It was only as night came on that we were able to make ourselves comfortable, having at last been left in peace. Our pagoda had three walls, made of bricks whitened by lime; the fourth side was open, as I have said, and sustained by beautiful wooden columns. Our ancient acquaintance, the Bouddha of Cambodgia and Laos, with its long features, hanging ears, and contemplative and devout attitude, had given place to two personages, life-sized, above whom a woman seemed to hover, seated on a cloud.

Of the three great religions spread over China, not counting Islamism, only that of Confucius seems to have remained pure from all mythological and superstitious mixture. The learned classes, who alone profess this doctrine, trouble themselves much less to seek religious notions in it, which indeed they would not find if they did, than a system of positive philosophy and practical morals. With the exception of the tablet of Confucius, which figures in the temples erected in his honour, and in all the schools, this worship has no images, symbols, or priests. The belief in Bouddha, on the contrary, introduced into China in the first century of our era, under the reign of Ming-Ti, soon passed to the court of the king of Tchou, prince-vassal of the empire, and to the hearts of the poor, the miserable, and the suffering. Flattered, but not fully satisfied, by the anathema of Bouddhism against activity and life, these wretched people grafted on the dogmas of Fo the superstitions which, in the absence of a well-founded faith and philosophic doctrines, grow so easily in the darkness of the human soul. Temples and images multiplied countlessly; but, at the present time, the Chinese bonzes, a race now ignorant and abject, are frequently unable to give a reason for the belief which they profess from necessity, and of the symbols that they worship from habit. Finally, Lao-tseu, born at the end of the seventh century before Christ, would appear to have played, contrary to his contemporary, Confucius, the part of an inspired prophet. Rising above the social horizon, going beyond the bounds of national tradition, and despising philosophy, he aspired to conduct his disciples to the heights of a cosmogony to which one cannot refuse a character of grandeur. He taught that supreme reason was preëxistent to chaos, and 'connected the chain of beings to him whom he called *one*, then to two, then to three, who, he said, made all things.'[1]

What is most clear in his book is, that a triune being formed the universe. Was this, as some affirm, a doctrine borrowed from the Jews by Lao-tseu, in a journey he made in the West, or, as others pretend, a remembrance of the ancient triune divinity of the Hindoos? I cannot here examine the point. I simply wish to indicate the three kinds of temples in which we were from this time called to take up our abode, and to return thanks to Lao-tseu, who furnished our first resting-place on Chinese territory.

His doctrines, disfigured by his followers, are becoming absolutely unrecognisable in the present day. His temples, like those of Fo, are filled with grotesque and grinning statues, objects of ridicule to the enlightened classes, who pursue the Catholic images also with their iconoclastic hatred.

---

[1] Abel Rémusat.

In the pagoda which we occupied there were, as I have said, a group formed of two men, who appeared to be under a female raised above them: it recalled to my mind the words of Lao-tseu, that 'all beings repose on the feminine principle.' A small lamp, placed on a table, burns always before the virgin, and three pans are constantly filled with incense. An old priest and two respectable priestesses sufficed for the care of the sanctuary. Never were vestals more accommodating. The sacred fire served to light our cigars; the tables were loaded with profane objects, and we took our meals on them.

The French flag planted at the top of the steps, the arms fixed to the columns, the mats stretched on the ground to serve as our beds—in fact, the thousand details of our daily life, did not appear to disturb our venerable hostesses, who came regularly every day to salute the idols. After having examined the oils of the lamp and the sawdust of odoriferous wood, they struck three strokes on a little bell, and prostrated themselves several times. These, with the addition of a pious lecture on certain days of the month, are the whole duties of their worship. These good old women seemed quite happy; they enjoyed their tranquil existence, and did not refuse themselves small gratifications. They had, for example, purchased two comfortable coffins, which was an evident proof they had not arrived at a complete self-denial. In Europe the Trappists dig their own graves, and no enemy of monastic institutions has ever reproached them for this custom, as being Epicurean. In China, on the contrary, to furnish oneself beforehand with a coffin is a luxury every one cannot aspire to; they are articles of furniture which cost very dear, above all when they bear the name of a renowned manufacturer.

One morning, the palace-guards brought M. de Lagrée the governor's visiting-card. Some Chinese characters on a piece of red paper signified that he wished to see us; such, at least, was the explanation given by one of ourselves, who, at the taking of Pekin, had been in the squadron of Admiral Charner. It is one of the advantages of the intense centralisation of which China has given Europe the example, that the traveller who has spent a month in Petcheli, does not feel himself a stranger in Yunan, at the other end of the empire.

To reach the hall of audience, we had to pass through a high arched doorway, which crowned two overhanging roofs, between which is arranged a place for two military posts. The governor received us in a room at the end of three courts. His excellency wore in his hat a ball of coral; but as he was a military mandarin, our respect for him was greatly diminished. We were aware that, in China, the *cedant arma togæ* is pushed very far; for civilians, as a rule, learned or unlearned, profess even for the greatest general a disdain which prudence does not allow them always to exhibit, though the prejudices of his compatriots justifies his feeling it. Besides, learned mandarins would be of as little use in the province of Yunan, as a university professor in a besieged town. Our host wore the usual Chinese costume, a furred cloak, long silk robe, and magnificent tail; he had large features, prominent eyes, and an open rather than a fine countenance, which bespoke benevolence and firmness. He would fain have added a certain air of majesty, but it did not succeed. He spoke little, smoked his pipe, and remained impassive till the moment when M. de Lagrée offered him a revolver. As soon as he comprehended the mechanism of this weapon, his eyes shone like those of a war-horse scenting the battle from afar: he sprang from his seat, forgetful of his dignity, and the six balls that he fired, one after another, would certainly have wounded several of his subjects, if they had not quickly turned his arm aside. The hall of audience was, in fact, invaded by a noisy crowd, who elbowed us, interrupting the conversation by their shouts of laughter, and mercilessly cutting short even the discourse of the governor himself.

He appeared to be animated with the best intentions towards us, though he showed some uneasiness as to the aim of our journey. One might have supposed he feared a secret understanding between us and the Mussulmans. He also informed us that all the western portion of the province through which the Mekong flows, which he called Kioulang-kiang (river of the Nine Dragons), was in the hands of these enemies of the empire. The experience we had gained in penetrating without passports amongst the Laotians, tributaries of Burmah, had taught us a lesson, and we did not feel disposed to incur new perils. M. de Lagrée, taking in the situation at a glance, renounced, not without regret, the plan of following the course of the Mekong, and determined, for two reasons, to turn his steps eastward. From the first he was convinced that, to penetrate at hazard into a disorganised country, overrun by undisciplined bands, intoxicated with murder and pillage, would only be to expose us to unpleasant occurrences, and to make us objects of suspicion to the faithful authorities of Seumao. On the other side, in presence of the certain development that the future reserves for our colonial establishment in Cochin-China, M. de Lagrée felt it would be useful to explore the zone watered by the Sonkoï. This river, which is not much known at this part, has its source in the north-west of Yunan, and falls into the sea in the Gulf of Tonkin, where our flag would be able to secure an easy entrance. The basin of the Mekong was, therefore, abandoned for that of the Sonkoï, and a purely geographical interest for a political one of the first order.

This determination, resolved on and announced at the governor's reception, appeared to give him great satisfaction; and, coming out of his diplomatic reserve, he at once became frank and pleasant. He promised us an escort; but he added that we must hasten our departure, for the war, though for a moment suspended, was on the eve of recommencing more furiously than ever, and the road which we were about to take was only separated by a three days' march from the Mussulman armies, which, chased from Seumao, were disposed to return again. This unfortunate town will long bear the marks of the combats which have taken place before its walls. The faubourgs and villages on the outskirts of the town, which contained a population of at least 30,000, have been destroyed; there does not remain one house in twenty. The conquerors appear to have directed their greatest violence against the pagodas; some having been entirely demolished, and others transformed into stables, whilst all have been desecrated; altars thrown down, headless statues, ornaments in pieces — present the signs, but too well known, of that horrible form of civil war called

a religious one.   I do not speak of the massacred populations, because nothing leaves less trace on the earth
than man himself: the most insignificant of his works at-
tests its existence by its ruins; but of himself there remains
nothing.

The inhabitants were actively engaged in repairing the
walls of the town, and in digging a large ditch round them.
On the platform were accumulated, at equal distances,
piles of stones to shower on the enemy, and every day the
troops were exercised in firing.   The siege-guns were long,
wide tubes of iron, half culverin, half musket.   One soldier
attends to the gun-carriage, a second points the gun, and
the third, who stands, match in hand, fires it.   All was,
therefore, in preparation for the approaching assault.   The
walls seemed to be strong enough to resist it; they were
thick, constructed of good bricks and freestone; the gates,
cased in iron, would stand, unless a powerful artillery should
be brought against them.   As to the violations of the rules
of the illustrious Vauban, the bad outline of the *enceinte*, the
want of bastions, the glacis of the scarp and counter-scarp,
it is not my province to speak of them.   The governor's
cabinet resembled the tent of a general in the field; at each
instant couriers arrived and left; he himself displayed su-
prising activity; it may be that the assurance his revolver
gave him had decided him on taking the offensive.   He had
received, besides, from Burmah, a quantity of European arms,
amongst which was a musket of Russian manufacture, taken
by the English, most likely, at Sebastopol.

Numerous files of horses and mules continually arrived
in the town, bringing cotton, firewood, and, above all, rice,
to warehouse in granaries, in anticipation of a siege.   The
richer classes had completely deserted the menaced town,
and there only remained shopkeepers, functionaries, and
soldiers.   Shoemakers, grocers, apothecaries, tailors, sellers
of opium, small traders of all kinds, braved the chances of
the war to gain some thousands of sapeques.   This was fortunate for us; for, whilst we provided ourselves with native
shoes, the men of our escort made us clothes of a quasi-Euro-
pean style from cloth made in Burmah.   We were anxious,
indeed, to make our nationality known by the cut of our

coats and of our hair. Our Chinese purveyors seemed quite indifferent to what we wore; all they cared for was that our money was good.

Whilst waiting our departure, I visited the shops, which much interested me, and I spent some hours in observing the working of the different trades, of which none exist in Laos, and which are one of the signs of civilised life. I was frequently invited by the shopkeepers, whilst strolling through the town, to enter and take a cup of tea; an offer which, in China, like that of coffee in the Levant, is the commencement of all conversation. The mandarins saluted me by bowing, in the same manner as European ladies; for a well-educated Chinese never uncovers his head. We received numerous visits. Our interpreter succeeded in making himself understood, by mixing with the language of the last Laotian province a small number of Chinese words; but the rumours he had heard had frightened him so much, that he did not dare to accompany us any farther in our journey. We had certainly never counted on his courage, which was easily shaken by the slightest appearance of danger; or on his devotion, which was not proof against money, or a woman's smile; but his quick and supple turn had fallen into new customs as insensibly as into a new language. He always managed to make himself understood, at least, by the lower classes, which was an immense advantage, as we soon discovered after he had left us. In fact, travellers in China always provide themselves with an interpreter, or, at any rate, with a vocabulary of all essential words, before venturing into the provinces of the interior. We were, on the contrary, thrown, without either of these resources, on the most distant frontiers of the great empire, separated, by an invincible barrier, from a refined and exacting society, and incapable of seizing even the literal meaning of educated conversation, and, of course, so much the more unable to find out what men, accustomed to make use of speech in order to disguise their thought, wished to hide under metaphors and amplifications.

M. de Lagrée fought against this new difficulty with the energy of which he had already given proof, and succeeded in triumphing over it. With a resolute character, but a tender

and sympathetic disposition, he had always found the way
to the affections of young people. Whilst acting as governor
of Cochin-China at Cambodgia, he liked to surround himself
with the pupils of the Catholic mission; many of them became his servants, and never deceived his confiding affec-
tion. He did the same in China. From the first day of our
arrival at Seumao, his benevolent manners drew towards
him a young Chinese without family or resources, like so
many others in this desolated province, and he made him
his teacher. By dint of work, patience, and gentleness, the
master and disciple became accustomed to, and finally understood, each other. In difficult cases, we had recourse to one
of our Annamites, who had learnt to write, as they taught it
in his country, before the establishment of the French schools
and the substitution of the European alphabet for ideographic
writing. He knew a certain number of the Chinese characters most generally in use. If a Chinese and an Annamite
cannot understand each other when they talk, they can at
any rate communicate by writing. For each of them, in fact,
these complicated signs, whose origin was the representation
of real objects, have an identical signification.

On the evening before our departure, a message came
from the governor to the chief of the expedition, begging
him to remain another couple of days. Accustomed to these
delays, M. de Lagrée employed the same means he had had
recourse to in Laos, and pretended to be very angry. After
long explanations, we at last understood that this was, on
the part of the mandarin, a very courteous proceeding, and
necessary form of politeness. It was good taste to appear
grieved at our departure, and to try and retain us, at least
for another twenty-four hours. If the desire of keeping us
longer with them, expressed in such an unexpected manner
by the authorities, was only a refinement of urbanity, the
population was animated by a much more sincere sentiment.
During the whole of our stay at Seumao, the court of our
pagoda had not ceased to be encumbered with the infirm,
the sick, and the wounded, to whom Doctor Joubert liberally
distributed remedies, counsel, and care. There, as everywhere, sickness was the sad companion of poverty; ulcers
showed themselves oftenest under tattered clothes; and our

establishment, at some hours, was almost like the porches
of Bethesda. One of the employés of the palace, who had
escaped at the moment of receiving correction for some
peccadillo, had been pursued by the soldiers, caught like
a hare, and literally hacked whilst lying on the ground,
exhausted and defenceless. Covered with deep wounds, he
was left for dead. We took him in, and repeated dressing
of his wounds soon restored him; a prodigy of European
surgery, at sight of which the joy of the friends of the
wounded man was only equalled by their gratitude. Our
reputation was at its height before we left, and we had the
satisfaction of leaving behind us regret and mutual good
feeling.

Our baggage-porters were poor creatures, who had been
compelled reluctantly to serve us. The commandant of the
escort was a mandarin of inferior rank, well fed, with a broad
straw hat, with brims sloping down, a number of cushions
below him, and his heels in the stirrups; a veritable Sancho
Panza on horseback; as to us, we could not afford such a
beast. Before him marched several men, carrying red flags;
behind were soldiers, some armed with lances, and others
with muskets slung across the shoulder. These last, from
time to time, attended to the smoking-matches of their gun-
locks. It looked as if we were very likely to come across
armed bands, and accordingly we kept our pistols loaded;
for our Chinese escort did not inspire us with much confidence. After leaving the town by the eastern gate, we followed a road which wound between hillocks covered with
tombs. The sky was cloudless and of the deepest blue; a
thin and scorched-up herbage covered the slight undulations
of the soil; a few trees survived against a red wall, or a
white gable, the shining brightness of which attracted the
eye irresistibly. We might have fancied ourselves transported
into the fields of Provence.

Instead of the narrow pathway which, in Laos, served
as a road across the rice-fields, we found here a paved causeway, which did not even end at the foot of the mountains.
It entered them, still maintaining a width varying between
one and three metres, and recalled to mind the Roman roads.
From time to time, when the way is too steep, a few steps

facilitate the ascent. We passed the night in an abandoned
pagoda at the foot of a monstrous idol, very much mutilated
and its inside torn open. The treasures of the pagoda
being often concealed in the body of the statues, miscreants
do not hesitate to treat them in this impious manner. Clouds
covered the summits of the mountains when we again started
on our journey, and the rising sun could barely pierce through
their dark veil. We perceived ruined villages, and walls
which afforded no shelter; not a house was standing, not an
acre in cultivation. The interruptions in the paving of the
road were frequent, and rendered the march difficult. Among
the blocks of stone which constituted the pavement, some
remain in the place they have occupied for centuries, and
others have sunk into the ground, or rolled into the ravines.
The time for such magnificent works has long since passed;
the administrative machine, which, in olden times, was so
well wound up, is now quite out of order; the empire is
threatened with a general dissolution; the government has
no longer either the money or the leisure necessary for the
keeping up of these great works, executed in times of yore
by all-powerful emperors, whose reign they still honour.
More than twenty-two centuries before the Christian era,
Chun, a simple labourer, associated with himself, by Yao, in
the imperial dignity, had commenced making dykes, to prevent the waters of the rivers from overflowing the country;
and Yu, raised to the throne, as Chun himself had been, in
consideration of his services and of his valour, achieved this
colossal enterprise. In the year 214 before Christ, Chi-
hoang-ti laid the foundations of that famous wall, whose
construction occupied several millions of men for ten years,
and is a lasting monument of the power of the Chinese. It is
to Chi-hoang-ti also that the honour is due for having laid
down these roads, which, after having first traversed the
Chensi and the Chansi, were afterwards added to, and finally
enveloped the whole of China in an immense network. Each
time a province was conquered, it was by similar benefits they
induced it to attach itself to the empire. To ameliorate by
improved laws, and enrich by works of great public interest,
the innumerable people successively grouped round the original kernel of the *hundred families*, was the method the Chi-

Plate 18 *Doctor Joubert providing consultation in Se Mao (Drawing by Émile Bayard. based on a sketch by L. Delaporte).*

Plate 19 *Savages from the surroundings of Ta Lan, Che Pin and Muong Pong (Drawing by Émile Bayard, based on a sketch by L. Delaporte)*

nese sovereigns pursued; it was thus that they cemented this gigantic unity, which required so many centuries to produce. Yunan itself, so often lost and reconquered, that one might almost consider it as a simple military colony, has not been forgotten by the imperial government; and the works of art which it has lavished upon it, lend to the wild grandeur of the scenery which surrounds them a singular and remarkable appearance. In the present day the roads are out of repair, the bridges tumbling down, and a desert is formed around these accumulated ruins. I could not have imagined such complete desolation. Strangers though we were, we felt ourselves overcome with sadness, and we followed in silence the windings of a road, over which death seemed to have passed.

All at once, in a narrow valley, we came across numerous houses, rising one above the other on the two slopes of the mountains. A long file of horses and mules, the sound of a waterfall, black eddies of smoke, with a powerful odour of coal, and the hum peculiar to manufacturing towns, roused us from our melancholy. We had, at length, reached a town sprung out of its own ruins; the Mussulmans had vainly tried to destroy it, for the greater glory of the Prophet; the energy of the inhabitants had prevailed, life had triumphed over death, and industrial activity had fought for three years against despair and misery. The secret lay in the fact that the hidden riches of the soil could not be carried away, neither could the enemy exhaust them. They might burn the houses, and overthrow the pagodas; but they could not fill up the salt-pits, or work out the coal, or destroy the pine-forests. A population of Chinese workmen carry on the works, and make use of the resources of all kinds which abound in this narrow space. If their methods are not yet perfect, they are, at any rate, very ingenious. The pits go down obliquely to a depth of eighty metres in the earth, sustained at equal distances by wooden frames. A large pump sends the air to the workmen who are at the bottom of the pits; and a series of smaller ones, each of which is worked by a man, pumps up the salt-water through a bamboo pipe, which empties it into a large reservoir, from whence they bring it into the caldrons. These,

Q

to the number of from twenty-five to thirty, are heated by means of wood and anthracite. The flaming mouth of the furnaces charm the eyes of the traveller, who arrives suddenly in this favoured spot, after having traversed barbarous or devastated countries. We saw a considerable quantity of lumps of sal., obtained in this manner by evaporation, warehoused, and ready to receive the stamp of the mandarin tax-collector. At the end of this small town, which is built like an amphitheatre, the pagoda lies in a nook removed from all noise and exhalation. Built on the side of the mountain, and shaded by beautiful trees, its brilliant colours, and a semicircular basin before it, covered with water-lilies in flower, delighted us. The Chinese pagodas, whose architecture is well known in Europe, do not in the least resemble the Bouddhist temples of Laos, which we had so frequently lived in. Notwithstanding that they cover a large space, they do not show the ample and sublime forms which give to some sanctuaries in Indo-China, as also to those in Hindostan, such an imposing majesty. They want that grandiose unity—noble characteristic of sacred architecture—which, without excluding the richness of a luxuriant ornamentation, reveals the profound sentiment from whence works, inspired by faith, appear to spring forth into one great plan. They have neither those upshootings towards heaven, which are in Teutonic Europe like an image of prayer, nor that harmonious development of architectural lines which bear witness among the Greeks to such a serene vision of ideal beauty. These pagodas are composed of long suites of sanctuaries, and small retreats, connected one with the other by terraces and galleries. The general appearance is flat, and seems on a level with the soil. One would say that the temples feared to approach the clouds, after the fashion of the Chinese belief itself; which dreads, above all things, to lose itself in abstraction. We found ourselves, however, as did also the men of our escort, very comfortable in them; and we not seldom regretted the pagodas, in places where the war has permitted some hotels to be kept open.

The second town in China in which we stayed was called Poheul. In order to arrive there, we had to traverse pine-forests, worked without method or measure by numerous woodcutters, by whom this richly-wooded country will soon be destroyed. Poheul is not so well situated as Seumao. Built in a narrow valley, two high mountains enclose and seem to crush it. On the summit a many-storied pavilion and an isolated tower produce a strange effect. These towers, of which the most celebrated is at Nankin, are often in China placed near the entrance to important towns. They appear to be connected with a religious sentiment. 'According to Indian tradition, when Bouddha died, they burnt his body; after which they divided his bones into eight portions, and enclosed them in the same number of urns, which, in their turn, were to be placed in towers of eight stories; and this, it is said, was the origin of these towers, so common in countries where Bouddhism has penetrated.'[2] These mountains are decidedly picturesque: the large black and white stripes of the calcareous rock blend with the green boughs of a shrub, whose roots are buried in the stone. The town of Poheul has suffered from the war, even more than Seumao. One street alone is inhabited. They had begun to dig a ditch, of some metres in width, round the walls; but this work of defence has been abandoned. Poheul seemed to be resigned to its fate; and the Mussulmans, who have already taken it once, will find it open to them as soon as they feel themselves strong enough to achieve the conquest of the province.

This town, which has renounced the perilous position of a place of war, remains an important administrative centre. About two hundred years ago it was raised to the rank of *fou*,[3] and the mandarin, who resides there, is conscious of his dignity. He had not sent any one to receive us officially; and M. de Lagrée having expressed some surprise at this circumstance, personages decorated with balls of all shades,

---

[2] The Abbé Huc.

[3] The territory of a Chinese province is divided into a certain number of *fou*, of *theou*, and of *hien*, which have, all, a chief town, fortified. The comparison that has been often made between these administrative divisions and our own (*département, arrondissement, canton*) is not strictly correct. The functionaries resident in the *theou*, in general submit, it is true, to those of a *fou*, but they are dependent, notwithstanding, sometimes, directly, on the provincial administration.

hastened to us, offering to conduct us to the prefect's palace.
The crowd followed us, but were not allowed to enter, as at
Seumao, into the court of the Yamen. The conference was
less noisy and more dignified. The governor was the type
of the Chinese mandarin, as they are represented in all our
caricatures,—short and fat, with half-closed eyes, and some
long hairs on the chin. He desired us to leave, as speedily
as possible, for Yunan-Sen, the capital city of the province,
and not to pass through Lingan; for he could not understand
the motives, which induced us to study the region of the
south-east, instead of marching quickly towards the north.
Strangers, who willingly lingered in Yunan, could not fail
to become objects of suspicion, when he would gladly have
paid a high price for the privilege of leaving it. In fact,
the mandarins in this part of the country feel themselves so
unsafe, that they would prefer, in place of the administration of a prefecture in Yunan, a simple canton in Setchuen. Having, for the most part, sent away their families,
and placed their wealth in safety, they consider themselves
encamped on a soil exposed to the incursions of the enemy,
and curse the short-sighted ambition, which has placed them
in this dangerous position.

During the whole of our stay, a great number of the
principal inhabitants, dressed in holiday attire, had not
ceased to pray, in a loud voice, on the threshold of their
door, before a pan of burning incense, accompanying themselves with monotonous beatings on a sonorous bell, and on
a piece of hollow wood, in the shape of a fish, bent into a
circle. They were members of the society of the Water-lilies,
a sort of freemasonry, whose avowed aim is to disseminate
books of morals, but who pursue, in secret, other designs.
The Pe-lien-kiao, or white water-lilies,—for there exist sects
who hoist other colours, — expect a great conqueror, who
must 'subjugate the whole universe. They distribute among
themselves the principal offices of the state, in the hope that
one of them will, one day, ascend the throne, and that they
will then, in reality, possess the dignities which they at present only enjoy in imagination.'[4]

[4] *General History of China*. Translated from the Tong-kien-kang-mou
by Father de Mailla. vol. xi.

It was to them that the emperor Yon-tching compared the Christians, when, in 1723, he resolved to proscribe the missionaries. Whatever may be the principles on which it rests, every organised society is certain to have enemies in its bosom. Despotism unites, against itself, men jealous of their dignity; under a liberal government, one sees a league of the envious and incapable formed. China has not only anticipated Europe in philosophy, science, and art; she has also undergone, before us, political revolutions. We were still in the height of our feudal system, when a daring innovator tried to effect a social revolution in the Celestial Empire. One might almost say that the human mind, left to itself, is condemned to revolve for ever in the same circle. In the second century of our era, towards the end of the dynasty of the Han, a great number of mandarins were put to death, under suspicion of belonging to a secret society. In the eleventh century, under the Song, Ouang-ngan-che commenced the application of a scheme which tended to give the exclusive property of the soil to the state; which distributed the seed, settled the sort of cultivation the soil should receive, according to its various qualities, fixed the tariffs, and suppressed, by these radical means, the proletariat and poverty; two problems whose solution torments us still. The empire was profoundly disturbed by these dangerously utopian theories, which aggravated the evils they pretended to cure. The actual sect of the Water-lilies has never made so much noise; but it deserves to be noticed as one of the numerous manifestations of that persistent spirit of revolt, always ready to inscribe seductive devices on its colours. It was thus that the Taepings, whose sole aim was pillage, stirred up a rebellion, in the name of national independence; saying, that they were called upon to overthrow the dynasty of the Mantchou Tartars, as that of the Mongols had been overthrown, five hundred years previously, by a renegade bonze.

M. de Lagrée, before advancing towards the east, and thus going farther away from the Mekong, which flows to the west of Poheul, desired to see it once more. The mandarin having objected to this, under pretext that it would be necessary to pass very near a camp of Mussulmans, there

was nothing to detain us any longer in this town, celebrated
only for the fine tea which is grown in its neighbourhood.
We announced our intention of leaving, and everything was
promptly prepared. The mountains were steep, and the rain
had made the roads very slippery. We stumbled at every
step, climbing up the steep slopes, which were covered with
rime, until we reached a large village, where the working of
the salt-mines is conducted on a considerable scale. The
pits from which they obtain this precious commodity are
very common in China, especially in the north and west, and
furnish a considerable revenue. The mandarin who ruled
in this district loaded us with presents—salt, pork, capons,
and a bag of rice. The reason why this subordinate showed
himself more generous than his chief, the prefect of Poheul,
was, that the military mandarin who commanded our escort
was charged to give him orders to that effect; and he certainly carried them out: for besides serving himself from the
forced liberality of our hosts, he hoped that his zeal would
call forth a larger remuneration when he left us.

Our horizon was constantly bounded by high and barren
mountains; ravines and landslips veined their black masses
with red earth, which looked like the bared muscles of
flayed giants. From the top of a peak, rising 1560 metres
above the level of the sea, we saw at our feet a deep valley,
into which we had to descend by an almost perpendicular
pathway. Between two banks of white sand the troubled
waters of the Papen-Kiang flow to swell those of the Sonkoï, and to lose themselves in the gulf of Tonkin. We were
soon to quit the basin of the Mekong.

Among the emotions of such a journey as ours must be
added those one experiences in passing the line which separates the basins of great rivers. At such a watershed, a
single step seems to take one on as far as if it were a week's
march. Water seems more living than the other powers of
nature, and it is doubtless to this it owes its attractions, so
strong and so mysterious. I liked to say to myself, whilst
crossing the smallest tributary of the Mekong, that its waters,
mingled with the waves of the great river, would reflect
farther down the tricolored flag; and when, by the direction
of the streams, I knew that they carried the tribute of their

waters to another master, I fancied I saw the last ties severed
which had united me for twenty months to a friend.

Villages had existed a short time previously in this gorge,
and their ruins still remained. We followed, for a long time,
the course of the Papen-Kiang, which we crossed at nightfall. Our Chinese made their horses dash into the stream,
whilst others, on the opposite side, shouted with loud cries,
to show the animals, who were accustomed to this performance, the place where they should land. Beyond this rapid
river, we saw, uneasily, that our road lay partly through
the bed of a winding torrent. In Laos, where bridges
are considered a useless luxury, we were resigned, beforehand, to enter all the marshes that came across our path.
Since our entry into China, such an occurrence was rare, and
made us doubly impatient, as if we were beginning to get
effeminate. Here, again, were vast pine-forests—a gloomy
setting to an occasional house in red brick, still left standing,
which seemed to solicit the paint-brush of some artist. There
was no longer anything tropical in the scenery. The aspect
of the country became more wild and severe; we were surrounded by mountains, the summits of some of them being
lost in the clouds. The paved road was so bad, that, far
from helping us, it only added to the difficulties of our march.
The traffic on this road is very great, on account of the salt,
which the traders come long distances to procure. This
most necessary article of consumption alone maintains commercial activity in this region, numerous caravans braving
the perils of the way to bear it off. After a long ascent,
we reached a high plateau, where we found numerous villages, and a cultivated soil. Fields of rice and black wheat
nourish a considerable population, grouped around Taquan,
an important village and a compulsory station on the road
from Poheul to Talan.

Four or five hundred soldiers, who were staying there,
notified their presence by the noise which are habitual to
Chinese armies in the field: crackers, musket-shots, bronze
gongs, copper cornets, and guttural cries, saluted our arrival. In times of peace, the journeys of the mandarins are
a heavy burden on the populations; but when it comes to
the question of supplying the soldiers with provisions and

transport, it becomes a veritable scourge. These warriors live by marauding, and commence by pillaging the villages they are appointed to defend. The detachment stationed at Talan was about to rejoin the valiant governor of Seumao. Our little mandarin, whose hat was adorned by a fox's tail, which on his head might be taken as an emblem, appeared delighted that the duty he was called on to perform as our escort took him farther away from the theatre of the war. He magnified our importance to augment his own, and also, as I have said, in the hope that the good entertainment he procured for us would likewise benefit himself. Stimulated by him, a blue-balled mandarin, residing at Talan, overwhelmed us with attentions, in the shape of courteous visits and quarters of pork. On the day of our departure this functionary headed us, without our knowing beforehand, and had a salute fired in our honour. Such honours puffed us up, and we blushed for our poverty, ashamed at being unable to acknowledge this noble behaviour better than by the offer of a small trumpet or a pewter teaspoon.

The farther we advanced towards the east, the ravages caused by the war became less visible. Ruins were not so frequent, and cultivation disputed the soil with the woods of pine. Villages again appeared on all the heights, but did not look so bright in colour as those of the Chinese villages properly so called. They are peopled by mountaineers, who recall, by their costume and the general cast of their features, the natives of the northern frontier of Laos. The population of Yunan is composed of elements so numerous, so different, and so changeable, that it defies all analysis. It would be necessary, in order to give any account of them, to remain a long while in this, perhaps the most interesting, province of the whole empire, and to make the manners and language of the different savage tribes a special object of study.

Yunan is one of the last provinces which has been added to the Chinese empire. In the third century before Christ, an epoch which may be termed recent, since the great empire had already had two thousand years of historic existence, this country, divided between several independent sovereigns, who were, in reality, only the chiefs of tribes, was included under the general and vague denomination of *country of the western barbarians*, and lay beyond the frontiers of China, which, under the Tsin, did not, on the northwestern side, go beyond the river Leao-Ho. The first emperors of the Han dynasty diminished still more the extent of their territory; and on that portion of the dominion they abandoned was founded the kingdom of Tchao-Sien, where the Chinese, in difficult times, found a sure asylum. Han-ou-ti, sixth emperor of the Han dynasty, put an end to this state of affairs, by taking possession of the country of Tchao-Sien, which he divided into four provinces, dependent on China. At the same time, he reduced the two kings of Lao-Chin and of Mimo, whose territories were situated partly in Set-chuen, and partly in Yunan itself, and conquered the principality of Tien, which corresponds to the town of Yunan-Sen and its dependencies. All the Chinese provinces have passed, in different degrees, through this process of slow agglomeration, of which it suffices to have given an example.

Under the influence of internal revolts, or political necessity, before settling into the limits which they occupy in the present day, they have undergone many alterations, which are scrupulously noted in long annals, to which I can only refer the reader. But what characterises several provinces of the empire, and, above all, those on the western frontiers, is the existence of certain races, which have shown a singular vitality: remaining distinct, in spite of conquest and annexation; their language, costume, and even, sometimes, the right of governing themselves by their own laws, having escaped, at least in some measure, the deadly grasp of a powerful centralisation. Yunan, from this point of view, merits particular attention. Stretching up to the masses of the Himalaya, it shares the wild character of that savage region, which banishes all effeminacy, and at the same time protects its population by its mountain ramparts. One must distinguish, amongst the numerous tribes, those who, still calling themselves by the name of Tou-kia (aborigines), have doubtless originally possessed the soil, from those descending from voluntary emigrants, who entered the country at a later period, and consisted of convicts, or of soldiers who had finally renounced their original homes. Of the first occupants of this vast territory, which to-day bears the name of Yunan, the most numerous are the Lolos and the Pai-y. The Lolos are divided into black Lolos, white Lolos, red Lolos, and Lolos of the rice-fields. It is on the colour of their clothes, and not on that of their skin, that the three first distinctions are founded. The fourth is easily understood. The emperors gained over these people, by according to their chiefs the rank of Chinese mandarins, and by giving them possession of their land. The Lolos of to-day still submit to a sort of feudal organisation. They have a chief of their race, whom they call *Toussen ;* but it is difficult to know what they gain by him, for he stands only in the place of a viceroy of the province, and exercises over his subjects a despotic power. Timid, lazy, and intemperate, they shun the stranger, leave to their women the care of cultivating their fields, and seek happiness in intoxication. The Pai-y, separated from the Chinese, like the Lolos, by their language, and even, it would seem, by the characters of their writing, resemble the populations of the south-west, and seem to be near akin to the Laotian race. The Chinese government has equally respected their customs.

In the first rank of the tribes, descending from emigrants come from other parts of the empire, must be placed the Pentijins. This race has lost, through contact with the Lolos, the intellectual superiority which a more advanced civilisation had originally given it over these natives. The Minkias, who are scattered chiefly in the western part of Yunan, say they came from the province of Nankin. They trace their origin to soldiers, who remained in the places where war had called them, and there founded a colony, comparatively civilised and even learned, which had its own language, and was rich in literary monuments; but the emperor of China, not being able any longer to tolerate such a sign of independence, gave an order to burn all the books belonging to the Minkias. Despots, not less severe on a book than on a conspiracy, have always proscribed thought. It was thus that the stern warrior, who, two hundred and fifty years before our era, inaugurated the dynasty of the

Tsin, incensed by the resistance he encountered from the learned classes, and their criticisms of his acts, in order to stop their mouths, had all books of history and morality burnt, and prohibited also the different sorts of Chinese characters then in use in the empire, allowing only one form to remain, that called li-chou, which is in use at the present time;[5] in the same way as the Tartars of Europe are now striving to proscribe the Polish language, by forcing the children of the vanquished to speak Russian in their schools. Nevertheless, in justice, it must be said, that Tsin-chi-hoang-ti, who may be called the principal founder of the Chinese empire, was not actuated exclusively by anger, or by pride, in this rigorous act of destruction, but was influenced rather by motives of policy; wishing, at one stroke, to efface history, always so powerful over the imagination, and to destroy the titles on which the vanquished feudal princes would have been able to found their rights, and perpetuate their pretensions.

The Lolos, the Pai-y, the Penti, and the Minkias are not the only tribes who live amidst the Chinese of Yunan, without intermingling with them, like the Khas amidst the Laotians; but I will go no farther in this enumeration. It is said, though I have had no means of proving it, that, from an intellectual point of view, the gradation is still broadly marked between the different inhabitants of this country. The missionaries do not hesitate to place the savages in the lowest rank; after them the Métis, half-castes of Chinese and natives; and finally the Chinese, who have at different periods flocked into Yunan from the neighbouring provinces, and more particularly from Set-Chuen. The multiplicity of the races has caused, as may be easily imagined, a great variety of costumes, and it was only in the streets of the towns that we ever found a crowd really Chinese as regards costume and manners.

At the crossing of a large river we met a caravan composed of more than a hundred beasts, who all courageously swam over. The water looked spiked with long ears, and the echoes repeated the loud protestations of the asses and mules. Scarcely had our porters finished the stage for which they had been requisitioned, than, without leaving us time

[5] Father Gaubil.

to pay them, they started off on their return home at a run;
for since we left the territory of Burmah, at Sien-Hong, our
baggage had been carried by government porters, to whom,
according to custom, no remuneration is due for their trouble.
The mandarin sent from Talan to meet us arrived, preceded
by banners of all colours.   His soldiers never tired of beating
on two gongs with different tones, which produced the effect
of two bells striking a funeral knell.   This music was intended to enliven us, and thus render the ascent of a very
steep mountain, which separated us from the valley of Talan,
less laborious.   Every person of any importance had a horse,
or even a palanquin; whilst our poverty obliged us to walk
always on foot, in spite of our uncomfortable shoes, and to
the great detriment of our dignity.   Notwithstanding the in-
equalities of the ground, the country in the neighbourhood
of Talan is highly cultivated.   The rice-fields, arranged in
the form of an amphitheatre, cover the mountains in semicircular terraces.   They sometimes overlook a spacious valley, and recall the theatres of antiquity, where the gaze of
the spectator takes in a vast sweep.   The houses, with their
gray colours and closely packed appearance, would give Talan
the aspect of a European town, were it not for a vast pagoda,
whose roofs, rising one above the other, prevent the imagination from wandering far from China.   Our escort made the loud-
est noise they were able, and the entire population, warned of
our arrival, rushed out to meet us.   They would have invaded
even the court of the pagoda into which we had been conducted, if two of our men, placed as sentinels, had not stopped
the inquisitive crowd at the entrance to the second court,
whilst we established ourselves in the most distant part of the
edifice.   On the altars here were no longer to be seen either
pot-bellied gods or grinning monsters; only tablets covered
with Chinese writing, and enveloped with a light veil of perfumed smoke.   It was the hall of the ancestors.   Not a sound
from the outer world could penetrate this sanctuary, which
was as bare as a mosque or a Lutheran church.   The spirits
of the dead, hovering over our heads, filled us with respect
for the great man who placed veneration for forefathers
as the basis of his creed.   Unable to raise himself by the
clear conception of the existence of the personal and im-

mortal soul, to the consoling dogma of the communion of the living and the dead, he contended against the nothingness to which every one after death was condemned, by doing honour to their memory. The ceremonies performed by the Chinese before the tablets of their ancestors, were, as is known, one of the two points which gave rise to the sad controversies from whence began the ruin of the Catholic missions, which had been so flourishing in the Celestial Empire during the seventeenth and part of the eighteenth centuries.

The Dominicans, who, at that time, were the most intolerant defenders of a strict orthodoxy, accused the Jesuits of authorising amongst the Christians practices which were not only of a political or civil nature, but which, having, above all, the character of religious observances, were tainted with idolatry. Presently, though it would have been quite possible to have arrived at an understanding, which, without sacrificing any principles,[6] would have protected interests of the greatest importance, personal rivalry envenomed the dispute. Without speaking of the conduct of Cardinal de Tournon, whose proceedings 'recalled the despotic temper of a Turkish pasha, rather than the paternal spirit of an apostolic legate;'[7] without reverting to the deplorable indiscretion of the bishop of Pekin, who rekindled the quarrels which had seemed to be dying out, I will say, whilst sheltering my incompetence behind a writer[8] not much suspected of favouring that which the Holy See has condemned, that, in this affair, the Roman Catholic Church lost one of the brightest ornaments of her crown. 'The Jesuits did for the Chinese nation what St. Paul did for the Athenians, and what the Fathers of the Church did for all the Gentiles; whilst the Dominicans sacrificed the spirit for the letter, and gave a blow to the growing Christianity of these vast countries from which it has never recovered.

When one travels in a country which has served as the theatre of historical events, imagination replaces the great

---

[6] The mandate of Cardinal Charles-Ambroise de Mezza-Barba proves this: whilst exhorting the missionaries to follow the Bull of Clement XI., it sums up and unites in eight articles the mitigations contained in it.

[7] Rohrbacher, *Histoire Universelle de l'Église Catholique*, tome xxxi.

[8] Ibid.

men who have lived there, and, mingling the emotion of
such recollections with the charm of nature, makes the enjoyment of the traveller more complete and more vivid.
This satisfaction had been wanting to us in Laos, a country
which has no history; and it would have been the same in
China, of whose annals I knew nothing, had I not been able
to carry back my thoughts towards the time when a pleiad
of heroic men merited by their labours the gratitude of the
Church and the literary world. On perceiving in the pagoda
of Talan these ancestral tablets, I could not help regarding
them with a feeling of bitterness, as the rock on which so
many hopes had been wrecked.

The curiosity of the Chinese soon interrupted these recollections of the past; for they contrived, notwithstanding our
sentinels, to creep into the court through holes in the walls,
in order to peep at us. It is true that, in our quality of mandarins, we had a right to use the stick, without giving offence
to the populace, and thanks to this, our walks through the
town were made possible. The paltry earthen fortifications
round Talan had not prevented it from falling, like Seumao
and Poheul, into the hands of the Mussulmans; but it had
been less badly treated by them, owing to the fact of its not
having the same commercial importance. The houses all join
together on each side of the streets; the shops are opened
at an early hour in the morning, and there is a crowded
market. There, amongst the numerous specimens of the
savage races, certain women greatly attracted our attention.
Dressed in a picturesque costume, which showed to advantage their vigorous and elegant figures; their marked features, and almost Grecian noses, formed an agreeable contrast
to the pale sickly Chinese women, dressed in a sort of sack,
and hobbling along on two crushed and distorted feet. The
inhabitants of Talan had, however, suffered greatly by the
frightful crisis which is taking place in this part of the empire. All the necessaries of life had reached very high prices,
and potatoes, which are not much appreciated in China, were
almost the only vegetables accessible to the poor. Our finances would not have stood a prolonged residence in this
desolated region, if we had been obliged to buy everything
at the price demanded; happily, thanks to the excellent re-

lations we maintained with the authorities, the presents we received amply sufficed to support us.

The season was temperate, and the month of November presented itself with the colours it shows in our own climates. The gray sky was a little rainy, the sun could not pierce the clouds, and the thermometer at mid-day did not exceed thirteen degrees centigrade. This would have been very agreeable, if we had had the means of warding off the wet; but sleeping on the floor of pagodas open to all the winds, without mattresses, and sheltered only by a slight covering, we suffered as only the poor do in France. Talan is, nevertheless, situated very near the tropics; but the elevation of the valley above the level of the sea caused this comparatively severe temperature.

The immense mineral riches enclosed in the mountains of Yunan have been long since discovered. For a long distance round Talan there are numerous beds, and at Sio, a place situated on the direct road to Yunan-Sen, iron is in great abundance. At sixteen kilometres from the town, gold is to be found; but the mines, abandoned to private industry, are worked by miserable wretches, who shiver on the mountain, where they have established their encampment, digging at random, and extracting the gold from the rock, by grinding it, and washing the dust produced by this operation. This labour seems to bring very small profits, but it is impossible to say what European intelligence might be able to draw from this mine. For a long time back, the laws of the empire have interdicted the searching for mines of precious metals, or opening them, in the fear that the attraction of a rapid fortune would divert the people from agricultural labours. The wish to preserve their subjects from the evils of the *gold fever* does honour to the philosophical emperors who have shown it; nevertheless, now that China is on the eve of entering into commercial union with the world, it is to be regretted that the greatest portion of its metallic riches is still unknown, or remains useless.

The mandarins of Talan, treating us as their colleagues had done ever since our arrival in China, would not allow us to leave without an escort. We passed along the outskirts of the town; the women, astonished, suspended their toilette, in order to look at us; and the boys shouted after us, without daring to come near. We had not passed the last house in the town, when we were already on the mountain. On the side of the road, a human head, fixed in a wooden cage, was a warning to vice, and an encouragement to virtue. The mountain, in which lay the gold-mines, appeared in the distance, haughty as a parvenue proud of her riches, and naked as though she disdained vain ornaments. A stream which flows from it yields morsels of gold, which are collected by the inhabitants of a village where we took a short rest.

Notwithstanding that we were accustomed to keep a watch over our baggage-porters during the halts, one of them had managed, by hiding behind a mat, to light his pipe of opium. When his load was again fastened on his shoulders, he reeled like a drunken man, and refused to go on. He was indifferent to menaces; a thrashing only made him moan; nothing could rouse him from his stupefaction. I do not believe there has ever existed a more terrible scourge than opium. The alcohol employed by Europeans to destroy savages, the pestilence which ravages a country, cannot be compared to it. It exercises an invincible attraction on all; the poorest beggar will smoke before dreaming of eating; and what makes it still more frightful is, that the habit once indulged in, one becomes fatally the prey of the poison. A great number of Chinese came to ask us for remedies against the temptation, to which they invariably succumb, even while cursing it. The only remedy would be the energy capable of enduring the sufferings of a smoker deprived of his pipe; but it is moral vigour, still more, perhaps, than physical strength, that opium commences by attacking.

It was now only as we approached villages that we again came to paved road; so that we knew by its reappearance that the place for a halt was not far off; and, in general, we pined for it, for our stages were long, and our march very laborious in this hilly country. Slopes, broken by rice-fields, made bends and capricious zigzags, almost like the walks of a huge garden. Sometimes a whole mountain was under culture from base to summit, and the water, pouring from terrace to terrace, looked like a gigantic cascade. A fine and penetrating rain, which almost froze the marrow of our bones, fell from the low gray clouds. The cold is a cruel enemy in a country, where the inhabitants do nothing to combat it; it gives fever quite as quickly as the sun. Wood was very difficult to obtain; and when we had succeeded in getting from the natives the means of a meagre and smoky fire, we stretched ourselves around it; then spoke of France, of the winter evenings, and of all that makes the heart beat, and the blood flow more quickly in the veins.

Amongst the works of public interest with which the emperors have covered China, the bridges are not the least remarkable. On arriving near one of these solid stone roads, boldly thrown across the torrent, we were able to realise the difficulties which the perseverance of the Chinese have sometimes had to overcome in their construction. Slabs of white marble, standing near it, told its history. According to the inscriptions, it took nine years to make it, the waters carrying away in winter the work which had been accomplished in summer. On the opposite bank a mountain covered with woods, convenient for ambuscades, stood out almost perpendicularly. Gray ruins scattered amongst the rocks gave a sinister appearance to this savage scenery. Our soldiers dressed their ranks, and we ourselves renewed the priming of our arms, for bandits infested the environs, and frequently attacked the caravans. A few days before our arrival, two hundred horses or mules had become their prey, after their drivers had been vanquished in a bloody fight. The native warriors who told us this story, made bold by our presence, had such a valiant appearance, that we felt quite at our ease. We clambered for two hours up so steep an ascent, that a handful of resolute men concealed on the heights, would have been able to stop a whole army; but no enemy appeared.

The road, hollowed out of the sides of the mountains, was suspended above narrow gorges; and we passed along through fogs, finding even in the vegetation the harsh look of the northern regions; but Yunan is, in this respect, a country of the most surprising contrasts. From the summit of a narrow mountain ridge, the view of an immense plain, traversed by a great river, filled us with

R

admiration. The sun, tearing open the curtain of mist, inundated with light one of the most beautiful landscapes that
it was possible to conceive. Two ranges of mountains, lofty
and arid, with the warm tints peculiar to the East, bounded
the horizon before us; ravines, cut out sharply by the
streams, marking their giant sides with deep wrinkles where
the rock stood out bare, like the bony frame of a Colossus;
close at hand the Sonkoï poured along its yellow waters
between banks of white sand, and the town of Yuen-Kiang,
on the edge of the river, lay surrounded with half-cut rice-
fields, areca woods, and fields of sugar-cane, which gave to
the plain an incredible richness of shade, admirably blended,
and bathed, as it were, in floods of light. We took a long
time to reach the paved road, which conducted us to the
gates of the town. There, all the mandarins awaited us in
robes of ceremony. Banners of all colours floated in the
wind. The noise of crackers and the firing of muskets
mingled with the sound of bronze gongs, and the lugubrious notes of a long copper trumpet, very like that which
will be used, according to Michael Angelo, by the angels,
when they summon the dead to judgment at the last day. We
had never before received so solemn a reception; it was, therefore, necessary to hold our heads very erect, and cast lordly
looks at the populace, to inspire them with sentiments of respect, for our outward guise was pitiable enough. The temperature had risen, and it seemed as though we had descended
into a privileged region, separated from the rest of the world.
A strange effect of our long wanderings in the mountains,
was what I might call the intoxication of the sun and the
plain. We found everything we could wish for in this oasis,
even to straw on which to sleep. Not content with having
come out to welcome us, the mandarins insisted on paying
us the first visits. They arrived, preceded, according to
custom, by soldiers carrying red papers, on which were
inscribed the names and quality of their masters, and followed by servants bringing a hog, a ram, and capons, and
loaded besides with packages of oranges and tea. When we
went to return the governor's visit, he received us most cordially. He showed us his son, an infant in arms, and told us
it was his only child. We knew that he had several besides;

but they were only girls, and they do not count in the Celestial Empire. He possessed quantities of European articles, which took away from the value of the modest presents we were disposed to give him. Watches, clocks, pistols, stereoscopes, all seemed to be of English providing; for the photographs represented scantily-attired courtesans, with the fair skin and red hair which revealed their origin. There is no prudery in commerce, even in prudish England.

The circumference of the town is great; but there are many empty spaces, filled with briers, or cultivated with vegetables. The market is considerable, and the shops numerous. Nevertheless, we soon discovered at Yuen-Kiang, notwithstanding certain appearances of prosperity, the signs of mourning and of poverty. Epidemics are permanently there, and a sort of cholera decimates the inhabitants. I continually saw coffins carried along the streets by four men; perfumed rods, alight, placed round the lid, exhaling a slight smoke as they passed. The country is also infested with bandits, against whom there is no guarantee for public security. The mandarins limit themselves to particular measures, according to the case, and on their own personal responsibility. As for the police, they never act seriously, unless the victim of the robbery or assassination have some social standing. The wealthy are always escorted by soldiers when they travel, or arm themselves and their servants; but the poor become the prey of the brigands. A poor Lolo from the mountains, who had come to sell us his potatoes, was seized on his way back to his village, and despoiled of the sapeques he was so joyfully carrying home; and we saw him brought back to us, his chest perforated by the stroke of a lance, to obtain surgical aid, which the gravity of his wound rendered useless.

The governor of Yuen-Kiang, showing himself full of kindness and expansive confidence, we endeavoured to take advantage of his frankness, which is very rare with the Chinese; but his ideas were confused, and his information imperfect. We profited by it, nevertheless, to go and examine a copper-mine, five days' march from Yunan-Sen, at a considerable village called Sin-long-chan, which is surrounded by walls, and constructed on a sort of circular mountain ridge, between larger mountains which overlook it. It is from these mountains they extract the copper. They are pierced with deep cavities, where the miner has followed the metallic veins, but the search appears to have been discontinued in the immediate neighbourhood of the village, where the streets are still paved with dross, the only works now being at the distance of nine miles from Sin-long-chan; where they were able to show us an establishment of small import-ance, made by poor people, incapable of conceiving or carry-ing out anything extensive. We saw several lumps of mineral, which awaited very insufficient treatment, accord-ing to our ideas, near a simple blast-furnace. The ore appears to be very rich, and to be spread over a considerable area. The red earth which covers it was dotted by the moving shadows of thinly-sown pines.

We knew that copper figured in the first rank of the mineral wealth of Yunan, the most richly-endowed pro-vince of the empire in this respect. Before the present troubles, it annually forwarded, to the treasury of Pekin, ingots of crude copper, to the value of a million of francs. But however abundant the mines of Sin-long-chan, under other conditions, may become, they cannot be compared to the argentiferous lead-mines of Sin-Kaï-tseu. Situated eighteen miles from Coqui, and near Tchao-Tong, at the north-western extremity of the province, these mines, which are above the level of the neighbouring river, employed, in peaceful times, 1200 workmen, simply to draw off the water. Money being very abundant in these parts, there was much gambling carried on, to take part in which travellers were stopped on their journey, only to find themselves, first, thor-oughly pillaged, and, then, forced to work in the mines, as the price of their liberation, at the rate of forty sapeques a day. Provisions being sold to them at high prices, they, in this way, remained slaves for a long time. Though it does not appertain to me to give an account of the minera-logy of Yunan—that task being reserved for Dr. Joubert —I cannot leave the subject without noticing the mines of zinc, tin, and silver which exist in the plateau of Tong-Tchouan, and also those of red and white copper (*pe-tong*), worked near Hoeli-Tcheou. The country is almost entirely stripped of trees; but coal, which is everywhere wasted, is often found near the mines, whose value it increases tenfold.

Since I am describing on the spot the part of the empire richest in mineral wealth, I find myself naturally led to explain, briefly, the monetary system of the Chinese. Civilised, and forming a firmly-organised society 900 years after the Deluge, these people were already in possession of a symbol generally adopted, which represented the value of things, and facilitated exchanges. It is to Hoang-ti, one of the six successors of Fo-hi,[9] first sovereign of the empire, that the honour is due of having invented money. He had it made of iron, a metal we have seen render the same service in some parts of Laos. Since then, money has changed very often as to its form and substance: shells have been employed, and also baked earth, and paper; but in the present day, and for a long time past, it is on the copper sapeque that the whole system rests. Whilst silver, exclusively considered as merchandise, remains in bars whose value is uncertain, copper money is coined by the state, and marked with its stamp. The copper-mines are the only ones of which the monopoly belongs to the emperor; who, by his exclusive right of coining, and of working the raw material, can, by this double privilege, raise or lower the value of the sapeques like that of the metal of which they are made, by melting-down a quantity, or, on the other hand, by setting the mines in more active work. 'There was a time,' says Père Duhalde, 'when the deficiency of copper was so great, that the emperor destroyed nearly 1400 temples of Fo, and melted all the copper idols, in order to make money.' Formerly private individuals were strictly forbidden to keep vases or other copper utensils, and they were compelled to deliver them up at the place where the money was manufactured. The government abused its right of coining to such a degree, at the time when the Europeans exported rolls of sapeques, that, when the civil war broke out in Yunan, and exhausted the princi-

[9] From the time of Fo-hi to that of the Emperor Yao, the Chinese chronology is wanting in exactitude. It was only from the reign of Yao, 2357 years before Christ, that veritable annals commenced, which from that time bear the impress of authenticity and historic accuracy. See Père Duhalde.

pal resources for obtaining copper, the working of the mines no longer sufficed for the demand. Alloy was then obliged to be used, for which zinc was largely employed. These small coins are circular in shape, and have a hole through the centre, which permits of their being strung together: a thousand are needed to make a roll. The dimensions vary in the different provinces, and are not always identical in neighbouring districts. Our first care, on reaching a halting-place, was to acquaint ourselves with the rate at which we should have to sell our silver, on the exchange. To change money is a much more complicated operation in China than in Europe; for eight francs cannot be changed without one's being burdened with at least one kilogramme in weight of copper coins. Mexican dollars were usually received with favour; and we exchanged gold in bars, and leaves, which we had procured in Bangkok, against silver ingots weighing one Chinese ounce, and worth about eight francs. These ingots are known by Europeans under the name of *tael*. Representing, in a small bulk, a rather large value, they advantageously replace, in all important transactions, the copper sapeque, whose chief merit is to permit what the Abbé Huc so truly calls the commerce of the infinitely small. Silver, whatever be the service it renders in the market, is nothing more or less than an article of merchandise, and every one cuts it according to his requirements; and, in consequence, every Chinese carries about with him a case containing weights and scales. In busy shops, they cut every day, with the aid of a hammer, a great quantity of silver; and the particles which escape, confounded with the dust of the shop, are swept into the street, and gleaned by the beggars.

However insufficient the geographical notions of the mandarin of Yuen-Kiang might be, M. de Lagrée did not hesitate to interrogate him. His experience had taught him not to disdain any source of information. How many times, in the course of our journey, had not some obscure piece of information been suddenly cleared up by the light of subsequent observation! Our expedition, besides, was not without some very valuable scientific documents, bearing the names of illustrious and devoted Frenchmen. It was, as every one knows, owing to the admiration caused by their works, that the Jesuits, admitted to the court of Pekin, acquired the favour of the Emperor Kanghi. They drew up, province by province, the whole map of the empire, so carefully that the positions of the principal towns were very accurately assigned. I may add, on the statement of the missionaries of that time, that, previous to their arrival in China, the Chinese had made great efforts to master the topographical configuration of their country.

Father Amiot affirms that 'the chapter Yu-koung of the Chou-King, which is perhaps the most ancient record of geography in the world, excepting the Pentateuch, contains a geographical description of China in the times of Yao and Chun,'—that is, more than 2000 years before our era. The learned missionary also adds, that the geography composed under Ming's dynasty served as basis to the *Atlas Sinensis*— the Chinese Atlas—of Martini, which 'is only a translation and abridgment of it.' I have myself seen a curious specimen of Chinese maps belonging to the governor of Yuen-Kiang. The author, anxious before anything else for the symmetry of his maps, had everywhere strewn them with uniform mountains, not very unlike sugar-loaves painted green. Whether he wished to trace a rivulet, or indicate the bed of a river, he gave an equal width to every stream of water, taking care to make them communicate with each other. The relative positions of the towns were pretty exact, which is explained by the Chinese having known the use of the compass long before ourselves. Their measure of distance, which they call Li, corresponds to a tenth of our terrestrial league. Our friend the mandarin replied to our questions by keeping his eye on this map, which was familiar to him, but which had the inconvenience of producing very absurd ideas in his head as to the mountain system, and the hydrography of Yunan. He confirmed our opinion, however, that the river, which bathes the walls of the town, empties itself into the sea, after having traversed Tonkin. Lying between the basin of the Yang-Tse-Kiang and that of the Mekong, it has its source in one of those southern ramifications of the Himalaya, which give birth at the same time to the Meïnam and the Canton river. It flows from the north-west to the south-east, still bearing the name of Hoti-Kiang at Yuen-Kiang, and only receives that of Sonkoï, at some little distance from the Tonkin frontier. From Yuen-Kiang to the level of the sea the barometer marks a difference of only 400 metres, which, for such a distance, would lead one to suppose that the Sonkoï flowed very smoothly. We remarked the existence of several rapids, however, and the information we received confirmed that of a cataract, impassable for loaded barques. This obstacle occurs on the Yunan territory; but from the first Annamite market, which is not more than three days' journey from Manko, the last Chinese one, merchandise can reach Kitcho, the capital of Tonkin, in sixteen days by the river, without having to undergo any disembarcation.

Before the war broke out, there was a good deal of commerce, especially in metals, between Yunan and Tonkin. A great part of the zinc, which served to manufacture the sapeques of the Annam empire, was brought by caravans to the first Tonkin market, where the Chinese received silver in exchange. This necessary and frequent intercourse had not, however, entirely effaced the remembrance of the bitter struggles which, in former times, distracted these two neighbouring countries. In the ninth century of our era, the barbarous tribes of southern Yunan rose, at the same time as those of Tonkin, against the authority of the Chinese emperors. The Annamite historians, who record this fact, affirm that even at that period a portion of Yunan belonged to Tonkin, and was only detached from it when the emperor of China had accepted the chief of the revolted tribes for son-in-law. Annamites are still forbidden to enter Yunan. The existence of a great number of half-subdued savages on the frontiers of that province, explains this measure in some degree; but, as may already have been suspected, the danger for China lies no longer in that direction. At a time when all Yunan threatens to escape from its laws, it is not against Tu-Duc's encroachments that it behoves the court of Pekin to arm. If my information does not mislead me, it is the sovereign of the Annamite empire, who feels uneasy at the stream of Chinese emigrants, who, forced to leave their country by its troubles, have passed through the valley of

Sonkoï, to establish themselves in the north of Tonkin. The strong position occupied by France in the southern extremity of the Indo-Chinese peninsula, compels us not to remain indifferent to the serious events, which, for different reasons, have awakened the fears of two Asiatic sovereigns; and our natural rôle at Pekin, as at Hué, consists in levelling, in the interests of all commercial Europe, the old barriers which separate the populations.

It has, perhaps, not been forgotten, that the project of uniting the western provinces of China to our Annamite establishment, was one of the motives which determined Admiral de La Grandière, in 1866, to propose to M. de Chasseloup-Laubat, then Minister of Marine, to have the Mekong explored. It will also have been observed, from the first pages of this narrative, that beyond the frontiers of the protected kingdom of Cambodgia, the river ceased to be practicable for steam navigation. The illusions, which remained, after the sad confirmation of this fact, had been dissipated little by little, and the interest of our journey came to be, in the end, concentrated on purely geographical questions. The fortunate accident, which obliged us to abandon the Mekong valley, threw open a larger field for our energies; till then too much confined to special studies, and it was with joy that we found ourselves able, in giving a new direction to our researches, to confirm a view which the men, who presided over the destinies of our young colonies, had long been led by their sagacity to entertain. The so long-looked-for communication, by which the plethora of the riches of Western China would one day flow into a French port, is to be expected by way of the Sonkoï, not by the Mekong. It was an undisputed truth, which would certainly cause the complete exploration of the Tonkin river.

For the time being it is necessary to reëstablish the commercial relations which formerly existed between the two countries, both of whom are now suffering from the cessation of traffic. It would be much wiser to make those numerous Chinese, who, in compact masses, have left their struggling country, assist in the restoration and development of these useful relations, than to behave suspiciously and haughtily towards them. It is, however, these hostile feelings, founded on inveterate hatred rather than on serious apprehension, that led Tu-Duc to drive back the victims of Chinese anarchy. It is no longer the time when the Celestial Empire, at the height of its power, compelled the neighbouring states to move in its orbit. It is undergoing too general and formidable a crisis for its interference in Annamite affairs to be dreaded. This is what is necessary to be understood, in order to cast down the artificial barriers raised, for political or other motives, between Yunan and Tonkin; but it will be difficult to make our ally comprehend it, till our influence can combat the men of letters—those intractable enemies of European ideas—who mould his policy. A protectorate, exercised directly as at Cambodgia, with power for immediate action, or, at least, complete commercial liberty, obtained in the ports of Tonkin, and guaranteed by the installation at Hué of an official representative of the governor of Cochin-China, — are the only means I see for escaping from the difficulties into which timidity without excuse, and scruples that are much too tender, would drive us.

When one observes attentively the persevering efforts made by England to attract to her Indian or Burman markets the commerce of Western China, one feels astonished at our indifference as to availing ourselves of an exceptional situation, and of circumstances which will not always be so opportune. To be the first arrivals, and to secure commercial connections, is an advantage more to be prized in the East even than in Europe, and this the present war would seem to offer us to an unhoped-for extent. This war, in fact, impedes the former channels by which the products of Yunan flowed into the valley of the Irawady, and opposes fresh obstacles to the opening of that route between India and China, sought for by the English with more perseverance than success. When one considers that it is a question of turning towards French possessions the products of a vast region, which comprises, without speaking of Northern Laos, four of the richest provinces in China, and of opening, in return, markets to our national industry, whose customers could be counted by millions, it must certainly be owned that such a result is worth our taking as much trouble about as our rivals take to obtain it. Is it a time, when, by good fortune, it depends on ourselves to precede them, that we should stop before the touchiness of a despot, who cannot conceive of free-trade without occupation of territory, and drives off our merchants as though they were the forerunners of our soldiers? When a war of conquest is decided on, it is clear that one accepts beforehand the consequences of success; and the opening of Tonkin is a necessary sequel to our establishment in the six provinces of Cochin-China. This part of the Annamite empire appears to be one of the richest countries in the world. A double harvest is annually reaped in its plains, which are cultivated by a laborious race; its mountains, which would be for Europeans living in Saïgon what certain ranges of the Himalayas are for the English residing in India—a place of repose and refuge from tropical heat—abound in metallic veins; and, finally, the missionary influence, so weak in Cambodgia, utterly wanting in Laos, and barely felt in China, shows itself there by an ever-increasing number of conversions to Christianity. The best-founded calculations reckon the number of Christians in the two apostolic vicariates of Tonkin at four or five hundred thousand. If experience teaches us not to trust too completely to the devotion of converts to European interests, it would be unwise to despise such a valuable aid.

To explore the Sonkoï, of which we had only obtained glimpses; to encourage the native coasting trade, already very active, between the mouth of that river and Saïgon; to exercise legitimate pressure on the rebellious will of the emperor Tu-Duc; to obtain a treaty from this prince, which would provide for our political and commercial interests; to seize, in fine, the opportunity of giving a downright contradiction to those who accuse us of incompetency in colonial matters,—is what should be undertaken with that confidence which insures success. Such were the plans I liked to think over, when, in the plain of Yuen-Kiang, I followed in thought the now unused course of the beautiful river which lay at my feet; and such is also the hope which I shall not be forbidden to express when, having returned to my country, I find France so strong, and the time so propitious.[10]

[10] Written in January 1870.

CHAPTER VII.

LANDSCAPES AND CHINESE SKETCHES IN YUNAN.

IN 1812, during the forced marches of the disastrous Russian retreat, our exhausted and worn-out soldiers often dropped down, to rise no more. Repose, for them, meant death. A danger of another description menaces travellers in distant lands; long halts are fatal to them; they are like death to the soul. When one has to labour daily, in order to supply the bare necessities of life, physical activity, over-excited by an incessant struggle, increases with the obstacles it encounters; and the mind, completely at the service of the body, appears to have no wants and no requirements of its own. But it soon avenges itself for this transitory subordination; and when material wants are supplied, intellectual privations become more painful. We felt this each time that a lengthened stay in a Chinese town brought us in contact with a civilisation which appeared complete, and yet still left our most imperious desires and most ardent aspirations unsatisfied.

Since the last sacrifices imposed, by the difficulty of transport, we were without a single book which might, in hours of lassitude, rouse up our thoughts, by making us forget ourselves. I will not attempt to describe this most cruel of our sufferings; any one who has undergone similar miseries—sailors wrecked on a desert island, or political prisoners immured in cells—will understand it at once. The last news we had received of France dated back more than a year. How many poignant uncertainties had we not experienced during this long period! how many events, happy or otherwise, might have befallen our family or country!

Our country! We had always been confident of seeing our efforts in these far lands contribute to her reviving great-

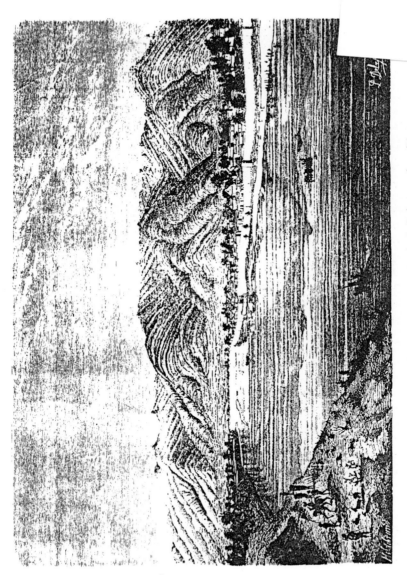

Plate 20 *The town of Yuen Kiang (Drawing by L. Delaporte, from life.)*

Plate 21 *The town and the lake of Tong Hay (Drawing by Th. Weber, based on a sketch by L. Delaporte)*

ness in the East; but it was especially on the shores of the great river, by which French influence could so easily penetrate into Western China, that the future appeared before us in its radiant splendour. Like those navigators who plant the national standard on a newly-discovered land, M. de Lagrée had the French colours hoisted on the barques which bore us along the current of the Sonkoï; whilst the salvos of musketry, with which the authorities of the town of Yuen-Kiang saluted our departure, drowned the loud hum of the assembled multitude. The sound gradually ceased; but still, for a long time, we saw the banners floating in the wind, the red umbrellas moving to and fro above the heads of the mandarins, and the lances and bayonets gleaming in the sun along the walls, whose battlements appeared in bold relief against the deep blue of the sky. The Sonkoï, becoming hemmed in between precipitous mountains, the plain and the town were soon lost in the distance, and the bright visions of a second Indian empire also disappeared as in the misty haze of a dream.

Our barques having been stopped by a rapid, we were obliged to land and resume our alpenstocks, to enable us to climb the difficult slopes, which, after a month's march, were to bring us to the high plateau on which is built Yunan-Sen, the chief town of the province of Yunan. Half way up the hill, in a hollow dug on the side of a barren mountain, the village of Poupyau first appears to view, like a verdant oasis in the midst of a desert. It is shaded by numerous arecas and gnarled tamarinds, the age of which would seem to carry far back the date of its foundation. The houses are made of earth hardened by the sun: they are one story high; and on their terraces the women turn their spinning-wheels, walk about, or look to their household duties. Oxen, asses, and pigs move about at liberty in the streets. Poupyau, which reminded me of the small towns in Central Egypt, enjoys the luxury of a surrounding wall. Sentinels keep watch every night at the gates. The inhabitants of this little fortified town belong to the Lolos race, represented on the banks of the Sonkoï by numerous tribes, over which the Chinese government exercises an authority which sensibly diminishes as one reaches Tonkin. When the action of

imperial power over even the Chinese is notoriously weakened in Yunan, it is easy to understand that the yoke is
still less heavy for people of a wild nature and different
origin, who live amongst mountains difficult of access, and
where surveillance is an impossibility. Whatever be the
future fate in store for these natives, it is impossible to
deny the advantages which they, probably unwittingly,
have derived from Chinese domination; numbers have followed their masters' example, and from wandering hunts-
men have become clever agriculturists. At Poupyau, for
example, they obtain their food from the soil. They have
turned the course of a torrent, some four kilometres from
the village, and have brought it through the mountains
into Poupyau itself, by an aqueduct constructed with the
first materials at hand, for they do not trouble themselves
much about elegance; though chance has so willed it, that
these materials are a splendid marble, whose worn blocks,
polished either by the water or the feet of the passers-
by, show the most lovely colours. The feathery plumes
of the arecas, and the strong branches of the gnarled old
trees, shade the cascade, where women come to draw water
in attitudes and costumes which recall old biblical memories.
They wear silver ornaments round their necks and arms, and
are clothed in a simple dress drawn in at the waist; a wide
plait over the forehead fastens the cap which conceals their
luxuriant hair: their beautiful proportions, their noble and
stately bearing, all combining to distinguish them from the
grotesque Chinese women, who look like maimed dolls, devoid of strength, freshness, and grace.

At this village we had some difficulty in finding a sufficient number of porters for our baggage; and it was with
surprise, soon followed by anger, that we saw the mandarins,
who were to conduct and supply us with these necessaries,
actually leading away a small caravan of government porters,
levied at their orders, and laden with merchandise gratuitously supplied by the village. Others were carrying their
palanquins, or saddles, the honest functionaries wishing to
spare their horses as much fatigue as possible. It would
have been waste of trouble to speak to them of humanity;
we could only insist on their fulfilling their duty towards

us, and supplying us with what was needful, before thinking of their own personal interests. Our rascally mandarins took notice, however, of our remarks; and to prove to us how zealous they were, they seized, at the evening halting-place, on the unfortunate chief of a Lolo village, guilty of having manifested no great desire to help us, put him into a pillory, and beat him unmercifully. We lodged with two good old women, easily made friendly by the offer of a few pipes of tobacco; and we passed the evening round the fire, whilst our hostesses, seated near us, their feet over the cinders of a brazier, smoked, and turned their spinning-wheels. A young female savage wandered to and fro, playing tricks on her grandmother, and after watching us a little, at length ventured on touching our long beards. Woman, more timid than man, is by her nature less suspicious; her sharper and surer instinct sooner discovers uprightness of intention, even under the most ferocious exterior. Towards midnight the chief, having. been released from his pillory, and rendered tractable by the beating, woke us up to offer us a fowl.

The next day our way lay through a valley, at first gloomy and wild. A torrent, which flowed at our feet over a bed of marble, dashed against variegated blocks formed of those hard concreted pebbles, called conglomerate by geologists. These natural mosaics, which would have adorned the palaces of Europe, have lain there for centuries, useless, waiting for an eye to admire them. On both sides, in the mountains, the calcareous rock had bared itself of the thin coating of soil to show its splendid colours. Little by little this gorge widened, and became populated and highly cultivated. Numerous villages lay sheltered under the great trees. The gray houses are built of dried earth, and the flat roofs support straw pyramids. They could easily be taken for the thatched towers of some strong château. The illusion is rendered still easier, because around the buildings are battlemented walls, of about the same height as the roofs. Everybody retires into his house, to defend himself against the highway robbers; but there is no barrier or wall strong enough to defend the peaceful inhabitant from official pilferers. All fled at the approach of our mandarins and soldiers. We suffered from these fears, of which we were the involuntary cause, and would hardly consent to halt in the hamlets. The following day we entered the town of Sheu-Pin, whose beauties, at first hidden by the promontories, which at the same time conceal the plain, suddenly reveal themselves to the enchanted gaze. Through an opening between two hills, the dazzled eye loses itself on a vast sheet of water, blue as the sky it reflects, and as calm as the air, undisturbed by the faintest breeze. It is a portion of the lake of Sheu-Pin. The town itself soon appears, like a floating city, joined to the land by broad causeways, and narrower paths through the rice-fields. Pedestrians, horses, palanquins, and boats move at the same time; small islands, covered with houses, are dotted over the azure lake: near us are buffaloes, up to their flanks in the water, harnessed to a species of harrow, on which an almost naked man is standing, like the genius of the sea, drawn by some slimy monster. At this novel spectacle, my sight became dimmed; I hesitated, and became for an instant incapable of distinguishing the limits between the two elements, earth and water appearing united, and confounded with each other.

The proper place for seeing, in their combined harmony, the town, plain, and lake, is a hillock surmounted by a large tower, which I ascended towards the evening, in order to escape the keen curiosity of a troublesome crowd. On my right, the sheet of water stretched out as far as the jagged mountains which formed its boundary; the waning day threw pale purple tints over all; on the banks the white gables of the numerous houses, which girdle the lake with villages, stood out against the shadow of the mountains; in the lake, fishing-boats, and tufts of water-plants stretching up to the light, sowed the surface with specks, at first scarcely seen, but gradually thickening as the town was farther off. Small reefs, inhabited, rose near at hand; then larger islets, crowned with pagodas, whose fantastic style, hidden a little by great trees, did not too much disfigure this wondrous landscape. The town itself, generally without character or relief, but then transfigured by the rays of the setting sun, appeared to me like a conqueror over the lake, which surrounds it and comes to die at its feet. The Chinese have had the very Chinese idea of building at the extremity of each jetty a sort

of entrance door, to mark where land begins and the other
element ends; not quite a superfluous precaution, and one
which, in reminding him of the city on the lagoons, makes
the traveller regret that the generations which constructed
Venice did not send emigrants into the plain of Sheu-Pin.

The governor endeavoured to persuade us, by his counsels, to leave without delay for Yunan-Sen; but we wanted
to visit Lin-ngan, and our persistence seemed to reduce him
to despair. At length he informed us that, as the Mussulmans
were hemming in this town, it would be very imprudent for
us to venture; and, in addition, the military mandarin, who
resided there, forbade us in formal and concise terms to
enter the place. This mandarin had such a reputation for
energy and ferocity, that nobody at Sheu-Pin could entertain the idea of six Europeans imagining the audacious project of going contrary to his orders, and braving him in
his own town. In Yunan, those men who are still faithful
to the empire, serve it in their own way; Lean-Tagen,[1]
governor of Lin-ngan, excited by the struggle which he
alone maintains in this part of the province, and exasperated by the treacheries which weaken him, no longer obeys
the commands from Pekin. Such were the observations
of the authorities when we showed them our passports.

M. de Lagrée cutting short all these discussions, which the
Chinese have the art of rendering interminable, announced
his intention of leaving, and remitted to the governor of
Sheu-Pin, more concerned for himself than for us, a declaration, which, if needed, would guard the responsibility of
this timid functionary with his chief. On this condition
the latter consented to authorise our embarkation on the
lake; whose waters, flowing into the valley of Lin-ngan, bore
us within a short distance of that town. The news of our
intended arrival had preceded us; for a mandarin awaited
it. Gravely and silently he signed to us to follow him,
and led us into a large building, situated outside the walls.
The doors were closed, but they were immediately besieged
and hammered at by the populace. This insatiable desire

[1] Tagen, that is to say, great man. It is an epithet, and sort of hono-
rary title, added to the names of personages occupying high civil or military posts.

S

to see us being thwarted, provoked great indignation; and brutal curiosity was soon transformed into furious hostility. Stones flew over the walls, and menacing shouts pursued us in our retreat. Just then M. Garnier rejoined us. Having left the expedition at Poupyau to explore the Sonkoï, some few miles below the obstacles which had stopped us, he had reached Lin-ngan two days before ourselves. He had a deep wound on his forehead; and owed to his revolver the fact of not being stoned by people, whose violence was unbounded.

This excitable populace did not wish for our lives; they only desired one thing, but they desired that imperiously: it was to approach, feel, and examine us at their leisure. The most audacious climbed the walls, and gave us from a distance, by gestures, orders to walk, sit down, eat, and even to sleep. They wanted to see how Europeans accomplished all the functions of life. Besides becoming very dangerous, if, like children who break a watch to study its mechanism, they took the fancy to inspect a European as critically, it may be readily conceived that this situation was intolerable. We were obliged, however, before resorting to force, to try every possible means of appeasing them. We informed the mayor of the town that we perceived we were mistaken, on entering China, to have counted upon our passports, rather than our arms; and, the emperor's word not being a sufficient guarantee against the violence of the inhabitants of Lin-ngan, we intended defending ourselves. Whereupon a placard was posted on our door, which caused the mob to hesitate for a moment, soon to return to the charge with renewed fury. Of all the mandarins at Lin-ngan, there is only one, the governor of Fou, who can still exact obedience and respect from the people; but, being annoyed at a journey, made without his previous authorisation, he refrained from taking any protective measures in our behalf. He bore us a grudge, and rejoiced in his revenge. Having, at last, been obliged to act by an energetic message from M. de Lagrée, he presented himself early one morning before us. He was truly colossal. He seemed humiliated at having yielded, and kept his oblique eyes fixed on the ground, which gave a most curious and constrained expression to his bull-like face. We have since been informed that this man is possessed of herculean strength: he can knock down an ox with a blow from his fist, cannot find any horse strong enough to bear him, and intermingles amusement with the rough work of war. He has theatricals, and assists at dances before going into battle. He abhors Mussulmans, both those who have remained faithful to the emperor and the insurgents. Report accuses him of having supplied himself with the red ball which he wears on his hat; but one thing is certain, and that is, that he refuses allegiance to the viceroy of the province. The latter having several times commanded him to report himself at Yunan-Sen, he replied, as one of our great feudal barons might have done: 'If you insist, I will go there, but with my soldiers.' His name is feared for twenty leagues round; and later on we were considered prodigies, when we said we had passed through Lin-ngan. This terrible general dryly authorised us to spend a few days in his town, and had a notice, sealed with his seal, placed on the doors of our establishment. The disturbance diminished at once, but even then, a large stone, passing between M. de Lagrée and myself, fell on the table at which we were writing. Two of our men rushed out and pursued the offender, whom they caught, and tied by his tail, regardless of his cries and excuses, to one of the columns; after which we delivered him up to the justice of the country. After being imprisoned in a pillory, he had his head cut off the next day, without our knowledge: for we should not have wished such a severe punishment. He was, in reality, punished for having infringed the commands of a chief, who maintains rigorous discipline over all those beneath him, whilst at the same time he frees himself from the bonds of his superiors. From that time, our abode ceased to be a prison, and it became possible for us to visit the town.

Lin-ngan, whose name is as well known in Laos as that of Yunan-Sen, is surrounded by a double wall. It is larger than Shen-Pin, but not so bright or cheerful. The houses are low, badly built, and dirtily kept. A single principal street leads from one gate to the other; it is broad and straight; with this exception, the inhabitants are crowded together in alleys. The pagodas are very numerous, occupy a good deal of ground, and yet more are being constructed.

The Chinese architects have devoted their energies to the decoration of some of these but it is more especially on the vast garden, which comprises several hectares in the centre of the town, that they have combined to lavish curious ornaments and costly futilities, such as columns supporting nothing, series of porticoes leading nowhere, and bridges beneath which no water flows. The garden itself is superfluous in this fortified town, and its doors are always closed. In all Chinese works there is something wrong and unfinished; one would say, that wishing to push to its utmost limits the theory of art for art's sake, they build at great expense an arched bridge on a flat surface, solely for the pleasure of erecting it, as in former times they raised on the northern frontiers of their empire that stupendous wall—a monument, at once colossal and useless, which marvellously characterises the genius of this singular race.

As far as the eye can reach, outside the town, tombs are clustered together, enclosing more than a hundred times the number of the whole living population. There is great uniformity amongst this funereal architecture. Small porticoes of bluish marble, or simple slabs, generally rectangular, let into the wall which supports the rising ground: are the usual shapes of the tombs. Their dimensions vary according to the importance and wealth of the deceased. Sometimes a spacious enclosure, filled with statues, and decorated with columns, to which a monumental door gives access, separates the body of a mandarin from ordinary corpses; but marble tablets, covered with inscriptions, are most in use. At Lin-ngan, these pretentious mausoleums are lost in the immensity of the cemetery as a whole; the columns dotting it over alone attract the eye. No trees, no flowers, no verdure; nothing but tombs, whose marble sparkles in the sun. This field of dead has no other enclosure than the yellow cliffs and bare mountains. One might fancy oneself transported into some necropolis of the Libyan desert. A road crosses this cemetery, so different from those one sees in France, leading to a lignite mine—a precious resource for this woodless country, where the cold is intense. Small straw-covered roofs protect the pits, at which four men work the whole day, letting down the empty baskets into the shaft, and raising those the miners have filled. These pits and the horizontal galleries under ground are strengthened by wooden frames; but they would not let us go down.

Reassured by the visit the governor had at last favoured us with, the other mandarins hastened to do the same, loaded with presents. To hear them, one would have thought the conduct of the mob at Lin-ngan had deeply grieved them, and they sighed at not having been able to proportion the punishment to the offence. This avowal of weakness we did not disbelieve, when we beheld the crowd follow after us, and invade the courts of the *yamens*, fill the audience-chambers, or hold fast by the windows, and for a better view tear the panes.[2] The resigned and abashed functionaries had to wait for some burst of laughter or noisy conversation to cease before they could speak themselves. We were not deceived as to the meaning of this astonishing tolerance, which was better accounted for by fear than by philanthropy. The mere caprice of a mandarin is enough to beat or behead a man; and yet they dare not meddle with a crowd. Things would, doubtless, have been different in the governor's palace; but he had received us so badly, that M. de Lagrée left the town without taking leave of him.

The direct route from Lin-ngan to Yunan-Sen being cut off by the rebels, we were obliged to return to Sheu-Pin, where we again received a cordial and hearty welcome. When we left it the next day, the principal mandarin wished to accompany us to the end of the plain, and quitted his chair to wish us good-bye.

The mountains soon assumed their usual uniform and severe aspect; the red earth appearing in places between the thinly-scattered cypresses and pines. Some steep declivities were deeply seamed by torrents. We passed along one hill so eaten away through this that the narrow path ran along the very edge of an abyss. For a long time back our daily marches might be described in a few words: first, to ascend, then to follow a straight road opened in the mountain-sides; and, finally, to descend some gorge or valley, to find a resting-place in the villages. The inhabitants of these hamlets, surprised of an evening by our sudden arrival, began to fly,

---

[2] Glass being very expensive in China, paper is often used in its place.

like the savages of Laos; owing, it appeared, to our great
resemblance, with our long hair and wild appearance, to the
Mussulman rebels.

'The brigands!'[3] was the very flattering exclamation
which saluted our arrival; whereupon the women hid themselves, and the men fled. The escort imposed on us by the
mandarins was increased at every halting-place. In fact, the
soldiers would not consent to go any farther, except in force.
They kept up their courage while we were with them, but
they trembled at the thought of the return. Some villages
take the most minute precautions for their safety. Some
have fortified and palisaded themselves; and have erected
towers about a hundred metres from their walls, where advanced sentries pass the night on duty. These soldiers only
have communication with the ground by means of rope-lad-
ders, which they let down or draw up as they please. Shouts
and pistol-shots redoubled during our marches; and I was
constantly followed, for my part, by an odious man with a
gong, who would not desist from deafening me with his
wretched instrument. I got more quickly over the steep
parts by the help of this diabolical music; being less tempted
to pause for breath, and fleeing from my torture as the bull
flees from the goad. Presently the green trees gave place to
red marl, dug out and cut away in a thousand forms by the
streams; now rising in pointed pyramids held on by their
base; or now, in columns detached from the mass, rising
isolated between two cypresses like the pillars of a ruined
temple. We reached without farther incident the town of
Tong-Hay, which is situated, like Shen-Pin, not far from
a lake, and is a military place of some note. It is the residence of a general, round whom swarmed the quilted uni-
forms of battered make-believe soldiers, insolent and brutal,
who live by pillage, and are hated by the population.

A detachment of these soldiers was appointed to guard
us, who amused themselves by pricking, with their lances
and knives, the faces of the inquisitive people who peeped
through the doors, purposely left on the jar. Enraged at
this treatment, the inhabitants, amongst whom were a large

[3] Kouïtsen, an injurious appellation, applied by the Chinese to the revolted Mohammedans of Yunan in particular, and to bandits in general.

number of Mohammedans still faithful to the emperor, rushed towards our dwelling, and just as we were going to dine, we learnt that an assault was preparing outside. Lances, six metres long, reaching to the top of the roof, were distributed amongst the soldiery, who took up a position in the yard of our lodging, whilst others lit their matches, and filled the pans of their guns with powder. A few slight wounds frightened the assailants, and night put a stop to this revolt of the inquisitive inhabitants : we insisted, besides, on the doors being left open. Here, as at Lin-ngan, they seemed especially anxious to see us eat. The European instruments, which took the place of the Chinese chopsticks, were the objects of thorough examination ; and I overheard one sagacious man explain to his neighbour, that the large soup-ladle was doubtless that of the chief of the expedition.

The town is surrounded by a rectangular brick wall well built. A large principal street, with shops on both sides, passes through its centre. The plain around is well cultivated, and numerous villages, pressing towards the lake, seem to dispute the cultivated land with the temporary pools of the receding waters. We could not stir out without dragging after us some thousands of men. The civil mandarin is a small, timid personage, who appeared terrified at occupying a post in this much-disturbed country. He abdicated in favour of the military mandarin, a sturdy fellow, decorated with a coral ball, and with a silvery moustache, who, on the contrary, appeared very confident: he laughed and spoke noisily, and drove away the crowd from the doors. On the 16th December the cold increased, and the next day we saw, not without some emotion, the snow fall heavily enough to cover the roofs, trees, and mountains. We were none the less obliged to leave Tong-Hay. The earth was hidden beneath a shroud, and in the morning one could not see twenty paces, for a thick fog. When the sun rose, the sad aspect of nature changed to a beautiful one : the bright colours of the pagodas and red earthen houses stood out wonderfully beneath the snow which covered their roofs : several trees, surprised in full leaf by this icy shower, seemed to regret their lost summer; others, more prudent, feeling winter approaching, had covered themselves with red leaves which, mingling with the snow, produced one of those marvellous contrasts, which force a cry of admiration from even the least enthusiastic. The flowers on the shrubs, with a drop of frozen water in their cups, held down their heads, as though dying; but the elegant palm-trees, bending under the snow, appeared especially as if they were the true inhabitants and characteristic illustrations of this intermediary zone, where extremes meet, and winter begins to strive successfully with the eternal summer of the intertropical regions. This almost forgotten spectacle produced an extraordinary sensation in us; and was no less novel to our Annamites, who, notwithstanding the suffering which the cold caused them, seemed struck with amazement, like blind men, who, opening their eyes at thirty for the first time, suddenly behold the curtain lifted on some grand scene of nature.

There could be few scenes more magnificent than those we gazed upon during that march. The white summits of the mountains were dimly visible beneath the sky, like pale floating clouds, of different and curious shapes. The villages, half-buried in snow, recalled those of the Alps; the monotonous rice-fields had also disappeared beneath a slight coating of ice, and our eyes wandered over a transfigured and dazzling country. We paid for these pleasures when we halted: badly-built pagodas, paved with cold slabs of stone, were our constant hotels; the wood, difficult to get, was damp, and one had to choose between the pure but icy air outside, and the smoky atmosphere of the interior, warmed with great trouble by a fire, lit in the centre of our improvised dormitory. At the same time it became necessary to observe, in reference to the population, in which the Mohammedan element became more frequent, certain rules of moderation and prudence, often omitted till now by our Chinese soldiers. They themselves, however, well knew when to submit: for, though insolent towards peaceable folks, and thieves when voluntary presents were the rule, they became humble and quiet when they thought the inhabitants of a town were secretly disposed towards the rebels.

Tchieng-Tchouan-Hien, a third-rate city, is also situated on a lake, whose waters spread themselves, from a river used for irrigation, into this immense reservoir surrounded by un-

cultivated mountains. This lake is different from those I have
formerly mentioned, in its larger dimensions, and the wild
nature of the surrounding scenery. On the stones standing
out of the water, and in the grottoes formed by the black
rocks which surround it, were several coffins, placed there
to be out of the reach of the wild animals, which feed on the
bodies. I went close to this lake whilst visiting the town of
Tchin-Kiang-Fou, built not far from its banks; the sky was
gray, the water colourless, and on the snowy breast of the
mountains great banks of clouds floated slowly in warmer
air. The lugubrious and dismal aspect of the scenery was
enough to make one shudder; nature seemed to have clothed
itself in funereal garments in preparation for the return of
war and pestilence, for those two ministers of death give no
respite to Yunan. Farther on, the town of Tsin-Lin-So has
fallen a victim to this double scourge. The unburied coffins
lay in close rows upon the ground, and we halted amidst the
dead, waiting for the mandarins who were to precede us.
We saluted them, after which a Chinese, fat, short, squat,
and chubby as a village minstrel, went in advance, blowing
on a sort of hautboy. Our cortége resembled a village wed-
ding passing through a cemetery; at every step heavy biers,
borne by four men, crossed our path. At the gate of the
town, the sharp sound of our fife was lost amidst the noise
of gongs and firing of guns, with which we were deafened,
by way of honour. The whole garrison was under arms, and
the joyous colours of the pennants floating at the ends of the
lances made a heart-rending contrast to the sad spectacle
afforded by the heap of ruins which was formerly the town
of Tsin-Lin-So. We were lodged as well as possible in the
first story of one of the few houses left standing, but even
it still bore traces of fire.

From the ramparts one could perceive the whole extent
of the work of destruction. Hardly a stone rests on a stone
in this unfortunate town: the ragged inhabitants have made
caverns for themselves under the remains of their dwellings;
and wander about amongst the ruins, appearing as far from
the resignation which ennobles grief, as from the despair
from which strength to combat it sometimes springs.

Outside the walls, the land for the most part remains un-

cultivated, and the dead, left exposed in the fields on whose
produce they once existed, await their burial.

Cypresses grow of their own accord, and are almost the
only trees around. Accustomed to see them shading tombs
in Europe, we were reminded of our cemeteries, when the
brilliancy and splendour of the landscape diverted our minds
from these gloomy thoughts. There is, besides, no comparison between the few square yards reserved in our country, by the municipal authorities, for the dead, and these
fields of rest, without other boundary than the horizon,
where the Chinese lay their corpses; instinctively choosing
a fine situation, as though the contemplation of nature, disdained during life, was to be the eternal occupation of the
dead. This liberty concerning burial proceeds from the only
elevated sentiment which exists amongst the Chinese: respect for the memory of those who are no more. The living
often suffer from this custom, which is a lasting and serious
evil for the public health.

We were approaching Yunan-Sen. From the summit of
a mountain we had already seen the lake which forms the
riches and beauty of this town. If the weather had permitted us to climb the highest peak of these mountains, we
should doubtless have seen the five lakes which marked the
different stages of our journey across this magnificent region.
After having left the basin of the Sonkoï, and skirted that of
the Canton river, we finally entered the valley of the Yang-
tse-kiang, called by the Chinese 'the Eldest Son of the Ocean.'
It was with indescribable emotion that I contemplated the
humble stream, slightly swollen by the snow, flowing tran-
quilly towards the north, sending its waters into Shanghaï,
as though to precede us. It was barely a metre wide, and
could not have borne a canoe; I saw it already in imagination, however, rivalling the largest rivers in the world, seven
leagues from one bank to the other at its mouth, and covered
with European steamers. Marvellous power of imagination,
which combats, by the hope of future joys, the effect of present sufferings, and, whilst pointing out the goal to the traveller, gives him strength to reach it!

Our porters, not knowing that we were in the habit of
paying for services, made forced relays at every village, and

compelled the peasants to supply them with substitutes. We
still came upon barely-closed coffins, laid along the wayside,
waiting till happier times and less sickness allowed Chinese
piety to throw a little earth over them—or place them, according to custom, in a small brick cave. We spent one night
in the town of Tchang-Khong, from whence we could see the
great lake, still ablaze with the setting sun, when the plain
was already in darkness; it was the time when demons,
riding on the moonbeams, descend to visit the dying, and
flutter around the dead. In the very pagoda we inhabited,
a crowd of men in white—a sign of deep mourning—were
keeping a funeral wake. The sound of cymbals, gongs, and
piercing shrieks, to drive away evil spirits, prevented us from
sleeping; and morning having at last arrived, we set out with
pleasure towards the great city, where we hoped to find more
comfortable quarters. The plain lay stretched out before us
in all its magnificence, and its vast proportions appeared the
more astonishing to us, because we were 1600 metres above
the level of the sea: but the bare mountains, which surround it, are too low for such an expanse. The eye, always
more bewildered, than charmed, by what raises the thought
of boundless space, looked round, regretting the absence of
anything on which to rest, and seeking—vain hope!—to discover afar some high monument, the top of a dome, the spire
of a minaret, or at any rate a town-wall with its battlements
and bastions. We passed through large villages; a broad
paved road, edged with fine cypresses, leading us into the
highly-cultivated plain, where the numerous population buzzed
around us, and a mixture of soldiers, and petty tradesmen,
revealed the vicinity of the capital. Situated in the lower
portion of the plain, Yunan-Sen cannot be seen until one is
within two hundred feet of its walls, and you are in its suburbs whilst you are still looking out for them. It is the misfortune of Chinese towns, that they cannot be distinguished
one from the other, except by the space they occupy. The
houses are built each on the same plan, devoid of elegance or
grandeur. Passing their lives in loading their memories with
sonorous, empty formulas, or in labouring, selling, or buy-
ing, the Chinese only understand and practise trifles: essentially material, selfish, and calculating, they have no sort of

enthusiasm. For them, the sky is without a God, art without an ideal, and towns without monuments. I was indulging in these reflections as I advanced along the principal street of Yunan-Sen, now walking, now being carried by the crowd, in the midst of which our little party seemed lost. With the exception of missionaries, they had never before seen Europeans, and the former, long obliged to hide themselves, have continued to wear the Chinese costume. Our beards, our long disordered hair, our strange garb, and especially our arms, excited the liveliest curiosity; and it was with a cortége formed of a large multitude, that we reached the palace of the baccalaureat examinations, where we were to reside.

This palace is a large building, occupying an immense piece of ground, at the extremity of the town, and consists of two principal sides, flanked with long rectangular buildings, in which it would have been possible to quarter a regiment. We were obliged to devote some time to a regular topographical study, to ascertain our whereabouts, in the midst of a labyrinth of courts, halls, and dilapidated corridors; and could only discover, from the broken benches and overturned tables, the places where, formerly, candidates laboured at those literary compositions, which serve as a basis for the political organisation of the empire. Diplomas are still competitive, but the posts are generally got by intrigue. Never, in any country, has the sale of offices, and the venality of functionaries, been carried so far. In Yunan, in particular, pacific strife, the courteous passage of arms, from which orators, poets, and moralists came out administrators and public functionaries, have all been abandoned. It is no longer with arguments that they fight. Since our arrival in this unfortunate province, as has been seen, we have followed the footsteps of the rebellion, and verified its deadly consequences, even in the departments still by name faithful to the emperor; but one had to come to Yunan-Sen, to be able to appreciate the whole extent of the evil.

In traversing the town, we remarked, amongst the crowd, numbers of Mussulmans who resist, or make believe to resist, the ambitious projects of their co-religionists. From under their large turbans, their fiery black eyes did not quail before menaces; their straight, prominent nose attested their origin, the strong imprint of which still survives, though they have been intermixed for several centuries with a different race. Their whole bearing breathes audacity, and their haughtiness impresses a stranger all the more, because they stand out in such strong contrast with the abject people who surround them, like fiery Arab steeds, who have strayed amongst a herd of beasts of burden. The mandarin Ku, who had come to bid us an official welcome, made use of his most winning and supplicating tones, to keep off the increasing crowd, at our request. This functionary, we were aware, bore the reputation of being cruel; so it was not without some amusement that we heard him, standing with his hands folded, dressed in a furred silk dress, address a robust but ragged fellow, who was determined not to leave the place. He implored him, calling him his grandfather, and great-grandfather, not to be so obstinate. We were obliged, at last, to place sentinels, and oppose, by force, all these ancestors of master Ku, insensible to the prayers of their grandson. These extraordinary attentions, paid to the crowd, would alone have sufficed to enlighten us as to the condition of the country.

The mandarins have everything to fear from these insubordinate people, whom an identity of origin, and of religious fanaticism, will, sooner or later, unite with the insurgents of the West, if, indeed, they are not even now leagued with them by a secret understanding. They have already been strong enough to foment a sedition in the city, to assassinate the Chinese viceroy, Pan, and proclaim in his place their grand muphti. The military commandant, a Mussulman, like themselves, was, during this time, shut up in Lin-ngan, which he had gone to besiege, by the inhabitants, who, after having opened the gates to him, had retreated into the plains, and held him blockaded in their own town. The giant Lean-Tagen, who had so badly received us, consented, notwithstanding the hate he felt towards a votary of Islam, to allow him to make his escape, on his asking leave to go and save Yunan-Sen. Once there, either because his attachment to the emperor was sincere, or that he did not think it a convenient time openly to declare himself, he reëstablished order, dragged the grand uléma from the mountains, where the new court had installed itself, and ordered him, after an ephemeral royalty which recalls that of Cardinal Bourbon when he was opposed by the league to Henry IV., to withdraw into the vast domains of spiritual matters, and not leave them.

The poor old uléma, shut up thus in his yamen, pretends, since that period, to care only about astronomy. At the time of our arrival, the viceroy, Lao, who had taken Pan's place, had just died. It was to him that one of Prince Kong's letters, of which we were the bearers, was addressed. His successor had been already nominated by the court of Pekin; but, not being at all anxious to take possession of such a perilous post, he wisely lingered at Setchuen, causing us to have resort to his temporary substitute, Song-Tagen, when we had any business. That dignitary received us with great solemnity; music played at the door of the yamen, near a brick screen ornamented with the classic dragon; and we were escorted, on our passage through the numerous courts, by the body-guards, several of whom wore symbolical and grotesque costumes, representing fantastic animals. The viceroy came towards us, robed in a splendid pelisse of dark fur, and the usual mandarin hat with cocked sides, also trimmed with fur; a fine peacock's feather, fastened into a clasp of jade, which was surmounted by a bright blue drop, farther enriching this headdress. Song-Tagen is a handsome old man, with white moustache, and a pleasing and gracious smile; the dignity of his deportment, which becomes his high position, is moderated by the urbanity of his manners; and he is thoroughly well-bred. As to his palace, like all those we have visited before, it betrays the precarious situation in which the Chinese functionaries live at Yunan. A crowd of mandarins in full dress, plumed hats, and embroidered silk dresses, remained standing in the audience-chamber, where we had tea, and exchanged, with Song-Tagen, the well-known polite commonplaces, which, even more in China than in Europe, are the indispensable preliminary to any serious conversation between those who have any respect for themselves.

Having reached Yunan-Sen, we had no longer any real difficulties to encounter, and our return by Shanghaï was virtually assured. But it must be remembered that we had been obliged to abandon the Mekong at Kien-Hong, in twenty-two degrees north latitude, 1200 miles from its mouth; and if the question of its navigability had been decided negatively, the question of its sources, which was the other part of our programme, remained unsolved.

Though we could no longer allow ourselves to hope completely to clear up this point, it was possible, at least, to try to see the great river again where it emerged from Thibet. To convince the viceroy of the geographical aim of our journey, and to make him aware, without awakening legitimate suspicions, that we wished to visit the west part of Yunan, held by the rebels, without any ulterior thought of political alliance with them, was a most difficult task, in which M. de Lagrée failed, notwithstanding all his mental resources, which had long been accustomed to Oriental diplomacy. In spite of all our caution in speaking on the subject, Song-Tagen resisted us, declaring that every attempt of this description would baffle and endanger us; after which he turned the conversation, without showing, however, any symptoms of anger. We had thus ourselves warned him of our intention, and did not act covertly; and this sheltered us from any reproaches of ingratitude towards a personage who had acquired, by a most loyal welcome, a right to our respect.

We had barely entered the garret we had chosen in the bachelor's palace, as the best-built part in the edifice, and the easiest to defend against a crowd or cold, when we received, on red paper, an invitation to dine from the Mussulman general Ma-Tagen, the commander-in-chief of the imperial troops, who was so cavalierly treated by the governor of Lin-ngan, his subordinate. Various reports circulated as to his secret intentions—reports often justified by his attitude; it was, therefore, very important for us, if he was really in secret league with the rebels, which was not at all unlikely, that we should keep in his good graces, and have his aid, if we needed it. The town was closely surrounded by the enemy's army; the advanced posts had already fallen into their power, and at any moment Yunan-Sen itself might be taken.

The inhabitants had already begun to make their escape. Two contrary streams jostled at the gates. The petty tradesmen sought to gain the mountain, to hide their money, while the population of the outskirts wished to get the protection of the town walls. The rich merchants had long left the place, and only the business people remained at their posts, being fully aware that every closed shop was certain to be mercilessly pillaged, in case the town were taken, or even if there were only disturbances inside. Under such circumstances, we accepted with pleasure Ma-Tagen's advances; and since he chose to feast, instead of going out to fight, there was no reason why we should pretend to be better Chinese than he was. So we put on the different portions of the curious costumes we had hastily contrived for ourselves, the remains of our European wardrobe being strewed about the forests of Laos, and reported ourselves at the yamen of the general.

We found him seated at a card-table, in the middle of the first court, surrounded by his companions, finishing a game of chess, which seemed to absorb all his attention. He scarcely rose from his seat to receive us, and had us conducted, by one of his attendants, into a sort of small drawing-room, elegantly furnished, where we partook of tea whilst awaiting our amphitryon. The sound of laughter and military jests reached even there, and reminded us, spite of ourselves, of those garrison scenes so often reproduced in some of our theatres. It was impossible to feel offended at the cavalier manners of Ma-Tagen. Having risen from a very low position, he was well aware of his deficiencies, and, instead of imitating the refinements of Chinese society badly, he rather affected a freedom of manner and bearing, which had the advantage of making his guests feel at their ease with him.

We leisurely examined the different rooms of the yamen. They were all comfortable, and betokened the presence of a man who felt sure of the future. Chinese paintings and Canton lanterns ornamented the walls and ceilings. In one of the small rooms off the salon, two young misses in chalk looked down, seemingly in astonishment at finding themselves in the possession of an old soldier, a fervent disciple of Mahomet. As soon as Ma-Tagen rejoined us, he began to question us concerning Medina and Mecca. The ramadan

had commenced. The diurnal abstinence had been succeeded
by nightly orgies, of which Ma-Tagen still bore the traces,
in his depressed and wrinkled appearance, his inflamed eyes,
and hoarse though powerful voice. Only one subject besides
the Prophet and the Koran interested him, and that was war
and warlike instruments. The courts of his palace were full
of piles of lances; the corridors, of sacks of balls, buck-shot,
and long-barrelled muskets. His armoury, which he made
us visit afterwards, still more astonished us; for it was well
stocked with European arms—double-barrelled guns, breech-
loaders, rifled carbines, revolvers, and pistols of all kinds.
Nothing was wanting, and I even saw some things which
had not come under my eyes in Europe. Ma-Tagen is a
powerful personage. He maintains, at Shanghaï and Canton,
agents who supply him with what he wants, and does not
distress himself about the very high prices which they ask.
Owing to the state of the province, he monopolises the customs, especially those on salt; and, by a confusion easily made
between the public treasure and his private fortune, he dis-
poses of enormous sums, which pay for the luxuries of his
house. This strange man passes whole days in practising
shooting; the walls, columns, pictures, all serve as targets
for his skill; and I perceived that the back of the chair, on
which I was sitting, was also riddled with at least twenty
holes. The whole house is in the same condition; and even
a servant, passing at the end of the court, has been known
to serve as a mark. Scandal accuses him of having killed
two of his children. He does not spare himself during a
fight. Being covered with wounds, he stripped himself entirely, to show us the scars, of which he is very proud. We
had not at all expected to meet, in China, a man of this disposition, who would have been better placed in the court of
the ancient sultans. But, however that may be, we had come
there for dinner; and, after having fully observed the riches
of the palace, and the curiosities of the proprietor, we sat
down to our meal.

Dry seeds of the water-melon were brought first, with
pine-apples, mandarin-oranges, in fact, a complete dessert.
Thinking we were the victims of a misunderstanding, we
resigned ourselves to seeing the dinner changed to a col-

T

lation; but, contrary to European customs, these feasts are always begun by dessert; and for three hours we saw the strangest and most delicate dishes succeed each other on the table. The resources of earth and sea are drawn upon by this upstart soldier; swallows' nests, worms of every description, fish-entrails, lichens, &c., are the more simple dishes which I have been able to remember; a number of hashed meats afterwards made their appearance, and the soup was served at the end of the repast. We each drank long draughts of hot tea, tasted rice-wine, and dried our fingers on bits of paper, which were used as napkins. Faithful to the laws of the Koran, Ma-Tagen fasted whilst watching us eat. Our want of formality delighted him; and we quitted him, feeling we had gained one friend more, a precious friend too, whichever side he chose to take.

The third personage, who might be of some use to us, was the old 'papa,' the venerable priest, whose ambition had unmasked itself for a moment after the assassination of the viceroy Pan, and who, as I mentioned before, had since lived in his yamen, amidst telescopes and maps of the world, making believe to embrace earth and heaven in his studies. These serious occupations did not suffice, however, to occupy his time. Intrigue, and even petty faults, such as irritability and vanity, shone through the cracks which universal science had made in his vast brain. We kept him waiting for our visit, and, had it not been for the wish to see strangers, and display his knowledge to them, he would not have forgiven us this delay. Twice we presented ourselves at his door, and twice he gave us to understand that he was at prayers. Finally, impelled by the desire to know what was the exact distance which separated the earth from the sun, or the time it would take a bird to fly from Yunan-Sen to the moon, or a cannon-ball to reach a star (for such were the subjects on which his conversation mainly turned), he allowed us to appear before him. His attendants, as gravely as though they were waiting on a god, conducted us, respectfully, into the sanctuary, where the oracle, a short old man, with an aquiline nose and white moustache, was enthroned. He wore a furred bonnet on his arched forehead: his eyes deep sunk in their orbits, and almost lustreless, but never resting, gave a kind of mechanical mobility to his austere features, their wrinkles revealing a crowd of fantastic thoughts as they changed each moment with the play of his countenance. Tea and candied sugar were brought in on our arrival. Our host, having formerly visited Stamboul, after a long time spent in Mecca, prided himself on knowing the habits of Europeans, and desired us to sweeten our tea. This gave the starting-point to a long geographical conversation, which was aided by a large planisphere, over which he drew a finger as lean as the leg of a pair of compasses, whilst his mouth, stupid with astonishment and admiration, repeated the different names of the foreign countries in a silly way, like a docile echo. At the island of Singapore, the old 'papa' stopped his forefinger. Having heard that at this place, being close to the equator, the days remain at the same length all the year round, he stayed there for a year to convince himself of the fact, placing sun-dials and measuring the shades. An Englishman, whom he consulted, had told him he was an ass; and this recollection almost suffocated him with rage. But it was on Arabia that he expatiated with greatest delight. This country, containing, as it does, the birthplace and tomb of the Prophet, assumed gigantic proportions in his eyes. He made the r sound out as he pronounced Arrabie, Arrabie. It was a magic word, like the 'Open sesame' of Ali Baba. His familiars in the end only pronounced the word Arabie in saluting us, and, when we wanted some favour of this idiotic old parrot, we presented him with an Algerian dagger, saying that it came from an Arab chief. After having thus explored the world, the shape of which was barely distinguishable on his map, we had to teach him how to use a telescope he had bought at Pekin, which had cost a good deal of money, but which he did not know how to mount. So much kindness dispersed the remains of his ill temper, the clouds vanished from between us, and it became possible for us to touch on the subject which so entirely preoccupied us. The hope of seeing it favourably looked upon had given us patience to support the tiring chatter of a conceited fool.

Hardly had M. de Lagrée explained the aim of our journey, and expressed our desire to visit the western portion

of Yunan, than the old papa replied : 'I can perfectly understand you; you travel exclusively for your instruction, as
I used to do for my own; but rest assured that, with the
exception of mine, all the heads in this country are too thick
for you to hope to get this fact into them. I am, however,
able to take away any obstacles. My authority, consecrated
by a pilgrimage to holy places, is equally respected by all
Mussulmans, whether imperialists or rebels. With one word
from me, you can travel freely through the whole land; and,
thanks to the passport in the Arabian dialect, which I will
present you with, you will be able to penetrate, if necessary,
even into Tali.'[4]

It was possible that this old gentleman, being a braggart
by nature, exaggerated his authority. We were assured,
however, that it was very great. And, besides, he must have
felt convinced of his power, not to fear his relations with the
mutineers being noised abroad, whilst he continued to live
in a Chinese town, and to receive from the imperial government the annual sum about of 3200*l*.

'*Cuncta religione moventur.*' It is long since Cicero said
so, and it is true, especially, of Islam. We took these offers
of service for what they were worth, and left the yamen of
the high-priest, who deigned personally to conduct us to the
street, an honour which he never accords even to the most
noble of his compatriots. Some few remarks on the zodiacal
signs, and observations concerning eclipses, had sufficed to
cement our friendship.

We were, therefore, on the best of terms both with the
civil, military, and religious authorities, and with the faithful
or disloyal subjects. We were able to await events, and to
make use, notwithstanding its critical position, of the resources the town offered to us. These must have been very
considerable in prosperous times, for, in spite of daily panics,
we found even then, with the exception of wine, abundance
of everything at all necessary to European life. Wheat-flour
is only used by the Chinese in the concoction of certain
pastry cakes; so we baked our own bread, delighted to taste
again this precious food, which rice does not replace, after
eighteen months.

[4] The chief town of the rebels.

The town of Yunan-Sen is built in a square, each side of which measures about four furlongs. It is surrounded by strong walls, pierced by six gates, the four principal ones surmounted by roofs, one above the other, like those of a pagoda; the other two narrow, and not so high. I discovered, whilst visiting one of the military posts over these gates, two heavy iron cannon; and it was not without some surprise that I deciphered, beneath the dust which covered them, a little bit above the touch-hole, the abridgment of that well-known inscription, '*Jesus hominum salvator*' (J.H.S.). It showed where they had been made; and, notwithstanding the shudder it gave me to see such initials engraved on cannons, I could not help feeling a sort of patriotic pride in it. Those Jesuits, who knew how to influence the emperor, as much by the worth of their labours as by their virtues, were mostly Frenchmen. Coming there for the salvation of souls, they turned astronomers, mechanicians, teachers of geography; they became philosophers and men of letters, without permitting science, which they illustrated by their labours, to be ever anything more with them than a humble auxiliary to their evangelical designs. These great apostles have successors at Yunan. This is not the place to relate, at length, the work of the Catholic missions, and this grave subject ought not to be merely incidentally spoken of.[5]

And here I take the opportunity of thanking Father Protteau, that humble priest, whose calm, absolute, and complete self-renunciation at first confounds the mind, then enforces admiration, when fully comprehended, and Father Fenouil, the ardent pro-vicar, whose heart, vibrating still at the names of mother and of country, joined so readily with ours, notwithstanding twenty years of expatriation—both for the joy we felt on seeing them, and for the services they rendered us.

A canal drawn from the great lake serves as moat around the fortifications. In the plain, outside the walls, are still to be seen the remains of a town, equal in size to the present

[5] To collect various documents, corroborated by his personal recollections, as to the state of the Catholic missions in the extreme East, was the last wish of the author. Death overtook him at the very moment when his failing hand was beginning to compile this work, on which he would have entered heart and soul.

one; it used to be the business quarter, and, as every one
knows, that part is the most important one of a Chinese city.
War, by stopping all traffic, has driven the life out of this
exterior town, which is to-day reduced to the condition of an
immense ruined suburb.

Two small cypress-covered hills somewhat relieved the
aspect of Yunan-Sen on this side. Numerous green trees,
many brilliantly-coloured pagodas, and some yamen roofs
with turned-up corners, decorated with curious devices, rise
above the lower houses, and break the monotony of the long
straight buildings. The principal street begins at the
southern gateway, and ends not far from the first hill. It
is very broad, and lined with regular shops, whose elegant
fronts are adorned with two sign-boards, painted black, and
covered with gold characters. Other signs in the same street
are fixed between two grooved posts. In this part live the
provision-merchants, over whose heads the wind shakes a garland of hams, fat fowls, and legs of mutton. The perfumers
show in their windows eau-de-cologne and French soaps; and
the fashion-plates, representing fresh Parisian faces, sufficed
to restore our courage, and take away from the Chinese women
their last chance of winning our hearts.

The women here, indeed, look like living puppets dressed
up in bags of blue cotton stuff, or particoloured silk, with a
bull-dog's head plastered with rice-flour at the top, and legs
as thin as those of a peacock underneath. They were enough
to make one regret the sturdy daughters of Laos. I must
also add, that if the sirens of this country do not make themselves more agreeable to their compatriots than they do to
foreigners, husbands must be perfectly happy in the Celestial
Empire; they can live in peace, and allow their wives' feet,
mutilated by an unjust excess of jealous distrust, to grow
properly. This jealousy is really one of the most plausible
explanations of the odious custom, owing to which the feet
of the girls are imprisoned in bands, causing the toes to double
up, so that the big toe alone being allowed to reach its proper
size, makes it possible for the fashionable ladies to wear those
pointed shoes, which a child of ten could not get its feet into.

There is a great deal of poverty at Yunan-Sen. A large
number of black skinny-looking beggars, clothed, notwith-

Plate 22 *A Pa-Y savage from Yunnan (Drawing by Janet Lange, based on a sketch by L. Delaporte)*

Plate 23 *Ma Cha, the northern end of the Ta Ly lake (Drawing by L. Delaporte, from life)*

standing the cold, merely with pieces of ragged felt, wander about the streets, like living skeletons; imploring alms of passers-by, or executing the most fearful music before the counting-houses where the merchants string their sapeques. I have seen a whole family, composed of father, mother, and six daughters, who had no other shelter than that of a hole in the earth, and whose only clothing was of the paper made from mulberry-leaves. The government, which in time of peace is venal and defective, is now only a heavy burden on the people, without advantages or compensation. Even the mandarins, placed between flight, which is ruin, and the insurrection, by which their lives are menaced,—between a river and a torrent, as a Chinese picturesquely called it,— inspired us with pity.

In theory, the political and social organisation of the empire is, in some respects, a model of democratic organisation. Hereditary and perpetual nobility exists only in favour of the members of the imperial family and the descendants of Confucius. Contrary to western usages, a man's renown merely reflects back on his ancestors; so that the son of a Chinese is not induced, as is often the case with us, to repose on his father's laurels. Appointments are open to all; there is only one legal line open for obtaining honour, that of the examinations, which attest the personal worth of the candidates. Were it not that this idea is a necessary consequence of the mere notion of justice — a notion nations, like individuals, find deep down in their hearts—we might believe that we had derived it from China, where the system of governing by *capacity* has been carried on for centuries; but this perfect equality, from want of its corrective, liberty, is now more a curse than a blessing. Officialism, that scourge of certain European democracies, is developed, beyond measure, in China, and the mandarins of every class constitute an essentially privileged order, which, even if their intellectual aptitude were never at fault, is generally without that other as needful quality, morality. This virtue, a delicate flower which one vainly seeks in the East, only flourishes in the light of publicity. Open day and free air are all it needs for growth anywhere; and if we have seen it, even in Christian countries, almost extinguished along with political liberty, we might well be surprised to see it prosper in China. The few newspapers printed in the empire are written to deceive public opinion, not to enlighten it; and it is not in the hollow speculations of their atheistical philosophy, that the Chinese will find a curb to their dominant passion, the love of gain. At this time government, at its last shift, hardly troubles itself to put its appointments up for sale; instead of leaving them to free competition, it sells its mandarin's buttons at heavy prices; and the one thought of the officials who buy them is to reimburse themselves for the cost from their posts. I have known a fratricide remain unpunished, because he had silenced the accusers, or bought the judge, with money. Father Fenouil told us, laughing, that having been worried by quarrelsome neighbours, he put a stop to their annoyance by threatening to load his mule with silver, and seek a mandarin.

The old papa, having sent the precious letter, which was to open even the gates of Tali to us, we had no reason for lingering in Yunan-Sen. A longer stay would have exposed us to finding ourselves, to no end, in the midst of the sack of the town, and another still more serious consideration was, that we should run the risk of seeing the Mussulmans invade the country lying between the capital and the Yang-tse-Kiang, cutting-off our march, and making a desert before us. In fact, their advance on Kut-sing-Fou was announced. M. de Lagrée therefore decided to leave without delay for Tong-Tchouan, situated at no considerable distance from the great river; wishing to penetrate from thence into the west of Yunan, and reach the conquered and pacific part of the country, so as to be, as soon as possible, where there were recognised chiefs and a responsible government. But our cash-box, which at our departure from Saïgon did not contain more than 25,000 francs (a thousand pounds), was nearly exhausted, and we could not, without farther resources, begin a long and perilous journey. The terror-stricken traders had hidden their money: nobody would have dared to confess that he possessed even so much as 100 taels; the viceroy declared himself unable to lend us anything. We were obliged, therefore, to have recourse to our friend, Ma-Tagen. He joyfully offered us 1000, or 10,000 taels, or whatever we wanted: money never troubled him. M. de Lagrée accepted 700, or about 6000 francs, payable in French rifles, &c., at Shanghaï. Our creditor had no more bounds to his demands than to his offers, and wished to obtain from us an agreement to send him a shipload of ball cartridges! He interrupted his game of chess to consult us on this matter; declared that we did him an injustice in offering him a receipt for our debt; took leave of us with the best possible grace, and then continued his game.

On the 8th January 1868, the commission left Yunan-Sen. Outside the suburbs, in which a crowd of petty tradesmen swarm and crawl, the large plain ends, between uncultivated and bare-looking hills. On the paved road, we came across long files of animals, and little narrow carts, laden with wood, drawn by buffaloes. The Yunanese, were they not so careless, might have at their doors firing sufficient for their wants; but they prefer to despoil the mountains of their last shrub, and then get wood from a great distance. They also burn anthracite; and at the village of Ta-pan-Kiao, where we first halted, they use a species of natural coke.

In this district, as in that we traversed before reaching Yunan-Sen, the ravages of the plague had succeeded those of war. Many coffins lay without burial on the ground. The Chinese think that the corpse of a victim of this strange malady, which makes its appearance with eruptions behind the ears, avenges itself on the living, if they commit the imprudence of burying it. War is, by common accord, suspended during the new-year festivities, by a kind of 'truce of God;' but the brigands give no respite, and we met with a detachment sent out to pursue them. Nothing could equal the disorder in which these warriors marched: each one did as he liked, and went in advance of his comrades, or after them, in such a way, that it was impossible, unless one stayed behind unbearably long, to avoid these wearisome companions. Ah, what a fine thing drill is, and how fully I now appreciated barracks and military discipline! We reached the village of Yan-Lin at the same time as this mob of soldiers, and had some difficulty in defending our door against their insolent curiosity, for they seemed disposed to make use of their arms, and force our weak defences. Three thousand men, vociferating loudly, demanded to see us dine, and the six of us could hardly find space in the little room of the inn. The staircase was narrow, however; our sentry's bayonet glittered in the darkness; and we finished our meal before the three soldiers, who were needed to form the first rank, had dared to advance against us. The tumult having been at length appeased, the chief of the troop hastened to appear: he apologised, and swore that, had he been informed before, he would have driven away the indiscreet imperti- nent fellows from our room. The poor man trembled, lest his men should know what he had said; but their curiosity seemed more excusable to us, when their captain revealed what it was that had so much excited them. They had heard that Europeans had an eye in the back of their heads, but on the other hand had no joints in their legs. On what can the first of these two popular ideas be founded? I do not know. As for the second, it must have been spread by a Chinese, whose imagination had been struck by the stiffness of some Englishman's way of walking.

Father Fenouil, who had accompanied us as far as Yan- Lin, left us to return to Kut-sing-Fou, where he resided. The emotion of this unfortunate priest, who perhaps, for the last time, had heard France spoken of, affected us deeply, and we set out sadly towards the north, across a vast damp plain, shrouded in a thick fog, through which the dark forms of the tall cypresses were barely visible. These large trees, growing on the hill-sides, sway to and fro in a melancholy way, and, like black curtains, conceal numerous villages, for the most part inhabited by Mussulmans, who although still in subjection to the emperor, spread around them such terror, that the frightened Chinese dared not rear their pigs except in secret, and even refused to sell us any, these animals being considered unclean by the true believers. Everywhere we met with ruined houses, and ragged, po- verty-stricken people. One day, being compelled by fever to walk slowly, I was following our caravan at some distance, when one of our porters came to warn me, by striking his neck with the back of his hand, that I was risking my life, and then, frightened, hurried back to rejoin the column. My beard sufficed to keep the bandits at a distance; but what an existence for the labourers, who did not dare to go as far as their fields! Huts, surmounted with a flag, on the roads, in which crouched a trembling sentinel, and at equal distances a patrol or two, were the only protective measures taken by the government in the vicinity of the chief towns. Labour is impossible without security, life impossible without labour; and that is the reason in this sad country why an honest labourer, from having a home in his village, becomes in his turn a bandit, when the village is destroyed, and there is nothing left of his abode but the walls.

The country was becoming desolate and wild; and the ruins, which are scattered over it, recalled to one's mind the image of a past prosperity. A stiff white plant grows up to the foot of the arid mountains: it is eaten here and there by large flocks of sheep, who are watched over by a shepherd clothed in a sheepskin, and his dog.

We had great trouble in finding shelter every night; the provisions, too, began to fail, as in the worst days of our travel in Laos; and the young Chinaman, whom, as soon as we had halted anywhere, we sent out to seek for food, often returned empty-handed. Being as much concerned as we were in the matter, he was neither wanting in zeal nor skill; but, unfortunately, production was at a standstill, and nobody would sell. The Mussulmans alone had in no way altered their habits; but we did not venture to treat with them. Our young purveyor, after a long march had sharpened our appetites, having unknowingly addressed one of these terrible followers of the Prophet, on discovering with whom he was dealing, fled in the midst of the negotiation, leaving behind him all the money he had been intrusted with; nor would any one of our escort consent to serve as intermediary in this affair. Soldiers, porters, mandarins, and interpreter, all trembled before a solitary man, who, with folded arms and a smile on his face, rejoiced in his triumph. At last, it being impossible to make ourselves understood, and out of patience with his arrogance, we decided on turning him out. To that, our Annamites did not make any objection; they had adopted our ways, habits, and prejudices, even the idea of honour had come to be theirs as well. They had rapidly passed from the respect which their nation professes for the Chinese, to a profound, and often ill-disguised, contempt. If we, with the money we had at our disposal, and the prestige by which we were surrounded in our capacity of foreign mandarins and our passports, had occasionally to endure hunger, the fearful sufferings borne by the population, and the extremities to which they were reduced, may well be imagined.

When one has seen, as we have, the livid inhabitants of a village waiting like vultures for the death of some miserable horse, to fight for its flesh, he is inclined, without personally knowing the fact, to believe even reports of cannibalism, which it is said often occurs in times of famine. Whatever the case may be, the Chinese government was in no way responsible for the troubles which the poverty of the land often caused us, since they had not engaged to provide us with provisions. The mandarins, who used so often to send us fowls, pigs, and sheep, generally did it in the hope of receiving some present in return; it was an exchange of friendly feeling, consecrated by usage; but our cash-box had long been empty, and more than once unfortunate functionaries, who had followed some succulent capon, sent to our lodgings, have gone away very much disappointed at being able to take with them only the sincere expressions of our gratitude. There was nothing of that sort to be expected in this inhospitable region, which was a very prairie, where poor herdsmen lived on potatoes and oats. Their welcome, however, was cordial and sympathising; they made room for us at their hearths, and relit their fires with small bricks of coal; for they could not have obtained a fagot, had they walked for miles round.

Our demoralised and home-sick porters, having taken advantage of the night to make their escape, we were obliged to procure others. Since nobody desired to let his shoulders, it was not without some repugnance that we found ourselves compelled to seize on passers-by, who murmuringly obeyed, and walked along, closely followed by our bayonets. We all felt it to be an urgent necessity that we should speedily reach Tong-Tchouan; and this reason was our excuse—if, indeed, we needed one—for these acts of violence, which were, however, but rarely committed, and always compensated for, to the satisfaction of the victims, by pecuniary remuneration.

In whatever direction one might choose to look, on the people, or on the landscape, nothing was to be seen but traces of misery or signs of barrenness. They cannot be called houses which men construct in this region, which is perpetually swept and parched by violent winds; they are simply fragile huts, easily built, and as easily destroyed. Having, at last, quitted these dismal heights, we descended, and followed the dried-up bed of a large torrent, enclosed by the mountains whose summits we had just trodden; and this led us to the village of Tay-Phou. The hotel-door was ornamented in our honour with red paper-hangings, and the military mandarin, who resided in this place, did his utmost to make us forget cold, fatigue, hunger, and the steppes. There was a fair at Tay-Phou, and the street was crowded with men selling scented sticks, roughly-coloured images, and dainties, which were fearful mixtures of flour, aniseed, oil, and onions. People come from long distances to make their purchases for the new-year feast; but it is difficult to fancy what rejoicings can be, held under mud roofs, battered by the winds; and I wondered how a new year can be inaugurated with joy amidst such surroundings. We ourselves were not unmoved in the midst of these noisy preparations.

It was the second time during our journey that we had seen to its close one of those years which are so short, and yet of which each of us sees so few roll by. Absence began to weigh heavily on our minds, and the hour was not distant when the measure of our moral torture was to be at its height. Our health too, that blessing so necessary—we were all, more or less, ailing—was beginning to be affected; and this year, which was hailed in the streets by a tumultuous crowd, seemed, from circumstances, to open very solemnly for us. During our last marches, the sick had followed us on an improvised stretcher; and M. de Lagrée was at last obliged to take his place there in his turn. The chief of Tay-Phou, who had been ordered by the mandarin of Tong-Tchouan to treat us well, took pity on our condition. He could not quite make out how such titled mandarins as we

evidently were, could be so badly dressed, and appear so
poor; but without waiting to discover the cause of this mystery, he fulfilled in a soldier-like manner the command which
had been given him. He thought it would spare us the
fatigue of travelling on foot as far as Tong-Tchouan, if
we went in a boat; and our satisfaction equalled our surprise, when he took us to the banks of the stream, down
which we were to sail. It was a thin strip of water, almost
too narrow for navigation, according to our French ideas;
but the Chinese thought differently. We all entered a flat
boat, made of long, flexible planks, which bent, but did
not break. It was pushed into the water, and we took our
departure, now floating, and then rolling over the pebbles at
the bottom, passing by rapids and cascades, till the torrent
widened and became a river. The country through which
this stream flowed excelled in ugliness any that we had seen
since we left Yunan-Sen. Monotonous mountains, and nothing but mountains, without a vestige of green, as bare and
red as though they had been cast out of the furnace below.
Narrow paths every here and there reach from their base to
their tops, seldom winding, but commonly going straight
up, as if those who had to scale their slopes would rather
bear the fatigue of the shortest road, though it were the
hardest, and spend as short a time as possible on ground so
uninviting. Once familiarised with the incidents of a mode
of navigation which had, at first, drawn our attention from
the landscape, the fearful aspect of the latter had, at last,
the effect of making us deeply discouraged. Never before
had we been so overcome by exterior influences.

Was it the effect of our utter weariness, or the foreboding
of a sinister presentiment? Even now, after two years, I try
in vain to explain to myself the weird impression this horrible country still gives me, where everything, except the sky
and the water, was literally the colour of deep-red blood.

We had been for some time drifting along a calm, deep
stream, drawn by two men, who walked with long strides
along a towing-path, when, leaving the river to our left, our
boat entered a narrow canal, which led us to the outskirts of
the town.

There were several bridges over the stream; and in

order to pass beneath the low arches, we were compelled to
lie down at the bottom of the boat, whose *patron* repeated
imperturbably in Chinese, for at least twenty times, the same
speech at every obstacle we encountered: 'There is a bridge;
bend your noble heads, O great men.' It was almost night
when we reached Tong-Tchouan. A mandarin was waiting
to lead us into an elegant pagoda, where the thousand fanciful designs of a superabundant decoration were lavished
upon the doors, ceilings, and platforms. Dragons and monsters of every description, winged, rampant, and corpu-
lent, stood out from wood deeply carved, mingling their
golden heads and red tongues with the garlands of flowers
and flocks of birds. Even there, we preferred, instead of the
more spacious apartments, the small cabinets and rooms
where the air could be warmed, and the inquisitive prevented from spying.

We took up our abode in a garret, formerly accessible by
a staircase, but now reached by a ladder; and there, after
having pasted paper round the windows, we made ourselves
at home amidst the old furniture and useless gods of the
pagoda — finding them a most precious resource, as they
were very dry, and the cold rendered a fire necessary.

Lean-Tagen, the governor of Fou, hastened to pay us the
first visit, notwithstanding his high rank in the military hierarchy. The following day we returned it. We had scarcely
passed the threshold of his palace, when crackers went off
in every direction; and guards wearing on their shoulders
thickly-quilted cotton by way of cuirasses, young pages
with rattan hats whose ugly shapes seem to have been imi-
tated by Europeans, and in long dresses, the sleeves coming
over their hands, began to shout at the top of their voice. It
was a flattering reception, to show how highly they thought
of us. The master, who wore a magnificent silk robe and
white fur mantle, conducted us through the numerous courts
of his charming yamen, till we reached a luxuriously decorated and tastefully furnished apartment. To see the carpets,
polished consoles, gilt lounges, lackered tables, and all those
thousand nothings which make a room agreeable, we might
have believed ourselves in a boudoir of the Chaussée d'Antin.
This dwelling surpassed in elegance, if not in richness, even

that of Ma-Tagen; and as for the proprietor, although as
much of a soldier as the former, he did the honours like a
gentleman, and it certainly could not interfere with his military endowments.

Lean-Tagen also possesses quite an arsenal of European
arms; but, being without agents at Shanghaï, he buys them
when they have already passed through the hands of several
intermediaries, and we drew back frightened at the prices
he named.

Tong-Tchouan is a middling-sized town, whose fortifications and public monuments are in good condition. It is
situated at some little distance from the Blue River, on the
commercial road leading from Sutcheou-Fou to Yunan-Sen.
Every one appears to live happily and peaceably there, and
the inhabitants do not seem to feel at all annoyed with their
chief, to whom the Mussulmans, being acquainted with his
weak point, have dispatched a fair negotiator, whose arguments he evidently approves. I did not notice many coffin-
makers about the town, and even the few did their work very
badly.

But M. de Lagrée's illness grew worse as time went on,
and the most perfect quiet had become necessary for him.
As far as he personally was concerned, there was only one
course to be taken; to wait at Tong-Tchouan till he should
be well enough to go on to Sutcheou-Fou, and from thence
to embark on a junk which would take him to Shanghaï. He
was quite incapable of making that journey in the country
of the revolted Mussulmans, which he had meditated from
the time we were at Yunan-Sen, and which he considered as
the crowning portion of his enterprise. On the other hand,
he was not unaware of the attraction which the idea of this
supplementary journey had for his companions. To study
the primitive civilisation which Islamism, transported so far
from its birthplace, had produced; to see the mosque side by
side with the pagoda; and revisit the Mekong at Likiang,
where, having barely issued from Thibet, it flows at the foot
of a mountain, measuring 5000 metres in height, and near
Yong-Tchang, on the extreme frontiers of Burmah, where,
six centuries before us, the Venetian, Marco Polo, had travelled; and, finally, to reach Tali, the youthful capital of a

growing empire,—such was the programme which had re-kindled our almost extinct ardour.

M. de Lagrée could not make up his mind to force us to renounce this expedition solely on account of his own health. Whilst he was still hesitating, the Chinese authorities did their utmost to persuade him to prevent our leaving; and a letter from Father Fenouil, frightened at the dangers which he was convinced we should undergo for nothing, at the end of a so far lucky expedition, put a climax to the anxiety of our unfortunate chief.

Fearing the perils which, with one accord, a hundred offi-cious mouths warned us of; dreading them all the more, too, because he would not be there to confront them with us; fearing, at the same time, to impose a sacrifice on us; tor-mented by a thousand conflicting sentiments, which revealed his clear-sightedness and generous disposition,—he assembled us all round his miserable bed, harder and not so good as even a camp one, and then gave us liberty to decide as we liked. Had we been able to foretell the future, and perceive the reverse which was awaiting us at Tali, and the sorrow we should undergo at Tong-Tchouan, perhaps our decision would have been different; but we were full of confidence, and we resolved to start.

CHAPTER VIII.

THE MUSSULMAN INSURRECTION IN CHINA, AND THE KINGDOM OF TALI.

IF Europe has nothing to fear, in the future, from Islamism, banished as it is within a decrepit empire, Africa and Asia are less fortunate. On the first of these two continents, it has so clearly shown us its energy, that we have always owned it by making concessions to the rebels, whom it has excited against us. It is not only northern Africa which the Prophet's standard covers with its deadly shade. It also influences most of the tribes lying in Central Africa, thus darkening the veil which, in spite of heroic efforts, still conceals from scientific eyes that mysterious country. The causes which elsewhere have secured the victory of the Crescent, have brought about the same results in distant parts of Asia. Carried, after Mahomet's death, by warriors and by trading Arabs, to the extremities of the old world, Islamism seduced or vanquished a great number of warlike tribes, both of the coasts and the interior. The success it has obtained among the Malays, those ferocious pirates, whose greed is now outwitted by steam, can be understood; but, not content with bending under its yoke the nomads and savages, the shepherds and pirates, it goes on attacking the oldest empires, and threatening to overthrow, with its strong blast, structures which have defied centuries. So far back as the thirteenth century, mosques rose in Bengal by the side of Brahmin temples, Mohammedanism having taken root on the banks of the sacred rivers of India. It has now broken out in China, where the ancient giant is in the throes of a rebellion, which owes part of its strength to religious feeling. The spectacle is not devoid of instruction.

Accustomed to profess a disdainful indifference towards all religions alike, the government of Pekin did not hesi-

tate, as we have seen, to intrust the command of the troops
sent against the rebels to a man, who could not fail to sym-
pathise with his co-religionists; and therefore seemed to be
compelled by his faith to favour the progress of those which
his political duty obliged him to combat: a strange error,
which, even in Yunan, excited the cautious censure of the few
generals who still remained faithful to the emperor. These
murmurings were always stilled, however, by the loud protestations Ma-Tagen transmitted to the deceived court. The
Chinese talk among themselves of certain battles, where the
imperial regiments never counted a wounded man in their
ranks, and fired in the air to acknowledge the good behaviour
of the enemy. They add, smiling, that a lieutenant of Ma-
Tagen, a suspicious observer, asked his chief, one day, to
exchange banners with him. The general dared not refuse,
but beat a retreat when he saw some of his guards fall round
him. But as though the sight of an inactive army, commanded by a general[1] favouring the enemy, was not enough
to show the neglect and blunders of the imperial government, the only man in Yunan who has prayed on the tomb of
the Prophet continues to receive an annual salary, and to
reside in a palace at Yunan-Sen, although he has been compromised in a former revolt. I am in a position to state that
he was not unaware of his power, and that he neither attempted to conceal his relations with the western rebels, nor
his influence over the Mussulmans who still remain faithful
to the emperor. From the manner in which the latter treat
the Chinese, it is impossible not to feel assured that they are
men full of confidence in their power. They do not comprise
one-tenth of the total population of that part of Yunan which
they have vanquished; but they are braver than their ene-

---

[1] I must state, however, that recent information which I have received,
does not confirm the opinion which I formed on the spot, touching the probable attitude of Ma-Tagen. Shortly after we had quitted Yunan-Sen, it was
invested by the rebel army. All the Mohammedan soldiers commanded by
Ma-Tagen went over to the enemy; but he remained faithfully at his post,
massacred those amongst his lieutenants whose loyalty appeared doubtful,
and bravely sustained the assault with the remainder of his army. He
was wounded on the walls. Perhaps his heart has changed, as the Chinese
say; or perhaps he is jealous of the rôle and importance of the sultan of
Tali.

mies, and possess, besides, pride, enthusiasm, and faith. The
generals who oppose them—men without honour or courage—command a low set of fellows, whose laziness is not
quickened by any patriotic sentiment. When one thinks that
the sovereign of three hundred millions of men was unable,
at the battle of Sagawane, to oppose more than fifteen thousand soldiers to the European armies who menaced his capital, one cannot feel astonished at the success gained by a
handful of rebels in the most distant province of the empire.
If they would accept, as bounds to the independent kingdom which they aspire to found, the limits of Yunan, the
government of Pekin would act wisely, notwithstanding the
riches it contains, in renouncing a territory which so long
stood outside Chinese unity; but it is to be feared that
they will not consent to this settlement. This revolt—and
it is that which makes it formidable—is condemned by its
double nature, to run its course, for those who guide it cannot check it as long as there are infidels to fight. Politics
may set limits to its conquests, even beforehand, but it is
very different with religious propagandism.

Report says, in fact, that the new sultan of Tali has dis-
dainfully rejected the offers of the Chinese emperor, and
replied to his conciliatory overtures by expelling the ambassadors charged with acquainting him with them. To engage
to respect the frontiers of the provinces round Yunan, when
they each contain a germ of dissolution, would be to betray
the Prophet, and call down God's judgment upon themselves. For example, Kionei-Tcheou is hardly less troubled
than Yunan-Sen by the insurrection of the Miao-tse, those
old mountaineers, 'Sons of the waste,' who, though often
beaten, are never daunted, and are always ready to shake
off the yoke which the feeble hand of the Celestial Empire
is no longer able to maintain. Setchuen itself is not free
from civil war, incessantly rekindled in that beautiful country by the Mau-seu, who were driven away less than two
centuries ago from Souitcheou-Fou, their capital, and forced
into Leanchan, a mountainous region traversed by the Blue
River.

In the prosperous times of the empire, these barbarians
lived unsubdued, protected by the fastnesses of the Hima-

layas, descending from time to time into the plain, and then quickly regaining their haunts, where they divided the spoil among them. Their audacity increases at this time in proportion as the restraint is weakened, and their efforts only too well second the designs of the Mussulmans, not to be favoured by them. Already the Yunan Mohammedans have availed themselves of the quarrels amongst the aboriginal tribes, and have made use of the Minkias, as of the Lolos, except that they have reduced and disarmed these good savages, who claimed to be treated, after the victory, as auxiliaries, not as slaves.

It is not only from this quarter that the Mussulmans have received an unlooked-for help. Leaving out of the question the social war of the *Taipings*, which has paralysed the strength of the empire in the south and menaced the very existence of the monarchy, and the capture of Pekin, which has destroyed the prestige necessary for absolute sovereigns, it is certain that the Yunan rebels have received material aid from their co-religionists in the northern parts, such as the Chensi and the Kansiou, of China; besides moral influence from their brethren in Eastern Turkistan, who took up arms at the same time that they did. Has the coincidence of these various combinations been accidental, or did it result from secret arrangement? That is a question, on which no light has yet been thrown, and which it would be rash to touch upon. And yet the last hypothesis would appear to be probable, when one knows, as I do, from unquestionable private information, that Islamism recruits adherents even in Thibet, mortally attacking Bouddhism in the holy city of the Lamas. There are implacable enemies of the Christian name, who now are exciting the popular feelings against our missionaries, recently driven from Roungs[2] by the bonzes; whilst the Mohammedans, little by little, are acquiring real power at Lhassa itself, adroitly making use as circumstances require, of violence or craft. They have frequent communication with the Yunan rebels; and the sultan of Tali distributes Arabic proclamations amongst their mountains, in which he endeavours to explain, in mystical language, the

[2] Advanced post of the Roman mission in Thibet, evacuated after the murder of two French priests, assassinated by the Lamas.

real nature of the revolution which is being accomplished. 'The true God,' he says, 'will triumph over all idols, and the kingdom of the believers will be established over the ruins of an empire polluted by the ancient abominations of infidels.' At what epoch was Islamism introduced into the central empire, and what is the origin of Chinese Mohammedanism? These are connected questions which it may be of use to glance at briefly, without any pretension to do more than bring the help of some information obtained on the spot to aid the solution.

From the earliest ages, dreams have been a means often used by the heavenly powers to communicate with men. Fable affords us many examples; and the Bible itself, if need be, will furnish us with others. The Chinese annals are not devoid of marvellous tales. The emperor Ming-Ti, having seen in his sleep a man in shining golden raiment, who advanced towards him, in some way understood—and the fact does credit to his sagacity—that there lived in the countries west of China an extraordinary being, more powerful than kings, and wiser than the most learned men. He immediately sent for the statue of the unknown teacher, and for the books containing his doctrine. The ambassadors discovered in India the images and precepts of Bouddha, and brought back these treasures; and this is how Bouddhism entered the empire in the seventh century before our era. Several Mohammedans whom I have consulted in Yunan say that Islamism made its entry in a somewhat similar way. Nothing is more sterile than the imagination of a barbarous people, which creates always the same chimeras, and continually makes use of the same plagiarisms. If, instead of shining raiment, one were to clothe the phantom in Arab dress, and if, in place of simple curiosity, to suppose that the emperor to whom it appeared had urgent need of help against internal troubles and extraordinary disasters, we should have the legendary explanation of the historical fact. It must, thus, have been an emperor of China who, in a critical moment, gathered round him the first Mussulmans; and these auxiliaries, when they had ceased to be useful, one can readily imagine, became dangerous; and, in accordance with the constant practice in the East, with masses of troublesome people, would be broken up throughout the empire, and confined to distant provinces, there to multiply. The Yunan Mussulmans have very confused ideas concerning their origin; but one can trace in all their versions of it, in the midst of fables which connect them with demons, a relation which the unhappy Chinese, however, would be very much disposed to admit—vague reminiscences of assistance given to the empire, and triumphs obtained over rebels—triumphs which were repaid by ingratitude. And these traditions are all confirmed by history.

The Chinese have not always been a laborious and peaceful race, wishing to live isolated, and for itself alone, occupied solely in resisting the invasion of foreign ideas, by a desperate resistance to the influence which drags it into the universal gravitation of nations. It has often carried its arms far beyond its immense frontiers; and it may be said that there is no region, throughout the continent of Asia, which has not been compelled to respect its name. Under the Thangs, it exercised paramount sway as far as Persia and the Caspian Sea to the west, and to the Altai mountains on the north. It received ambassadors from Nepaul, India, the Roman Empire, and protected the king of Persia against the Arabs, in the seventh century of our era.[3] From the eighth century it fought against the Caliphs, who completely defeated the Chinese emperor's troops, about the same time the Moors succumbed, at Poitiers, to Charles Martel; and yet, notwithstanding the still recent recollections of this, in the year 757 Sout-Song, menaced by a formidable insurrection, did not hesitate to call upon the Mussulmans and solicit the aid of the Caliphs against its own rebellious subjects. Abou-Abbas and Abou-Giafar-Almanzor, chiefs of the family of the Abbassides, and founders of Bagdad, dispatched troops into China, which Father Gaubil supposes to have been Arab bands, garrisoned on the eastern frontiers of Khorassan and Turkistan. These forces, combined with the Chinese army, a troop of western Tartars, and the contingent furnished by the Oïgours, formed a force powerful enough to enable Sout-Song to rout his enemies com-

---

[3] Klaproth, *Tableaux Historiques le l'Asie.*

pletely. The battle took place in Chensi, not far from Sin-Gan-Fou, at that time the capital of the empire. Taissoung was obliged, like his father, to invoke the aid of foreigners, numbers of whom, wearied with their long journey across Asia, settled on the soil they had come to defend.

On the other hand, the Chinese had commercial relations with the West, often represented, it is true, in their annals as the enforced tribute of vassals to their lords, but the true character of which cannot be questioned. Among those nations which, from the most remote ages, sent forth their traders into the empire, the Arabs have always had a foremost place, and at the very time when their co-religionists were fighting in the north under the imperial standard, they did not shrink from sacking and burning Canton, which was even then a great commercial city, with which they drove a rich traffic by sea. Commerce and war were thus the two great causes which brought the Chinese and Mussulmans into contact several times in those ages; the Mussulman inroads being made at various epochs, and from different points. This agrees both with the traditions still surviving in China, though corrupted, and with the study of facts; but in submitting it to the reader, I can only send him to the sources, if he is curious to learn more minutely respecting the formidable shocks of which ancient Asia has been the theatre, and of which Europe has often felt the reaction.

...bout the thirteenth century, Mussulmans were so numerous in Yunan, that Marco Polo, writing in 1295, represented the population of Yachi as being 'a mixture of idolatrous natives, Nestorian Christians, and Saracens, or Mohammedans.'⁴ The city called Yachi by the illustrious traveller, appears to be the same as Tali, which was called Y-tchéou by Tan-Oudi, who founded, after having carried his arms beyond the Ganges. This celebrated city, which is now the centre of the rebellion, received the name of Yao-Tchéou

⁴ The learned editor of Tong-Kien-kang-mou gives most curious information concerning the different religions practised at the court of the Tartar Manjo-Khan, religions which Marco Polo found existing in the city of Tali, but principally respecting the Christian sect founded in the fifth century by Nestorius.

under the Thang dynasty, then that of Nan-tchao,[5] after it
had cast off the Chinese yoke; and, finally, it was called
Tali, after its capture by the grandson of Gengis-Khan.
Since that epoch, dynasties have changed in China; the
Mongols have been replaced by national sovereigns, and
these have, in their turn, been overthrown by Mantchou
Tartars: but yet, in spite of all, the kingdom of Tali remained, for six centuries, incorporated with the empire. In
1857, it again detached itself; for what motives, and under
what circumstances, I shall endeavour to explain.

The doctrines of Islamism have not been spread in China
by the preaching of a wandering apostle; they have per-
petuated themselves among the descendants of ancient immigrants, settled in the Chinese Empire, without any considerable aid from the conversion of those around. There is
reason to believe that the degenerate Christianity of the
Nestorians, and the modified Islamism of those whom Marco
Polo called Saracens, have been blended into one creed,
based on the dogma of the divine unity, and that this common
belief has induced amongst its disciples a scorn of atheists
and polytheists, which is easily turned to hatred. These
feelings have betrayed themselves hundreds of times, by
partial revolts, which might have sufficed to enlighten a government less blind than that of the Chinese as to the causes
and extent of the danger.

The first disorders appear to have broken out in 1855,
among some miners, who were ill-treated by the mandarins
superintending the works. The majority belonged to the
Mohammedan religion. Exasperated by violence, and feeling
themselves strong enough, they assassinated the Chinese
officers, and spread themselves, in armed bands, through
the country, calling upon their co-religionists to join them.
As the result of this movement, the Mussulmans grew everywhere still more insolent, refused to pay taxes, braved the
agents of the law, and showed a profound disdain for the
Chinese population. They killed all the swine in the name
of the Prophet, and violated the young women in that of

[5] The kingdom of Nantchao is one of the four which the Chinese call
the scourges of the empire. It has acquired new claims to this name
since the Mohammedan revolt.

Allah. They attempted, in 1856, to assassinate all the
Chinese mandarins in Yunan-Sen at once. An energetic
man, named Changsou, who had proved his valour in the
war with the Taipings in Kouang-Si, now thought the
moment had arrived to make a decisive stroke. Being the
governor of Hokin, a town situated a day's march south
of Likiang, and not far from Tali, he resolved, in concert
with the mandarin of Likiang, and another Chinese chief,
to organise, for the same day, the wholesale massacre of
Mussulmans throughout the province of Yunan. He killed,
in fact, some hundreds round the environs of Hokin—an act
of cruelty too incomplete not to be dangerous—and thus
provoked a general insurrection. By way of reprisals, the
numerous Mohammedans in Tali murdered all the Chinese
officers in that city, and prepared themselves for war. The
mandarin of Hokin came, in 1857, to besiege the place, which
is the second in importance in Yunan—perhaps the first, if
looked at from both a literary and commercial point of view.
He acted, in the name of the government, against rebels,
already abhorred, who had not had time to prepare, or to
procure arms, and yet he was beaten. A sortie, made by
some twenty determined Mussulmans, sufficed to disperse the
besieging army, composed of outcasts more accustomed to
the fumes of opium than those of powder. The son of a horse-
dealer, poorly educated, a native of Monghoa, bearing the
name of Tou, was then proclaimed sovereign. The Mohammedans call him Soliman; the Chinese have added to his
name the title of Uen-soai, and he governs by the aid of a
council composed of four military mandarins. The whole of
the western portion of the province has rapidly fallen under
his yoke. In the first flush of victory, his troops advanced as
far in Burmese Laos as Sien-Tong; but, having been driven
back by the king of that country, they withdrew, as we have
seen, to the south of Yunan, towards Scumao and Poheul,
which they have taken and lost; and they continue to hold in
check the brave governor of Lin-ngan. The Mussulmans only
kept Yunan-Sen long enough to partly destroy that large and
beautiful city.[6] Owing their power more to their bravery

[6] As I stated in a former note, they have again invested it. This second
siege has lasted more than eighteen months. I have just heard that they

Plate 24 Man Tse people (Drawing by Janet Lange, based on a sketch by L. Delaporte)

Plate 25 *Min Kia people (Drawing by Janet Lange, based on a sketch by L. Delaporte)*

than to their numbers, they reign by the terror which they inspire. Report says they bury or flay alive any prisoners who fall into their hands. Wherever they have co-religionists they have partisans; their enemies, struck down in the dark, amidst their own soldiers, die either by the dagger or poison. It was thus they got rid of their implacable adversary, the mandarin of Hokin, who, whilst shut up at Ten-Huen-Chen, in an intrenched camp, began to quarrel with his generals, whereupon the soldiery, profit ng y these disputes, which sprang from personal jealousi s, disbanded; and, not very long after, the terrible Changs u v as found assassinated in his bed.

Without enumerating in d tail the efforts made by the government of Pekin to stop the progress of the insurrection, it may be stated that they have only served, by exposing the powerlessness or the venali y of the Chinese, to redouble the confidence of their enemies. The military mandarins either appropriate to themselves the money provided to raise an army, or come to an understanding with the rebels; as in the case of Lean-Tagen, governor of Tong-Tchouan, whom we visited in the month of January 1868, who fled, without profiting by a brilliant victory he had gained, and left his soldiers to be massacred.[7]

Dreading our having any communication with Mussulmans, who might enlighten u concerning his conduct, he never ceased offering a desperate resistance to our journey into the west; but our determination was not to be shaken. Sinister prophesies, and gloomy pictures. alike remained without effect on imaginations so accustomed to such things as ours. If we had not felt M. de Lagrée's hand tremble in ours as we parted from him, and had we not seen Dr. Joubert, who was to remain alone with the invalid, looking pale with apprehension, the day of our departure would have been one of rejoicing.

---

have been repulsed, at last, more than thirty leagues from that capital, and obliged to fall back on Tali. From these alternate successes and reverses, we may infer that this portion of the empire will be long destined to endure anarchy.

[7] He has since been recalled from his post, had his rank taken away, and been exiled to Setchuen.

I have already said, that, in accordance with a custom, in use from Cambodgia to China, foreigners are not allowed to visit these countries, unless they have taken the precaution to provide themselves with passports. We were ignorant, at the time we left Saïgon, of even the existence of the growing kingdom of Tali, and had, besides, no means of communicating with it. On the other hand, we were unable to find among the Tong-Tchouan Chinese, a creature who would venture to go on before us, to the Mussulmans, and be the bearer of a letter to them. We left, therefore, somewhat at a risk, without any other guarantee than the note, written in Arabic by the old ulema of Yunan-Sen, and not feeling at all too confident of success. It was possible, however, that the same feeling which made the Chinese functionaries regard our journey with so much displeasure, would secure us a welcome on the part of the Mussulman authorities. A handful of resolute men resisting an immense empire, might give a good reception to the representatives of one of those European governments, whose mighty power, heightened by a mist of exaggeration, is admired by the most savage tribes; and it was not impossible that the rebels would hasten to make friends with us. The principal events of the Chinese war are well known, in spite of official lies, throughout the Celestial Empire; and if some episodes in that memorable campaign have confirmed the Chinese in the belief that we are barbarians, we had yet given proof of strength and bravery, two highly-esteemed qualities at Tali. War having rendered the direct road from Tong-Tchouan to Tali impracticable, we decided on making a circuit round the enemy's country, before penetrating into it, and then reaching their capital as soon as possible, by following the frontiers of the Chinese province of Setchuen.

Our caravan, reduced to four officers[s] and five guards, set out at ten o'clock in the morning of the 30th January 1868. We again entered the valley which we had long followed before reaching Tong-Tchouan. The mountains surrounding it still looked red and desolate. Yet when one sees them rising behind him, and closing the horizon, it is not with-

[s] MM. Garnier, Delaporte, Thorel, and De Carné. The escort was composed of two Tagals and three Annamites,—in all, nine persons.

out a feeling of pleasure, the inevitable effect of distance, by which scenery profits as well as men. The road, a rocky path running either along the river or on the mountain, was encumbered with palanquins, pedestrians, and gaily-dressed horsemen, all in their holiday clothes. It is the custom in China, as in Europe, to bid a welcome to the new year. Even the horses and mules, laden with salt, are all decorated with garlands and coloured ribbons.

We made our first halt in a village, which was being fortified. The inn was poor and dirty; the beds, which need no making, were of stone, with stone pillows. We stretched our mats over these granite couches, for we had not hitherto taken the plan of Chinese travellers, of carrying blankets, mattresses, &c. on the saddles of our horses. But as M. de Lagrée did not allow us much time, and as it would therefore be necessary, if we wished to obtain any result without going beyond it, to march very quickly, we decided on procuring horses. Nothing can be easier in Yunan. Horses abound in that mountainous province, which is less provided with navigable streams than other parts of China, and where the loads are carried either by men or horses. The latter are 'small and stand low, but are strong and hardy.'[9] They are probably, writes Marsden, of the same race as the horses of Lower Thibet, which are brought to Hindostan for sale. The inhabitants of Bhootan told Major Rennel that they obtained their horses from a country thirty days' march from their frontiers.[10] Tardy though this help was, yet it spared us many fatigues. From Crachè[11] to Tong-Tchouan, M. de Lagrée had been obliged to keep within the straitened limits of an insufficient purse; and, indeed, he had suffered more than any of us from an economy which he was obliged to practise whilst deploring its necessity. The loan so happily procured from Ma-Tagen placed us, as regarded financial difficulties, in a much better position, and permitted us to buy horses. For my part, I have preserved most pleasing recollections of those first days, during which I advanced at my ease, without any anxiety concerning the road, since my horse, accustomed to guide himself, carried me with as much

---

[9] Martini.　　　　　[10] Marsden's *Travels of Marco Polo*.
[11] Our starting-point in 1866.

composure as he had before carried bags of salt or bales of
cotton.

In the beginning of the month of February, the earth,
quivering with the approaching spring, still hid the germs
within it, and remained uniformly gray. Only a rash blade,
here and there, heralded the approaching birth—the wondrous and universal breaking out—of life. Numerous fruit-
trees lined our road. They were all budding. The rising
sap burst through the bark, and the more forward were already in pink or white blossom. A forest of apple, apricot,
and almond trees were preparing to sprinkle with their snow
the green carpet which the growing rice would soon stretch
out at their feet. These smiling scenes, however, were soon
to be replaced by others of a totally different nature.

On reaching by an almost imperceptible ascent a more
elevated position, there rose suddenly before our eyes an
immense entanglement of gray mountains, bare, and seamed
with ravines. We saw that we were amidst the sources of
a great river, towards which an irresistible attraction was
drawing all the torrents roaring down the gorges. A solemn
feeling seemed to announce its presence. The hand of God
appears to have surrounded the great arteries of the physical
world with impassable barriers, as it has taken care to en-
velope in shade and mystery the fountains of life within us.
We were obliged to descend slowly into the gulf by narrow
paths clinging to the mountain-sides. On one hand the
smooth wall, sometimes bending over us, rose above our
heads, passing into arching vaults like those dug by the
sea out of the cliffs; at our feet yawned an abyss deep
enough to make one giddy. However imperfect it may be,
such a road must have taken great trouble to construct.
Opened in the calcareous rock, which forms, in a great measure, the body of the mountains, it is often so slippery as
to add another to the many perils of the journey.   Over
large spaces the declivities are too steep to hold the earth,
and the rocks everywhere show themselves sharp and blue,
like congealed lava of a volcano which has destroyed in its
course the smallest germ of life. One feels crushed by the
immense proportions of inert nature, between the heights
which hang overhead and the abysses which draw on to-

wards them beneath. The caravans appeared in the distance like ants hurrying home before nightfall. Horses and
badly-trained mules, walking without due care and easily
alarmed, often roll over the precipices when they chance to
meet in perilous places. Hence, before venturing on such
passes, the mandarins send a scout ahead, to tell the traders
and merchants to stop and stand aside at certain parts
arranged for that purpose. The governor of Tong-Tchouan
had, of his own accord, and without telling us, taken this
necessary precaution on our behalf.

Miserable habitations perched on little terraces, like eagles'
nests clinging to the rocks, shelter here and there some poor
family, which lives on the sapeque laid by each traveller,
near the bowl of cold tea which he drinks on his way. The
heat is, in fact, very great, even in the month of February.
All these stone walls, exposed to the burning rays of the sun,
which there is not a single leaf to turn aside, get heated
very quickly, and it becomes hard to breathe in the glowing
air of this immense furnace. At last, after a long and painful
march, we perceived at the bottom of the cradle, formed
for it by two steep mountains, the Yang-tse-kiang, whose
waters, notwithstanding its name of Blue River, are as green
as those of a calm sea in a creek.

Remembering the look of the Mekong, we expected to
see the Yang-tse as boiling and muddy; but, on the contrary, it flows calmly along, glittering with light. It was
with joy we hailed this river, which alone gives life to a
region where everything is dead; a peaceful and rich image
of life, in the midst of all that is sterile and wild. It appears, however, from information we received, that there are
rocks in the bed of the river, a short distance above and
below the village of Manko, where we took a day's rest.
This village, one of the stations where travellers who go by
this route to Setchuen must halt, has almost the importance
of a small town. However, it contained no functionary who
had the power to impress men to carry our baggage. We
therefore hastened to hire some; and for the sum of two
francs twenty-five centimes a day, we had men who walked
bravely, and did not need us to be constantly watching
or urging them on. The regular government porters often

run off, when they think they can escape the penalty which
the law inflicts for doing so. Besides, one is continually
obliged to dispute with them as to halting-places, and the
length of the march, which we should have found impossible
to do; for we had left Tong-Tchouan absolutely dependent
on ourselves, without any interpreter, or any one we could
trust in the midst of this unknown world.

The following day, after an hour's waiting, which I
spent on the bank, watching the Blue River as it flowed
500 leagues from its mouth, a large boat left the opposite
side, and slowly advanced towards us. Our whole caravan,
including the horses, entered it. This heavy machine, with
stems of thin trees hardly shaped, for oars, was then put in
motion, and bore us to the opposite bank of the deep river,[12]
which serves as a boundary to the two most westerly provinces of the Chinese empire, Setchuen and Yunan. Then
began one of our longest and most wearisome ascents. Our
horses entered a path which seemed barely practicable for
goats, and up this we climbed, almost in a straight line,
with the river at our feet, dotted here and there with banks
of glittering sand.

Fields of sugar-canes formed green and regular patches
on the edges of the river. Manko was still to be seen immediately under us; but it grew smaller and smaller, furnishing in its lessening size the only proof of our advancing.
At last the road ran along the crest of a side valley; the
slope became less steep; and we admired, whilst pausing for
breath, the magnificent panorama of high mountains which
marked the course of the river behind us. We still obtained
occasional glimpses of it, winding along like a thin green
serpent with glittering scales, gliding and turning without
disturbing the obstacles it could not pass. But it was in
the morning that I liked most to gaze on the mountains.
When the aurora, that immortal magician, threw its gold
and purple over the bare forms of these children of the
Himalayas, their peaks, rising little by little from the darkness, became gradually surrounded with a glorious aureola,
and the light, peering at last through every veil, illuminated

---

[12] A cord, ten fathoms long, with a stone at the end of it, thrown into
the middle of the stream, did not reach the bottom.

the whole range at once, reflecting it in the river as in an emerald mirror. We still kept climbing, and, having had more than 25° of heat on the banks of the Yang-tse-kiang, were now shivering in our cloaks, as much surprised by this sudden change as bathers would be, plunged into vapour-baths and then deluged with iced water.

There is something very strange about the sensation which one feels at a great height: no sound reaches it; the air is rarefied, and the atmosphere seems to have attained a sensible transparency. This calm and peaceful feeling was in no way affected by the wild landscape beneath; the deep gorges, the rocks of every description heaped up around, eloquent witnesses of past disturbances,—these things did not matter; when one has overhead nothing but the blue sky, he seems to participate in its high serenity. Not a living being would willingly inhabit this chaos. I perceived, at a great distance beneath me, a flock of yellow sheep, driven along by a herdsman, and seeking a meagre pasturage of scorched-up herbs. They moved slowly amidst the blue rocks which pierced the soil, creeping, one might say, like the vermin on the ragged coat of a beggar. My horse, to avoid the roughness of the path, preferred walking on the narrow strip of green where the precipice commenced: I allowed him to do as he liked; he cared for existence as much as I did, and I thought my reason was less to be trusted than his instinct.

Ta-Chao is a very picturesque village, with its wooden bridge and white houses, sheltered by large trees. A little verdure and a little commonplace landscape give so much pleasure to the eye, after the grand sight of the wild, bare zone through which we had passed! We lodged in one of the numerous inns of the village, where caravans usually stop. Large stables shelter considerable numbers of horses and mules. In the evening, a long fiery serpent illuminated the mountain ravines facing us, consuming the remainder of the small amount of vegetation which existed there. From Cochin-China to this place, we met everywhere with traces of that aimless devastation, which destroys in a few hours what it takes nature centuries to create. Winter periodically recalls to the Chinese the necessity of keeping themselves

X

warm, and they would most probably be more careful of
their wood, if they had not, everywhere, in the countries we
visited, a combustible mineral easy to extract.

Not far from Ta-Tchao, the road again enters the rugged
sides of the mountains. The cold seized us as before ; and an
icy wind blew in our faces, sweeping over the snowy crests
of the higher peaks. These peaks, which have a vegetation
peculiar to themselves, are the last refuges of certain savage
races, who are no longer met with in the plains. Clothed
in stiff plaited felt mantles, their heads covered with a high
twisted cap, these last representatives of an oppressed race
watched us pass, motionless, and crouching silently behind
the rhododendrons and stunted pines. They build their
poor villages in the hollows, and cultivate the slopes, but
the harvest is frequently carried away by the torrents of
rain to the bottom of the abyss, with the soil that grew it.
After having vanquished these unfortunates, the Chinese
insult them; horrid paintings cover the walls of their pagodas, representing one of these fine savages in national
costume, chained, and without arms, enduring the outrages
of a group of Chinese soldiers: a vengeance worthy of the
cowardly people who find a gratification in it.

Our baggage porters, who had come from Tong-Tchouan
to Manko by order, but had been hired from that station,
were still gay and active, notwithstanding the fearful ascents
which tried both ourselves and horses. They are wonderfully sure-footed, and though heavily laden, never stumbled,
even in the steep paths, the paving of which, broken continually, formed a long succession of steps and quagmires.
The inns were, for the most part, sickening dens, crowded
with travellers. In the best bedroom of one, candles were
needed in broad daylight, and the only window was over
the stables,—a narrow shed which served for both pigsty
and privy. We were more lucky in the village of Tchang-
Tchou, where we joyfully installed ourselves in rooms opening on a raised gallery above an inner court. The troubles
and fatigues of the day were quickly forgotten in the evenings, where we found a good supper and good bed ; for the
rest we cared very little. At Tchang-Tchou, however, where
we arrived frozen, after a long march across the snow, we

tried to make punch with the bad rum of the country. The
flame rose and flickered about at the caprice of the wind,
which penetrated through the badly-joined partitions. We
thought of the cheerful fires, with their leaping flames,
which had thrown the same short-lived light on so many
youthful scenes; but the reality chased away such dreams.
When we came to sip the concoction, we found it as nasty
to the taste as to our sense of smell. The people outside,
seeing through the t⸱ ⸱a paper, which adorned our windows,
a man with a long reddish beard, in a room devoid of any
other light, kindling a fantastic fire, which seemed to run
over the table, took us for sorcerers about to compose a
charm, and fled in terror; and the innkeeper, wishing to
make himself agreeable towards strangers, who were versed
in occult sciences, immediately struck up the serenade with
which it is the custom to honour mandarins; an old drum
and tin pan forming the orchestra.

After leaving Tchang-Tchou, we entered a valley shut in
by mountains, which in some places pushed out great spurs,
in others sank into green lagunes. The sky was clear, and
the snow, sparkling like silver beneath the mid-day sun,
seemed to vie, in its metallic brightness, with the white
vapour of the clouds. This valley is full of villages; the
houses are new or freshly built; and every now and then one
is reminded, by some group of buildings, of the well-cared-
for villas of our retired merchants. This part of Setchuen
seems to breathe freely, and profit by the sad condition of
the neighbouring province, depopulated by war, pestilence,
and famine.

With these consoling symptoms of calm prosperity are
combined, round Hoéli-Tcheou, signs of animation and commercial activity. This village is surrounded with a strong
enclosure; bastions are being completed, and other fortifications are in course of erection: beyond this, the inhabitants of Hoéli-Tcheou seem very little troubled by passing
events. It was more than ten days since the new year,
and they were still celebrating this periodical event. Arches
of triumph, in painted wood, as wide as the street, arose
at short intervals amongst the stirring crowd. The small
low houses, with wooden façades decorated with many-

coloured lanterns, looked like hastily-constructed sheds of a fair. An acrobat, his face hidden by a grotesque mask, was performing on a pyramid of props; we passed by, and notwithstanding his efforts to keep the lookers-on around him, the whole crowd followed us, delighted to see an exhibition of real Europeans. It was with difficulty our horses found room to pass up to the hotel to which we were conducted. This establishment looked pleasant, and had an inviting air of cleanliness, as delightful as it was rare. Above a long narrow inner court was a wooden gallery, giving access to cells without windows, where complete darkness reigned. It appears that the Chinese, when they travel, only stop at a hotel to sleep, or smoke opium. In fact, I saw through the half-open doors, by the light of the small lamp, which an opium-smoker is never without, men lying on mats, inhaling the white vapour, which at first seems to exhale but little odour, but which soon affected me so much that I have often seemed to steal part of his drunkenness from the sleeping smoker.

Hoéli-Tcheou is essentially a town of transit, and it has adapted itself to this destination. The houses are vast shops, filled with lumps of copper and salt, bales of cotton, and cases of medicinal plants and dye-stuffs. Whole streets are inhabited by makers of pack-saddles, sellers of horse-harness, and other things necessary for caravans. The yamen of the governor, whom we visited, did not answer at all to the reputation which this personage has earned for himself of being greedy of gain and thoroughly extortionate. He levies a considerable tax on the merchants who take goods to the coppermines; besides taxing on his own account many other industries, to such an extent, that they have ceased to use boats, within the limits of his circumscription, on the navigable parts of the Blue River. But notwithstanding all these extraordinary resources, his yamen is very simply furnished. We only stayed at his dwelling long enough to repeat the few Chinese sentences of our vocabulary, appropriate to the occasion, which was quickly finished, and we withdrew, leaving him not much enlightened as to our projects, and visibly uneasy at our resolve. In the evening a messenger brought us a very incomprehensible letter, which gave some trouble to the most learned of our Annamites to translate. In this curious epistle, the governor informed us that stars had been observed making the most curious movements in the firmament, and that they had finally disappeared. Was this astronomical statement a delicate allusion to our journey to Tali, the object of the special anxiety of the Chinese authorities, and to the fate which awaited us amongst the Mohammedans? We never knew; but if this interpretation be the true one, we must confess that the mandarin of Hoéli-Tcheou had found means to renew, by the flattering and fanciful form he had given it, a prediction often before made to us. This personage, however, treated us as mandarins, and took on himself, without consulting us, to send away the baggage-porters whose shoulders we had hired, replacing them, on our departure, by government ones obtained at his command. Besides these, we were escorted by five or six petty chiefs, who paid us every attention, endeavouring to divine our wishes even before they were formed, and only leaving us alone when an occasion for drinking presented itself. These men disguised themselves very badly in their quality of spies, under the mask of devoted servants. We had nothing to conceal, and plainly told them that we had resolved to enter Tali, which rendered their task much lighter.

The road continued very steep. The mountain-sides were covered with bushes of pink camellias and rhododendrons, remarkable for their various sizes and colours. Amongst these latter shrubs some have red flowers, which stand out in such contrast with the dark background of the foliage, that the eye is quite dazzled; others have clustering white flowers, as exquisitely delicate as those of an azalea. In the plains, the pale blossoms of the poppy, which is largely cultivated, balance themselves on their long flexible stalks, pleasing the eye, and impregnating the air with a strong scent which gets into one's head. Animals even, they say, cannot resist vertigo; bees, for example, greedily plunder these vegetable sirens; and when the petals have dropped off, and man has gathered the poison for himself, the intoxicated and *blasé* bees disdain the juice of other plants, and die of inanition. Rats, which had taken up their abode in an opium distillery, have been found dead in great numbers, shortly after the closing of the establishment; having been accustomed to breathe the vapour exhaled from the caldrons. they died when it failed them. Horses and pigs, which have tasted poppies, refuse every other food, and perish after the opium harvest,—a striking picture of the perilous intoxications of life!

We got as far as the village of Hompousso without an interpreter, but had been preceded by a letter from the governor of Tong-Tchouan to that of Hoéli-Tcheou, whose authority reaches thus far—and in fact had only had to allow ourselves to be transported and conducted. Here we reached the limits of the provinces in subjection to the Chinese government: at a few leagues from us was war, terrible and pitiless war, especially so for the peaceful inhabitant, equally pillaged by both armies. It was important for us not to enter at hazard on the route which led to the capital of the Mussulman kingdom. We had no information, and supposing that a Chinese could have helped us, we should have been unable to understand what he said.

We had been told at Yunan-Sen, that at two days' journey from Hompousso there lived a Chinese Catholic priest. In the midst of our trouble it was an unlooked-for happiness; and nothing can explain the delight I felt on receiving a note written in Latin, in which this unexpected interpreter announced his arrival. It was quite like a miracle to find a Chinese, who not only spoke a known tongue, but was, in the nature of things, of the same ideas and opinions as ourselves, and that in the midst of an inquisitive and malevolent crowd, in a hamlet far away from the civilised world. To whatever belief one may belong, this great result of Catholicism, noiselessly obtained, in a place where there was so little else of good, strikes the mind with admiration and respect, when a fortuitous circumstance brings it suddenly to light. Father Lu had barely entered our house before he was assailed with questions; which he answered with a very good grace, of which his timidity heightened the charm. He consented to accompany us as far as the village of Machan, where he resided: but he could not go farther without interfering with the annual visit to his converts, and compromising himself with the imperial government: drunken Chinese had already insulted and menaced him, because he had made himself useful to Europeans. It was arranged that we should go in company to Machan, and when there, with the help of Father Lu, we should choose, among the divers routes which lead to Tali, if not the most direct, at any rate the safest.

We again met the Yang-tse-kiang, whose waters, always green, flowed through a less lovely country than that which served them as frame at Manko. After a few hours' painful walking on the sandy bank, we saw the great stream divide, and found ourselves in the presence of a geographical problem, whose solution the Chinese for centuries have disputed, without being able to come to any decision. The question is, which arm—that from the north, or that from the west— is the veritable Blue River? Science usually settles the question in favour of the western arm,[13] which bears the name of Kin-cha-kiang (the river with the Golden Sand); whilst its rival bears that of Pe-shoui-kiang (the river with the White Water). The name of Yang-tse-kiang is only applied, after the confluence, to the two united streams.

On the left bank of the Kin-cha-kiang, the volume of whose waters is much reduced above its junction, coal abounds in many parts of the valley. We visited a pit about two leagues from Machan. The mineral belongs to the proprietor of the soil, who sells for 600 sapeques the right of extracting 1000 Chinese pounds. Every one comes to take the quantity he desires to consume, and extracts it at his own expense. Reduced to a glutinous powder in the shape of cakes, much employed in the native kitchen, this coal sells for double the price of the other, 1200 sapeques, or a half tael, the 1000 pounds. They do not trouble themselves to push the works very far; and, without hollowing galleries, are contented to scrape the surface of the soil. Some of Father Lu's converts came on horseback to meet us, and we made a solemn entry into Machan. Machan is a poor village, which has been destroyed several times, and is often assailed by bands of ferocious wolves, which, descending from

[13] The western arm soon turns also to the north, and after Likiang it flows long in a parallel direction with that of the Pe-shoui-kiang.

the mountains, carry away animals and children, and often
worry even men.   We rested there a day, whilst preparing
for our departure.

We were on the borders of Yong-pé.   This district belongs to Yunan, which forms, on the left bank of the Kin-cha-
kiang, a curious enclosure in the Setchuen territory.   This
country is in great measure peopled by turbulent savages,
who revolted in 1859 against the imperial government, and
committed the imprudence of calling the Mussulmans to their
aid, who invaded them, and imposed a new yoke, which is
harder to bear than the old one.   On entering this region,
which traverses the ordinary route from Setchuen to Tali, we
should have run the risk of being stopped on our way by a
timorous chief, who lived too far from the centre of the Mohammedan kingdom to enable one to appeal from his decision to that of the sultan of Tali.   By offering very high
pay, we managed to collect some courageous men, who consented to serve us as guides and porters.   They told us of
an almost deserted route, very tedious, and destitute of resources, but which, not being frequented by the soldiery, had
no other inconvenience than that of being exposed to the
inroads of brigands ; and our experience made us dread the
thieves much less than the warriors charged with watching
over them.   We should have 300 kilometres to go instead of
200, which is about the length by way of Yong-pé.   Although
they were ardently seconded by Father Lu, our efforts to find
a messenger who would be the bearer of a letter, and the
Arabic note of the *papa*, to Tali, remained unsuccessful.

By their perseverance, even more, perhaps, than by their
daring, the English have acquired a preponderating reputation as explorers of the globe ; and it is no little satisfaction
to succeed in any part, where they have constantly failed.
This satisfaction, which springs from a fruitful spirit of emu-
lation, and not from a feeling of petty vanity, we had already
felt at being the first to pass from Indo-China to China, and
from Laos to Yunan.   Now that we are about to set foot
upon Mussulman territory, it may not be uninteresting to recall the obstacles before which Colonel Sarel, the chief of the
last English expedition, who, on leaving Shanghaï, went up
the Blue River, deemed it necessary to withdraw.   That officer

did not go beyond Pinshang, the extreme limit of navigability of the Yang-tse-kiang, which we have been fortunate
enough to come upon, and whose course we have followed
more than 300 miles above that point.

That this result was not without importance, one may
judge by the words of Dr. Barton, a member of the English
expedition, who, after having mentioned the reasons for
which Colonel Sarel was obliged to stop at Pinshang, con-
cludes in the following terms, in which one can trace, notwithstanding final failure, a sort of patriotic pride: 'Thus,
after having ascended the Yang-tse-kiang for 1800 miles,
being 900 miles more than any other European, except the
Jesuits, dressed in the Chinese costume; after having penetrated to the extreme western frontier of the empire (for
we were only a few miles from the country occupied by the
independent tribes), we found ourselves obliged to abandon
every hope of accomplishing our original plan of reaching
India by way of Thibet; and we were compelled to return
to Shanghaï after an absence of five months.'[14] 'In fact,' said
an English writer, a great admirer of Colonel Sarel's, 'this
officer did not abandon his enterprise till he had reached a
country plunged into rebellion and anarchy, which no guide
would venture to cross with him.'

However, before venturing into a country a prey to rebellion and anarchy, we availed ourselves, for a day, of Father
Lu's hospitality. This young priest loaded us with delicate
attentions. He did not hesitate to deprive himself, for us,
of a bottle of port, which, except what was necessary for
the sacrament, was all he had in his cellar, — a precious
beverage, given to him by a former bishop of Yunan, now
living on the frontiers of Thibet. The best Johannisberg or
Tokay will never have such a delicious flavour for us. Father
Lu's church is about a league from Machan. It is poor, ornamented with a few rough images, and serves both for draw-
ing- and dining-room, as soon as the cotton handkerchiefs
which cover the altar have been removed, after mass, by the
native sacristan. The missionary's room is close to his church.

[14] *Journal of the Royal Geographical Society*, vol. xxxii.: Notes on the
Yang-tse-kiang, from Hankow to Pinshang, by Lieutenant-colonel Sarel
and Dr. Barton; London, 1862.

I spent some hours, which fled only too quickly, in this modest cell, looking over his library, which was contained in a narrow trunk, and devouring the books as I chanced upon them. The Bible—the book of books—was the first which I came across. These pages, impregnated, as they are, with austere philosophy and glowing poetry, where the religious idea, alternately soft and terrible, shows itself, on one page, under the awful form of an angry God, dictating his laws amidst storms; on another, under the features of a fair Jewess, invoking the burning kisses of a lover; the mixture of solemn gravity and mystic grace it contains: all this produced on me, after such a long abstinence from moral food, an effect which I might in vain try to describe. What vague ideas and mysterious sensations must have passed through the brain of a young Chinese, meditating before the image of the holy Magdalene, after reading the Song of Solomon! Father Lu was not a Chinese when at college; and I thought, as I looked at his gentle countenance, that the seeds of consumption had not been the sole causes of his pallor. The charming beings whom he had only known by his books, could not fail sometimes, in his dreams, to become embodied before him; and though, from infancy, accustomed to refer everything to God, above all, love, I suspect he sometimes wept over himself, and honoured with a tenderness which would not, perhaps, be supported by the analysis of a rigorous orthodoxy, those saints of another race, who, with their fair hair and blue eyes, no doubt appeared to him nearer the angels than the dingy women of his adopted country. We conversed with him in Latin, and in a Latin which must have made Virgil and Cicero shudder in their distant graves. On the morning of our departure, this excellent missionary, become our friend so quickly, advised us to load our weapons carefully; and, convinced that we were playing with our lives, left us with emotion, to go to the altar to implore the benediction of God upon us.

We crossed the Kin-cha-kiang in small boats, which almost overturned at the least movement made by either of the two horses. The waters of the stream are always green, and the banks always free from woods. The great forests only reappear at the height of Hokin and Likiang. They

belong to the government; but, following a custom used,
I think, in Norway, the company which fells these forests
throw the trees into a river, after having marked them
with the imperial seal, and stop them when they reach
Souitcheou-fou. We disembarked on Yunan territory, and
determined on taking a road, which, perhaps, had existed
formerly; but there was no trace of it left, and we each
made our way, as well as we could, through the briers,
climbing the rocks, and hanging on by the roots and
branches. Our baggage-porters—who were paid very highly,
on account of the risks to which they were liable—laid
down the law to us, and demanded to halt, after a few hours'
march, in an isolated house, from which the inhabitants had
fled on our approach. On this frontier, so often crossed by
the Mussulman bands, peaceful folks were more timid than
elsewhere. An old woman, who had exposed herself to all
sorts of dangers rather than abandon her dwelling, at length
came out from behind a box, and, reassured by our behaviour, began to call her people. After an hour of persua-
sive entreaties, six robust fellows quitted the hiding-places,
where they had crouched like hares; and, each helping,
we soon had a table, benches, and beds made of planks.
The horses were placed beneath a shed; and I opened
a coffin,—a piece of furniture which had already served
me on former occasions to put my horse's forage into,—but
it was occupied by the proprietor. The pigs lived under
the same roof as this corpse, and cooking was carried on
close by. After the harvest, when they have time to spare,
and money to spend on the funeral, our hosts will probably
think of burying their father.

The country was absolutely deserted; and we journeyed
some time without meeting a single traveller. We at length
reached, not without some curiosity, the first village of the
Mussulman kingdom. It was very quiet, and did not justify
the terror of our porters. There was nothing to prevent
the insurgents from carrying their frontier as far as the
river: and yet they have left, between the Kin-cha-kiang
and their domain, a sort of neutral territory, where the red
flag of the imperial troops still floats, as a form; but where
the functionaries, far from loyal to a government which had

fallen of itself by the flight of the mandarins, are inhabitants of the country, and true chiefs of the national guard, enjoying a half independence, and exercising, without control, the power which they have seized for themselves. It often happens that the constituted authorities name these military personages destined to replace them. The motive which determined the new sultan of Tali to stop the progress of his arms was solely commercial; and it is worth while mentioning this fact, because it throws a light on one of the most original sides of the Chinese character. The white flag, adopted by the rebels, might have frightened away the traders, had it been planted on the very borders of the river; and it was too soon to make a change. The Chinese government has never tried to shut up its enemies in those barriers, which are one of the most powerful means used in Europe by belligerent nations for starving, or mutually impoverishing, each other. They never have blockades. The armies fight, and travellers are stopped; but on either side merchandise is a surer guarantee than a passport.

Vegetation profits from the absence of man; and the pine-forests, burnt up elsewhere, are here healthy and green upon the mountains. Our eyes were refreshed and gladdened by the sight of bushes of rhododendrons and camellias, which flourished in the damp soil of the ravines, beneath the shade of the trees; they looked all the more beautiful, because we were accustomed only to see them growing in the narrow beds and the unwholesome atmosphere of hot-houses.

We passed in front of the first Mussulman custom-house, round which several traders were assembled. A functionary visited the bales, baskets, packages, and received the sapeques. We made him understand that we were not merchants, and he refrained from inspecting our baggage. In the village of Ngadati, the population is, in great part, formed of savages of the Lissougn race. The costume of the women of this tribe is composed of a short petticoat, reaching to the knees, made of hempen cloth;[15] and of a large open bodice, trimmed, as well as the shirt, with a

---

[15] Hemp is not generally used, except among the savages. The Chinese dress themselves in silk or cotton only.

blue border. Their headdress is a sort of elegant mantilla, whose variegated ends fall down the back.

We were amusing ourselves with watching this interesting fraction of the great human race, when firing, shouts, and lugubrious blasts on the Chinese trumpet, announced the arrival of the military chief of Ngadati. He was the first Mussulman functionary we had met on our journey. He had a free-and-easy manner, and, from a distance, appeared to be dressed like a gentleman of the court of Louis XV. Beneath a sort of three-cornered hat, his long black hair fell on both sides of his shoulders, and was only caught up near the middle, and made into a thin short queue. The sultan, who is not unmindful of details, has already occupied himself about his subjects' costume. He has ordered them to wear a queue, on the double condition that they do not shave the front of their heads like the Chinese, and that they do not add to their natural appendage the long silk plait, which reaches to the feet of the dandies in the Celestial Empire. The military chief of Ngadati seemed anxious to visit us; he did not ask to see our papers, and in no way tried to give us any trouble. We had been informed that the chief of Peyouti was the only one powerful enough to cause us any embarrassment on this deserted route. We hastened to reach this village, and encounter serious difficulties at last. We had been warned of so many dangers, that we felt somewhat disappointed at not meeting with a single obstacle. In fact, a calm tranquillity reigned over this country, accounted for by the poverty of the district, but which we had not expected. A few merchants preceded, or followed us. They were, for the most part, laden with salt; a merchandise which is the object of important, though local, commerce; for the Chinese law, preserved by the Mussulmans, assigns limits to each salt-mine, outside which its products cannot be sold. Tea, opium, metals, and medicinal plants are the only considerable exports of Yunan. The prestige attached to us as Europeans preserved us from any attempts on the part of brigands, who are much dreaded, by solitary travellers, in this country, which would seem to have been made on purpose for ambuscades. A few signs were all that revealed to us the existence of these invisible enemies. Cross-shaped

gallows, the moveable beam of which has an iron hook at
each end, waved their great arms, as though calling for their
human prey. Now and then some skull reflected the rays of
the sun, like a block of rounded quartz, or marked the dark
sky with a white speck, which was not very awful-looking.
A small cold rain fell, whilst the mountains were covered
with snow, which produced on the branches of the green trees
those happy effects so often described. In this region, the only
inhabitants are herdsmen, watching their flocks, and savages,
crouching by the side of a stream, near a smoky fire, occupied
in threshing hemp. The vegetation is very healthy; it appears, in China, to be always the opposite of the population.

A dozen mud-huts, scattered, without order, on the top
of a mountain, and as many more houses in ruin, made up
the village of Peyouti. It has a singular appearance. The
roofs are composed of planks of wood, overlapping each other,
and kept in their places by heavy stones, in such fashion as
to give one the idea that a hailstorm of flints had fallen on
these wretched dwellings. One often sees, even in the large
towns, the same system of roofing employed. The means
of obtaining a livelihood in Yunan are so uncertain, that the
inhabitants do not even trouble themselves to construct a
dwelling-place. The rain fell in torrents into the deserted
hut where we were lodged, in default of finding a pagoda,
or hostelry, to receive us.

As to the formidable chieftain, whose presence people,
either ill-informed, or desiring to amuse themselves at our
expense, had announced, he never appeared. We could
easily have levelled his village with the mud from which it
had been constructed. One has to ascend, for a very long
time after quitting Peyouti, and follow the bed of a torrent,
which looks like a black winding line in the melting snow.
At the summit of the ascent, the view embraces a splendid
collection of mountain-peaks, bathed in clouds, which resemble the wreaths of smoke rising above a manufactory;
and these clouds shed a lurid hue over the landscape.
Numbers of peasants reside, with their families, on the borders of their fields, in huts formed of intertwined branches,
and await, in abject misery, peace and sunshine, or death.
They avoid the great thoroughfares as much as possible, lest

the passing soldiers should carry off their scanty harvest, and prefer the chance of being pillaged by robbers, as less exacting and more humane. Men, at very long intervals apart, are supposed to watch over the public safety. They stand sentinel, trembling in miserable sentry-boxes, three or four together, but seldom possess more than a single lance between them.

After several days of long marches, sometimes amidst deep gorges, sometimes on the tops of perpendicular ravines, through a very poor, and almost uninhabited, country, we arrived at the extremity of a spur of the mountain, where the view commanded a magnificent plain, such as we had not seen since leaving imperial China. Numerous little groups of houses, on whose walls we soon discovered the deadly traces of war, appeared to be bathed in a sea of verdure. The imperial soldiers had only recently set fire to everything which the persevering proprietors had rebuilt after a former disaster of the same kind.

We searched in succession three small towns, without finding a single house where we could pass the night, under shelter from the wind and snow, and, at last, only found lodging in the fortified town of Pinchouan. It is a populous place. The streets are filled with men, remarkable for their costume, their long hair, marked features, and a certain air of savage insolence, which characterises them. It was easy at once to recognise them as Mussulmans, if only by their haughty demeanour. One of them rudely entered our room, while we were at our meal. Upon being desired to leave, he replied by drawing his sword. Our Annamite sergeant, carried away by his courage and indignation, without waiting for orders, rushed on the impudent fellow, disarmed him, and thrust him violently out at the door. The military mandarin of Pinchonan came to us, on hearing of this occurrence, and, after a friendly conversation, requested to have the letter of the 'papa' read to him. When he had heard the praises with which the old astronomer had been kind enough to write of us, a visible degree of respect was joined to the cordiality with which he had, at first, treated us. This Mussulman commandant had conceived the idea of attracting merchants to the town, by guaranteeing to indemnify them for any robberies that might be committed on them in his territory. This measure compelled the inhabitants of the villages, upon whose shoulders the payment of the indemnity would really fall, to trace out the brigands, and act as police.

The proud snowy peaks of the mountains, which skirt the shores of the lake of Tali, were already visible; the other mountains, that were nearer to us, appeared rounder and smaller. Small plains became more frequent, and gave indications of the great plain to which we were to come. In the plain of Pien-ho, not a single village remained standing. The ruins, made alternately by the imperialists and by the rebels still serve as a precarious shelter to a large number of families, who continue to sow, because they can gather the harvest in six months, but who do not think it worth while to build. We were conducted to the house of Father Fang, a Chinese Catholic priest, short and thick, with a flat Tartar face. We were ignorant of his existence, and he had not received notice of our arrival. We took him by surprise, whilst reading his breviary; and it would be difficult to describe his astonishment. *Vox faucibus hæsit;* the Latin remained sticking in his throat, and only eventually came out in monosyllables, perfectly unintelligible. Recovering, at length, from his surprise, he left his prayers, in order cordially to do the honours of his house to us. Father Fang possesses the only house in the village; he built it himself. He has had the opportunity of developing his talents as an architect, for his present residence is the fourth that he has been obliged to erect. The others had been burnt for sport by passing soldiers. We slept in the chapel, which, as soon as mass has been said, is devoted to common purposes.

The calendar of Father Fang informed us that it was Shrove Tuesday. Less fortunate than the celebrated Curé de Grosset, who was able, in three days, worthily to perform all the duties of Carnival and Lent, we allowed the last hours of this day, marked by so many mad pranks in Europe, to slip away without doing them honour of any kind. We were as little inclined to fête the *bœuf gras* as to share the doctrines of which that overfed animal seems to be the symbol; for I have, in fact, always entertained the idea that the Catholic Church is opposed each year more and more to the doctrine of brute force and fattened flesh. To receive from a Chinese priest, and in the company of Chinamen, the ashes which typify the origin, the redemption, and the common end of humanity—what a rude lesson for the pride which is so apt to spring up in the brain of every European absent from home!

The *memento homo quia pulvis es*, which must, at all times, cause us to reflect, produces thoughts still more grave and solemn in a time of misfortune, such as has now overtaken this country. Civil war, famine, epidemics, and emigration, are proved, upon reliable evidence, to have reduced the population of Yunan by more than one-half, in the space of ten years. One has but to wander ever so little from the highways to run up against the mutilated bones of victims of murder, either unknown or unpunished. It has often happened to me to make such discoveries as would fill the imperial police agents in France with joy. At some miles from the dwelling of Father Fang, in a spot separated from it by a mountain, resides another priest, a Frenchman, who has concealed his house in a dip of the ground, about half-way up the hill-side. He lives, as it were, from one day to another, without having seen, for fourteen years, a single compatriot, adopting children, forcing himself in the midst of danger, to sustain the sinking courage of some few Christians, who surround him; and endeavouring to collect about him a sufficient number of just men to save Sodom. The details which he gave us respecting the new Mahommedan empire, which was then in course of formation, made us shudder with horror; and one does not know whether to feel most indignant against the sanguinary and lascivious tyrant, or against the population, ten times more numerous, who bear the shameful yoke, not without complaint, but without any attempt to shake it off.

Father Leguilcher lives in complete retirement, far away from the high-roads, holding no communication with the Mussulman authorities, against whom he has no protection, and who almost ignore his existence. When the sounds of war, rising from the plain to his asylum in the mountain, become too threatening, he seeks refuge in a deep cavern, a

Y

place considered holy by the Thibetians, who make pilgrimages to it. Still strongly attached to France, though he has renounced the hope of ever revisiting it, he consented, in order to serve Frenchmen, to throw off the caution which prudence, no less than his own tastes, had hitherto imposed on him, and to accompany us to Tali, where we dared not venture without an interpreter. To have penetrated, as it were, into the suburbs of that city, without having received any safe-conduct or authority, might appear to savour somewhat of rashness; but as no messenger would consent to carry our letters, the only course open to us was to deliver them ourselves. We had always been fortunate for two years, and we counted on our lucky star. Father Leguilcher had, however, a very limited confidence in the success of our enterprise; but if it succeeded, it would have the advantage of giving to his position, as missionary, a sort of official sanction, by which his Christians, the sole object of his thoughts, might hereafter benefit. It was this consideration that determinined him to share our fortune.

It was necessary to descend at hazard from the heights, on which the French priest had concealed his dwelling, in order to reach the level of the inhabited country; for the capricious zigzags of the path, which led to the plain, had more the appearance of being traced by the running of water than by the feet of men. Our horses were useless to us till we were able to regain the high-road from Yong-Pe to Tali. A fortress, occupied by a considerable military chief, commands this road. We caused ourselves to be formally announced, and entered the fort, without giving the mandarin time for consideration. He was quite taken by surprise at our sudden arrival; dropped his pipe of opium, and appeared half-besotted as he advanced towards us, and gave some orders to his people, who ended in blowing with all their might into some discordant clarionets. We were loaded with honours. The commandant of this fortress has not embraced Islamism; he has remained mild and tolerant, like a Chinese, and, without losing the confidence of the sultan, has frequently opposed the violence of the soldiery. A band of these Mussulman warriors having demanded of him one day, with a purpose easily surmised, to replace the men who carried their baggage by young girls, he had them seized and bound, and ordered that they should be smeared all over with hog's-lard, saying, 'You desire to defile our women; you shall first be defiled by our swine!' In spite of all the efforts of this personage, the villages have been destroyed round the citadel, which was constructed to protect them, and heaps of bricks alone mark the spots which they occupied. When night came on, we had great difficulty in finding a house standing; it was a sorry place, dark and uninhabited. We placed our horses in the inner court, and lay down on the pavement by their side, redoubling our usual vigilance. At no great distance from us, on the hills, dwelt some savages called Chasu, who from time immemorial have plundered travellers. The peasantry pay them an annual tribute, called in Chinese the robbers' rent, upon the condition that the half of what has been taken from them is reimbursed. The cultivator does not lose anything; a handsome benefit is still left to the brigands, and every one is satisfied; a curious tacit understanding, a sort of *camorra* connived at by the government, and accepted by all, as a natural servitude imposed on a certain district.

On the following day our route lay through a series of low undulations, into a narrow and long valley, which appeared to be hermetically sealed, at its farther end, by the great chain of the Tien-song mountains. These seemed to separate and recede as we advanced. At length we perceived right before us the magnificent expanse of the mountains of Tali. Their feet were bathed by the beautiful lake, whilst their summits, crowned with snow, were lost amidst the clouds. A large carpet of verdure was stretched at our feet, in the midst of which groups of houses, built of red brick, with their tiled roofs and white gables, glittered in the sun. Around us all was light, colour, and purity. If we had been compelled to stop here, we could not have regretted our long marches, our anxieties, and our fatigues. After a first burst of admiration, criticism resumed its rights. If this landscape was not one of the most magnificent which could be imagined, it was entirely the fault of the Chinese, who have not allowed a tree to remain either on the great mountains or on the smaller hills, which would be so ornamented by shade and foliage. On the other hand, kitchen-gardening is admirably understood; we observed beans, cabbages, and all kinds of common vegetables; the rice-fields also occupied a large space. The peasant population, that resides on the borders of the lakes, is an indigenous race, belonging, in great part, to the Minkias. Of the five hundred villages which once stood in this plain, scarcely two hundred and fifty can now be counted, and of these only one is inhabited exclusively by Chinese.

We passed along a paved road, on which workmen were employed. It was the first time, since our entry into Yunan, that we had seen a road either in course of construction or repair. This road leads to a fortress, whose walls rest against the mountains on one side, whilst on the other they are prolonged down to the lake, so that it absolutely closes the road. The commandant of the place informed us that he had sent for orders to the sultan, and that we must await the result.

These orders arrived the next day, and we felt ourselves relieved of a heavy load of anxiety, when we heard that they were favourable. We passed through the fortress, a regular mouse-trap, where it would have been easy to imprison us in a moment; but as a mandarin had been sent from Tali with some soldiers to act as escort, we felt reassured, and did not suspect that any snare was laid for us. On the other side of the fortress the plain opened out, and was traversed by the road, which we followed. As soon as the walls of the town, dominated by the high mountains, appeared in the distance, our porters were seized with a panic. The Christians, who had chosen to follow Father Leguilcher, prudently retired, proposing to rejoin our caravan as soon as they heard what sort of a reception we had received. Very bad reports were brought to us: fourteen Europeans had recently been put to death, and, according to our frightened attendants, we should soon see their heads stuck on the walls. By the Chinese all strangers are called Europeans. The men massacred by order of the sultan were probably Burmans or Hindoos, for their skin was nearly black. Nevertheless, we entered without obstacle into this formidable city. The main street, at first almost deserted, became filled by degrees. We ad-

vanced, closing up to each other, with eyes on the watch, and
our hands on our arms. A mandarin, magnificently dressed
and mounted on a valuable horse, cast a contemptuous glance
on our woollen garments, shabby and without gold embroidery, and our jaded thin horses: he desired us to dismount.
We were then assailed by an enormous crowd, shouting and
excited, which swarmed from all the side streets, oscillating
backwards and forwards, like the waves of the sea, and
threatening to crush us. The soldiers pressed upon us behind, and violently tore off our hats. This insult was followed
by a brawl, in which we were compelled to use the butt-end
of our muskets; our three Annamites and their two companions used their swords bravely, till at length the mandarin, who had at first remained passive, tardily interposed,
at the moment when a Mussulman soldier fell wounded.

This incident, which might have had such fatal results,
and of the origin of which we were ignorant, had been caused
by the curiosity of the sultan. He had been watching us
from the ramparts of the citadel, and it was to enable him
to examine at his ease our European features that our hats
had been so brutally pulled off, after we had been compelled
to dismount. He himself gave the order to conduct us out
of the town, and lodge us in a place which he pointed out.
We had scarcely been installed in our dwelling, when mandarins came to make excuses on the part of the sultan, to
offer an audience for the next day, and regulate the ceremonial, a point upon which they showed themselves very con-
ciliating. They insisted, however, on one thing—a promise
that we should present ourselves without arms. They then
conversed respecting the purpose of our journey; but the conversation, in spite of the courtesy of its terms, became a
regular cross-examination. Whether the exclusively scientific object of our expedition had not been sufficiently maintained by us, or whether their heads were too thick to believe in such disinterested motives for so toilsome an expedition, as the high-priest of Yunan-Sen had predicted, it is
certain that, on the following day, we found the friendly
disposition entirely changed.

At the hour which had been fixed for the audience, a
mandarin came to inform us, that there were still some

details to be arranged; that it was necessary to have a clearer and more complete explanation; and ended by saying, that the sultan required to see Father Leguilcher. After the fortunate issue of our previous negotiations, in which we had already received proofs of the wisdom and intelligence of the missionary, we thought that the interview with the sultan would be advantageous, and without danger. Father Leguilcher, less confident than ourselves, nevertheless went, like a man accustomed to face all dangers. He returned, safe and sound, after an hour's absence; but having heard the most violent menaces uttered, first against himself, for having introduced people of *our sort* into Tali; then against us, who had come to reconnoitre the roads, measure the distance, and to make maps of the country, with the intention, evident, in spite of the effrontery of our denial, of taking possession of it. 'Go and tell,' the sultan had added, 'go and tell these Europeans, that they may take all the country watered by the Lant-san-Kiang (Mekong) from the sea, as far as Yunan, but they will be obliged to stop there. Even had they conquered the whole of China, the invincible kingdom of Tali would still prove an insurmountable barrier to their ambition. I have already put many strangers to death; these insolent fellows, who shed the blood of one of my soldiers under my very eyes yesterday, may expect a similar fate, if they remain longer in my country. I spare them now, because they have been recommended to me by a man venerated by Mussulmans; but let them return at once to the place from whence they came; and if they attempt to reconnoitre the river, which flows from the lake of Tali (the Mekong), woe betide both you and them!'

This sovereign, who reigns by terror, lives in a state of perpetual fear. The walls of the citadel, which is constructed in the centre of the town, are the strongest and finest possible. The sultan remains shut up behind these ramparts. Two cannon, always loaded, stand pointed at the door of the hall of audience. No one, except his most devoted servants, approaches him; and very few of his people even know him by sight. The suspected are summoned, one by one, into this den; and seldom return alive.

Plate 26 *View of the interior of the pagoda of Ta Kouan (Drawing by E. Thérond, based on a sketch by L. Delaporte)*

Plate 27 *The fortified mansion of the bishop of Yunnan in Long Ki (Drawing by L. Delaporte, from life)*

When the Christians, who had mingled with the crowd, saw Father Leguilcher on his way to the audience, they burst into tears, quite convinced that he was going to his death. It was not, however, so bad as that, as we have just seen. After the account given by the missionary, we were not only compelled to renounce all hope of seeing the Mekong again, but even of visiting the town; and it was necessary that we should remain close prisoners in our dwelling, till the next day. We loaded our arms; for there was everything to fear from a man so much alarmed as the sultan. After the inexplicable change which had already taken place in his disposition to us, we felt that we might dread, in this eccentric tyrant, some fresh impulse, which might materially aggravate our position. We were, in truth, absolutely at his mercy; and although we were quite determined to defend ourselves, it was impossible to entertain any illusion respecting the result of the contest, if it really came to that. At night our whole house, with the exception of the portion in which we were actually lodged, was filled with soldiers. Our own sentinels were, in consequence, obliged to retire into our very rooms, and under the feeling that some great calamity was impending over us, we passed the night in constant observation of the soldiers, who, on their side, were equally watchful of our movements.

At the first glimpse of dawn our gaolers entered the courtyard, and offering no resistance to our departure, prepared to escort us, armed to the teeth. Everything went well till we came to the fortress, which commanded the entrance into the plain. There the mandarin, commanding our guard, ordered us to halt; and then quickly left us. Fearing that he had gone to communicate with the commandant of this place, and suspecting that, in order to get rid of us, there might be an idea of imprisoning and making away with us, we assembled all our baggage-porters, and pushing them before our horses, we passed, at a hand-gallop, all the fortifications that stopped our way, in spite of the shouts of the sentinels and the orders of their chief. Fortunately for us they were very badly guarded; and once out of this dangerous spot, we had space before us, and did not fail to profit by it.

At ten o'clock at night, when we had taken possession of a deserted house, easily defensible, in order to pass the night there, a small number of soldiers asked quietly to be allowed to enter. They came to inform Father Leguilcher that the commandant of the fort, the very same from whom we had had such a friendly reception three days before, required him to appear before him immediately. They were also charged to purchase, in the name of the sultan of Tali, the revolver which we had intended offering to that capricious personage as a present. In spite of the urgency with which they pressed on us this double negotiation, these indiscreet ambassadors were conducted to the door. To compromise the missionary, by making our escape in the night, would have been a want of prudence; and to sell a weapon to a man who had neither deserved it as a gift, nor had had the courage to take it for himself, would have been a want of dignity. So the soldiers left us murmuring, and we spent the night in consolidating our barricades. These, however, turned out to be unnecessary; and this alarm was the last. The chief of the new Mussulman empire spared us, from the fear of provoking against himself the intervention of Europeans; and his fanatical subjects were kept in awe by the secret terror with which our arms had inspired them. On returning to the hermitage of Father Leguilcher, we at once became aware, by the consternation visible on all countenances, that the news of our ill-success had preceded us. Christians were flocking to it from all parts of the mountain, filling the chamber and the oratory, pressing round the priest, whom they were afraid to question—silent, like persons who felt that some great misfortune was impending. On the following day, when Father Leguilcher, whose life would have been endangered by a longer stay amongst them, departed with us, sobs burst forth; men and children desired to accompany their benefactor. As to the women, it was really sad to see them, with their mutilated feet, striving to keep pace with the horses, and bathed in tears, whilst they laboured up the steep mountain. They held by the robe of the priest, who did not turn round, for fear of giving way. We carried away with us the soul of this little Christian world, surrounded by enemies on the side of Thibet, as well as on that of China, feeling that it would possibly, after our departure, and in consequence of our imprudence, be persecuted on account of its faith. This was a bitter thought, which, added to the inevitable sympathy, to which all human suffering, when sincerely expressed, gives rise, drew from us the first tears which we had shed for two years.

The mountain Li-kiang soon showed itself, with its imposing form, on the horizon; it looked, in the distance, like a huge white phantom, which appeared to guard the entrance to Thibet. We had set out, at first, from the low plains which had been gained from the sea by the alluvial deposits of the Mekong, and could, at length, gaze upon lofty summits and eternal snows, and have a glimpse of that hazy country, to which our dreams had so often led us. But at the same moment we lost all hope of ever being able to penetrate it; though the serious difficulties, which now occupied our thoughts, left us little time for regret. As long as our journey continued to be through Mussulman territory, it was necessary to press on, and encamp only in safe spots, and at a distance from populous places. It was, therefore, with great satisfaction that we, at length, arrived at the tract which was, by common consent, considered by both belligerents to be neutral. Our itinerary, on the return journey, was the same, with one trifling modification, which I have described in conducting the reader to Tali; so that I need not lose time over it. We had the satisfaction of obtaining from the mandarin of Hoéli-Tcheou the punishment of a soldier who had insulted Father Lu; and also the publication of the last imperial edict in favour of Christians—an edict of which the population had hitherto been kept in ignorance.

Meantime, thanks to the missionary, who served us as interpreter, the conversation of travellers, innkeepers, and merchants—people who are, in all countries, curious and talkative—was no longer a sealed book to us. Our adventures were generally the chief subject of talk; and in the account of them, truth already began to give way to fiction. We listened to these stories without taking any part in them, and it was thus that the first news of the invalid of Tong-Tchouan came, after our long absence, to grieve our hearts.

We succeeded in unravelling from the extravagant details with which an opium-smoker embellished his narrative, that an operation had been performed on M. de Lagrée. Of what nature had the operation been? What had been its results? To all the questions which hurried to our lips, no serious answer could be obtained. It was not till three days before our arrival at Tong-Tchouan, that our apprehensions changed to certainty. M. de Lagrée had died on the 12th of March 1868, of a liver-complaint, with which he had been ill for more than sixty days. Dr. Joubert, who had, in the highest degree, enjoyed the friendship and confidence of our chief, came to meet us. He was himself much enfeebled by the fever, and still suffering from the impression made on him by the painful duties which he had had to perform—the post-mortem examination and burial of the corpse. M. de Lagrée had retained his senses to the last. The feeling of the responsibility which rested on him never left him; when at the point of death, his greatest grief was, to remain in ignorance of our fate. This is not the place in which to pay him, at length, the tribute of praises which he had so justly earned. I will only say now, that the success of our long journey had been his work, and that all the honour belongs to his memory. It remained for us to gain Shanghaï. The narrative of this rapid passage through China will be the subject of the last portion of this work.[16]

[16] This voyage on the Blue River can be easily followed by the help of a map of China.

CHAPTER IX.

At Tong-Tchouan, our journey of exploration ended. Our
strength, as well as our resources, was exhausted; and,
under the heavy blow inflicted on us by the loss of our chief,
all our thoughts turned towards Shanghaï. It was still necessary, however, to traverse, in order to reach that city, almost the whole of China, in its widest part; but this seemed
easy to us with the assistance of the Yang-tse-Kiang, that
'*grand chemin qui marche.*' After having so long contended
against the current of the Mekong, through an unhealthy and
almost deserted country, we were, at length, to find compensation for our past fatigues; we were about to be borne
upon one of the mightiest rivers of the world, through one
of the most densely-populated countries, towards a European
city. Nevertheless, we had not yet arrived at the spot where
this great artery is continuously used by junks of large ton-
nage. Some stages still separated us from Souit-cheou-Fou,
an important town of Setchuen, where it was our intention
to embark; and we were in haste, like the Hebrew captives
of old, to commence this march towards our deliverance. But
there still remained a duty for us to perform at Tong-
Tchouan itself.

The Chinese government always avoids placing at the
head of a province any individual who has been born in
it, and consequently possesses there his family, fortune,
and interests.[1] On the other hand, respect and religious
veneration for the dead having alone, among the educated

---

[1] The Mantchou conquerors were the authors of this policy. They
desired to prevent the Chinese functionaries from taking root in their
government, and thus to preclude any possibility of their creating round
themselves centres of insurrection.

classes survived the shipwreck of all other beliefs, the value
which the children of a functionary attach to the possession
of his corpse admits of easy explanation. 'A son,' says Father Duhalde, ' would live without respect, especially in his
family, if he did not cause the corpse of his father to be buried
in the tomb of his ancestors, and a place would never be
assigned to his name in the hall where they honour them.'
From this cause it is that one so often sees those solemn
funeral processions, which traverse the country, and weigh
down the population, which is compelled to offer to the living
mandarins presents worthy of the personage whose corpse
they are escorting. When we wished, in the forest of Laos,
to open the tomb of Henri Mouhot, in order to assure ourselves that it contained his remains, it was opposed, as being
a sacrilege. In China, on the contrary, it was possible for
us to exhume the body of Commandant Lagrée, without
doing violence to prejudices, or contravening customs; only,
sad to relate, neither curiosity nor ill-will had been arrested
by death, and the hideous populace, without any respect for
our grief, insulted the sailor, who was fulfilling this sad
task, and went so far as to stone the coffin. On the spot,
where he had reposed for some days, in the garden of a
pagoda, Messieurs Joubert and Delaporte had raised, with
their own hands, a pyramid of stone, which will recall to
Europeans, who may hereafter visit this place, the recollection of one of the longest journeys that was ever made in
Asia, and also the name of the Frenchman, who died before
he could gather the fruits of the success which he had in-
sured.

We easily found a Chinese undertaker, who agreed to
convey the coffin to Souit-cheou-Fou, and we ourselves left
Tong-Tchouan on the 7th April 1868. We were still accompanied by Father Leguilcher, who had been obliged, as we
have seen, to flee from a persecution which was imminent,
and was going to rejoin his bishop, on the frontier of Setchuen and Yunan, and seek from him an asylum and instructions how to proceed. He was good enough to supply the
want of any other interpreter; and, thanks to him, we were
enabled to obtain information of the commercial movements
that were going on, the activity of which is testified by the

number of caravans which preceded us, or crossed our road.
The inns are numerous on this frequented route, which joins
Yunan to Setchuen by Souit-cheou-Fou; but they are usually mere dens, where man and beast live in promiscuous
and insupportable filth. The dungheap charms the sight of
this agricultural people, without wounding their olfactory
nerves; and these utilitarians think there is no use seeking
privacy to do what they regard as a beneficial and produc-
tive work. The beds furnished by the innkeepers consist of
thick mattresses, upon which the traveller can place cushions.
These mattresses are not fit for use, for every traveller leaves
on them his tribute of vermin; so that they harbour myriads
of filthy insects, and we found ourselves frequently obliged
to stop and have our clothes boiled, and rub our bodies
with spirit, distilled from rice, in which tobacco had been
steeped. The greater number of inns are kept by men, who
have come from Kiangsi, the province where most of the
porcelain is manufactured, and which sends to Yunan for the
most of the salts of lead employed in the preparation of the
glazing.

The town of Tchao-Tong is the last of any importance
in the province of Yunan. Its streets are filled with mud,
blackened with coal, and unceasingly pounded by the feet
of the horses and mules of the caravans. It is populous,
though the mandarin, who visited us, evidently exaggerated
when he carried the number of inhabitants up to 80,000.
Even if this number was reduced a full third, a sufficiently
large field is still left for the vanity of a municipal officer.
But what appeared to be essentially wanting in the intellect
of this high functionary, was the capacity to understand quantity: hence at the dinner to which he invited us, an inconceivable number of dishes appeared upon the table. This
festival was the last to which we were invited by a Chinese;
and, as I shall not have any other opportunity of describing what is prescribed, under similar circumstances, as the
puerile but accepted code of etiquette in the Celestial Empire,
I take this one, and borrow from the book of Father Duhalde some of the formalities essential for persons of good
society when they entertain each other.

'A feast must be always preceded by three invitations,

which must be sent, in an equal number of written notes, to the intended guests. The first invitation is sent on the day before; the second on the morning of the day fixed for the repast, as a reminder, to the guests, of the invitation that has been sent to them, and to beg them anew, not to fail to attend to it; finally, the third note is sent when everything is ready, and the master of the house is free to receive his guests. This is carried by one of his servants, and expresses the extreme impatience which he feels to receive his friends. According to the ancient customs of China, the place of honour is given to strangers, and amongst them to the one who comes from the greatest distance: the master of the house always occupying the lowest place. When the giver of the repast introduces his guests into the dining-hall, he salutes them in turn. He then pours some wine into a porcelain cup, and, having bowed to the person of the highest rank amongst them, he places it before him. The guest replies to the civility, by gestures which he makes, to induce the host not to give himself the trouble; and he, at the same time, asks for wine to be brought to him in a cup, and taking some, steps forward, to carry it to his host, who, in his turn, stops him by some customary words of civility. The feast is always begun by drinking unmixed wine. The host, with one knee on the ground, in a loud voice invites all the guests to drink. Then each one takes his cup with both hands, and raises it to his forehead; then lowering it beneath the table, and presently carrying it to his lips, he drinks slowly, with three or four pauses, the host never omitting to urge them to empty their cups, which he does, first of all, himself; showing the bottom of his cup, pointing out that it is quite empty, and begging every man to do the same. At the commencement of the second course, each guest makes his servant bring him divers little red-paper bags, which contain trifling sums of money, for the cook, the *maitre-d'hôtel*, for the actors who perform, and for the servants who wait at table. . . Little or much is given, according to the rank of the person who entertains you. But this present is only given when the feast is accompanied by comic acting. The amphitryon always makes some difficulty about accepting what is offered to him.

The master of the house, on showing his guests out, never omits to say, " We have entertained you very badly," &c.'

Everything, even to simple inclinations of the head, is prescribed by rules, in its least details; indeed it is all set out in printed instructions. The whole question of these rules of good breeding is elevated to the rank of a social science; and at Pekin, a council of ceremonies watches over these grotesque customs, with as much jealous anxiety as is shown by a political party, in Europe, for the maintenance of a constitution. If one has to pay a visit to a mandarin, the first step is to send him your card. This card is a small piece of red paper, on which one writes his name, followed by some polite but empty phrase, such as: 'The tender and sincere friend of your lordship, and the constant disciple of his doctrine, presents himself, in this quality, to pay you his respects, and make a reverence, down to the very ground.' If the mandarin is disposed to receive you, he advances to meet you, and begs you to pass in first. You answer, 'I dare not;' and, after an infinity of prescribed gestures and set phrases, the master of the house presents the chair on which the guest is to sit, and slightly flicks it, with a fold of his robe, to wipe off the dust. If one desires to write to a person of importance, it is necessary to use white paper, which has ten or twelve folds, like a screen. You begin the letter on the second fold, and write your name at the end. The smaller the writing you use, the more respectful it is considered. When the letter is finished, you place it in a small paper bag, outside of which is written, 'The letter is within.' If you have papers which are to be sent to court, you fasten a feather to the packet; and this symbol indicates, to the messenger, that he must have wings. We have ourselves received the visit of ten mandarins at a time, and, according to custom, offered them tea, commencing with the one of highest rank, who made a gesture as if to offer it to the second, then to the third, and so on to the last. Not until all had politely refused did he commence drinking. The second mandarin, in his turn, presented his cup to the eight others; and so on through the whole number, till the last but one, who did not fail to receive a polite refusal from the last. All this was

carried on with imperturbable gravity; and, to prevent ourselves from bursting into laughter, we were obliged to call
to mind the shades of language, and good manners, which
distinguish good society in Europe.

One thus sees that education, if a minute formalism be
dignified by that name, is pushed as far in China as with us.
How often must we have appeared, to these refined mandarins, people of coarse manners and incongruous customs!
What astonishment they must have felt, for instance, when
we took off our hats to salute them, who think it an im-
pertinence to uncover the head![2] If they had been writing
in France respecting us, we should certainly have had reason to fear, lest they should repeat the testimony which the
Lipou, or council of ceremonies, once gave respecting the
ambassador of the Grand Duke of Muscovy. This answer,
translated, by order of the emperor, into Latin, by the missionaries of Pekin, commenced thus: ' *Legatus tuus multa fecit
rusticè.*'[3]

The country round Tchao-Tong is as much ravaged as
the rest of Yunan. A short time before our passage through
it, the Manseu hordes had come down from their mountains, and harried it with fire and sword, and the bands of
imperial soldiers completed its ruin. The population, still
very numerous, in spite of the calamities which decimated
it, finds shelter where it can, in mud-huts, or in caverns in
the rocks. Its misfortunes have been so great, that it sees
an enemy in every unknown face. In an excess of zeal, the
mandarin of Tchao-Tong had given us an order to press porters, who were to be changed at every village; but we never
found a single hamlet that was not deserted on our approach,
so that we had to make a regular man-hunt. Fearing to be
retained by force, and made furious by this apprehension, our
porters went at this odious work with the keenest ardour.
Each one hunted for a man to take his place, and brought
him in triumph, often covered with bruises from the blows he
had received when caught.

[2] To conform to this way of thinking, the missionaries have asked
leave from the Pope to use a special headdress, something like the caps of
ceremony of the mandarins, at the celebration of mass. The Thibetians
salute each other by pinching the ear and putting out the tongue.

[3] Père Duhalde.

The roads are well laid out and broad; they only require a little keeping up. Here and there a few old women give an occasional stroke with a pickaxe, and hold out their hands to travellers, who profit by their voluntary labour; an ingenious pretext for begging, and also a useful protest against the negligence of the public authorities. The greater part of these roads are constructed on projecting slopes above rivers and torrents, which are affluents of the Yang-tse-Kiang, and traverse a region, upon which the troubled appearance of the mountains that bristle over it, gives the impress of a severe kind of beauty. Some of the larger villages have the arrogant look of our old feudal fortresses; for example, that of Tahou-anse, built half-way up a jagged hill, and having a large entrance-gate, recalls the threatening profile of a strong tower. Every here and there, the heads of decapitated brigands or deserters serve as food to birds of prey. Coal is often visible in the gorges, and is much used; it does not appear, however, that any effort is made to discover the seams, or to increase the working of it. Those mines only, which accidental circumstances have discovered, are worked, and these are quite sufficient for the very limited local consumption. The metals show themselves everywhere abundant; iron at Hé-hi; silver lead at Sinkaitsen, not far from Tchao-Tong. I have already mentioned this mine, which appears to be exceedingly rich.

On leaving a narrow defile, we saw the village of La-oua-tan, which was separated from us by a rapid river. Below the close rows of houses, which cover the declivities of the mountains, there was a large number of junks in course of building; some lying on the sand, others firmly moored to the bank. Thus, exactly one year after taking leave of our canoes, and setting foot in Burmah on the banks of the Me-kong, we again found vessels in China, upon an affluent of the Blue River.

The vicar-apostolic of Yunan resides at Long-ki, not far from Lo-oua-tan. The friendly assistance which had been rendered us by the priests of the mission made it our duty to pay our respects to this old man, now approaching the termination of a long career, which persecution had several times nearly cut short. Monsignor Poucet had arrived in China at the close of the Restoration, and had never seen France

z

again. Since that time, he has spent his life in the mountains of Yunan; and it was at the summit of an almost inaccessible height, that we had to seek the episcopal *palace*. The mandarins, who, for a long time, persecuted the missionaries, no longer possess the power to protect them. At the present moment, these last protect themselves against the invasions of the wild tribes, and sometimes even afford to Chinese, who are not Christians, shelter behind their walls, which the Manseu do not care to approach too nearly. They are, however, terrible enemies, these Manseu, who lie in ambush on the borders of Setchuen and Yunan. In a single year they are said to have reduced to slavery, or to have massacred, more than a thousand travellers. Ferocious and intemperate, they gorge themselves in their dens with meat and brandy, the fruit of their plunder; when they are satiated they sleep like boas, and soon afterwards start again on expeditions. Jealous of their own independence, they seek for no support outside their own tribes, and have exterminated a detached band of the army of the Taipings, without thinking of forming an alliance with them against the imperialists. The necessity of defending themselves, and especially of protecting the numerous children who come to Long-ki, and to the college of Chen-fou-chan, to seek the instruction which is freely given to all, has developed in some missionaries qualities, which it is strange to find under their garb. Their activity, their vigilance and bravery, reminded me of those immortal types, furnished by our military orders to romance and history. The native Catholic clergy is, in part, recruited from the pupils of these establishments. At Chen-fou-chan, amongst sixteen youths admitted to, and educated in this hospitable house, only one on an average takes orders. The others, with hearts educated on principles of Christian morality, and minds fashioned on the European model, by the study of Latin, obtain employment in different occupations at the missions, and, freed from the prejudices of their countrymen, place themselves in connexion with strangers in the ports which are open to European commerce.

When we had finished this last excursion, the river La-oua-tan, ministering to our impatience, bore us along with furious rapidity. We shot rapids, where the water, hemmed in by rocks, has a very visible fall. An oar fixed at the prow of the junk serves as a rudder in these dangerous places, where a false turn of the tiller would cause a catastrophe. Soon afterwards, the river broadens out, and opposite Souit-cheou-fou has the appearance of an arm of the sea. We had, finally, left Yunan. On entering the territory of Set-chuen, we thought, that, furnished as we were with pass-ports, we could count upon the mandarins for protection, and trust to them to insure us respect from the common people. But from the first moment of our arrival at Souit-cheou-fou, we had to give up this hope, and provide for our own security. The town was full of aspirants to military bachelorship, who, having completed their rough exercises, before a jury of examination, in the Champ de Mars, desired to give themselves the pleasure of a siege at our expense. The first, who attempted to enter our domicile by force of arms, was a bachelor of the watch, insolent, and dressed in rags. He received a sword-cut on the head. He was a vigorous fellow, come from Yunan to take his degrees. The soldiers of Yunan have a great reputation at Setchuen, and are renowned for their bravery. All the other candidates took offence at his treatment, and prepared to avenge him. Proclamations affixed to the walls, tumultuous meetings, passionate harangues, nothing was omitted by these valiant soldiers, to excite each other to the murder of five strangers. All this hubbub, which the Christians came trembling to tell us about (the Christians always tremble in China), lasted for three days, at the end of which we received the excuses of both infantry and cavalry.[4]

The mob remained quite indifferent to the quarrel, and the mandarins did nothing to allay it. The police is, never-theless, organised in all Chinese towns, and is by no means destitute of the power of acting. There is a special func-

[4] These bold warriors watched our departure, and when they were quite certain that the current of the great river had decidedly carried us away, they broke into our former dwelling, fired shots, and searched every corner to discover where we were concealed. After this glorious expedition, of the stirring details of which pompous announcements were made on the walls, the soldiers scattered themselves about the town, boasting to the people that we had disgracefully fled. These particulars reached me only quite re-cently.

tionary for each quarter; in every house the father of the
family acts. The inhabitants generally are, in part, responsible for the crimes committed by their neighbours, and in
consequence take some share in watching them. Hence arise
many violations of the sanctity of private life; but no one
thinks of complaining.

At the present time, however, everything even in penal
affairs ends in China in a question of money. Whether the
culprit has incurred the penalty of ten strokes or of death,
on most occasions a little ingenuity, and some few *taels*,
enable him to get out of prison safe and sound, and be again
proclaimed an honest man.

One of us having been insulted, one day when we were out
walking, by a group of idle people, we picked out the one
who appeared, from his dress, to be the best off, and seizing
him by his tail, whilst his companions ran away, we dragged
him through the town to the palace of the mandarin. During
our passage to it, his relations and friends came discreetly
to offer to buy his freedom. Our compatriot might have
done a good stroke of business on that day. However, he
preferred answering these propositions by some good strokes
of a whip, to which the mandarin added at once, and in
a public place, a sound bastinadoing. This took place in
Yunan, where the military mandarins possess a real suprem-
acy, in consequence of the state of the province, and generally, as has been seen, gave us proofs of their favour. We
encountered, on the other hand, from the learned officials
who governed those portions of the empire that were at
peace, a very different treatment, of which the impunity,
granted to the brawlers at Souit-cheou-fou, was a disquiet-
ing symptom. But it is easy to explain whence arose the
favour of the generals, and the hostility of the prefects.

One regrets to observe that the profession of arms is
valued too highly amongst many nations of the West, but it
is assuredly placed too low in the scale among the Chinese.
Since the Tartar invasion, the Mantchou emperors, placed on
the throne by their soldiers, could not fail, both from policy
and gratitude, to endeavour to secure some prestige to the
military profession. It may be said that they have failed
against the league of the learned professions, who coalesced

and have nearly reached the term of a laborious career, spent
not in the acquisition of the eighty thousand characters of
their language, but in deciphering them, and themselves
painting large numbers of them (for in that consists the
whole knowledge of a learned Chinese),—foresee in European
science, ways, and writing, rivals, with which they decline to
contend, because they are aware that the struggle would
be fatal to them. If by any new process, means were found
to teach the pupils of our lyceums to read and understand
Chinese, as readily as they read and understand English or
Italian, how great would be the disgust of certain Chinese
linguists, who are well salaried by our learned bodies to give
instruction, which is little attended to, and as little overlooked!

This is the cruel extremity clearly perceived in China by
those who possess the most foresight, vaguely guessed at
by others, and, not without reason, feared by all. That which
is now passing at the very door of the Celestial Empire, in a
country long attached to it by political ties, and still its tributary in literature, and a slave to its pictorial writing,
has nothing reassuring in it. There is a newspaper now
printed at Saïgon, which has substituted our phonetic characters for the Chinese hieroglyphics; and the young An-
mites instructed in the colonial schools are enabled to read
this journal after some months of study. This reform, effected without noise, contains, none the less, in spite of its
simplicity, the seed of a renaissance for this part of the extreme East, no less fruitful than that which, in Europe, followed the discovery of printing. In a country like China,
where one emperor has been seen burning the libraries, and
casting members of the learned class into the flames, another,
better inspired, may possibly be seen who will take the European alphabet under his protection, without permitting himself to be stopped by the despairing resistance of an egotistical
caste. Although this deliverance of thought does not appear
to be very near, the educated classes seem to have a presentiment of it; and, in consequence, encourage, by under-
hand means, violence against strangers in the lower orders,
who in all countries are so easily made the blind instruments
of the skilful.

At Souit-cheou-fou the storm had dispersed, but not without giving us a salutary lesson and a useful caution. The anger of some, and the indiscreet curiosity of others, did not prevent us from exploring the town. It is admirably situated on the Blue River, at a point where the latter receives a very considerable affluent. It is regularly built, and overlooked by a hill, which is crowned by a pagoda. This sanctuary is reached by a long flight of stairs, of easy inclination, which our Yunan horses, accustomed to more difficult ascents, mounted without difficulty. The view is splendid from this elevated spot, and we were able to enjoy it in perfect tranquillity, for the crowd had not followed us. I found there, upon the altar, a statue of Fo, which was a reproduction of the features so long familiar to us in the Cambodgian and Laotian Bouddha. This face, calm, and with long features, from which a sort of passive, but ecstatic and contemplative, expression has driven all animation, is rarely met with in China. In the beginning, as we know, God made man in his own image; but since that time, one may say with truth that man has certainly done the same thing to Him on a generous scale.' To speak only of the Chinese, in adopting the great Indian ascetic, who lived on wild herbs and roots, they have given him a monstrous paunch, which could have only been produced by the most substantial nourishment. This belly, however, is symbolic. A people who clothe themselves in white when in mourning, who get angry when one uncovers before them, who eat their soup at the end of dinner, have a perfect right to contradict us in more important matters, and to place the seat of intelligence elsewhere than in the brain. In fact, the stomach, if not in their thoughts, at any rate in their manner of speaking, takes the place with the Chinese which the head holds with us. Thus they say: 'I keep that in my stomach;' that is to say, in my memory. Or, again, 'This man has some stomach;' meaning that he is a man distinguished for intellect. Bouddha, therefore, has no just ground for complaint.

Placed at the entrance to Yunan, on the confines of the country, where the mountains become lowered in height, and separate, in order, as it were, to give liberty to the Yang-tse-kiang, hitherto but a colossal torrent, to take the calmer

submission; principles, no doubt, very respectable, but which have the grave inconvenience of all principles, of being absolute. Their results are, on one side, strict dependence; on the other, unlimited and uncontrolled power — results unacceptable in family life, and supremely unjust in the state adopting the doctrine, which is not less dear to the Son of Heaven than that of divine right to our own ancient kings.

Assisted by the current, and urged on by our oarsmen, who were ever attentive to furl or unfurl our great straw sail, according to the direction of the breeze, we descended so swiftly, that it was impossible to seize the details of the vast picture which unfolded itself before our eyes. An immense river, whose waters, at each instant increased by the tribute of innumerable affluents, are ploughed by fleets of junks; banks at one time overlooked by rocky precipices, at another, and more frequently, formed by the last undulations of the mountains, which, as seen from the middle of the stream, appeared scarcely to rise above its level; white and red houses, towers, pagodas, fortified hamlets, cultivated fields, the incessant witnesses of human activity in the midst of a fertile landscape—made up the spectacle which we saw constantly renewed, day after day. At night we found a shelter in our junk, which we infinitely preferred to the inns.

Tchon-King is a large city in Setchuen, said to contain nearly a million of inhabitants. We could not pass by without making a halt at so important a commercial centre. This populous town is built in the form of an amphitheatre; a happy arrangement wanting in most Chinese towns. A large number of war-junks, decorated with the various mandarin ensigns, were at anchor before the broad and steep stairs, which lead from the end streets to the water-side. They formed the noisy convoy, which was escorting the body of the viceroy of Setchuen; and made an unpleasant encounter for us, since we too were transporting a coffin, for which it was more difficult to insure respect than for ourselves; since the contrast between the splendid pomp of the Chinese escort, and the indigent simplicity of our own, was too great to escape the ill-natured acuteness of the assembled crowds. Leaving four armed men on board the junk which contained the corpse, we succeeded, with great difficulty, in forcing our way to the nearest inn. There we proceeded to install ourselves quietly, disregarding the clamour and deafening noise, from the throats of ten thousand men, out of doors; and shouts, which appeared to be a confused mixture of threats—when suddenly one of those unknown friends, whom the sainted labours of the missionaries have raised up for Europeans, burst into our room. According to this man, the mob, collected from all parts of the city, finding it impossible to reach our junks, which were anchored some fathoms from the shore, was preparing to stone them, and a heavy stone, hurled by some one amongst them, had already profaned the humble bier of the great French mandarin. Our men in charge had replied to this aggression of the mob by presenting their firelocks at the ruffians, who had hesitated at the sight of the pointed barrels. Our volunteer messenger said that he had left when this occurred, and that it was high time for us to interfere.

In spite of frequent messages sent to them, the mandarins persisted in not showing themselves; so we had no hope of help from them. Meantime, the three Annamites and the French sailor, left in the junk, might be in serious peril. So, three of us rushed into the street, revolvers in hand. Surprise made the mob open a passage, which was closed as soon as we passed. The cries, hushed for a moment, were redoubled, and pursued us to the shore. We there found our men, who had had the coolness not to fire, but had courageously landed, and seized and led off a prisoner, his hands tied behind his back, amidst the most formidable collection of ruffians I have ever seen, not one among whom had dared to attempt the rescue of their comrade from three resolute Europeans.

I may say, in passing, that this simple fact readily explained to me the meaning of the whole Chinese war. As regards the prisoner, he was at once claimed by the prefect of the city, who undertook to punish him. We let him go, with a halter round his neck, quite convinced that, the moment he was out of our sight, he would be set free, and, very possibly, rewarded. At nightfall, some sedan-chairs arrived in front of our inn. They had been sent by the Vicar-apostolic of East Setchuen, whose yamen we succeeded in reaching, after passing, *incognito*, through the whole city. In this vast residence, consisting, like those of the great Chinese mandarins, of numerous buildings, separated by enormous closed courts, we found rest, and, what had a still greater charm in our eyes, the warmest hospitality. Beneath the Chinese costume, Father Favent has preserved all his natural kindness of heart, and Monsignor Desflèches,[5] the Bishop of Setchuen, all the vivacity of the French intellect. We were disposed to judge very severely of the Chinese; and it was with secret pleasure that we heard these two men, indulgent as they were, draw up, in chance conversation, an act of accusation against this hateful race.

Tchon-King, situated, like Souit-cheou-fou, at the junction of the river with an affluent, which is navigable for several days' journey, is a vast entrepôt of all the merchandise that goes up the Yang-tse-Kiang, or descends from Setchuen to Shanghaï. The mere local consumption and production would cause a very considerable commercial movement. Since the opening of the ports to Europeans, this movement has greatly increased. The price of certain commodities has risen enormously,[6] and many of them are now almost beyond the means of the mass of consumers. The Chinese foresee and dread this necessary consequence of the treaty, imposed on them by our arms. Abundantly supplied by nature with the most various products; feeling no wants which they cannot liberally satisfy from their own resources; on the other hand, warned of the value set by European nations on their trade, by the efforts, humble for long, but now more and more urgent, made to secure it—the Chinese have obstinately refused to make modifications in their commercial legislation, from which they expected to realise no

---

[5] This prelate is now in Rome. He has united, with many of his brethren, in attesting that the infallibility of a single person will be more readily accepted by the populations he directs, than that of an assembly. The projected definition, indeed, will not frighten Asiatics, as any one feels, who knows them. As to liberty of worship, we are delighted to believe that it will find, in the vicars-apostolic, vigorous defenders, well stored with arguments, in the bosom of the council.

[6] For instance, the oil used for varnish, and in which the tow used in boat-building is dipped, was formerly sold at twenty sapeques the pound; it now costs one thousand sapeques.

profit themselves. This legislation was wholly based on a
tariff rigorously prohibitive, though not intended to protect
the national industries against foreign competition; for this
proud race believed, à priori, that all other manufactures
must be inferior to their own. The economists of the Celestial Empire entertained other apprehensions, and pursued
another aim. The emperor has always taken very seriously
his position as father and mother of his subjects. He is
bound to watch, in the private retirement of his palace, over
their well-being and repose. Not only does he, by fastings
and mortifications, take on himself a share of their suffering
when misfortunes overtake them, he is also considered to be,
in a certain degree, responsible for disasters he has been unable to prevent. A local famine, or even a simple scarcity,
which frequently occurs in this vast country, where the slow
and difficult communication is farther trammelled by innumerable internal custom-houses, is often sufficient to raise a
revolt, unless the state intervene in time, by opening its
store granaries.

Under such conditions, supposing an emperor on the
throne of China sufficiently enlightened to understand the
advantage of reforms, he may still be excused for recoiling
from the danger of originating that transitory period of suffering, which even the most legitimate economic revolutions
generally produce. To reserve the whole national produce
for home consumers; to guarantee them from excessive dear-
ness of all articles of consumption, and, at the same time,
to preserve them from dangerous contact with Europeans—
were the chief objects of the imperial government. We know
how force has overcome these scruples, and triumphed over
resistance. Unfortunately, the first act of the struggle—the
war of 1840, which was to be concluded later under the walls
of Pekin—was an odious attack on morality; and the old
repugnance of the Chinese to grant free access into their
ports to European vessels, was shortly justified by the forced
introduction of opium.[7] From that time, the salutary law
which prohibited the culture of the poppy in the empire,

[7] In 1867, on 300 millions of francs, which represented the total im-
portations at Shanghai, opium figured at 150 millions. (Report of M. Siegfried to the Minister of Commerce.)

ceased to be applied. The poison distilled from this deadly plant multiplied its ravages; and at the present day, in certain localities of Setchuen and Yunan, the proprietors, speculating on the high price of opium, have neglected the cultivation of alimentary substances, to the great detriment of the people, who lie, dying of hunger, on the borders of fields where the poppy has supplanted rice.

Leaving Tchon-King behind us, and continuing to descend the river, we landed, for some hours, at the town of I-hang-Fou. Here, barely 360 miles separated us from Hankao; and we thought that, within so short a distance of the first European establishments, we might display our strange costumes and faces with impunity. We advanced, without distrust, and unarmed, into the winding streets of the town, but were compelled hastily to regain our junks under a shower of stones. As soon as we had got on board, and were in possession of our means of defence, it would have been, assuredly, very easy for us to avenge this last insult; but, after accomplishing so long a journey without having the death of a single man to weigh on our consciences, was it not better to exercise a last effort of self-restraint, and to avoid firing on the crowd, at the risk of killing an innocent person? Something, however, had to be done. In spite of the French flag, which floated at the stern of our junk; in spite of the lanterns[8] at our prow, large as gourds, which they resembled in form,—we found that we must cease to anchor in front of the large towns. Between Ichang-Fou and Hankao, there were no departmental chief towns upon the banks of the river, which, after passing the first of these points, flows between the two provinces of Honan and of Houpé.

At some miles above I-chang-Fou, the mountains approached so closely as to form a gorge; and, for a moment, the river resumed the appearance which had been so familiar to us in the defiles of Yunan. It boils up, and precipitates its waters over the rocks; amongst which our junks, skilfully steered, descended with fearful rapidity. Below Souit-cheou-Fou, we had passed several rapids, which are

[8] These lanterns were covered with characters painted in red, and visible from a distance, signifying, 'Great Ambassadors of the West.'

modified and altered in position according to the season, changing with the level of the river, which is influenced by the summer rains, and the melting of the snows in the Thibet mountains. But what a difference between these not very numerous obstacles, through which the largest junks are without hesitation taken, and the long succession of rapids that commences on the frontiers of Cambodgia, and makes of the Mekong a stream with difficulty used, even by canoes! Steam navigation—which, according to treaties, ceases at present at Hankao—is certain, some day, to break these bounds; and the existence of numberless coal-deposits in the basin of the Yang-tse-Kiang, and even on its very banks, makes its extension still more certain. In default of Europeans, the Chinese themselves will be, doubtless, tempted to employ, on the Blue River, this means of transport; the quickness of which they have learned to appreciate in the passage from Hankao to Shanghaï, a passage which they make in large numbers on board the American steamers. In what degree will the rapids, scattered at considerable intervals from I-chang-Fou to Souit-cheou, be an obstacle to the development of this navigation? This is a question beyond my personal competence to answer; and I should not have touched upon it, if I had not had sailors as colleagues, whose opinions agreed with that given by Captain Blakiston and his companions in 1861.[9] According to this double authority, it is only by adopting a particular form of construction that steamboats could ascend the Blue River without danger, from the rapids of I-chang-Fou, as far as the frontiers of Yunan; and farther, it is possible that, in some spots, it might be always necessary to have recourse to towing and cables. This operation, which, however, it would not be necessary to repeat often, would be a trifling inconvenience, in comparison with the immense advantages which would be obtained, both in a political and commercial point of view, by the establishment of a service of steamboats upon a river which traverses China from one extremity to the other, and whose current is, at the present time, with difficulty ascended by junks. When the wind renders sailing impossible, it is by the sheer force of their arms that the

[9] *Five Months on the Yang-tse*, by Thomas Blakiston; London.

Chinese go up the stream; they row standing, and keep stroke to a regular cadenced song. Our crew, more fortunate, had only very trifling labour; they husbanded their strength for the return journey. We were, in fact, approaching our destination; palaces on the banks and palaces on the water, consulates and steamers—for these our eyes, wearied with Chinese sights, were longing; and these they at length perceived, when we cast anchor before Hankao.

This town, situated on the left bank of the Yang-tse-Kiang, and of a considerable stream called the Han, flowing into it, is, in some sort, the third quarter of an immense city, of which the two other parts, erected on the opposite banks of the same streams, are called Hanyan and Vouchang. The Abbé Huc estimated at eight millions the population, packed in these three towns; which are, he says, 'as it were, the heart, which communicates to the whole of China its prodigious commercial activity.' On the first point, the exaggeration is manifest; although the disasters, which have fallen on this portion of the empire, have produced an enormous decrease in the population since the travels of the Lazarist missionary. At present, it does not amount to two millions; and, terrible as may have been the Taipings, it cannot be credited that they have, in so short a space of time, destroyed six millions of men.

As regards the importance of these places in a commercial point of view, it has increased, though in some degree it has been modified, since the time of the Abbé Huc. It is here that European commerce, having at length succeeded in its struggle for freedom, has planted its flag, until the time comes when fresh concessions open the other ports of the Blue River to the enterprising ardour of western merchants. It is not necessary to dilate on the subject; France retains distinguished agents at Hankao, as well as at Shanghaï, who watch with constant solicitude over her interests, and furnish her with every useful information.

Our mission was accomplished; and I, for my part, neither felt courage to take notes, nor to interrogate M. Gueneau, the acting consul, or the other Frenchmen, whom we met at his table, respecting China. Besides, in order to satisfy our hosts, we had to answer their questions. The commandant of the English gunboat, stationed at Hankao, not satisfied by verbal accounts of our adventures, insisted on our donning our costume as travellers in the Laotian forests—a costume, by the bye, which pretty much consisted in wearing nothing at all—and he wanted to photograph us in this simple attire. After having so long been an object of curiosity to the Chinese, we were now threatened with the same fate amongst civilised people. I must not, however, omit to say, that the courteous reception which we met with upon this occasion, made the curiosity more than pardonable.

It is easy to understand with what eagerness the intrepid merchants, who have pitched their tents at 200 leagues from the sea, on the extreme frontier of the China which is open by treaty, scan the western horizon. We too were most anxious for news. The last courier who had reached us in the forests of Laos, and the first scrap of a newspaper which had rejoiced our eyes in the house of a missionary in Yunan, had acquainted us, the one with the catastrophe of Sadowa, the other with the sad tragedy of Queretaro. These two thunderclaps, followed by a long silence, had shaken our courage. Wounded on both continents, would France retain the wish, still more, would she possess the strength, to play a part in the extreme East? Would not our enterprise, begun under happier auspices, become a useless exploration, —a work barren in results for our country, and from which others would reap the benefit? Thanks be to God, the first hour of our stay at Hankao dissipated these apprehensions. Not only was Cochin-China, the base of our operations, not deserted by our flag, but such was the confidence entertained for the future of the colony, that the governor, in spite of the European complications, occasioned by the events in Germany, had been able almost to double its territory, without causing the slightest embarrassment to France, which would at this moment, when the pacific acquisition of three provinces was obtained, have with difficulty denuded herself of a single battalion. This considerable event increased our anxiety to arrive at Saïgon—that French town where our departure had been saluted, as a pledge of future prosperity, and where so many friendly hands would soon clasp our own. But we had still, before reaching the Donaï, to leave the Yang-tse, to traverse a part of the Yellow, and the whole of the Chinese Sea.

We embarked on one of those American steamers which ply between Hankao and Shanghaï. As I went on board, I was filled with surprise and delight at the proportions of the magnificent vessel, and I felt as a savage might feel when he for the first time gazes on the apparition of these floating masses, propelled by neither oar nor sail, and only moved onward by the beating of their own hearts of fire. But with the first marvel of civilisation which we encountered, we also came in contact with the prejudices of civilised men. We were the only European passengers, and a number of first-class berths were unoccupied. The Chinese, on the contrary, were crowded together, and confined in a narrow space—a kind of 'Jews' quarter.' On board these merchant-vessels, the rule enforcing the separation of races is very stringent; and, in spite of all our remonstrances, our Tagals and Annamites were separated from us, and shut up apart, as if they were lepers. Two years of peril, suffering, and rigid self-denial, had raised these men to the level of the best; and they bitterly felt the outrage offered them by the Anglo-Saxon captain's proud strictness.

Entirely given up to the pleasure of being alone in a cabin, and finding a bed furnished with sheets; absorbed by the novel enjoyments to which my every movement gave rise, I permitted myself to be carried on, for a length of time, without troubling myself to go on deck and observe the banks of the Yang-tse. We made a halt before Kiou-Kiang, the second station of European commerce, situated near the mouth of the great lake Poyang. There also, along the straight line of the quay, are erected luxurious hotels, of which the solidity and fine proportions should make the native architects reflect on the inferiority attributed to Europeans in the arts of peace.

After having learnt, to their cost, that we know how to destroy, the Chinese must learn, at last, that we know how to build. That which chiefly strikes the traveller, who, in passing, contemplates the European establishments in the Celestial Empire, is, the permanent character which is impressed on them from the beginning. The treaty had scarcely been signed before palaces began to be erected; and the rush made to take possession, on a soil so long interdicted, was so impetuous, that one cannot sometimes refrain from asking, whether the goal has not been overshot. For example, at Kiou-Kiang, business, so long interfered with by the rebellion of the Taipings, does not seem to have acquired, in the hands of Europeans, a development commensurate with the considerable expenses which were necessarily incurred in its first establishment. In the towns of the interior, the native Chinese merchants, everywhere dangerous rivals, enter into formidable competition with foreigners, especially since the complete submission of the rebels. These latter inflicted on the very richest portion of the empire ravages, of which we have often seen the traces on the banks of the Yang-tse-Kiang, but which were nowhere more horrible or prolonged than in the lower basin of that great river. We arrived in the night before Nanking; and though this city was opened to foreign commerce by the treaty of 1858, we did not stop there. An ancient capital of the empire, renowned for its schools, the guardian of the tombs of an illustrious royal family, Nanking fell, in 1853, into the power of the Taipings, who, during eleven years, made it the centre and focus of the insurrection. It was there that their chief, for a moment able to think himself finally victorious, meditated founding, to the south of the Blue River, an independent kingdom: a gigantic dream, with which, in spite of the appearance of a strict neutrality, a portion of the foreign colony associated itself. Though it is already beginning to rise from its ashes, Nanking, at the time of our passing it, was not an object of much interest; and had it been left to my decision, I would not have wasted the two hours which we spent in visiting it, thus retarding for that time our arrival at Shanghaï. The town of Tchin-Kiang is more worthy of attention than the ruins of the Porcelain Tower. In 1842, the Tartar troops in garrison there defended it valiantly against the English. It commands the entrance of that famous canal, which, starting from the chief town of the maritime province of Tche-Kiang, cuts the Blue River and the Yellow River, traverses 300 leagues of country, and was formerly the main water-highway of the empire from its extremities to its centre. It was by it that far the greater part of the taxes in kind was conveyed to Pekin. The province of Yunan alone annually sent by this route 1200 junks, laden with ingots of copper. This colossal work, more worthy than the Pyramids of Egypt or the Great Wall of Tartary to excite the admiration of the world, has for the moment lost its importance; but since the insurrection has been repressed, the junks, preferring the safe and easy navigation of this internal artery, are, by degrees, abandoning the sea, and, resuming their old habits, again begin to crowd the channel of the Grand Canal. Tchin-Kiang is the last port of the Blue River in which European vessels coming from Hankao are authorised to remain; Shanghaï itself is situated more than five leagues in the interior, at the point where the Houang-pou joins the Vou-song, which empties itself into the Yang-tse-Kiang, in face of the lower island of Tsoung-ming. Our steamer anchored, on the 12th of June 1868, in front of this great dépôt of European commerce; and while it discharged the teas and the silks which it had taken in at Hankao, we directed our steps to the French quarter, seeking for the French consulate, where the graceful hospitality of Madame Brenier de Montmorand made us, in two days, forget the miseries of two years.

The European establishment at Shanghaï is placed in a peculiar position, not in accordance with the ordinary rules of international law. It, in fact, constitutes a regular European colony, divided between English, French, and Americans, administered by each, according to their own municipal laws, with the assistance of a mayor and council, elected under the superior authority of the consul.

This local organisation, independent of the Chinese functionaries, was, not without reason, considered indispensable. Instituted at a time when the rebels surrounded Shanghaï, it has survived those difficult times, and is based on the belief in two facts—the weakness of the Chinese government, and the incompatibility of the laws of the empire with western civilisation. It is a decisive step on the road which the son of the Celestial Empire has been compelled to enter, the bayonet at his back, and one cannot but see in it a concession which may, without rashness, be considered as the prelude to more extended sacrifices.

It is on account of the depth of the port, and the excellent position which Shanghaï holds in the neighbourhood of the tea and silk-producing districts,[10] that it has been chosen as the principal entrepôt of foreign commerce with the Celestial Empire. This choice having been made, nothing has been neglected which could contribute to the erection of a superb city, worthy of the mission assigned to it by its founders, by the side of the Chinese town of this name. The monotony of the site, and the moist unhealthiness of the climate, recall the plains of Lower Cochin-China, which are as flat and fertile as the Kiang-Sou. Nature often chooses to unite in this manner ugliness and fertility.

Were I to pass over in silence the numerous proofs of sympathy so prodigally given us by the French colony, I should be ungrateful, and my narrative would be incomplete. The fraternal banquet, to which our compatriots were so good as invite us, proved that France, though behind England, America, and Russia, in that part of China, in her commercial greatness, still counts at Shanghaï sons both numerous and worthy of her. But I have too often given the reader an account of our fatigues and sorrows, to allow him to underestimate the joy which a manifestation, so flattering, gave us at the close of our journey.

The passage from Shanghaï to Hong-Kong took place, without incident, on board the Duplex, a vessel belonging to the Messageries Impériales, which had had the good fortune, a short time previously, thanks to the coolness and experience of Commander Noël, to escape one of those fearful cyclones, which render the navigation of the Chinese seas so perilous. The Yang-tse, seven leagues wide at its mouth, resembles the Kin-cha-Kiang, which we had traversed at 2200 miles from this spot, as the oak resembles the acorn; but its waters had lost in transparency what they had gained in volume, and the green river, which we had seen flowing at Han-kao, between two precipitous mountains, had as-

---

[10] Seven-eighths of the 40,000 bales of silk, and a third of the seventy-five million kilogrammes of tea, exported annually from China, come from Shanghaï. (*Sixteen Months round the World*, by M. Siegfried.)

sumed the appearance of a muddy ocean without shores. The swell of the waves showed our near approach to the sea; and was in my case followed by that faint sickness, which resembles the intoxication one would find in a cask of cider, or adulterated wine. Present sufferings always appear most painful; and I anathematised the tossings of that perfidious element, whose rude motions made me think kindly of the rough gait of the Laotian elephants. This was, as may be imagined, only a passing impression, soon dissipated by the appearance of the British island; and it will be believed, that even when my trouble was at the worst, I had no inclination to regain Europe by land across the whole of Asia. A journey of 10,000 kilometres in Indo-China and in China had satisfied my ambition as explorer.

The history of Hong-Kong is known to every one in Europe. This island, which is not ten leagues in circumference, has become in thirty years[11] the fortunate rival of its neighbour, the ancient Portuguese colony; and Victoria, like a rich millionaire, appears from the summit of her rock to look down upon Macao, over which the memory of Camoëns, and the past greatness of Portugal, seem to throw a poetic veil of melancholy. The safety and magnificence of the roadstead induced the English to fix their choice on Hong-Kong. They have gained a victory over nature, which does credit to their obstinate genius, assisted as it has been by a marvellous instinct. The increasing development of Shang-haï has notably diminished the extent of business at Canton; and Hong-Kong itself, placed at the mouth of the river which connects the great mart of Southern China with the sea, has itself suffered in its commercial prosperity. But with resources of all kinds comprised within a narrow territory, with its deep water overtopped and sheltered by mountains, and its dry-docks, it has, nevertheless, continued to be the great centre of steam navigation in these latitudes. The French company of the Messageries Impériales persist in maintaining their chief station at Hong-Kong, though it had engaged with the government to establish it at Saïgon. Capitalists, who readily listen to the whisperings of interest,

[11] It was ceded to the English government by the treaty of Nanking in 1842.

are deaf to the cries of patriotism; and I must add that it would be unjust, on this account, to quarrel with a great company, which does so much honour to our flag in these distant seas; but still, since a dock has been built at Saïgon, one can hardly understand this delay on the part of the Messageries, largely subsidied as they are by the State, in the execution of an agreement, profitable to our growing colony, and which in some degree touches the national dignity.

The consequence to us of this organisation of the service, which is to be regretted for more serious reasons, was that we had the annoyance of disembarking, and of quitting the Dupleix, which is specially assigned to the passage from Hong-Kong to Shanghaï, and of going on board the Impéra-trice, which runs between Hong-Kong and Suez.[12] China disappeared behind us, and the shores of the Annamite peninsula soon began to appear above the horizon. We coasted them towards the south-west, as far as the promontory, which terminates them, and marks the entry of the river of Saïgon.

On an evening in December 1865, I had seen from a great distance the feeble ray of light which streams from the summit of Cape St. Jacques, glimmering over the water. Thirty months afterwards, having returned to the same spot, I saw the white column of the lighthouse glittering in the midday sun. Yielding to the superstitious inclination, which so readily rises in the mind of one who has long lived in intimate communion with nature, I fancied that I saw, in such very different spectacles, what seemed a symbol of the modest beginning of our colony, and a presentiment of its future development. In entering the river of Saïgon, we approached the Mekong, to which the Donai is joined by an inland canal; but we were not again to see the great river that had so long borne us on its waters. I would not, indeed, have consented to take the smallest trouble in order to procure me this sentimental satisfaction. For my part, I was in

[12] Since the opening of the Suez Canal, the packets run from Hong-Kong to Marseilles. They have thus forty days consumption of fuel, while the English are trying hard not to exceed twenty or twenty-five days. This is another reason for making Saïgon the head of the line.

that frame of mind, when it even annoys one to be obliged to turn round with the earth, if one thinks of it; for after two years of wanderings, absolute immobility and complete repose seemed to me to be supreme happiness.

Warm as had been our reception by the French residing at Hankao and Shanghaï, that which greeted us at Saïgon was still more cordial. All those warm-hearted men, who whilst courageously doing their duty in that land where they suffer so much, but which they cannot help loving, rejoiced with us at our safe return, and shared with us our mourning sorrow. The entire colony, having at its head Admiral Ohier, the successor of Admiral de La Grandière, accompanied the body of Commandant Lagrée to the cemetery. He reposes amidst his companions in arms, fallen, like himself, for a cause which has already made so many martyrs. The English have raised bronze statues in honour of the energetic men who were the first to force their way into the far inland forests and prairies, and paid with their lives for the honour of opening the Australian continent to their countrymen. May we not expect from France that she will erect a durable monument to the intrepid chief, who, struggling at once against climate, nature, and men, lost in this grand effort a life already distinguished by so many eminent services in Cochin-China, and especially in Cambodgia, where he was the chief instrument in establishing the French protectorate? I may be permitted to stay a short time by the side of this tomb, in order to throw a rapid glance over the results obtained from this exploring expedition of the Mekong. It will be the fittest funeral oration for the illustrious dead, and the most natural conclusion for this humble work.

The readers who have been good enough to follow me, from the frontiers of the kingdom of Cambodgia to the cemetery of Saïgon, are aware that our mission has done more service to the general progress of science, than to the particular interests of the colony, whose funds supplied its cost. As to what concerns the first part of the programme, which was marked out for us, our long sojourn in the valley of the Mekong, and our numerous excursions on both banks of the river, have corrected the errors, and set at rest, by lifting the veil from the doubts which had hitherto led geographers to false and uncertain conclusions, in describing the eastern zone of the Indo-Chinese peninsula. The capricious windings of the Mekong; the prolongation of its course to the west, at the eighteenth parallel of latitude; the importance of its affluents; the strength and volume of its waters, and, if I may venture to say so, the proof of its individuality, which, contrary to the received opinion, continues to the end of its course;[13] the certainty of its entry into Yunan, where it receives the waters of Lake Tali, and into Thibet, where it has its source—all these obscure points were cleared up. In a word, we brought back precise information respecting the whole course of an immense river, that rises amidst the snows, and completes its course under a burning sun. On the other hand, there are the exact observations and seemingly well-founded information respecting the other rivers of Indo-China;[14] as to their position in different parts of their course, and the limits of their basins; and, in addition, many particulars respecting a part of China itself, which had been, hitherto, the least known. These, I ask permission to call the discoveries of the expedition directed by M. de Lagrée, in the domains of geography—discoveries which certainly constitute the larger part of our booty; and I am the more ready to state them, from having not directly contributed to them.

Although in political and commercial matters our success was not so great, still even here our efforts were not entirely fruitless.

Without entering into details of the subjects, thoroughly sifted by M. de Lagrée, before the commencement of our journey, I will only call attention to the light which the labours of the commission have permitted him to throw on the persevering work of absorption, which the court of Bangkok is constantly pursuing, in Indo-China. This absorption is effected by the aid of the embarrassments, which Europeans

[13] That which supposes the union of the Mekong and Meïnam.

[14] The Meïnam and the Tongkin rivers are, in comparison with their powerful neighbours, only secondary streams, which take their source in the last ramifications of the Himalaya mountains. The Irawady, Salween, Mekong, and Kin-cha-Kiang, on the contrary, penetrate into the very heart of the great range. These three rivers coming nearer each other as they flow away from their sources, follow, for long, almost parallel directions.

have, created, between those ancient rivals, the Burmese and
the Annamites. Its result has been, to leave nothing existing of the Laotian nationality but a name, and to make of
Vien-Chan, its principal centre, a mass of ruins. It is still
this ambition, so long favoured by fortune, which, after having forced back the emperor of Annam from the valley of the
Mekong, to which river his dominions formerly reached, has,
by keeping alive the antipathies of races, at this day, rendered any resumption of commercial relations, between the
Annamites and Laotians, impossible. We have, also, been
able to obtain evidence that the yoke of Siam, in itself toler-
ably light on the people, weighs heavily on the pride of certain great vassals; for instance, on the king of Luang-Praban, whose friendship might be very useful for us. It will be
recollected, that his states border on Tongkin; that they are
inhabited by a vigorous and pushing race; and that we found
in his capital a considerable commercial activity, evinced by
a daily market, the only one, probably, which exists in the
whole of Siamese Laos. On the day when our advice, given
with prudence, and firmly pressed, shall have effected a
union of subjects by curbing the ambition of their princes,
Annamite merchants, replacing the Burmese pedlars, will
start from the banks of the Tongkin to carry to Luang-
Praban, and thus to the greater part of the middle and
lower valley of the Mekong, the tissues and other manufactures of Europe, at present introduced almost exclusively
by Bangkok.

The course of the great river, utilised by means of large
rafts, would then render important services to this commerce, restored to its natural channel. As to steam navigation, it is useless to expect to extend it beyond its present
limits. This first delusion, which was rudely dissipated at
our very starting-point, went near to spoil our whole journey.
But there was a compensation in reserve. To enter China
in spite of the probabilities to the contrary, to escape from
the hands of the Burmese with only the sacrifice of some
health, and the loss of our whole wardrobe, and to disappoint the English, was assuredly a success. But the colony,
which had conceived the idea of our expedition, expected
from our efforts an effective result in a material point of

view. We could say to it, it is true, that Saïgon is for ever separated from China by a long series of cascades and rapids, and in this manner destroy the most favourite of its dreams; but these would have been words painful to utter, and still more painful to hear. As often happens, we found consolation for this disappointment in a quarter where we least expected it, in consequence of a forced change in our programme, introduced by M. de Lagrée. I must mention that this modification, which was subsequently acknowledged to have been necessary, was, when first announced to us, severely criticised by all. We were compelled by the Mussulman revolt to leave the Mekong, in order to gain the Sonkoï; to abandon geography, and solve a problem of more practical and immediate importance. It does not appear to me now, that there is any reason for regretting this circumstance, especially as, having sought and made acquaintance with the rebels, we were edified by their hospitable virtues.

I have already explained the importance of the information we acquired respecting the river Tonkin at the time of our passage to Yuen-Kiang. In my opinion this is a principal point, which I do not think it will be useless to mention again. In default of a protectorate over the whole of Annam, which the change effected in the ideas of Tu-Duc and his mandarins, since the seizure of the three provinces of the west, may some day cause to be accepted at Hué, it is a first necessity that our commerce should have free access to all parts of that empire; that it should be able to ascend, without being disturbed, the course of the navigable waters of upper Cochin-China and of Tonkin. Among the latter, the Sonkoï deserves particular attention. Both from what we were able ourselves to see, and still more from the reports which we heard, it promises to realise all the hopes and expectations which the Mekong destroyed. Uniting China with a country which cannot long escape French influence, it is predestined to carry to the sea the productions of Tonkin itself, and the wealth of a portion of Yunan, Setchuan, Kouei-tcheou, and Kouangsi. To speak only of Yunan, I find by an English document, that in 1854, the year which preceded the Mussulman insurrection, an interchange of traffic took place between that province and Burmah, representing a value of half a million sterling. This commerce, carried on by means of caravans, which took twenty days to go to Bahmo[15] from Tali, crossing the Mekong (Lantsang-Kiang) and the Salween (Loutse-Kiang), was fed by Yunan and the neighbouring provinces. Russian fabrics, coming by way of Siberia, even entered Burmah by this route. There is reason to believe that the kingdom of Ava, which furnishes to the Chinese a great quantity of cotton, would continue to attract a certain number of traders; but it is easy to perceive, that if the trade was set free from trammels and prohibitions, and encouragement were given to it, it would spread of itself, and be extended over the valley of Sonkoï. The disturbance caused in Yunan by the civil war affords us a precious occasion to make an effort, the advantages of which may be measured beforehand by the umbrage it already gives to our rivals.

There is something beyond this. Like a corpse preserved for a long time under the bell of an exhausted receiver, whose dissolution is hastened when it comes into contact with the outward air, China is being decomposed by the breath of European ideas. This empire, the oldest that exists under the sun, is, in its turn, falling into ruin, its hour is approaching, and it would have in all probability already come, but for the mutual jealousy which is felt by its heirs. The progress of Russia in the north, the strong position held by the English in the west, the concealed projects entertained by other powers, of which the marks of sympathy given to the chiefs of the Taipings was a curious symptom—in a word, the force of circumstances, and the weakness of the Chinese themselves, enable us to foresee the dismemberment of that ancient empire, whose foundation was laid, thousands of years ago, by Fohi. In the presence of such an eventuality France should be prepared. Her part is traced out by the position which she already holds on the Annamite peninsula. It is absolutely neces-

---

[15] Steamers can ascend the Irawady as far as Bahmo. From this place one can reach in six days, across a mountainous country, inhabited by independent savages, the large village of Langchankai, situated south-west of Yonhtchang, between the Irawady and the Salween, which is the first market in Yunan. It is this short distance which the English have, as yet, been unable to pass.

sary that she should exercise a paramount influence at Tonkin, which is for her the key of China, and that, without
hurrying by any impatience the course of events, she should
show her flag to the people whose protectorate may some
day fall into her hands.

It requires perhaps some courage, at the present hour, to
announce such a conclusion, and to speak to France of her
interests in the East. As the wind blows towards Byzantine
discussions, and in favour of searchers for the philosopher's
stone, since the doctors, done with prescriptions, take the
course of consulting the sick man, the first comer may point
out a remedy. This remedy for the evil which oppresses
us is, assuredly, not new; but it has the merit of having
been proved by the experience of others, and may be summed
up in two plain words—emigration and colonisation.

For more than half a century, constantly expressed in
terms, at bottom identical, the problem of the proletariat and
of poverty will continue to be a permanent cause of sterile
agitations for us, so long as the theorists of socialism, con-
centrating their thoughts on the narrow territory of their
native country, confine their efforts to exciting those who
possess nothing against those who possess anything. A
considerable portion of the globe still remains unexplored,
and in the regions already known and described, all the pro-
letariats of France, if they had the courage and the intelligence, might possess themselves of vast domains, by the
right of first occupation. Thanks to the solitudes of Africa,
this will remain true for a long time to come; as regards the
remaining portion of the globe, time presses; and the Latin
races have not a moment to lose, if they do not wish to be
permanently excluded from it. The Anglo-Saxons are grasping the world; and if our destinies accomplish themselves
in the manner already predicted by men, whom an ardent
love for their country has inspired with a sad eloquence,
France, with her forty millions of inhabitants, will cease to
be anything but a school of political casuists, where the lords
of the universe may come to hear fine discourses on the
sovereignty of the people. 'China will be, according to all
probability, for Australia, what India has been for England;
and should England be some day eclipsed, it is not less pro-

bable that India also would fall into the hands of the Australians. But let us leave on one side all these conjectures, though they present themselves to the mind with all the appearance of truth, and confine ourselves to drawing the sole conclusion which interests us from facts already established. Whether Australia or the United States, some day, get the command of the Chinese seas, of India, and of Japan; whether England continue to hold her own empire there, or yield it up to the two young rivals, who have sprung from her own bosom,—our children are no less certain to see the Anglo-Saxon race mistress of Oceania, as well as of America, and of all parts of the extreme East, which can be ruled, occupied, or influenced by those who hold possession of the sea. When things have arrived at this point (and it is a great deal to say it will require two centuries for this), will it be possible to avoid confessing, that from one end of the globe to the other the world is Anglo-Saxon?' (*La France Nouvelle*, par M. Prévost-Paradol.)

With their enervating climate, which confines Europeans to the transactions of commercial affairs, and forbids them, on pain of death, to attempt labour or production, our Annamite provinces are rather a counting-house than a colony, properly so called. But India also is a counting-house, and yet it is far from useless to the grandeur of England. Nevertheless, perspectives full of the deepest interest and attraction open from Saïgon, beyond the mountains of Tonkin, over the fertile and healthy countries of Western China and Thibet. Fortune, which has so often in our colonies made us pay for her favours of a day by lasting betrayal, appears to have become less cruel. Louisiana and Canada escaped from our hands, in spite of our efforts, at two periods which were fatal to our maritime power; Cochin-China, on the contrary, has survived; and has prospered notwithstanding the hesitations of the government. One may say of it, that of all our distant enterprises, this one has been the least premeditated and the most fortunate, the most slighted and the most fruitful, the most obscure and the most useful; it is the work of our fortune rather than of our will.

THE END.